HISTORY
OF RUSSIA

Sergei Mikhailovich Soloviev

The
Academic International Press
Edition
of
Sergei M. Soloviev

History of Russia From Earliest Times

G. EDWARD ORCHARD
General Editor

Contributing Editors

HUGH F. GRAHAM

JOHN D. WINDHAUSEN

ALEXANDER V. MULLER

K.A. PAPMEHL

RICHARD HANTULA

WALTER J. GLEASON, JR.

WILLIAM H. HILL

G. EDWARD ORCHARD

LINDSEY A.J. HUGHES

NICKOLAS LUPININ

GEORGE E. MUNRO

DANIEL L. SCHLAFLY, JR.

ANTHONY L.H. RHINELANDER

PATRICK J. O'MEARA

PETER C. STUPPLES

T. ALLAN SMITH

MARTHA L. LAHANA

ANTHONY V. KNOWLES

HELEN Y. PROCHAZKA

ALEXANDRA S. KORROS

GARY J. MARKER

MARIAN J. RUBCHAK

RALPH M. CLEMINSON

CATHY J. POTTER

BRIGIT A. FARLEY

SERGEI M. SOLOVIEV

History of Russia

Volume 22

The Reign of Tsar Alexis
Poland, Turkey, and Ukrainian Cossacks,
1667-1674

Edited and Translated and With an
Introduction by

Cathy J. Potter

2002
Academic International Press

The Academic International Press Edition of S.M. Soloviev's
History of Russia From Earliest Times in fifty volumes.

Volume 22. *The Reign of Tsar Alexis, Poland, Turkey, and
Ukrainian Cossaks, 1667–1674.*
Unabridged translation of the text of Volume 12, Chapters 1-3 as
contained in Volume VI of S.M. Soloviev's *Istoria Rossii s
drevneishikh vremen* published in Moscow between 1959-1966, with
added annotation by Cathy J. Potter.

ISBN: 0-87569-240-0

Composition by Ethel Chamberlain and Llano F. McCowen

Printed in the United States of America

A list of Academic International Press publications is found at
the end of this volume.

ACADEMIC INTERNATIONAL PRESS
Box 1111 • Gulf Breeze FL 32562-1111 • USA
www.ai-press.com

CONTENTS

Weights and Measures   *viii*

Preface   *ix*

Introduction   *xiii*

I   **RUMORS DISTURB LITTLE RUSSIA**   1

Turkish Schemes—Zaporozhia and Bishop Methodios De-
nounced—The Tsar's Envoy Ladyzhensky Murdered—Lady-
zhensky's Murder Reported to the Hetman—Investigation of
Cossack Complaints—The Tsar Admonishes the Cossacks—
Sheremetev Courts Doroshenko—Doroshenko Responds—
Bishop Methodios Breaks with Moscow—Methodios Calum-
niates Moscow—Tukalsky Convinces Briukhovetsky to Be-
tray Moscow—Rebellion Erupts in Little Russia—The Tsar
Writes to Briukhovetsky—Uprising in Little Russian Towns—
Briukhovetsky Appeals to Don Cossacks—Poles Respond to
Cossack Rebellion—Briukhovetsky's Downfall—Doroshenko
Retires to the West Bank—Archpriest Simeon Adamovich in
Moscow—Archbishop Lazar Baranovich Petitions the Tsar—
Further Adventures of Bishop Methodios

II   **RELATIONS WITH UKRAINE, POLAND AND TURKEY**   38

Tatars Proclaim New Hetman—Difficulties for Doroshenko—
Two Hetmans Correspond with Sheremetev—Little Russian
Embassy in Moscow—Archpriest Simeon Adamovich Writes
to Tsar—Sheremetev's Envoy Reports to Moscow—Mnogogreshny Elected Hetman—Petitions to Moscow—Relations
with Poland and Sweden—A Russian Candidate for the Polish
Throne—Ordin-Nashchokin's Last Service—Ordin-Nashchokin Corresponds with Tsar—Ordin-Nashchokin Corresponds
with Chancellery—Ordin-Nashchokin Meets Polish Commissioners—Ordin-Nashchokin's Dismissal—Polish Ambassadors
in Moscow—Negotiations—Negotiations Concluded—Russian Mission to the Turks—Events in the Crimea

III DISTURBANCES PERSIST IN ZAPOROZHIA   81

Anxiety about Little Russia—Archbishop Lazar Baranovich
Writes to Moscow—Archbishop Lazar Champions the Treaty
of Glukhov—Hetman Mnogogreshny's Precarious Position—
A Curse Against Mnogogreshny—Archbishop Lazar Baranovich's Pretensions—Tsar Responds to Archbishop—A Muscovite Embassy in Constantinople—Doroshenko's Declara-
tion—War on West Bank—Hetman Mnogogreshny's Complaints—Moscow Dispatches Envoy to Mnogogreshny—Cossack Elders Denounce Mnogogreshny—Mnogogreshny is
Seized—Accusations Against Mnogogreshny—Interrogation
and Exile of Mnogogreshny—Serko's Exile—A Cossack Council in Kozachia Dubrova—The Election of Hetman Samoilovich—False Prophet Appears in Ukraine

**IV THE TURKS GO TO WAR. A PRETENDER IN
ZAPOROZHIA**   124

Turks Attack Poland—Battle of Batog—Kamieniec Podolsky
Falls to Turks—Moscow Responds to Turkish Attack—Serko
is Liberated—Samoilovich Sends His Sons to Moscow—News
from Left Bank—Khanenko Petitions Tsar—Metropolitan
Tukalsky's Position—Romodanovsky and Samoilovich En-
counter Problems—Public Opinion in Ukraine—Attack on
Azov—A Pretender in Zaporozhia—Tsar's Emissaries and the
Pretender—Doroshenko Negotiates with Moscow—Samoilo-
vich Opposes Reception of Doroshenko—Romodanovsky and
Samoilovich Cross to West Bank—Khanenko Writes to Prince
Trubetskoy—Samoilovich Elected Hetman of Both Banks—
Doroshenko Petitions to Become Subject of Tsar—Moscow
and Zaporozhian Pretender—Serko Sends Pretender to Mos-
cow—The End of the Pretender

V DOROSHENKO BROUGHT TO HEEL   158

Doroshenko Refuses to Submit to Tsar—Tatars Come to
Doroshenko's Aid—Doroshenko's Brother Defeated and His
Emissary Seized—Ivan Mazepa—Mazepa's Testimony in
Moscow—The Tsar Refuses to Release Samoilovich's Sons—

Romodanovsky and Samoilovich Attack Chigirin—Sultan and Khan Mount New Offensive—Russian Army Retreats to East Bank—Hetman Opposes Uniting Russian and Polish Forces—Romodanovsky Reports to Tsar—Archbishop Baranovich Denounces Simeon Adamovich—Hetman Samoilovich Denounces Serko—Hetman Complains About Simeon Adamovich—Serko Corresponds with Moscow—Trouble in Kanev—Discussions About New Campaign on West Bank—Russian Army Campaigns Alone—Doroshenko's Position Becomes Untenable—Serko Seeks to Mediate for Doroshenko—Moscow Rejects Serko's Mediation—Events on Don

Appendix
   Cossack Ranks in the Hetmanate   192

Illustrations
   Tsar Aleksei Mikhailovich   *xx*
   Jan Kazimierz   *xxi*
   Stepan ("Stenka") Razin   *xxii*
   Ivan Astafievich Vygovsky   *xxiii*
   Afanasy Lavretievich Ordin-Nashchokin   *xxiv*
   Artamon Sergeevich Matveev   *xxv*
   Main Entrace to the Kievan Caves Monastery   *xxvi*
   Turkish Military Formation of the Mid-Sixteenth Century *xxvii*
   Courtyard of the Chancellery for Foreign Affairs   *xxviii*

Notes   195

Index   247

The Editor and Translator   267

Linear and Surface Measure

Arshin: 16 vershoks, 28 in. (diuims) 72.12 cm
Chetvert (quarter): 1/4 arshin, 1/2 desiatina, 1.35 acres (sometimes 1.5 desiatinas or c. 4.1 acres)
Desiatina: 2,400 square sazhens, 2.7 acres, 1.025 hectares
Diuim: 1 inch, 2.54 cm
Fut: 12 diuims, 1 foot, 30.48 cm

Obza (areal): c. 10 chetverts, 13–15 acres
Osmina: 1/4 desiatina, 600 sq. sazhens, .256 hectare
Sazhen: 3 arshins, 7 feet, 2.133 m
Vershok: 1.75 in., 4.445 cm, 1/16 arshin
Verst: 500 sazhens, 1,166 yards and 2 feet, .663 miles, 1.0668 km
Voloka (plowland): 19 desiatinas, 20 hectares, 49 acres

Liquid Measure

Bochka (barrel): 40 vedros, 121 gallons, 492 liters
Chetvert (quarter): 1.4 bochkas, 32.5 gallons
Korchago (wine): Rus, unknown

Kufa: 30 stofy
Stof: Kruzhka (cup), 1/10 vedro, c. 1.3 quarts, 1.23 liters
Vedro (pail): 3.25 gallons, 12.3 liters, 10 stofy

Weights

Berkovets: 361 lbs., 10 puds
Bezmen: c. 1 kg, 2.2 lbs.
Chetverik (grain measure dating from 16th century): 1/8 chetvert, 15.8 lbs.
Chetvert (grain measure): 1/4 rad, 3.5 puds, 126.39 lbs., c. 8 bushels
Funt: 96 zolotniks, .903 lbs., 14.4 oz., 408.24 kg
Grivenka: 205 grams
Kad: 4 chetverts, 14 puds, 505.56 lbs.
Kadka malenkaia: 12th-century, small measure

Kamen (stone): 32 funt
Korob (basket): 7 puds, 252 lbs.
Osmina (eighth): 2 osmina to a chetvert (dry measure)
Polbezmen: c. 500 g, 1 lb.
Polosmina (sixteenth): 1/2 osmina
Pud: 40 funts, 36.113 lbs. (US), 40 lbs. (Russian), 16.38 kg
Rad: 14 puds, 505.58 lbs.
Zolotnik: 1/96 lbs., 4.26 grams

Money

Altyn: 6 Muscovite dengas, 3 copecks
Bel: Rus, pure silver coin
Chervonets (chervonnyi): gold coin of first half of 18th century worth c. 3 rubles
Chetvertak: silver coin equal to 25 copecks or 1/4 ruble (18–19th centuries)
Copeck: two Muscovite dengas
Denga: 1/2 copeck
Grivna: 20 Muscovite dengas, 100 grivnas equals 1 ruble, 10 copecks
Grosh: 10 peniaz
Grosh litovsky (Lithuanian grosh): 5 silver copecks
Kopa grosh: 60 groshas, one Muscovite poltina, 1/2 ruble
Kuna: 12th-century Rus coin comparable to Westerns denarii or Eastern dirhems. Varied in value by region. Replaced late 14th century by the denga or serebro (silver). Also a marten skin.
Moskovka: 1/2 copeck
Muscovite denga: 200 equals 1 ruble
Novgorod denga: 100 equals 1 ruble
Novgorodka: 1 copeck

Peniaz: 10 equals one grosh (Lithuania)
Poltina (poltinnik): 50 copecks, 100 dengas, 1 ruble
Poltora: 1 1/2 rubles
Polupoltina (-nik): 25 copecks, 50 dengas
Rezan: 12th century Rus coin. 50 rezan equals one grivna kuna
Ruble: 100 copecks, 200 dengas
Shiroky grosh (large silver coin): 20 Muscovite copecks
Veksa: 12th-century Rus small coin equal to one squirrel pelt (belka)

Foreign Denominations
Chervonnyi: c. 3 rubles
Ducat: c. 3 rubles
Dutch efimok: "lion dollar" or levok, 1 thaler, 2.5 guilders
Efimok: foreign currency, 1 thaler, .75-1 ruble, 1 chervonets or chervonnyi
Levok: Dutch silver lion dollar
Thaler (Joachimsthaler): c. 1 ruble, 1/3 chervonets or chervonnyi

Note: Weights and measures often changed values over time and sometimes held more than one value at the same time. For details consult Sergei G. Pushkarev, *Dictionary of Russian Historical Terms from the Eleventh Century to 1917* (Yale, 1970).

PREFACE

This volume is an unabridged translation of Chapters 1, 2 and 3 of Volume XII of Soloviev's *Istoriia Rossii s drevneishikh vremen* (History of Russia from Earliest Times, 29 vols., St. Petersburg, 1851-1879). The text is translated from the *Mysl'* edition of Soloviev's *Works in Eighteen Books* (Sochineniia v vosemnadtsati knigakh) published in Moscow, 1988-1998, in which the original Volume XII appears as the second half of Book VI, and the translated chapters are found on pages 336-480.

Soloviev embarked on his ambitious project as a young historian of thirty and spent the remaining twenty-nine years of his life, working in the archives and at his desk, to produce his extraordinary *History of Russia*.[1] Only his death in 1879 checked the flow of volumes. The last volume, which brings the history to 1774, was published posthumously. In its breadth and its depth, as well as in the sheer volume of hitherto unexamined archival material it incorporated, the work remains unsurpassed to this day. Since many of the sources which he quotes at length in his text remain unpublished and some have been lost or misplaced with the passage of time and the vicissitudes of war, revolution and reconstruction, his work remains invaluable to scholars. Moreover, the story he presents is an exciting one, a sweeping epic replete with tsars and pretenders, with swashbuckling bogatyrs[2] and bandits, with war, pilgrimages and pageantry. Russian publishers have assured that Soloviev's work is accessible to scholars and those who read the Russian language, with two new editions in the past forty years. The goal of the series and this volume is to make Soloviev's history of Russia accessible to the widest possible range of readers in the contemporary English-speaking world, in a translation that is both accurate and readable. In pursuit of this goal some compromises were necessary.

Most Russian terms were translated, with the exception of those which have become familiar in English, such as boyar, tsar, cossack, khan. Less common words either are transliterated (chaika or murza) or translated (rada or krug) with an explanation provided in the endnotes upon their first occurrence. In the translation of terms the goal has been consistency, insofar as possible. To the rule of consistency, the title voe-voda is a notable exception. In seventeenth-century Russia it was a title given to men serving in a variety of capacities. It could be equivalent to a military commander, a military governor, a mayor or a provincial governor. It is translated with an English term appropriate to the context and the function of the individual. Cossack ranks in this period of the hetmanate are translated in accordance with George Gajecky's useful reference work, *The Cossack Administration of the Hetmanate*, 2 vols. (Cambridge, Mass., 1978). A brief overview of the administrative organ-ization of the hetmanate and the important ranks and their duties is provided in the Appendix.

Transliteration follows a modified Library of Congress system. Dia-critical marks and ligatures are omitted. The Cyrillic letters transcribed as "ia" and "iu" have been maintained within words, but rendered as "ya" and "yu" at the beginning (thus Belaia not Belaya; Yaroslav not Iaroslav). The suffixes "-ii" and "-yi" have been replaced with "-y", the suffix "-oi" with "-oy", and the "-iia" common to many feminine names has been simplified to "-ia" (Dmitry not Dmitrii, Donskoy not Donskoi, Maria not Mariia). The apostrophe commonly used to indicate a soft sign is dropped or, in some cases, replaced with an "i" (tsar not tsar', Soloviev not Solov'ev). Plurals of transliterated Russian terms have been anglicized (efimoks not efimki). The aim has been to achieve a compromise between scholarly accuracy and simplicity for those readers not familiar with the Russian language, and also to maintain consistency within the series.

Russian personal names are directly transliterated except for those which English usage has made familiar with respect to Russian historical figures, such as Alexander, Alexis, Michael, Peter, etc. Non-Russian names, locations and terms are given in their native form, where this can be determined. Turkish, Tatar, Persian and other names and terms are transliterated in accordance with guidelines established by the editors of this series. If the original cannot be determined, the name or term is directly transliterated from Soloviev's Russian. Ukrainian names, loca-tions and terms are the exception. In the text they have been transliterated directly from Soloviev's Russianized form, in conformance with the preceding practice.

Literal translation and a graceful, readable English text are incompatible. Nonetheless, translator intervention has been applied judiciously and with restraint. All material in parentheses is Soloviev's own, and material in italics is in accordance with his usage. Explanations and elaborations on information provided within the text are provided in endnotes. In some cases, if the nature of the Russian text requires free paraphrasing to convey its true sense in English, the Russian as well as a literal translation is provided in an endnote. Occasionally information has been inserted in the text, in which case it appears in brackets. There are a few exceptions to this rule. To clarify some of the longer quotations which Soloviev includes, phrases such as "the tsar said" or "the ambassador asserted" have been added freely, without indicating the supplement. In addition, Soloviev typically indicated the year of events once, in January, with subsequent dates being indicated only by month and day—until the next year appeared. To assist the reader the year occasionally has been added to dates without the identifying brackets.

Soloviev, in accordance with Russian custom, identified individuals by their given name or a diminutive, or their given name and patronymic, or by their title and family name, or by their title alone. For non-Russian readers this can become confusing. Wherever possible, at the first instance of a name, the title and full name is used: given name, patronymic and family name. Diminutives are identified in the endnotes. Occasionally the family name of an individual has been added later in the text, to identify more precisely and unambiguously the individual in question. Finally, in this period the forms and spelling of family names, particularly among the Zaporozhian Cossacks, were not necessarily firmly fixed. Reflecting this, as well as the vast amount of archival material he was perusing, Soloviev's usage also is not firmly fixed. When different variants of a family name appear throughout Soloviev's text the most common variant has been chosen and used consistently throughout. Other variants are indicated in an endnote and in the index. When Soloviev or later editors appear to have erred in the identification of individuals the correction has been made and this is indicated in an endnote.

The three chapters of the original text have been divided into five, and many of the very long sentences and paragraphs have been broken into more tractable lengths. Soloviev's topic headings which appear at the beginning of each chapter in the original have been recast into subheadings and incorporated into the text at appropriate points. Some of these headings have been combined or omitted when the discussion related to them was a paragraph or less in the original. In other cases, where Soloviev allowed one topic heading to stand for a complex discussion covering dozens of pages, topic headings have been added. Finally, Soloviev's original bibliographic notes have been omitted. They consist primarily of archival references which are no longer current and are of no interest to the general reader. The specialist may consult one of the Russian language editions. With the noted exceptions, Soloviev's material has been presented in its entirety and, within the constraints of English syntax, the order of presentation has been retained.

Cathy J. Potter

INTRODUCTION

The present volume focuses on the Ukraine and the struggles and divisions within the Zaporozhian Cossack Host during the tumultuous years from 1667 to 1676, a period known in Ukrainian history as "a time of heavy weeping." It continues the narrative and the themes presented in Volume 20 of this series [Book 11, Chapters 1-3], which is devoted to the Ukraine from the death of Hetman Bogdan Khmelnitsky in August 1657 to the conclusion of negotiations between Russian and Polish representatives, culminating in the signing of the Treaty of Andrusovo in January 1667.

The Andrusovo treaty concluded the thirteen-year war between Poland and Russia, a war which for a time also involved Sweden. In regard to the cossacks of the Ukraine, although cossack leaders continued to refer to the Pereiaslav agreement of 1654, the Andrusovo treaty effectively superseded the earlier pact. The terms signed at Andrusovo provided for a thirteen-year armistice between Russia and the Polish-Lithuanian Commonwealth during which discussions were to continue to achieve a permanent peace. The Commonwealth conceded large areas of Belorussia, the Smolensk and Severia regions and the Chernigov district, as well as the Left Bank of the Ukraine. The Right Bank of the Ukraine remained under Polish control. Russia was granted jurisdiction over the city of Kiev until April 15, 1669, when it was to revert to the Poles. Russian control of the town of Smolensk also was to be temporary, limited to thirteen and one-half years. In fact, Russia never relinquished control of the two cities, and probably never intended to do so. A treaty signed in 1686 confirmed Russia's permanent possession. Jurisdiction over the Zaporozhian Camp (Sech), the stronghold of the Zaporozhian Cossacks below the rapids of the Dnieper river, was to be shared by Russia and Poland. The Zaporozhian Cossacks were expected to defend both tsar and king against Turkish or Tatar attack.[3]

The Treaty of Andrusovo shaped the future of the Ukraine. Its provisions made it exceedingly unlikely that the cossack administration in the Ukraine, the hetmanate, could succeed in forging a unified and autonomous political entity in the region. The cossack hetmanate was established in 1648. Bogdan Khmelnitsky's successful insurrection of that year challenged the control of the Commonwealth over a large territory in the Ukraine. In 1649 the Polish Sejm[4] (Diet) recognized the hetmanate as an autonomous unit within the Commonwealth. Although some historians have identified the hetmanate as a Ukrainian cossack state, from the very beginning its status was precarious.[5]

Following the signing of the Treaty of Pereiaslav in 1654 Bogdan Khmelnitsky shifted his allegiance to the Russian tsar and the hetmanate entered the Russian sphere of influence. Khmelnitsky's death shattered the fragile unity of the hetmanate. The years leading to Andrusovo were marred by factional struggles among the cossacks in which the Moscow government actively interfered in pursuit of its own interests. Moscow could not unilaterally dictate events in the Ukraine. Yet over time Russian influence inexorably increased in the area, even as the power and international stature of the Polish-Lithuanian Commonwealth declined. The Treaty of Andrusovo was a pivotal event in the decline of the Commonwealth and the rise of Russia. It was an equally portentous event in Russia's assimilation of the Left (Western) Bank of the Ukraine, a long process which this volume does not follow to its conclusion.

The current volume opens in January 1667, shortly after the signing of the Andrusovo agreement. On the Right Bank, Peter Dorofeevich Doroshenko had served as hetman since 1665. He adopted a pro-Turkish policy in an attempt to unite all of the Ukraine and escape the constraints and encroachments on cossack autonomy imposed by both Poles and Russians. Ivan Martynovich Briukhovetsky was hetman on the Left Bank. In 1663 he was elected to the position by a full cossack council, in elections orchestrated by Russian officials. Shortly after his installation as hetman Briukhovetsky was received in Moscow with honor, elevated to the rank of boyar and married to a daughter of one of the princes Dolgoruky. Officers in his retinue were enrolled in the lists of Russian noblemen. This proved to be the zenith of his hetmancy. Briukhovetsky's pro-Russian policy earned him neither praise nor support in the Ukraine. When Russian policy towards Poland changed as a result of negotiation of their differences at Andrusovo, Briukhovetsky's position became untenable.

Chapter I recounts the complex conspiracies and counter-conspiracies culminating in the downfall of Briukhovetsky. The Turks threatened from the south. The Zaporozhian Cossacks in the field grew restive. Their loyalty to Briukhovetsky, never strong, wavered. Murdering a Muscovite envoy, they justified their action with complaints against Russian policies and Russian soldiers in the towns, at the same time toying with the idea of uniting with Doroshenko on the Right Bank. The Moscow government was equally equivocal in its support of the hetman. Even as Moscow reassured Briukhovetsky of resolute support Russian representatives entered into discussions with Doroshenko, seeking to persuade him to abandon his Tatar alliance in favor of submission to both the Polish and the Russian sovereigns. Only the naïve could believe that Doroshenko would exact no price for such an action. Moreover there could be little doubt that the asking price for Doroshenko's loyalty would be the post of hetman over a united Ukraine.

Tangled secular politics in the Ukraine intersected with equally tangled and intertwined religious and ecclesiastical politics. From the perspective of Moscow, control of the Ukrainian church was a step towards political control in the Ukraine. From the Ukrainian side, an autonomous church and an autonomous Ukraine were intrinsically related. The post of metropolitan of Kiev, head of the Ukrainian Orthodox church, a bone of contention since 1659, remained unfilled after the death of Dionysios Balaban in 1663.[6] Thus rivalry over the hetmancy was complemented by rivalry over the Kievan metropolitanate. By 1667 the intrigues and machinations of Moscow's appointee as vicar of Kiev, Bishop Methodios, had alienated many. His support in Moscow was fading. Metropolitan Joseph Tukalsky stood at the shoulder of Hetman Doroshenko on the Right Bank, searching for a means to unite both the Ukraine and the Ukrainian church. Archbishop Lazar Baranovich of Chernigov, replaced by Methodios as vicar of Kiev in 1661, retained an interest in regaining the lost position. Seeking a solution to his myriad problems, Methodios turned to conspiracy. Encouraged by Hetman Doroshenko, he enticed Hetman Briukhovetsky to embark on rebellion against Moscow.

For Methodios and Briukhovetsky the rebellion ended in disaster, with Methodios in prison and Briukhovetsky dead at the hands of his own cossacks. Hetman Doroshenko, the chief instigator of the affair, was not permitted to savor his victory for long. Chapter II opens with the appearance of another claimant to the post of hetman. Peter Sukhovey or Sukhoveenko, supported by the Crimean khan, challenged Doroshenko's position. Soloviev relates Doroshenko's efforts to retain his position and autonomy as he was squeezed by the Tatars, Turks, Poles and Russians.

As Doroshenko danced a council at Glukhov confirmed the election of a new hetman for the Left Bank, a man not unsympathetic to Doroshenko, Demian Ignatovich Mnogogreshny.

Moscow's troubles with the Ukrainian cossacks did not unfold in isolation. In Chapter II Soloviev shifts his focus to the broader diplomatic context of Ukrainian turmoil. He presents a detailed discussion of the diplomatic negotiations to complete the Andrusovo agreement and the downfall of the chief negotiator for the Russians, Boyar Afanasy Lavrentievich Ordin-Nashchokin, head of the Chancellery for Foreign Affairs. Cossack insistence that they be present along with the Polish and Russian ambassadors at the renewed Andrusovo negotiations and their fear that Kiev would be returned to the Poles exacerbated tensions with Moscow. Though the cossacks were denied representation, Muscovite diplomacy successfully avoided the return of Kiev to the Poles. This did not mollify dissatisfaction in the Ukraine.

Chapters III and IV return to Ukrainian difficulties and struggles following Hetman Mnogogreshny's election at the Council of Glukhov. Cooperation between Moscow and the new hetman, Mnogogreshny, soon evaporated. Distrust quickly undermined relations and intrigues flourished. By 1672 Mnogogreshny was removed from his post, convicted of treason and exiled to Siberia. Ivan Samoilovich took his turn as hetman on the Left Bank.

On the Right Bank the situation was equally unstable. In 1671 Hetman Doroshenko suffered harassment from the Poles. By 1672 a greater threat loomed as a large Turkish army invaded Polish Ukraine menacing Kiev and other towns on the Right Bank. Polish defeats made manifest the vulnerability of the Left Bank, consequently Russia was drawn south into war against the Turks.

The Russian army assisted by Hetman Samoilovich and the cossacks of the Left Bank campaigned against the Turks and Tatars, and their ally Hetman Doroshenko and his cossacks. Simultaneously Moscow continued to correspond with Doroshenko, seeking to persuade him to change his allegiance and submit to the tsar. As Doroshenko's position weakened the Muscovite blandishments grew more attractive and more difficult to refuse. Chapter V relates the complex negotiations and discussions ultimately leading to Doroshenko's submission to the tsar, his exile and the proclamation of Ivan Samoilovich as hetman on both banks of the Dnieper.

Unity was fragile and ephemeral. The tumultuous and tragic story of the Ukraine does not end with this volume. Another decade passed before Russia and the Commonwealth signed an agreement recognizing their respective interests and claims in the Ukraine and finally bringing an end to this chaotic and catastrophic period of Ukrainian history known as "the Ruin." The ratification of this "Eternal Peace" divided the entire Ukraine among the surrounding powers.[7] Soloviev relates the details and complexities of these subsequent events in Volumes 23 through 26 of this series.

Soloviev does not present a unified and integrated history of the Ukraine. First of all, he never intended the different parts of his monumental *History of Russia* to stand alone. He viewed history as an unending, organically developing process, molded by a people's environment, their character or "national physiognomy," and the play of external pressures. His classic work, unmarred by what he would have seen as false periodization, reflects that belief. Second, although even as he wrote a nascent Ukrainian national consciousness was stirring, Soloviev was a Great Russian writing a history of Russia. He was not unsympathetic to the difficulties of the Zaporozhian Cossacks and the Ukrainian people, nor was he unfair. A scrupulous historian, true to his sources, he exposed the duplicity and treachery of cossacks and Russians, Turks, Tatars and Poles alike. Nonetheless, in his history the Ukraine is a part of the tapestry of Russian history, not a tapestry in its own right.

Soloviev's presentation of events in the western and southwestern territories is subordinated to his synthesis of Russian history. The work of Soloviev's near contemporary, Nikolay Ivanovich Kostomarov (1817-1885), and the younger Mykhailo Sergeevich Hrushevsky (1866-1934) sought to redress the balance. Kostomarov's work is colorful and lively although less fastidious than Soloviev in its use of sources and more inclined to go beyond the limits of what the sources reasonably could support in the interpretations. Hrushevsky was a skilled historian as well as a notable political figure. He died before he could complete his majestic work on the history of the Ukraine. The final volume ends with the events of 1658, thus he did not cover this critical period for the Ukraine which Soloviev relates in this and subsequent volumes.[8]

Scholarly conventions regarding citations have changed considerably since Soloviev's time. The original text of this translated volume contained only one explanatory footnote. A brief paragraph at the end of

Soloviev's original Volume 12 indicated the author's sources. Soloviev made extensive use of archival material from the Moscow Archive of the Ministry of Foreign Affairs, the Archive of the Ministry of Justice and the State Archives. The material from all these collections is now preserved in the Russian State Archive of Ancient Acts (RGADA) in Moscow.[9] Soloviev also used several published sources including the chronicle of Samoil Velichko for information about the death of Hetman Briukhovetsky,[10] the writings of Jan Chryzostom Pasek for details about the adventures of Ivan Mazepa,[11] and Dr. Samuel Collins, *The Present State of Russia, in a Letter to a Friend in London* (London, 1671), regarding the hostility between Afanasy Ordin-Nashchokin and Bogdan Matveevich Khitrovo.[12]

Readers who do not read Russian or Ukrainian and who wish to delve more deeply into any of the topics introduced in this volume will find that the literature in English is scattered and uneven. The emergence of Ukraine as an independent state has stimulated an increasing interest in the Ukrainian past manifested in a flow of historical studies. The majority of this work is in Ukrainian or other Slavic languages.[13] The Harvard Ukrainian Research Institute, the Canadian Institute of Ukrainian Studies at the University of Alberta, and other institutes devoted to Ukrainian studies[14] are actively engaged in the publication of monographs and translated sources related to Ukrainian history. A lacuna remains for the second half of the seventeenth century.

Although based on observations made in the years 1630-1647 Guillaume Le Vasseur, Sieur de Beauplan's *Description d'Ukrainie*, first published in Rouen in 1660, contains a wealth of ethnographical information about both cossacks and Tatars which remains relevant for the second half of the seventeenth century. This is available in an excellent scholarly English translation prepared by Andrew B. Pernal and Dennis F. Essar, *A Description of Ukraine* (Cambridge, Mass., 1993)

The annotations at the end of this volume offer suggestions for further reading on specific topics in Western languages when available. The bibliographies and citations in these cited works will help to guide the reader through the scholarly literature. General histories of the Ukraine, such as Paul Robert Magosci, *A History of the Ukraine* (Toronto, 1996) or Orest Subtely, *Ukraine. A History*, 2nd ed. (Toronto, 1994), also include useful guides to literature about the specific periods and topics covered by their work. Philip Longworth's general history *The Cossacks* (London, 1971) provides guidance in its notes and bibliography as well. For brief definitions, explanations and bibliographical suggestions, the reader should consult *The Modern Encyclopedia of Russian, Soviet and Eurasian History* (abbreviated as MERSH), edited by Joseph L. Wieczyński, et al. (Academic International Press, 1976-). For information about topics relating to church and religion, *The Modern Encyclopedia of Religions in Russia and Eurasia* (MERRE), edited by Paul D. Steeves (Academic International Press, 1988-) is useful. Finally for the committed and tenacious, journals such as *Harvard Ukrainian Studies, Journal of Ukrainian Studies, Ukrainian Quarterly* and *Ukrainian Review* offer scholarly treatments of important issues.

The best starting place for this period in Ukrainian history remains Soloviev. The volume opens in January of 1667 with a cossack emissary in Moscow pleading for assistance against an anticipated Turkish and Tatar attack.

TSAR ALEKSEI MIKHAILOVICH

IOANNES CASIMIRVS DEI GRATIA REX POLONIÆ MAG:DVX
LITHVANIÆ,RVSSLÆ,PRVSSLÆ,MASOVLÆ,SAMOGITIÆ,LIVONIÆ,
SMOLENSCIÆ,SEVERIÆ,CZERNIHOVLÆQVE NEC NON SVECORVM,
GOTHORVM VANDALORVMQVE HÆREDITARIVS REX.

JAN KAZIMIERZ

King of Poland

Engraving

STEPAN ("STENKA") RAZIN
Detail from a seventeenth-century English engraving.

IVAN ASTAFIEVICH VYGOVSKY
Hetman, 1657–1659
Unknown artist.

AFANASY LAVRENTIEVICH ORDIN-NASHCHOKIN
Unknown artist.

ARTAMON SERGEEVICH MATVEEV
Unknown artist.

MAIN ENTRACE TO THE KIEVAN CAVES MONASTERY

TURKISH MILITARY FORMATION OF THE MID-SIXTEENTH CENTURY

Engraving

COURTYARD OF THE CHANCELLERY FOR FOREIGN AFFAIRS

Seventeenth century

HISTORY OF RUSSIA

Volume 22

The Reign of Tsar Alexis
Poland, Turkey, and
Ukrainian Cossacks,
1667–1674

I

RUMORS DISTURB LITTLE RUSSIA

TURKISH SCHEMES

Important events engrossed Moscow in the year 1667. On one hand, the difficult Thirteen Years War was coming to an end.[1] On the other an unprecedented church council, held in the presence of two Eastern patriarchs, moved toward the condemnation and confinement of Nikon and a solution to the question of the religious schismatics.[2] At the same time, at the end of January 1667 emissaries of the Zaporozhian Host, Colonel Yakov Kondratievich Lizogub of the town of Kanev and a chancellery official named Karp Mokrievich,[3] brought *information* from the boyar and hetman Ivan Martynovich Briukhovetsky.[4]

As usual, the hetman begged help against enemies and false friends, declaring that in his poor and inadequate opinion requests for peace from the Crimean khan should be rejected. "The Muslim wishes only to make a false peace," asserted Briukhovetsky, "then he will attack Little Russian towns. The Greek merchants speak truly when they report that the sultan has ordered the Moldavian and Wallachian hospodars to go to war in the Ukraine.[5] Everyone fears the approach of the infidels and traitors. They petition for an increase of [Russian] soldiers in the Little Russian towns. Neither the boyar, Hetman Briukhovetsky, nor Governor Peter Protasiev have regular troops. They have all dispersed and gone home. In Targovitsa, that traitor-town, Muslim money is minted at the order of the khan and at the request of Peter Dorofeevich Doroshenko. Supposedly this money is made of silver rather than copper.[6] It is hoped that once this money is put into circulation all the people will listen to the Muslims. Likewise, Chigirin and other traitor-towns must be destroyed totally. While they stand intact there will be no peace in the Ukraine.

"According to Christian custom," Briukhovetsky's messengers continued, "for the sake of the tsar and the Orthodox faith the hetman ordered a church built in honor of the Forty Martyrs near Konotop, on the site of the bloody battle.[7] He petitions the sovereign to grant assistance from the treasury for church construction. He also requests the donation of two cannon for metal to cast the bell. In addition, he informs his majesty the tsar that some of the clergy are insubordinate. They allow people of both sexes to live in an unlawful manner and to be divorced. If the great sovereign conferred upon us an incumbent for the metropolitanate of Kiev[8] he would eradicate much disorder. The clergy are pulled in two directions. If the patriarch of Moscow sent a metropolitan to the metropolitanate of Kiev, all vacillation in the Ukraine would cease.

"The wife of the late Bogdan Mikhailovich Khmelnitsky[9] came to Kiev from the side of the traitors [from the West Bank] with the daughter of Grishka Gulianitsky[10] and they are living in the Caves monastery. Moreover, in all of the sovereign's towns the governors allow peasants to distill spirits and sell as much as they can. This is unacceptable. It leads to quarrels, deforestation and grain shortages. The great sovereign must order the governors to decree that only cossacks, not peasants, may distill spirits."

Finally the messengers reported that Colonel Matvey Gvintovka of Nezhin was at fault for having refused to sign the articles when he was in Moscow.[11] Several colonels on their return from Moscow notified the hetman about Gvintovka's dereliction of duty. The previous year at Chigirin he displayed patent treachery. When the hetman reprimanded him, Gvintovka answered "Nowhere are men ordered to make war on their own people." He even told the hetman to call a council and lay down the mace.[12] "Now," the envoys declared, "Gvintovka sits in Gadiach under guard. In his place the full assembly of elders elected Artem Martynov [as colonel of the Nezhin Regiment]."[13]

A table attendant, Ivan Telepnev, was sent to Little Russia with responses to all these articles and an announcement about the conclusion of the Treaty of Andrusovo.[14] The great sovereign generously praised and rewarded the hetman for his service and for his warning about the khan. Soldiers would be sent quickly to the Little Russian towns. A directive from the tsar would be forthcoming about a metropolitan for Kiev. The sovereign ordered that Gvintovka be dealt with in accordance with law of the [Zaporozhian] Host.

ZAPOROZHIA AND BISHOP METHODIOS DENOUNCED

Hetman Briukhovetsky, after a service celebrating the universal joy that greeted the peace with the Poles, announced to Telepnev that the Turkish sultan himself wanted to go to war against the Poles in Kamieniec, which the Armenians wished to surrender to him. Then the hetman implored the sovereign to send him to another town because in Gadiach there was nothing for him. The place was deserted. As before, Hetman Ivan Martynovich cautioned Telepnev about Zaporozhia. "The cossacks go in droves to Zaporozhia," he noted. "Somehow [the tsar's] soldiers must be moved into Koidak and Kremenchug[15] lest grain be permitted to pass into Zaporozhia. If there are mobs of cossacks in Zaporozhia we can expect trouble from them."

After meeting with Briukhovetsky, Telepnev was directed to proceed to Kiev and meet with the governor, Boyar Peter Vasilievich Sheremetev,[16] who had complained about the cossacks, saying "The cossacks impose large taxes on the burghers, who respond by dispersing. The soldiers are deserting because of hunger. In Kiev there is a total of 3,177 cavalrymen and foot soldiers."

Soon new information came from Briukhovetsky about Zaporozhia, along with a denunciation of Bishop Methodios.[17] "Quickly, as soon as possible, send me soldiers lest the population on this side of the Dnieper despair," wrote Hetman Briukhovetsky. "I am sending the Zaporozhian Cossacks all kinds of presents and trying to persuade them in every way possible to behave. If only the duplicitous clergy were not such an obstacle to me. They incite the Zaporozhians to all kinds of evil. The most holy bishop of Mstislavl, for example, fans the flames of dissension and innocent Christian blood flows. Now that this bishop is not in the Ukraine, it seems to many that they live in a different world. Let the bishop live in Moscow, or wherever the sovereign pleases, save in the towns close to Zaporozhia. It would have been difficult to pacify the Pereiaslav rebellion[18] had not the bishop gone to Moscow last year. The bishop persuaded the cossack, Chief Justice[19] Peter Zabela, to send his son to Zaporozhia. What for? Zabela himself is old and was never in Zaporozhia, and his son only visited there a long time ago. They were just at the court of the Polish king, where they obtained privileges for themselves. Then he decided to send his son to Zaporozhia, to torment people and to incite the Zaporozhians to evil deeds. I petition the great sovereign to forbid the cossacks whom I have sent, particularly the Zaporozhians, to meet with the bishop in Moscow. He will incite them to every kind of evil. Some of them told me that the bishop secretly summoned starving Zaporozhians and complained that thanks to me he receives no alms to distribute from the tsar's treasury."

THE TSAR'S ENVOY LADYZHENSKY MURDERED

Briukhovetsky's fears concerning Zaporozhia were realized. His gifts proved to be in vain! In April 1667 Table Attendant Fedor Abrosimovich Ladyzhensky crossed the Dnieper on his way to the Crimea together with the khan's couriers. On the road they were joined by about a hundred and fifty Zaporozhians who had wintered in Little Russian towns. Two nights passed peacefully. On the third day the band of Zaporozhians fell upon the Tatars, slaughtered them, pillaged their property and went into hiding. Arriving in Zaporozhia, Ladyzhensky demanded that the cossack field ataman, Zhdan Rog, order a search for the culprits and escort him to the first Crimean town. "Thieves committed this evil deed without our knowledge," Field Ataman Rog responded. "They did not appear in the Camp,[20] nor can they be found."

A few days later a council was convened. After the council the cossacks seized all Ladyzhensky's papers and money, examined them and hid them in the Camp. The cossacks then announced that they would not allow Ladyzhensky to leave because he had no documentation from either the sovereign or the hetman.

As soon as this was known in Moscow a good friend of Ladyzhensky from Little Russia, Table Attendant Vasily Petrovich Kikin, hurried to Briukhovetsky in Gadiach. "If you wish to show your service and zeal," he exhorted Hetman Briukhovetsky, "send some available, trustworthy men to Zaporozhia to ensure that the field ataman and the whole Host find the thieves quickly, execute them in accord with the ancient law of the Host, return all that was pillaged and allow Table Attendant Ladyzhensky to leave." By this time Ladyzhensky already had departed.

On May 12 a new council caused a sensation in Zaporozhia. Zhdan Rog was removed from the post of field ataman and Astap Vasiutenko was elected in his place. Following the election the council discussed Ladyzhensky's release. The council decided to allow him to leave. Then the old field ataman, Rog, made a speech asserting that a search must be mounted for the cossacks who slaughtered the Tatars. "Search for what?" the cossacks shouted at him from the circle. "You yourself knew about this. Right now you have the Tatars' belongings in the Camp."[21] They ran to Rog's quarters in the Camp and brought the things as evidence. "The cossacks brought me these objects as a gift," answered Rog. "They did not say where they acquired them." Thus the affair ended in the Camp.

Field Ataman Astap Vasiutenko himself was dispatched with forty cossacks to accompany Ladyzhensky down the Dnieper. They had traveled barely two versts[22] from the Camp when cossacks caught up with them in boats and ordered them to come to the bank. The Muscovites obeyed. The cossacks stripped the wretches naked and set them ashore. Then they surrounded them with armed soldiers and ordered them to run into the Dnieper. When the Muscovites began to run a musket volley rang out behind them. Mortally wounded, Ladyzhensky sank. The bullets did not hit the others because they were already close to the other bank, but the murderers chased after them in boats, seized them and slaughtered them.

Having declared war with Moscow in this Zaporozhian form the cossacks discussed how they would unite with Doroshenko, drive the Muscovite soldiers from the Little Russian towns and refuse the Muscovite tsar any kind of tribute from their fathers and relatives. The Zaporozhians boasted that the colonel of Poltava was on their side. In fact, in Poltava Governor Prince Mikhail Ivanovich Volkonsky informed the sovereign that there was great turmoil in that town. "There is a firm order, buttressed with strong threats," he wrote,"from the Poltava colonel to the cossacks and the burghers that those who wish to serve you loyally, great sovereign, must not come to me, and no one may associate with Russian people. They will beat to death anyone who associates with us. The colonel threatens to beat to death the burghers elected as sworn officials for collection of customs duties. Therefore they will not collect transit duties for you from those passing through Poltava with merchandise."

LADYZHENSKY'S MURDER REPORTED TO THE HETMAN

The cossack field ataman Vasiutenko personally informed Hetman Briukhovetsky about Ladyzhensky's murder. "We are very distressed this spring," wrote Astap. "No one cares about our safety. Owing to our sins, those who gave us bread in the past now plan to give us a stone.[23] I do not know who would be grateful for a stone, because it is not fit to eat. His majesty the tsar amuses us with sheets of paper, as children are amused with apples. He writes urging us to serve loyally while he, having concluded a peace with the Polish king, together with the king immediately confers with the khan promising to decrease our numbers in return for the khan's friendship. We see that this already has begun. Why do they so harass a poor people destroyed by war?

"The faces of many people here are awash with bloody tears. The sovereign refuses to protect us, his fledglings, under his wings. Only divine mercy will save us from this bitter yoke, which formerly was sweet.

He who wishes to prepare a field for his descendants first cuts out the thorns. In such a fashion our ancestors, not grudging their health, tore the thorns from the fatherland so that it would bring forth freedom for us. This freedom we consider priceless, just as it is sweet to the fish and the birds and the beasts and all creation. As the great river overwhelms many other streams so too, with the assistance of the all-powerful God all schemes of earthly monarchs are overwhelmed.

"There is occasion not only to act but also to think about how our fatherland is being brought to utter destruction. If a wild beast had human reason even such a beast would feel pity at this sight. I know that the table attendant (Ladyzhensky) was put to death without our knowledge. This happened because in the towns the people suffer great abuses from the Russians. Nonetheless, we wish to live in love with your magnates as before. Kindly report to his majesty the tsar that I have forbidden my soldiers to engage in any kind of activity in the towns. Let the cossacks live as before. Unless the Russians cease their harassment a great conflagration will erupt because as long as we live we will safeguard our rights and protect our liberties. If the Russians try to infringe our rights and liberties, then truly they will cut off their own heads. They will not succeed. Like the blind they will fall into a hole. Let the monarchs consider that man proposes, God disposes."

Briukhovetsky sent a cossack, Aide-de-Camp Fedor Donets,[24] to investigate Ladyzhensky's murder. On May 26, 1667, Trinity Sunday,[25] Donets arrived at the Camp. A council was convened, the hetman's paper was read and arguments began. The Zaporozhians who came from the eastern side of the Dnieper, as well as those from the western side who had lived for a long time in Zaporozhia, attacked the newcomers from Doroshenko's side of the river [the West Bank]. "This evil happened thanks to you, not us," they charged. "It is not our fault that such evil has occurred in Zaporozhia." A fight erupted. The field ataman, approaching Donets, warned him "You had better withdraw to the Camp, for who knows what may happen? They might murder you."

The cossacks from the western side showed papers taken from Ladyzhensky. "Look at what is written here!" they shouted. "The Muscovite sovereign and the Polish king have made peace with the Turkish sultan and the Crimean khan. Why have they made peace? Obviously in order to demolish Zaporozhia. This is why we drowned Ladyzhensky!" They shouted and dispersed, having decided nothing.

The old cossacks grumbled among themselves in the villages. "We do not know what to do with these hotheads," they moaned. "You see how many have come! They do not listen to us or the elders!" The cossack field ataman, the elders and the old cossacks told Donets that the big trouble-maker, the cossack who drowned Ladyzhensky, was a man called Strakh. They seized Strakh and chained him to a cannon. After getting the guard drunk and beating him almost to death Strakh smashed the lock on the chain and fled. He hid in the Crimean town of Islam where the Tatars, recognizing him as having murdered some of their own, hanged him.

Donets returned to Briukhovetsky with a document from the cossack field ataman, who wrote that the Zaporozhians themselves would be happy to execute those guilty of such an evil deed, but so far these criminals had not appeared in their camp. At the same time Vasiutenko informed the hetman that the murderers of the Tatar couriers could be pardoned. "The words of one of the couriers," he wrote, "evoked anger and cruel rage in the cossacks. The Tatar said that his majesty the tsar freed the khan so that he might extirpate us, the Zaporozhian Cossacks, and destroy our homes. There would be no more mercy for us."

The field ataman did not consider it necessary to explain who had heard these words of the Crimean courier, insofar as his murderers allegedly had not appeared in the Camp. Vasiutenko, reporting these words as indisputably true, continued at length, as usual, with complaints against the Muscovite sovereign, asserting that nets were being cast on three sides against the cossacks. In conclusion, the field ataman asked that the tsar forgive the Zaporozhians for the murder of the Tatars and Ladyzhensky, promising in return that they resist all enemies coura-geously.

Briukhovetsky did in fact tell Kikin that the sovereign should pardon the Zaporozhians for this double murder and the pillaging of the treasury. Otherwise, he argued, this cossack company would remove itself from the sovereign's protection and join the Crimean khan and Hetman Doroshenko on the other side of the Dnieper. "In due time," Briukhovetsky declared, "I will exterminate the evildoers and troublemakers." Donets said the field ataman directly told him "If the sovereign pardons us we will gladly serve him. If he is angry, be assured that we will unite with Doroshenko and the Tatars to make war on the sovereign's border towns."

INVESTIGATION OF COSSACK COMPLAINTS

First of all, it must be determined whether the Muscovite governors were not acting foolishly toward the cossacks. A series of complaints was presented against the Poltava governor, Prince Volkonsky. He was accused of listing several cossacks as burghers and of taking money and copper quitrent from them.[26] The same Kikin set off from Gadiach to Poltava to investigate this business. He compared the names of the petitioners with Volkonsky's report and with the register of burghers. He found that the names of many people did not tally with their nicknames. Then he turned to the Poltava colonel, Grigory Vitiazenko, requesting that he send all the petitioners to him in person to be questioned as part of a genuine investigation.

"They cannot be sent for questioning," answered Vitiazenko. "Now is the time for working the ploughed field and the hayfield. The cossacks will not put aside their work and they will not come. Moreover many cossacks are not at home. They are away in Zaporozhia. So what if the nicknames of the cossacks do not tally? In the Ukraine it is customary for people to be called by various nicknames. Some people have three or four nicknames. They are referred to according to their father, or their father-in-law, or their mother-in-law, or their wife. This is why one and the same person is recorded on the governor's list of peasants with one nickname, and on our regimental cossack list with another.

"Moreover, in the past when registrars were sent to Poltava from Moscow they recorded many absent cossacks as peasants because at that time the cossacks were all with me on campaign near Kremenchug, and others were in Zaporozhia. The registrar himself lived in Poltava and sent clerks around the district to record information. These clerks listed absent cossacks as peasants without truly ascertaining who was a cossack and who was a peasant. Owing to the clerks' laxity, the peasants intentionally identified cossacks as peasants so that the cossacks would have to pay various dues and help provide transport."

Kikin inquired whether the governor's denunciation of the colonel was just. He turned with a question about this to Archpriest Luka. "The colonel is hostile to the governor," replied the archpriest, "and has forbidden the cossacks and many of the burghers to go to Prince Volkonsky. Please don't say I said this though, or the colonel will be angry and will persecute me."

In the evening, Regimental Justice Klim Chernushenko came to Kikin. As they conversed the justice confirmed the opinion of the archpriest.

Chernushenko was more loquacious and described his own experiences, relating how they all suffered from the colonel. "Colonel Vitiazenko is often *enraged*," Chernushenko said. "He beats us cossacks unjustly. He unjustly beats and dishonors his own wife and ours. If a cossack or a peasant commits the smallest infraction the colonel confiscates all his property, his horses and his livestock for himself. He rounded up the millers from the Poltava Regiment and made them work for him, and the peasants from the village were forced to cart timber for the construction of his house. He built himself a house grander than that of the hetman himself. Our whole town of Poltava has deteriorated and is in ruins. No one is happy about this colonel. We warn him of this discontent but he does not listen! We would like to petition the great sovereign and the hetman to remove Colonel Vitiazenko. His wife and his regimental chancellor, Iliash Turansky, encourage him in all kinds of evil deeds. We do not trust the regimental chancellor because he is from the other side of the Dnieper. What can be expected from him but treachery? He made a second regimental seal and keeps it secretly, without the colonel's knowledge."

After this Kikin asked around the villages as to whether the collection of dues was carried out lawfully. It turned out that in the registers cossacks were listed among the peasants, including long-time cossacks who were made cossacks in the time of Khmelnitsky, but who later were mixed in together with the burghers. When it came time to pay taxes they remembered their old cossack rank. In addition, real abuses on the part of the Muscovites[27] appeared. Clerks traveled around the villages drunk and they took money, a grosha[28] or two per man. Cavalry Ensign Dolzhikov, the man assigned to collect the tax, did not collect it himself. Instead he sent one of his orderlies who took another chekha[29] per man over and above the government quitrent for himself. Kikin corrected the abuses. For this, Briukhovetsky and all the Poltava cossacks thanked the sovereign.

THE TSAR ADMONISHES THE COSSACKS

To remove any cause for rebellion, the abuses were corrected in accordance with the cossacks' petitions and an admonitory letter in the name of the tsar was dispatched from Moscow to all the regiments of the Zaporozhian Host. "Muscovite soldiers live with you in the Little Russian towns," the document explained, "not because we suspect your loyalty, but for your defense. They are there to strike terror in the hearts of your enemies. We hoped you would receive the truce with the Polish king with particular joy because you started the war and Christian blood was spilled in your defense. Instead of universal Christian joy, desperate opposition and terrible bloodshed occurred in your towns. Who has ever heard of messengers being murdered? Among you are lawless men who attack their own kin and scorn divine justice. They have committed such criminal and unchristian deeds that their infamy is known to the whole world. We expected you, as loyal subjects, to undertake the investigation of these criminals and banish them from the community of righteous Christians. With astonishment we now hear that despite your oath and the regulatory articles trouble is erupting among you, disturbing the whole population. You wish to hold an unauthorized council, with what intention we do not know! Refrain from such an evil undertaking! Fire is not usually extinguished with fire. We must extinguish the flame with the water of peace, which the merciful God has provided in abundance. We should drink peacefully from the vessels and scoops of sincerity, filled from these saving streams and proffered in our Christian hands to extinguish the bloody flame of war and to soothe the intense heat of insult, which is withering human hearts. Among you are some frivolous people who wish to follow Hetman Doroshenko along the evil path, whereas Doroshenko himself should remember the single font of Christianity. Be ardent about this godly affair!"

The archimandrite of the Caves monastery in Kiev, Innokenty Gizel,[30] did wish to be ardent about this godly affair. In accordance with his ecclesiastical obligations Gizel entreated Doroshenko not even to think about submission to the Muslims, who in accordance with their own law exterminated Christians to gain their own salvation. Gizel endeavored to persuade Doroshenko to submit to the Orthodox sovereign of Moscow.

For its part the Moscow government also worried about this godly affair and released Hetman Doroshenko's brother Grigory from captivity. For this kindness the hetman sent the tsar a letter of thanks in November. In the letter "he preached mercy, praised clemency, confessed inexpressible thanks, bowed his head to the ground with all humility, promised all joy, and vowed not to permit any hostility towards the sovereign's people."

SHEREMETEV COURTS DOROSHENKO

The governor of Kiev, Peter Vasilievich Sheremetev, sent a message to Doroshenko telling him that he could prove his gratitude for the release of his brother by abandoning the Tatars, returning to Christianity and serving both great sovereigns, the Muscovite tsar and the Polish king.

"I would willingly sacrifice my life in gratitude for the generosity of the great sovereign," responded Doroshenko, "only right now I cannot leave the Tatars and place myself under the sovereign's hand. I will make an agreement with the king at the Sejm on the basis of an agreement made with Hetman Jan Sobieski.[31] Sobieski promised to give me Belaia Tserkov,[32] but I have yet to receive it. After the Sejm, if they will not give it to me, I will take it myself."

The boyar's envoy also demanded from Doroshenko that he not allow the Tatars to cross the Dnieper river into the sovereign's Little Russian towns. "I know nothing about the Tatars' plans," replied Doroshenko, "but if the Tatars come, then their enemy, my enemy and the enemy of the whole Zaporozhian Host [that is, the Poles] will be closer to the sovereign's towns."

"I served the Polish king with the cossacks for many years," continued Doroshenko, "and risked my life for him. For a reward the Poles turned our holy churches into Uniate meeting houses.[33] The king will give us all kinds of liberties and privileges and universals,[34] then will send Poles and foreigners to take these liberties away from us and other Orthodox Christians. They will beat and torture not only simple cossacks, but even the colonels and the elders. They will exact all kinds of taxes from us and in many towns they will curse and burn the churches of God. They will turn other Orthodox churches into Latin churches. No Orthodox Christian can tolerate this. We will stand for the Orthodox faith and for our rights. I do not want Christian blood spilled. If I send Tatars against the sovereign's towns, may my own blood flow. Were I to serve the Russian sovereign as I have served the Polish king I would receive favor from his majesty the tsar. I have long desired to be under the hand of the great sovereign, but I have not been called before. I cannot break with the Tatars immediately. Before the sovereign's regiments could arrive in defense the Tatars would destroy us. The Tatars repeatedly have urged me to march with them to destroy the sovereign's Little Russian towns, yet I have restrained them. I have written to Boyar Sheremetev warning him to beware of the Tatars, and I will continue to write. I want to be under the hand of the great sovereign. I do not want boyar rank from him or anything else. I desire only the sovereign's favor, that the cossacks may retain their own rights and liberties. According to the Treaty of Andrusovo Kiev must be surrendered to the Poles, but I and the whole Host will give up our lives rather than surrender Kiev to the Poles."

The emissary also visited both Metropolitan Joseph Tukalsky[35] and the monk Gedeon (Yury) Khmelnitsky.[36] He told them they must persuade Doroshenko to part with the Tatars. Both promised to do so. All of them, Peter Doroshenko, his brother Grigory, Tukalsky and Khmelnitsky, told the envoy in secret that they would certainly provide Boyar Sheremetev with much secret information. In return they expected the boyar to show them great love, to honor their messengers and provide them with food and drink, and bestow great presents upon the hetman and his messengers.

Sheremetev was not sparing of gifts. He only hoped they would win over the dangerous Doroshenko, upon whom now depended the peace of the Eastern Ukraine, and whose name so agitated the Zaporozhians.

In Moscow, Boyar Afanasy Lavrentievich Ordin-Nashchokin[37] vigilantly followed events in Chigirin. He sent Crown Agent Vasily Mikhailovich Tiapkin[38] to Pereiaslav for a meeting with Grigory Doroshenko to discuss the inclination of Hetman Peter to break from the Tatars and place himself under the protection of the great sovereign since an alliance with Poland was no longer a possibility. Tiapkin informed Nashchokin that Tukalsky was trying to persuade Doroshenko to submit to the Muscovite sovereign, thinking thereby to achieve the metropolitanate of Kiev. Bishop Methodios, on the other hand, would have been happy not to hear about Tukalsky, much less to see him, for precisely the same reason that Briukhovetsky did not wish to hear about Doroshenko. Methodios feared he would be deprived of his honor. The burghers and the cossacks, particularly the tax-paying peasants on both sides of the Dnieper, very much loved and honored Tukalsky and Doroshenko.

"Let it be known," Tiapkin wrote to Nashchokin, "that the archimandrite of the Caves monastery and Tukalsky are very close friends and they have influence over the populace. It would be beneficial to gratify the archimandrite with a commendation from the sovereign and a letter from yourself, which he greatly desires. It would also be good to write to the other abbots and brethren of the Kievan monasteries because through them all things can be arranged, for good or for ill. In Pereiaslav there are no loyal and good people of any rank. All are rebels and pernicious spies. We cannot believe a single word from anyone. The only way to turn them onto the true path is to send about three thousand soldiers. Then they will be frightened into loyalty. There are few soldiers now in Pereiaslav and these are all naked, barefoot and hungry. They are deserting because of poverty. The worst of it for me is that I cannot find a loyal man here. I would give the world to find one, but these evil men swear falsely. They take oaths and then tell lies."

DOROSHENKO RESPONDS

Pereiaslav was not the only place where lies were rife. Lies were also ubiquitous in Chigirin even though here its independent position made mendacity unnecessary. On January 1, 1668 Peter Doroshenko wrote a sharp letter to Tiapkin asserting that he could not submit to the tsar. Genuine reasons could have been found for this refusal, instead Doroshenko filled the letter with falsehoods and slander. Bogdan Khmelnitsky, according to Doroshenko, not only handed White Rus over to Moscow but also all of Lithuania with Volhynia. He brought the tsar's soldiers to Lvov (!) and Lublin and inspired many executions. What gratitude! The Muscovite commissioners did not allow the hetman's ambassadors into Wilno before the negotiations! They established Ivan Vygovsky[39] as hetman and, in addition, advanced Martyn Pushkar,[40] Mikita Bezpaly,[41] Yakov Barabash,[42] and Silka[43] against him! At Andrusovo they advised both monarchs to pacify, that is to say to exterminate, the cossacks. Doroshenko even decided to excoriate the Moscow government for the return of White Rus to Poland. Following this action, he asserted, the Orthodox churches again suffered persecution by the Catholics. Doroshenko's audacity finally crossed the line, passing over into confusion, even into buffoonery.

"On what basis," he queried Tiapkin, "did you decide to abandon one city and to surrender another, *without us*, since you acquired them not by your own force but with the help of God and our bravery?"

At the very same time Doroshenko and his brother Grigory, in discussions with Tiapkin, constantly reiterated that they were subjects of the king. What right had they to rebuke the Moscow government for concessions of land to the king's side when they were proclaiming themselves the king's subjects? Still worse, knowing full well that their apostasy from the king to the sultan was well known to all, they asserted that their present alliance with the Tatars was based on the Treaty of Gadiach[44] with Poland concluded by Vygovsky, according to which the cossacks fell under the king's authority and at the same time in alliance with the Tatars! When it came time to boast of their importance, all this was forgotten. They claimed that Moscow was obligated to the cossacks for the Andrusovo truce since they, along with the Tatars, had attacked the Poles, forcing them to make peace quickly with Moscow. They wreaked such terrible damage, political confusion and chaos among these unhappy people that they lost all self-respect or regard for the integrity of their own words.

The cossacks could not force a renegotiation of the Treaty of Andrusovo. This was not because Moscow was forced to conclude the truce on the condition of *who possesses what* and to give up the western bank of the Dnieper, thanks to the cossacks. Rather it was because Andrusovo was a peace between two governments, each of which had sufficient cause to be displeased with the cossacks. This was a dangerous situation for the cossacks, who suspected collusion between the two sovereigns directed against themselves. They were not satisfied simply with voicing their suspicion. They directly asserted that such collusion really existed. They unburdened their hearts, threatening Moscow with a disruption of the peace.

"The treaty will not be fulfilled by the Polish side," Grigory Doroshenko told Tiapkin. "The Princes Wiśniowiecki[45] and other senators and gentry who had towns, settlements and villages in Little Russia now have lost all of these properties. There is no way the king can compensate them. Therefore Poland will have to break the peace treaty."

In his fantasies about the guilt of the Moscow government in relation to the cossacks Grigory Doroshenko did not differ with his brother. "The great sovereign," he maintained, "gave the cossacks the right to elect their own candidates to the post of hetman and to all the ranks. Now the great sovereign has selected as hetman one who is not a native Ukrainian cossack. Many of the colonels are also foreigners, Wallachians, and not native cossacks. This is why the Zaporozhian Host is most unreliable. In contrast, the hetman and the elders beyond the Dnieper are all native cossacks. For this reason there are many rebellions in the Zaporozhian Host. Now they establish a hetman according to the order of the great sovereign and arm him with charter, mace and standard. Later they select another hetman, in secret, and arm him with charter, mace and standard. So here are all these hetmans, Vygovsky, Pushkarenko,[46] Barabash, Silka, Bezpaly, Iskra.[47] Each desires to retain the honor given to him. They cause internecine strife in the Zaporozhian Host. These non-native hetmans and colonels free outright thieves. By contrast, loyal servitors of the sovereign, men such as Hetmans Yakim Samko,[48] Vasiuto Zolotarenko[49] and Aniky Silich of Chernigov,[50] are harshly executed."

Audacity and recriminations were interspersed with timidity and polite requests. Hearing rumors that the tsar was coming to Kiev on pilgrimage Grigory Doroshenko turned to Tiapkin with a petition. "When his majesty the tsar, God willing, comes to Kiev with great forces, we are very afraid and all the people are terrified by the thought that the Poles might then attack us, counting on the forces of his majesty the tsar. We beg the great sovereign's mercy and ask that he forbid his army to help the Poles. Our people are very apprehensive about his majesty the tsar's visit to Kiev. They do not believe he comes just to pray. Should the Poles alone attack us and should we raise the Tatars against them, we beg his majesty the tsar not to be angry with us nor send his regiments against us."

Finally Grigory Doroshenko announced to Tiapkin a secret request. "We wish to be under the high and powerful hand of his majesty the tsar, as long as there are no local Muscovite governors, nor soldiers with all kinds of leaders, and as long as our cossack liberties and rights remain inviolate. Peter Doroshenko must be hetman on both sides of the Dnieper and no taxes or collections of any kind are to be taken from the burghers and the tax-paying people. In accord with the bounty of the great sovereign Hetman Briukhovetsky will be allowed to live even without the hetmancy because he was granted the very highest honor and many favors."

Even as he demanded that Moscow award him the hetmancy on both sides of the Dnieper Doroshenko, together with Tukalsky, was agitating to gain the hetmancy by other means, raising rebellions against Moscow on the East Bank and deceitfully provoking Briukhovetsky himself to rebel.

The very fears voiced in Chigirin with regard to an alliance of both realms against the cossacks also were voiced in Zaporozhia. The Zaporozhians and other cossacks, generally by their own behavior, in fact did quickly push the Moscow government to view cossacks with hostility. It is easy to understand the impression produced in Moscow by the news of the slaying of the Crimean couriers, followed by news of Ladyzhensky's murder and of riots throughout the Ukraine. Then Briukhovetsky wrote that the sovereign should pardon the Zaporozhians or it would become worse! It is understandable that thereafter, in Moscow, cossack emissaries could not be met with smiling faces and open arms! Thus the standard bearer sent by the hetman spent only three days in Moscow and was refused an audience with the sovereign. He left with nothing and on his return told how Ordin-Nashchokin dismissed him, saying "Now it is for God to absolve you!"

Afanasy Lavrentievich, a man of order, an authoritarian, really had no love for the cossacks. In the eyes of the cossacks Ordin-Nashchokin was the culprit in the Andrusovo truce and rapprochement between Moscow and Poland. Thus he appeared hostile and formidable. He was blamed also for the fact that the sovereign granted a million in compensation to the hated Polish gentry who were deprived by the cossacks of land in the Ukraine. It seemed to the cossacks that Nashchokin would finish this business with them. Thus among them spread a rumor that Nashchokin was coming to Little Russia with a large army. What good could the cossacks expect from Nashchokin?

All of these fears, rumors and tumult among the cossacks would have produced no significant consequences on the eastern bank of the Dnieper river were it not for the fact that the boyar, Hetman Briukhovetsky himself, the most humble among the tsar's boyars,[51] stood at the head of the movement against Moscow. What at this moment convinced the boyar-hetman suddenly to turn into a cossack and openly voice his sympathy for Stenka Razin?[52]

BISHOP METHODIOS BREAKS WITH MOSCOW

Briukhovetsky's enemy, Bishop Methodios, was in Moscow in 1666 and the beginning of 1667 in connection with the Nikon affair. His behavior in Kiev in regard to the metropolitanate and his bitter enmity toward the hetman, so detrimental to peace in Little Russia and the interests of the realm there, could not but weaken the favor the bishop earlier enjoyed in Moscow. Although experience should have taught that not all denunciations emanating from Little Russia were credible, the constant and strong accusations of the boyar-hetman could not be ignored. Methodios perceived the change. The respect he had enjoyed earlier ceased. Once he asked for sables and was refused. Upon his departure to Little Russia sternly he was ordered to desist from his agitations and make peace with the hetman. The prelate departed Moscow in high dudgeon and made for Gadiach, the hetman's capital. News had arrived already of Methodios's departure from Moscow. The boyar-hetman was greatly alarmed.

A bevy of cossack nobles rushed from Gadiach to Smelaia, a property of the Kiev Caves monastery where the archimandrite, none other than Father Innokenty Gizel, was living. The cossacks brought an invitation summoning the archimandrite to Gadiach. It was essential that the boyar-hetman see him. Gizel was alarmed. He and Hetman Briukhovetsky did not get along at all. The archimandrite was given no choice in the matter.

Unless he agreed to go voluntarily the cossacks would take him against his will. He went.

"Why are you angry at me," the hetman asked, "and why do you not pray to God for me at the great holy Caves lavra?"[53] In such fashion did Briukhovetsky greet Gizel.

"We do not wish you any evil," answered Gizel, "but we see your animosity. Many times we have written to you with anguished and tearful appeals because the cossacks were destroying our lavra of the Caves. They beat the peasants in our holdings, they steal horses and oxen and every kind of goods and grain, and they dishonor and beat me and my brothers, monks and honorable people. You are without mercy. You have scorned our letters and our tearful appeals. Owing to your hostility to the holy cloister, we have not prayed to God for you."

"It is true," replied Briukhovetsky. "The cossacks have caused great evil to the holy cloister. I trusted them, but shall do so no longer. I hear that Bishop Methodios is coming from the capital. Hitherto there has been peace among us. Now the bishop is coming. Does this not bode ill for us? Have a talk with him, father archimandrite. Persuade him to make peace with me, to curb the evil and live in concord, that people in all of Little Russia may live in peace and work for our great sovereign with pure hearts."

The boyar-hetman worried unnecessarily. Methodios himself came to him with words of peace. All was forgotten except the friendship which prevailed before 1665. As a sign of the renewed friendship a match was proposed between the daughter of the bishop and a nephew of the hetman.

The hetman and the bishop did not become friends and relations in order to work for his majesty the tsar with pure hearts. Methodios transmitted to the uncle of his son-in-law [Hetman Briukhovetsky] all his dissatisfaction, all his irritation against ungrateful Moscow. He conveyed to him his own observations and his fears that Moscow was preparing something fearful for Little Russia.

METHODIOS CALUMNIATES MOSCOW

Secret conversations with the hetman did not satisfy Methodios. From Gadiach he travelled to his native city, Nezhin. Here in his home with guests he inveighed against the Muscovite magnates and prelates. He denigrated the morals of the Muscovites and vowed never again to set foot in Moscow. In the same vein he spoke of Archpriest Luka in the presence of the tsar's governor, Ivan Ivanovich Rzhevsky, such that the governor considered it appropriate to leave without waiting for dinner. Methodios did not hide the cause of his dissatisfaction with Moscow. He was treated dishonorably there. He was not given as many sables and provisions as he desired. Moreover Methodios, while speaking of insults he himself suffered, did not shrink from suggesting that insults were also being prepared for all Little Russia. "Ordin-Nashchokin," he declared, "is coming from Moscow with many soldiers. He comes to put Kiev and all the Little Russian towns to the sword, to burn and raze them to the ground."

These speeches were reported to Tiapkin in Pereiaslav, who deliberately hurried to Nezhin to ask Methodios from whom he had heard this. The bishop claimed he learned this from Muscovite traders traveling with goods into Lithuania and Poland, who then visited Little Russia. "They are telling the burghers," he said, "that Boyar Afanasy Lavrentievich is coming to Little Russia with many soldiers in preparation for the return of Kiev. This was not announced to the hetman and to me in the great sovereign's document about Kiev and the Little Russian towns. The hetman and I are very distressed and disturbed." Methodios also let it be known that in Moscow there were rumors that Kiev and all the Ukrainian towns were about to be ceded to the Poles. He wrote that, remembering the great sovereign's generosity, he was announcing this because he perceived that all the people were confused.

Hearing about Methodios's speeches in Kiev, Governor Sheremetev quickly dispatched Ivan Timofeev Lopatin, a captain of the Moscow musketeers, to tell the bishop that all rumors disturbing the Little Russians were foolish. "The great sovereign," Lopatin advised, "made peace with the king so that in the tsar's ancient patrimony, in the city of Kiev and all the Little Russian towns, all the Orthodox might live benevolently, in virtue, peace and joy. Now the great sovereign wishes to come to Kiev to visit his patrimony and worship at its shrines. He desires to see the city of Kiev, the Little Russian towns and the loyal Zaporozhian Host. He wishes by his visit to give joy to the soldiers and all the inhabitants and to make them eternally firm in their faith and allegiance. He dispatched his boyar Afanasy Lavrentievich Ordin-Nashchokin to the Little Russian towns in advance of himself, an old custom proper to the the sovereign's rank.

"Before the sovereign's travel boyars and councillors will be sent to prepare supplies and to proclaim the tsar's journey to everyone. The standard bearer's report of the words of Boyar Ordin-Nashchokin is preposterous. Boyar Afanasy Lavrentievich is an intelligent man. He bears responsibility for numerous great affairs of the realm. Not only would he never utter such words to the standard bearer, he would not even think them secretly. Such words were sown by an enemy of the cross of the Lord, a helper of Satan, a hater of the Christian community. Hearing that a mischief-maker, the standard bearer, has spread such tales, it is for you, my lord bishop, to deny them."

These admonitions were ignored. "For God's sake, do not blunder," Methodios wrote to Briukhovetsky. "As I see it, this affair is not just about a small strip of territory but about all of Little Russia. Be assured of this, the honorable Nashchokin is coming to take us by the neck and hand us over to the Poles. How do we know that the Russian and Polish sovereigns did not take an oath to one another about this? There are many signs that they are haggling about us. It would be better if they did not beguile us and behave so perfidiously towards us! Live with great caution and indulge the Zaporozhians in all ways. Fortify yourself with as many of them who turn out and watch the border towns with your men lest Moscow settles more people there. Such is my advice, because they will crowd in and appropriate our territory.[54]

"Has not Lord Vasily Dvoretsky[55] been sent to you on some kind of military business for his majesty the tsar? He will have come from Nash-chokin and will have wormed something out of him. He will tell you. He has his own problems. He is slandered by Sheremet[ev][56] and complains bitterly about his dishonor. It is not a good sign that Sheremet[ev] welcomes the most useless Poles and entertains them. He does not honor the cossacks, although they are honorable people, on account of these Polish dogs, and he boasts against them. Yet he corresponds with Doroshenko! God knows, is this not all to spite us? You must be very cautious. Do not go to Nashchokin, even should he tempt you. My native land is sweet to me. God save us if they take us by the neck and hand us over to the Poles or if they carry us to Moscow. Death is better than an evil life. Be careful they do not send you to the Poles as a gift, locked up in a Muscovite prison wagon like the late Barabash."[57]

TUKALSKY CONVINCES BRIUKHOVETSKY TO BETRAY MOSCOW

Simple caution did not satisfy Briukhovetsky. He immediately turned traitor and raised a rebellion against the tsar. Did Briukhovetsky decide to do this simply because Methodios informed him of his own irritation and fears? Did Briukhovetsky act only because of the encouragement of the bishop? There is no doubt that Methodios encouraged the hetman to turn traitor. Ultimately Briukhovetsky decided on this course for other, much more compelling reasons. The kinds of ideas being nurtured on the

West Bank of the Dnieper, in Chigirin, have been mentioned. Doroshenko wanted to be hetman of both sides of the Dnieper. Tukalsky wished to be metropolitan of Kiev and all Little Russia. Tukalsky was not averse to achieving his goal with the help of Moscow and Doroshenko was prepared to be named hetman by the tsar. At the same time the old accomplice of Vygovsky did not wish to be hetman on Briukhovetsky's terms, but now it was difficult to receive other terms from Moscow.

Doroshenko and Tukalsky cast about for a way to tear the East Bank of the Dnieper away from Moscow with the help of Briukhovetsky himself. Tukalsky embarked on a correspondence with Briukhovetsky, suggesting that Doroshenko would yield his mace to him. Thus Briukhovetsky would become hetman of both sides of the Dnieper. First he must drive the Muscovite governors out of the Ukraine, break with the tsar and place himself under the sultan's protection. Doroshenko himself wrote that the tsar had sent Tiapkin to him, calling upon him to assume the post of hetman on the eastern side of the Dnieper.

Briukhovetsky succumbed to temptation. The encouragement of Methodios achieved its goal. Briukhovetsky by indulging Moscow had earned the hatred of the cossacks, yet what good could be expected from Moscow? Bishop Methodios knew this. The standard bearer knew this. Briukhovetsky must escape this difficult position between two flames, between the hatred of the cossacks and Muscovite intrigues. The means was at hand. By rising against Moscow, against the tsar's governors, Briukhovetsky would gain the favor of the cossacks, Doroshenko would relinquish the hetmancy, and Ivan Martynovich Briukhovetsky would sit on the throne of Bogdan Khmelnitsky.

Hetman Briukhovetsky called the colonels to a secret council. Colonel Artem Martynov of Nezhin came to Gadiach. After Gvintovka's removal as colonel of Nezhin by Briukhovetsky, Martynov was named to his place. Colonel Ivan Samoilovich of Chernigov (the future hetman)[58] also arrived in Gadiach, as did Kostia Kublitsky of Poltava, Rodion Dmitrashko-Raich[59] of Pereiaslav, Gritsko Apostolenko of Mirgorod, Lazar Gorlenko of Priluki and Vasily Dvoretsky of Kiev.

The council deliberated. What must they do first? How were the Muscovites to be driven from the Little Russian towns? At first the colonels listened to Briukhovetsky with suspicion, thinking he was trying to deceive them with these words. Briukhovetsky observed this and kissed the cross, swearing to his sincerity. The colonels also kissed the cross, swearing their support.[60]

REBELLION ERUPTS IN LITTLE RUSSIA

By the end of 1667 news circulated among the cossacks that Briukho-vetsky no longer was content to be the most humble of the tsar's boyars. Rebellion flared. In the Baturin and Batman districts cossacks of the Pereiaslav Regiment pillaged the peasants, beating and torturing them. They took charge of the money and collection of all taxes. As a consequence the peasants stopped delivering money and grain to the tsar's treasury.

In January 1668 in Mirgorod many burghers registered as cossacks, refusing to pay tax to the treasury. Briukhovetsky's servant came and forbade the millers to give grain to the treasury. In Sosnitsa nothing was collected from the burghers or the peasants because they were dispersed by the cossacks' pillaging or had registered themselves as cossacks. The very same thing occurred in the Kozeletsk district. In Priluki, in the upper part of the town, a signal cannon stood in the square. The regimental lieutenant ordered the cannon be taken and set at the entrance gates. When the governor sent soldiers to take the cannon to the citadel the lieutenant beat the soldiers and refused to surrender the cannon. "We will remove all the cannon from the fort!" he shouted. Thanks also to his incitement the burghers and villagers all stopped paying taxes. The tax-collectors risked death if they showed their faces in the districts. The cossacks pillaged the burgher tax farmers, cut off their beards and bluntly told the burghers "Join us, or you, the governor and the Russians will be dead by Shrovetide."[61]

In Nezhin the tax farmers were not burghers. There the burghers were even angrier at the tax farmers than elsewhere but, being satisfied with Governor Rzhevsky, they acted in a legal fashion. They sent petitioners to Moscow asking that the sovereign grant them exemption from the payment of the duty for one year. "In regard to the liquor franchise," they explained, "charters were given specifically to the town but now a musketeer is assigned to collect the dues, causing great offence to the groaning community. With documents they claim the receipts of the town council[62] including the weighing fees, the fees for the measuring of goods at the customs house, the taxes from the sale of horses, from the tar trade, from tobacco and from the Avdeevsk grain mills. Musketeer Spitsyn seized all these receipts along with the great tax. According to the charter granted to the town in the case of gross injustice in the court the magistrate is not to be called before the boyar governor, he is to be summoned to Moscow. Now the Chancellery for Kiev[63] has destroyed all of this."

Who was to blame for these innovations, for the uncertainty in relations? The petitioners directed attention to a curious case. While a guest of the Trinity priest Ilia, Petrushka Sasimov, a Nezhin burgher, caused some unknown annoyance to Councillor[64] Gavril Timofeev. "You have dishonoured my wife," the councillor said to Sasimov, "and now you dishonor me. I shall seek justice against you!"[65] Petrushka, thumbing his nose, replied "Here is your justice for you!" The burgomaster Yakov Zhdanov was present. Offended by such profanation of justice he went to the town office to report this incident to the governor. The governor handed Petrushka over to the municipal court. Then Petrushka sent his wife to Kiev, to Boyar Sheremetev, with a petition. Sheremetev ordered the bur-gomaster and councillor brought to Kiev. They were imprisoned in the chancellery in chains for more than two weeks. Then they lived in Kiev on bail for twelve weeks. There was no court or confrontation with anyone although the town office extorted two hundred and twenty rubles for some unknown reason.

A document was immediately sent from Moscow to Kiev demanding that Sheremetev clarify this affair. He was reminded that members of the council should not be remanded from Nezhin to Kiev in response to petitions. The people of Nezhin also petitioned the sovereign to allow Governor Rzhevsky to remain with them because he was a good man. He lived among them, fearing God, and forbade any kind of trouble, pillaging or thievery. At the same time they petitioned against the archbishop of Chernigov, Lazar Baranovich,[66] who had given them great grief and taken two villages.

At the end of January Governor Sheremetev in Kiev was notified that a council was in session in Chigirin attended by Doroshenko, Metropolitan Tukalsky, Gedeon Khmelnitsky, the colonels, all the elders, Crimean envoys, a monk sent by Methodios and a delegate from Briukhovetsky. Doroshenko could not endure the latter. "Briukhovetsky is a bad man," he told Briukhovetsky's envoy. "He is not even a native-born cossack. Why does he take such a great burden on himself and accept an honor to which he is not entitled? He handed the cossacks over to the Russians, who subjected them to all kinds of unprecedented requisitions."

"Briukhovetsky did this against his will," answered the emissary. "He was taken to Moscow with all of the elders." Doroshenko feigned satisfaction with this answer. With all the elders he confirmed that along both sides of Dnieper river the inhabitants would be united. They would live autonomously and pay tribute to the Turkish sultan and the Crimean khan, as the Wallachian prince did. The Turks and the Tatars would defend the cossacks and go to war with them against the Muscovite borderlands. The voice of the monk Khmelnitsky was heard. "I will retrieve all my patrimonial goods and give payment to the Tatars, if only to escape the power of the Muscovite tsar and the Polish king," he proclaimed. "I wish to renounce the monastic garb and be a layman."

At this same council it was decided to kill the tsar's governors and soldiers in the Little Russian towns. Emissaries from Zaporozhia were at the council and took the oath for their brothers to submit to the authority of Doroshenko. The Tatars stood near the Black Forest.[67] Doroshenko wished to send some of them with his brother to attack Poland, and to go himself with the remainder against the Muscovite borderlands.

THE TSAR WRITES TO BRIUKHOVETSKY

In early February 1668 Sheremetev's report reached Moscow with news about the unrest in Little Russia. A communiqué from the tsar was dispatched to Briukhovetsky. "The cossacks do not provide money and grain to distribute to our servitors," the letter charged. "The governors wrote to you about this but you do not believe them nor do you restrain the willfulness of the cossacks. The cossacks brazenly register taxpayers on the cossack list as they please. They starve our soldiers and subject them to all kinds of other pressures to the point that those who do not desert will be compelled to disperse. Our couriers travel among Little Russian towns in dire need of transport, which the cossacks refuse to provide. There is disobedience and audacity in all that they do.

"Your obligation as hetman is to keep the cossacks in order. This is also the obligation of the colonels and the elders who have been rewarded by our great benevolence and whose crimes all have been forgotten. In your letter you called yourself the loyal hetman of the Host, yet you remain constantly with the cossacks and fail to restrain their hostile activities. Loyalty to the Host is not incompatible with your promise to us, which must be honored in deed as well as in word. Those who honor promises with their lips whilst their hearts are distant will be judged by God.[68] Gross deviations are known, not only from our authority but from the Christian faith, thanks to such willful cossack deeds. By renouncing the living God and the defense of Christendom they will hand themselves over to the Muslims in eternal damnation.

"They think Kiev will be ceded to the Polish side, therefore they seek to place themselves under the Muslim yoke prematurely. They do not consider that hitherto Christian souls have sought to save themselves from bloodshed and from Muslim captivity. Can true Christians be proud to assume the burden of such evil murder on their own souls? For the reassurance of Christian people and in order to bring justice against those who are evil, the nobleman Ivan Afanasievich Zheliabuzhsky[69] is being sent to you with an announcement which will inspire hope. He will read to you and the colonels the articles fixed by treaty with the Polish king. With the agreement of Bishop Methodios and the colonels and all the elders you will gather in one place. You will speak with the spirit of meekness and reassure the faint-hearted, lest Christian people be troubled with ideas about the surrender of Kiev. For God's sake, go now to pacify peaceful Christians without insults. Having accepted great losses in war, we have not given up the Ukraine!

"If the faint-hearted are troubled and therefore refuse to bring the grain and money collections to our governors, or prefer to take responsibility for these collections themselves, let all the Little Russian populace petition us openly. We will receive their request kindly and consider what is easiest for the people and most pleasing to God. We have directed the colonels, together with the burgomasters and prefects, to collect the taxes from the tax-paying peasants according to custom, without any affront. We have directed that the collection be disbursed to the servitors in the form of provisions and clothing. Moreover, we have directed the governors not to send tax collectors themselves. Henceforth when you send envoys to us with letters select reasonable and loyal men to serve as your envoys. Do not send people like your standard bearer, who instead of bringing our sovereign favor, conveyed hateful and stupid words to the people."

UPRISING IN LITTLE RUSSIAN TOWNS

This document was written on February 6, 1668. On February 8 the boyar-hetman launched his rebellion in Gadiach. On this day Governor Yury Postnik Grigorievich Ogarev and the colonels of the Muscovite army, as was the custom, went to pay their respects to the hetman at his home. Briukhovetsky was at home but did not appear. The dwarf Luchka ventured from the residence and said "The hetman went to pray in the church near the hill." Ogarev sent the orderly to the church to find the hetman. The orderly found no one there.

Ogarev himself attended mass and the colonels went home. In the middle of the church service Briukhovetsky sent for Colonel Yagan Gults and said to him "Colonel Sokha and a field ataman came to me from Zaporozhia with the cossacks. 'We are not happy that the tsar's governors are in the Little Russian towns,' they said to me. 'They collect many taxes and commit offenses.' I wrote to his majesty the tsar about this but there was no response. So, you colonels, leave the towns."

In response to this Gults, a German,[70] said "Come along [and speak] to the governor and my comrades." Briukhovetsky abused the governor. "If you do not leave town," he shouted, "the cossacks will kill you all!" Frightened, Gults said "If we leave the town, will you order them not to attack us?" Briukhovetsky crossed himself, saying "There will be no provocation from the cossacks if you leave peacefully."

Gults went to the governor and reported his conversation with the hetman. The governor called on Briukhovetsky. The hetman did not appear for a long time. Finally he came and declared that the Muscovites should leave town.

Ogarev announced to his soldiers it was time to depart because there were insufficient troops to oppose the cossacks. There were only about two hundred Muscovites to stand against the cossacks and there was no fort in the town. The Russians gathered and marched away. When they arrived at the gates they found them locked with cossacks standing by them. Gults and the civil officials were allowed to leave but the musketeers, the soldiers and the governor were halted. Ivan Bugay threw himself on Ogarev and the cossacks attacked the soldiers. The governor with a few followers fought his way beyond the town chased by the cossacks. They also caught up with Gults and his comrades. The Russians struggled, insofar as their strength allowed, but the cossacks prevailed. Seventy musketeers and fifty soldiers fell under the knives of the murderers. About thirty musketeers succeeded in escaping the town, then froze to death along the road. A hundred and thirty of the leading servitors were captured by the cossacks. Governor Ogarev was wounded in the head and carried to the archpriest for medical treatment. The barber served as the doctor. The cossacks showed no mercy to the governor's wife either. They defiled her, dragging her around the town by her hair and cutting off one of her breasts. Then they dumped her at the almshouse.

Having disposed of the Russians in Gadiach, Briukhovetsky circulated pamphlets to all the other towns exhorting them to follow his example. "We did not do this alone, we had the support of a council of all the elders," he proclaimed. "We have broken with Moscow for important reasons. The Moscow ambassadors and the Polish commissioners agreed to destroy the Ukraine from both sides, and they confirmed this agreement with an oath. They swore to destroy our sweet fatherland, exterminating all who live there, both great and small. For this reason Moscow gave the Poles fourteen million dengas[71] to hire foreign regiments. We learned about this evil, unfriendly Polish intention through the Holy Spirit. To escape destruction we renewed the union with our brothers. We did not wish to drive Muscovites from the Ukrainian towns with the sword. We wanted to escort them to the borders in safety. The Muscovites themselves, with evil in their hearts, announced they would not go peacefully on the road allowed to them. Instead they would declare war. Then the people rose up and did to them what they intended to do to us. Few were left alive! I beg you, in the name of the whole Zaporozhian Host, if you wish the unity of your fatherland, the Ukraine, think about your enemies at home! Think about the Muscovites! Cleanse your towns of them! Fear nothing, because we have come to the desired agreement with our brothers on the other bank. If necessary, they will not be slow in coming to your aid! The Horde too is prepared to assist on this side, although not with a large force."

BRIUKHOVETSKY APPEALS TO DON COSSACKS[72]

A document was sent from Gadiach to the Don. "Polish deception and the corrupt malice of Orthodox boyars almost caught me and the whole Zaporozhian Host in a thickly woven net. I complain about them to you, my brothers, and to all the main cavalry regiments, and present what follows for your consideration. Has Moscow behaved righteously, acting like a brother to the Poles, these longstanding enemies of Orthodox Christianity? The Poles have caused Orthodox Christians living in the Ukraine, people of all ages, even small children, to be destroyed by the sword. The Muscovites have seized settlers and driven them like cattle to Siberia. They have sought to destroy the glorious people of Zaporozhia and the Don and ultimately to exterminate them. As a result these places where Orthodox Christians lived by their own blood, sweat and toil have become wild fields, the abode of beasts. Yes, this they have done so that foreigners from impoverished Poland can be settled here. The Moscow boyars, assisting these ruined Poles, gave them fourteen million dengas and confirmed their eternal friendship with an oath. I think they did this only to weaken the tsar's authority so that just like in Poland, in accordance with Polish custom, they could possess towns, for in Poland the senators are all like kings and refuse to have one lord. Thus these boyars bring all innocent people and their tsar, given to them by God, to poverty and misery. In the end they will destroy themselves. We subjected ourselves to the great sovereign voluntarily and without coercion only because he is an Orthodox tsar but the Moscow tsarlets, the godless boyars, conspired to bind us to themselves in eternal servitude and slavery. I trust that the all-powerful right hand of God will free us.

"I present the following to you for consideration. When Moscow concluded a truce with the Poles, Jews and other non-Orthodox prisoners who had been baptized and married in Moscow were released to Poland. As soon as they left Moscow these people repudiated the holy cross and reverted to the faith of their forefathers with their ancient pagan customs. Is this right? They refuse to release our brethren, Orthodox Christians, wishing instead to lead them into greater servitude and misery. Their cruelty surpasses that of all pagan peoples and their own ungodly deed bears witness to this. They dethroned their highest pastor, the most holy father Patriarch [Nikon], refusing to obey his commands.[73] He taught them to have mercy and love towards their neighbors. For this they imprisoned him. The most holy father admonished them not to join the Latin heresy. Now they have accepted both the Union and the Latin heresy and they allow Roman Catholic priests to serve in the churches. Moscow already has begun to write with Latin letters rather than Russian.[74] The towns which the cossacks took by the sword, Moscow returned to the Poles.[75] In these towns the persecution of the Orthodox has already begun.

"You, my dear brothers, are accustomed to glory and victory, and to living in freedom. Be joyful, my lords, about the golden liberty through which God gives all wealth, and be not tempted by the deceitful Muscovite gifts. I warn you, as soon as they pacify us they will turn their attention to the eradication of the Don and Zaporozhia. Their evil intention already has been announced. Not long ago near Kiev, in the towns of Brovory, Gogolev and others, they slaughtered all the inhabitants, not even having mercy on small children. I beg you a second time, and I warn you, do not be tempted by their wretched money. Act in brotherly accord with Lord Stenka [Razin]. Thus we will be in unbreakable union with our brothers beyond the Dnieper."

The Don did not respond to Briukhovetsky's appeal since, fortunately for Moscow, Lord Stenka and the "naked ones"[76] of the Don were diverted to the east. The Little Russian cossacks of the Ukraine did rise up against the tsar's soldiers.

By January 25, 1668 Colonel Ivan Samoilovich of Chernigov (the future hetman)[77] assisted by the cossacks and burghers was beseiging the tsar's governor, Andrei Vasilievich Tolstoy, in the lower town, having dug entrenchments in a ring around the town. On February 1 a priest came to Tolstoy with a proposal from Samoilovich to evacuate the town. Hetman Briukhovetsky with all of the Ukraine had denounced the sovereign and taken an oath to the Crimean khan[78] and Doroshenko. In response Tolstoy staged a sortie, burned the citadel, killed many of the besiegers and seized their standard.

On February 16 a document was presented to the governor from the hetman himself. His majesty the tsar's *boyar* and *hetman* wrote to his *friend*, Tolstoy, that the whole *loyal* Zaporozhian Host and the whole Ukrainian community from all the towns intended to expel the tsar's soldiers, who had inflicted great injustices and unbearable offenses on the inhabitants. Briukhovetsky also suggested to his *friend* that he depart from Chernigov, abandoning his artillery, following the examples set by the governors of Gadiach (!), Poltava and Mirgorod.

Tolstoy did not accept the friendly suggestion. Governors Vasily Bogdanovich Likhachev of Sosnitsa, Kirill Alexandrovich Zagriazhsky of Priluki, Timofey Dmitrievich Klokachev of Baturin and Miron Lavrentievich Kologrivov of Glukhov were taken by the cossacks. In Starodub, Governor Prince Ignaty Grigorievich Volkonsky was killed when the town was taken by the cossack colonels Sokha and Boronia.

Governor Isay Maksimovich Kvashin remained under siege in Novgorod-Seversk. Several times the cossacks sent him proposals to evacuate the town. "I will die, but I will not give up the town," answered the governor. On February 29, at dawn, three captains[79] appeared with the same proposal. Kvashin ordered the messengers be executed. The enraged cossacks mounted an assault and took the town, but the governor sent more than ten cossacks to the next world before he himself was wounded with a musket ball. It was reported that Kvashin wished to kill his own wife. He struck her with a saber about the ear and shoulders, but the blows were not fatal. The fate of the governor's wife in Gadiach explains Kvashin's behavior.

The cossacks made two assaults on Pereiaslav and Nezhin, but in vain. Colonel Vasily Dvoretsky attacked Oster but could not take the town thanks to help sent from Kiev by Sheremetev. The position of Sheremetev himself was not enviable. He wrote to the sovereign that in Oster, Pereiaslav, Nezhin and Chernigov the soldiers bravely repulsed the cossacks. "But if the siege is maintained for long," he warned, "there will be a shortage of grain reserves in the towns and great misery! Everywhere traitors have established strong barriers and the burghers are not permitted to enter or to leave Kiev to purchase grain. Moreover if Oster falls, Kiev will become even more crowded. There is no money in the treasury in Kiev and grain supplies are very low. In March we distributed only half the normal ration of grain to the soldiers. In April they will be sustained somehow, though in great want. If horses are fed there will not be enough for more than two months. Doroshenko awaits the Tatars and soon will descend with them on Kiev. We have few soldiers and even they are naked, hungry and totally impoverished. Many have not eaten for three and four days, and no one gives charity in the name of Christ."

POLES RESPOND TO COSSACK REBELLION

At this time the Muscovite emissary Ivan Pavlovich Akinfov was in Warsaw. Hearing of the events in Little Russia he demanded of the senators that the king, in accordance with the conditions [of the Andrusovo treaty] send his army against the rebels to assist the tsar's army.

"The cossacks' treachery is already well known to us," the senators replied. "Now Doroshenko has written to Hetman Sobieski saying that if the king does not order his royal army be dispatched he, Doroshenko, will act to assure that both sides of the Dnieper support the king. This is patent deceit. As if this would oblige his majesty the king, who himself was under pressure from the Turk for a long time. As if the cossacks of this side would rebel in order to subject themselves to the Turk! Now we must conciliate the khan in some way, lest he join them. The king has dispatched universals to the crown hetman and the Lithuanian hetman instructing them to collect armies and send them with the tsar's governors."

Michał Pac,[80] the Lithuanian hetman, told Stepan Polkov, the clerk sent to him, "Both sovereigns, uniting their armies, must slash and burn all these traitor-Cherkassians[81] until their places are devastated because they will never adhere to their oath to both sovereigns. Nor can we ever expect any good from them. They have knelt to the Turkish sultan, who will find it difficult to defend them every year because of the distance. Thus it will be possible for their majesties, the tsar and the king, to ruin them, the dogs!"

The Polish king, Jan II Kazimierz, himself wrote to the tsar informing him that he had ordered the crown hetman to bring his army to join the tsar's army. The king requested that some Russian regiments be transferred to the western side of the Dnieper for protection against the Wallachians. Poland offered only promises. The Russians would have to rely upon their own resources.

The tsar's commanders, Prince Konstantin Osipovich Shcherbaty [or Shcherbatov] and Ivan Petrovich Likharev, defeated the cossacks near Pochep in April and near Novgorod-Seversk in June. On the return path to Trubchevsk for about twenty versts along the sides of the road they destroyed many settlements and villages. Prince Grigory Grigorievich Romodanovsky[82] surrounded the towns of Kotelva and Oposhnia with his own forces.

BRIUKHOVETSKY'S DOWNFALL

What about Briukhovetsky? He was in no mood for Romodanovsky. The colonels on the eastern side of the Dnieper had disliked him before. Now they hated him even more because he surrounded himself with Zaporozhians and allowed them liberties. The Zaporozhian rank-and-file did as they wished within the towns.

The colonels summoned Doroshenko. Together with Tukalsky, Doroshenko sent a message to Briukhovetsky telling him to bring his mace and make obeisance to him. Briukhovetsky could keep Gadiach with its subject towns for life. Having been deceived, Briukhovetsky was enraged and immediately broke off all relations with Chigirin. He seized Doroshenko's cossacks and dispatched messengers to Constantinople to make obeisance to the sultan.

On April 2, 1668 the emissaries, namely Colonel Grigory Gamaleia, the cossack scribe Lavrinko[83] and the cossack quartermaster Ivan Bezpaly, arrived in Adrianople where Sultan Mehmed [IV] then lived. They petitioned that Hetman Briukhovetsky and all Cherkassians be taken under the sultan's hand in eternal subjugation, on the condition that no dues be collected from the Cherkassians and that the sultan assure their protection from the Moscow tsar and the Polish king.

In Gadiach a crowd of Tatars under the direction of Cheli-bey[84] came to take the oath. Briukhovetsky had to give the guests seven thousand gold ducats and present to Cheli-bey a large coach with horses and hangings, as well as two Russian maidens. Briukhovetsky left Gadiach with the Tatars to oppose the tsar's soldiers and stopped near Dikanka, waiting with his regiments. Suddenly news arrived that Doroshenko was approaching.

Sorrow overwhelmed Hetman Ivan Martynovich. He begged the Tatars to send Doroshenko away to his own side of the Dnieper. The Tatars chose not to intervene in the affair and quietly waited to see how it would end. First, a dozen cossack captains came to Briukhovetsky, repeating Doroshenko's earlier proposal that he voluntarily relinquish the mace, the banner, the staff and the regalia. Briukhovetsky beat the captains, fettered them and sent them to Gadiach. The next day Doroshenko's regiments appeared. Quickly the cossacks of both sides united. A cry resounded among the elders and the rank-and-file cossacks. "We will not fight for the hetmancy!" they shouted. "Briukhovetsky has done us no good. He only provoked war and caused more bloodshed!" Immediately they ran to plunder the eastern hetman's wagons. Doroshenko sent Captain Drozdenko to seize and bring Briukhovetsky. Hetman Ivan Martynovich was sitting in his tent in an armchair when Drozdenko entered and seized him.

At this point the Zaporozhian colonel Ivan Chuguy, a loyal friend of Briukhovetsky who had been inseparable from him since the beginning of his hetmancy, struck Drozdenko on the side with a musket barrel, such that he fell to the ground. This did not save Briukhovetsky. A mob of cossacks from the eastern side of the Dnieper burst into the tent with shouts and curses, seized the hetman and dragged him to Doroshenko.

"Why did you write to me so harshly," Doroshenko asked him, "refusing to relinquish the mace voluntarily?" Briukhovetsky spoke not a word. Receiving no answer, Doroshenko gave a sign with his hand. The crowd threw themselves upon the wretched man, cutting off his clothing and beating him with a pole, with gun barrels, iron bars and bear-spears. They murdered him like a rabid dog and threw him out naked. Chuguy bravely defended him even then, though alone with but a few comrades he could do nothing. Doroshenko assured Chuguy that he had not at all desired Briukhovetsky's death.

Doroshenko himself almost suffered the same fate. In the evening the cossacks of both sides were drinking and carousing. They began to shout that Doroshenko should be murdered also. Doroshenko, scarcely able to calm them, rolled out several barrels of vodka. At night, with all of the elders, he retreated to the edge of the wagon camp for safety. He ordered that Briukhovetsky's body be buried in Gadiach, in the church he had built (June 1668).

DOROSHENKO RETIRES TO THE WEST BANK

Having destroyed his rival and proclaimed himself hetman of both sides of the Dnieper Doroshenko moved to the town of Kotelva, which Boyar Prince Grigory Grigorievich Romodanovsky had placed under siege. The governor retreated. Doroshenko did not pursue him. He returned to Chigirin, taking Briukhovetsky's property and the army's artillery (one hundred and ten cannon) and plundering everyone identified as wealthy.

As a consequence of Briukhovetsky's treachery Moscow lost forty-eight towns and localities occupied by Doroshenko, 144,000 rubles, 141,000 quarters[85] of grain reserves, 183 cannon, 254 arquebuses, 32,000 rounds of shot, and about 74,000 items from the personal belongings of the governor's servants and the soldiers.

On the eastern side Doroshenko left Colonel Demian Ignatovich Mnogogreshny of Chernigov as deputy hetman. Soon Hetman Doroshenko abandoned the East Bank. Then the East Bank reverted to Moscow. Events following the Russian defeats at Konotop and Chudnovo were repeated. Prince Romodanovsky collected a considerable force and marched on the offensive. The [Novgorod-]Seversk deputy hetman, as Mnogogreshny was called, did not have the force to oppose him. Besides, under whose banner would he show resistance? Initially he sent to Doroshenko with a request for help, but received the answer "Defend yourself!" Romodanovsky took the new town[86] in Chernigov by assault. With no hope of saving the old town, Mnogogreshny entered into negotiations with the tsar's governor.

ARCHPRIEST SIMEON ADAMOVICH IN MOSCOW

On October 25, 1668 Archpriest Simeon Adamovich of Nezhin, Vasily Ignatovich Mnogogreshny, the acting hetman's brother, and Matvey Gvintovka, formerly colonel of Nezhin, arrived in Moscow. They announced that Prince Romodanovsky had sent them, together with couriers including his own son, Prince Andrei Grigorievich Romodanovsky, Alexander Petrovich Skuratov and Mikhail Andreev Tolstoy, from a camp beyond Belaia Vezha. On the road Tatars fell on them and captured Romodanovsky's son and his comrades. The Muscovites questioned the Little Russians separately.

Gvintovka said that before Briukhovetsky's treason he was imprisoned by Briukhovetsky and kept at Gadiach in chains. In his place Artem Martynov was made colonel. When the sovereign's people were killed, he was brought to Nezhin under guard. Following the murder of Briukhovetsky he was freed. At the same time Vasily Mnogogreshny was freed from prison in Veprik. Mnogogreshny had been imprisoned because he beat his wife and she died from the beating. Gvintovka and Vasily Mnogogreshny together went to the village of Sednevo, to Hetman Demian Mnogogreshny, to urge him to place himself under the authority of his majesty the tsar as before. Demian rejoiced at this advice and released them to travel to the regiment, to Prince Romodanovsky. Colonel Peter Roslavets[87] of Starodub was also with them at this council. When the two men reached Romodanovsky a correspondence was initiated between Romodanovsky and Demian. The affair ended with Demian and Roslavets kissing the cross in the presence of two Muscovite colonels sent by Romodanovsky. Later, in the town of Devitsa, Demian met with Romodanovsky. "I heard from Colonels Demian and Roslavets," Gvintovka added, "as well as from others, that their hetman, who stood at the head of the army, was given to them by his majesty the tsar and elected by the cossacks. If the tsar's soldiers approached the Cherkassian towns and negotiated with them, all the towns would surrender."

Describing their adventures, Gvintovka and Vasily Mnogogreshny announced that Demian Mnogogreshny and Roslavets strongly urged them to seek a reassuring document from the merciful tsar and especially to obtain from the Moscow patriarch a document of absolution for breaking their oath. As soon as they returned to Demian and Roslavets cossack messengers would be sent with all speed to his majesty the tsar to obtain the sovereign's permission for them to have a Russian hetman with an army. Then they would support the tsar in Korobovo and the cossacks would feed the tsar's army with provisions to its complete satisfaction. The sovereign should direct that receipts be taken collectively from the regiments, not as it was done in the past. Rather they themselves would assess what each regiment must pay. Demian and Roslavets had spoken with Prince Romodanovsky about all these articles.

ARCHBISHOP LAZAR BARANOVICH PETITIONS THE TSAR

At the same time that Mnogogreshny and Gvintovka were conveying such welcome news in Moscow a document arrived from the archbishop of Chernigov, Lazar Baranovich, indicating that the deputy hetman's unconditional obedience could not be taken for granted. Nor could it be assumed that he desired to see a Russian hetman, appointed by his majesty the tsar, placed over him.

It will be recalled that at one time Lazar served as vicar of the metropolitanate of Kiev and was replaced in this post by Methodios.[88] To understand the character of Lazar's political activity the primary interests which shaped the struggles in the Ukraine must be considered. The interests of the Host, or of the cossacks, diverged from those of the town population. The cossack council of elders struggled to gather all power into its hands and sought to minimize governmental control. Thus the cossacks were firmly opposed to the presence of the tsar's governors in Little Russian towns.

The town population viewed things differently. From their point of view, the cossacks and their colonels were the source of oppression. Therefore they viewed the tsar's governors as protectors, both from external enemies and from the cossack colonels' violence.

In relation to these two opposing goals the clergy could not maintain a unified point of view. The view of the prelates, the ecclesiastical powers, was different from the view of the urban parish clergy. The prelates sympathized with the goals of the cossack elders. From their standpoint it was important that the area be kept as independent of the Moscow government as possible because this was a necessary condition for their own personal independence. The primary desire of the Little Russian prelates was to remain nominally under the jurisdiction of the patriarch of Constantinople, avoiding subordination to the patriarch of Moscow, who would not be satisfied with the mere shadow of power. Consequently the interests of the ecclesiastical elite corresponded with the interests of the cossack elders.

The parish clergy, on the other hand, were tightly connected with the urban population and naturally shared their goals. It was no accident that the archpriest of the town cathedral, a very important individual at that time, appeared in Moscow as a representative of the urban population to inform the great sovereign that the people wished to have the tsar's governors among them. Archpriest Maksim Filimonov of Nezhin [before he became Bishop Methodios] acted in this fashion, as did the other archpriest, Simeon Adamovich.

Now the Chernigov prelate Lazar Baranovich, who in the eyes of the Moscow government appeared to be a man unsympathetic to its interests, took upon himself the role of mediator and peacemaker. He assumed this role to ensure that the demands of the cossack elders in regard to the recall of the Russian town governors would be met.

Lazar entreated the tsar to pardon the felonious cossacks. "These are people," he wrote, "obstinate and greatly distressed yet they wish to work zealously for us [Baranovich is associating himself with the Moscow government] without sparing their lives. These people, with their glo-rious force, assisted the Poles at Khotin[89] and in various battles. These people also desire freedom. They fight not from compulsion but voluntarily. To what folly will the Poles succumb when the Zaporozhian Host abandons them? Now the cossacks are at odds. Various cossack factions interpret the situation differently and assert diverse opinions. Nonetheless, their greater zeal is to your most illustrious majesty the tsar. The cossacks and the whole Ukrainian community grieve about the actions of some of the [Russian] governors in the garrison towns. Some people are prepared to flee to Lithuania and others to Poland to escape these gov-ernors in the Ukrainian towns. They are encour-aged by the usual teachings of the barbarians.[90]

"By the liberty with which Christ has blessed us, free them, most illus-trious tsar anointed by God. Yes, they firmly maintain their freedom. Yes, truly they will labor for you and they will forsake the barbarians in all ways if you free them! As a sign of his conversion Demko Ignatovich Mnogogreshny, the [Novgorod-]Seversk hetman, is releasing his cap-tives. Like the hemorrhaging wife whose flow of blood stopped when she touched the hem of the robe of Christ,[91] so too when the Zaporozhian Host falls with humility and touches the edge of the robe of your most illus-trious majesty, O tsar, I think this flow of blood will cease."

Accompanying his petition Baranovich included the letter he had re-ceived from Mnogogreshny stating the conditions under which the cos-sacks would subordinate themselves to the tsar. "Having consulted with the regiments of this side of the Dnieper," wrote Mnogogreshny, "we wish to live in conformity with those liberties known to belong to the rank of cossack. When the great sovereign wishes to preserve for us, his subjects, the original liberties confirmed to the late Bogdan Khmelnitsky of glorious memory in Pereiaslav, and to remove his soldiers from all our towns, from Pereiaslav, Nezhin, Chernigov, then your grace, kindly write to his majesty the tsar. If he will receive us graciously, protect our liberties and forgive what happened under the influence of Briukhovetsky, (and what was done in response to the violence of the governors and the viola-tions of the liberties of the Zaporozhian Host), I am prepared to submit to his majesty the tsar with the regiments of this side of the Dnieper and re-turn our forces to wherever the tsar directs. If his majesty the tsar disdains our service, we are prepared to die for our liberties. If the governors remain they will perish one after another, for we do not want them." In answer to all these documents Moscow sent responses to Baranovich and Mnogogreshny in November. The sovereign pronounced a pardon for the cossacks, assuring them of his favor. No conditions were stipulated nor were any more definite promises made.

FURTHER ADVENTURES OF BISHOP METHODIOS

While Lazar Baranovich was assuming the task of mediation between the cossacks and the great sovereign, what was the other prelate, Bishop Methodios, doing? Up to this point he occupied the senior ecclesiastical post in the Ukraine as vicar of the metropolitanate of Kiev. He had been disappointed in his calculations, just like his son-in-law's father. Briukhovetsky's downfall inevitably entailed misfortune for Methodios as well. Just as Doroshenko could not tolerate Briukhovetsky by his side, Joseph Tukalsky could not tolerate Methodios. Initially Methodios was held under guard in various places on the East Bank. Then the cossacks took him across the Dnieper and settled him in the Chigirin monastery. Tukalsky sent a message to him there, demanding that he abandon the archiepiscopal mantle. "You are unworthy to be a bishop," Tukalsky ordered his envoys to tell Methodios, "because you accepted consecration from the Moscow metropolitan." Methodios was transferred from Chigirin to the Uman monastery where he plied the monks guarding him with drink and escaped to Kiev.

There Methodios's first act was to visit Boyar Peter Vasilievich Sheremetev and denounce the Kievan archimandrites and abbots for having relations with Doroshenko, Tukalsky and Briukhovetsky. When interrogated the archimandrite of the Kiev Caves monastery, Innokenty Gizel, responded that Briukhovetsky had sent for him to mediate with Methodios, whose arrival the hetman feared. Justifying himself, Gizel described how in Nezhin Methodios dishonored the Muscovite magnates and prelates. In response to the accusation that he was in contact with Doroshenko, Gizel replied that he really had written to the Chigirin hetman to ask him to prevent the cossacks from plundering the property of the Caves monastery. He added that he also had written about this to Tukalsky.

Under interrogation Abbot Alexis Tur of the St. Nicholas hermitage emphasized that Methodios's accusations were hearsay and could not be confirmed in any way. Abbots Feodosy Safonovich of St. Michael's monastery, Melety Dzik of St. Cyril's monastery, Varlaam Yasinsky of the Brotherhood monastery, Feodosy Uglitsky of the Vydubits monastery and Ivan Stanislavsky of the Mezhigorie monastery testified that they maintained relations with Chigirin with the knowledge of Boyar Sheremetev. All agreed emphatically that while Methodios was in Moscow all was quiet. The moment he arrived in Little Russia and became related to Briukhovetsky the disturbances began. The burghers of Kiev came to Sheremetev with similar tales. Doroshenko also sent a document denouncing Methodios. He enclosed a letter which Methodios wrote to Briukhovetsky, inciting him to rebel against Moscow.

Methodios's position was unenviable. He completely lost his head, not knowing what to do, nor to whom to turn. He had wormed himself into the favor of Sheremetev with denunciations against his own people. To Feodosy Safonovich he wrote that he had quarreled with Sheremetev because of the common good, for the integrity of the fatherland, the church of God and the freedom of the people. Sheremetev thought it best to send Methodios to Moscow since given the chance he would foment rebellion in Kiev.

The captain of the Moscow musketeers, Ivan Alekseevich Meshcherinov, took Methodios to Loev by way of the Dnieper river. From Loev they took the road to Stary Bykhov. In this town Major Yuditsky came to Meshcherinov and asked where he was going and whom he was taking with him. When Meshcherinov informed him that he was taking Methodios, Yuditsky cautioned "Serving as I do both great sovereigns [the Russian tsar and the Polish king], I must warn you, do not go to Mogilev. There the headstrong peasants are in rebellion and they will seize the bishop from you. They are as obstreperous as the Zaporozhian Cossacks. The day before you arrived two monks were brought in from there. They said they were from Kiev, from the Caves monastery. They were taken through Mogilev and I know for a fact that there they incited the peasants to rebellion. It is better to go through Chausy and Smolensk." Meshcherinov took heed and proceeded to Chausy. Here Methodios scolded the company commander. "God is good to you," he said. "Had you gone through Mogilev you would have seen there what they would have done to you!"

In Moscow, in response to all accusations, the bishop answered merely that he did not know about the treachery of Ivashka[92] Briukhovetsky until the sovereign's people were murdered in Gadiach. He was placed under guard in the New Savior monastery in Moscow where he died.

The kinsmen by marriage, Briukhovetsky and Methodios, paid dearly for the trouble caused and Doroshenko, its chief instigator, did not celebrate for long. The Tatars did not prevent Doroshenko's separation from Briukhovetsky. Soon he heard some terrible news. The Tatars had established another hetman in Zaporozhia

II

RELATIONS WITH UKRAINE, POLAND AND TURKEY

TATARS PROCLAIM NEW HETMAN

A Zaporozhian scribe, Peter Sukhovey, or Sukhoveenko, a young man of twenty-three years, cultured and learned, was sent to the Crimea for negotiations at the end of 1668. While there he succeeded in pleasing everyone, so much so that his hosts wrote to Zaporozhia "Henceforth would you send us the same kind of cultured people? This is the first time you have sent such intelligent people to us." The Tatars proclaimed this cultured and learned man hetman of the cossacks.

Doroshenko ground his teeth. "I still have not renounced my intention," he said, "of turning the Crimea head over heels with my saber, as my grandfather Mikhail Doroshenko[1] overturned the Crimea with four thousand cossacks!"

Sukhoveenko wrote to Chigirin announcing that he was hetman of his majesty the khan, and that Doroshenko should not be so bold as to sign himself Zaporozhian hetman. The khan's seal, a bow and two arrows, was on the document, rather than the ancient seal of the Zaporozhian hetman, a man with a musket. Doroshenko ordered that Sheremetev be informed of his intention. "I am going to smash this bow and arrow," he vowed. Doroshenko placed his hopes on the division within Zaporozhia. Of the six thousand cossacks, half were for Sukhoveenko and the other half supported Doroshenko. Six Zaporozhian notables arrived in Chigirin bringing a letter to Doroshenko from his supporters. "Come to the steppe," they wrote, "to a black council.[2] We will bring Sukhoveenko to the field by force and kill him. We will break the khan's arrows with our muskets."

Doroshenko dismissed the Zaporozhians with honor, giving each a fur coat, fine leather boots and hats and sent them back to Zaporozhia with presents for the cossacks consisting of supplies of grain and vegetables.

DIFFICULTIES FOR DOROSHENKO

Other news arrived from Zaporozhia to the effect that if a black council were convened it would turn out badly for Doroshenko. Caught between Poland, Moscow and the Tatars, things went badly for the Chigirin hetman. He was corresponding with all sides, offering enticements, prevaricating and deceiving. He communicated with the Tatars, offering to buy Sukhoveenko from the khan. The khan set a high price, requesting that Doroshenko give him Serko in return for Sukhoveenko![3]

Doroshenko corresponded with Sheremetev and with Romodanovsky, assuring them of his devotion to the great sovereign. His missives told of how many times he had called the colonels together, arguing "Should we not submit to Moscow? Should we not send envoys to the tsar?" The colonels preferred to remain in subjugation to the sultan. They were convinced that if they submitted to the Moscow tsar he would order all cossack elders executed. Likewise, if they submitted to the Polish king, he would take revenge on them.

Little Russia exploded. Sukhoveenko stood with the Horde at Lipovaia Dolina, a settlement not far from Putivl. Rumors spread that he had become a Muslim and now was called by the Tatar name, Shamay. The cossacks of the Poltava, Mirgorod and Lubny regiments joined him, but the Priluki colonel continued to support Doroshenko.[4] Instead of receiving a delegation of a hundred Tatars, he had them all slaughtered.

Grigory Doroshenko, appointed acting hetman by his brother, stood with the Host in Kozelets. He wrote to Sheremetev in Kiev asserting that he wished to serve the great sovereign, yet when Sheremetev sent an envoy to receive his oath he told the messenger "I did not write to the great sovereign promising to serve him and swear an oath. I wrote to announce that I had not come to Kozelets with the regiments to make war, lest the tsar's officials be alarmed and see this as a military provocation. How could you force me to take the oath anyway? Now I soar in accord with my own will like a blue-grey eagle. We fought for cossack liberties. It will be difficult to force us into submission. For our liberties we will die to the last man. If the great sovereign directs the governors and soldiers to withdraw from Little Russian towns, joyfully will we obey the great sovereign. The Zaporozhian Host is a stone wall between Muscovy and Poland."

The [Novgorod-]Seversk acting hetman, Demian Mnogogreshny, continued to reiterate the same. "The current war with the great sovereign," he wrote to Lazar Baranovich, "arose with the blessing of his grace,

Father Methodios Filimonovich, bishop of Mstislavl, and his disciple, the Nezhin archpriest Simeon Adamovich. I hear that Prince Romodanovsky sent this archpriest with my brother Vasily and Gvintovka to the great sovereign. He sent him to assure the final destruction of our poor Little Russia and of the whole community. Yes, and thither as well, to Moscow, went Father Methodios! Worst of all, they went to agitate his majesty the tsar with unnecessary schemes and to incite the boyars and all the councillors to calumny. If the great sovereign refuses to confirm our liberties, established during the reign of Bogdan Khmelnitsky then, like it or not we will bow to the pagans. On whom then will the sin fall? On Bishop Methodios, yea and on the Nezhin archpriest. Go, your most holy grace, to his majesty the tsar and petition that he not believe these slanderers who sow evil."

Baranovich sent this document to Moscow together with one of his own wherein, citing the words of scripture, he sought to persuade the sovereign to fulfill Mnogogreshny's request. "Turn your face from their sin and these impious ones will return to you. Entreat your slaves, lest in despair they harness themselves to the yoke of the non-believers, the Muslims."

In Moscow the demands of Mnogogreshny and Doroshenko were recognized as cossack demands or, more accurately, as those of the cossack elders. To refute them it was decided to give voice to all Little Russia, to all the component parts of its population. "Let Demian and the Zaporozhian Host," replied the tsar to Baranovich, "send us respected people from their midst, from the clergy and the laity, from the serving men and the burgher ranks and from the villagers, to request they be taken under our sovereign hand. Then we will present our gracious edict to them about liberties and rights." Accompanying this summons was a missive to Mnogogreshny and the whole Zaporozhian Host.

TWO HETMANS CORRESPOND WITH SHEREMETEV

In the meantime Doroshenko did not cease corresponding with Sheremetev, continuously affirming that he would agree to be under the hand of the great sovereign when the Muscovite governors were removed from Little Russia. "I am greatly astonished," responded Sheremetev, "that Hetman Peter Dorofeevich Doroshenko gives orders about such matters! What good will come to you if there are no governors or soldiers on the eastern bank? In this current unstable period, given the banditry of the Pereiaslav colonel, Dmitrashko-Raich,[5] if there were no soldiers in Pereiaslav the territory would belong to the Tatars. Those who wished to drive all of you to the Crimea would have made Pereiaslav their capital and have fulfilled their desire."

"Muscovite soldiers must be removed from Little Russia," argued Doroshenko. "In years past the Polish king ordered his soldiers removed from Korsun, Uman and Chigirin, and the Little Russian people rejoiced. Hetman Doroshenko and the whole Zaporozhian Host, seeing such royal favor, were placated and acted according to the will of his majesty the king."

"Yes," retorted Sheremetev, "we saw how it was done according to the will of his majesty the king. The Polish commander from Chigirin took the field alone. Then the hetman called the Tatars, invaded Poland and destroyed many towns, settlements and villages. If the tsar's soldiers are withdrawn we must fear the same thing will happen in Little Russia. The enemy would attack, the cossacks would go against him in the field and who would remain in the towns? The timid burghers would surrender."

Sheremetev also corresponded with Mnogogreshny seeking to persuade him to abandon his demands with regard to the governors. "Boyar Peter Vasilievich Sheremetev," the governor's envoy assured Mnogogreshny, "never thought that you, his friend, would be a disloyal servitor to his great sovereign. He constantly recalls your just mind, your courage and commendable zeal, and the blood you shed when you served the great sovereign loyally and fought zealously against his enemies. Your liberties and rights were never infringed. The bandit Briukhovetsky quarreled with those like himself, with Vasko Dvoretsky[6] and with the prelate. In the towns the governors have acted in everything according to the articles upon which you agreed. Your rights and liberties were never infringed in any way. If these articles were in any way unacceptable to you, this was not according to the will of the great sovereign but according to the petitions of the bandit Briukhovetsky."

LITTLE RUSSIAN EMBASSY IN MOSCOW

Despite persuasion Mnogogreshny and his colleagues did not yield. In January 1669 a large Little Russian delegation appeared in Moscow. Abbot Jeremiah Shirkevich[7] of the Maksakov monastery represented Lazar Baranovich. Hetman Demian Mnogogreshny sent the quartermaster Peter Zabela, the general aide-de-camp Matvey Gvintovka, Justice Ivan Domontov, six cossack captains, two cossack atamans, a regimental justice, a military clerk and forty-six rank-and-file cossacks. Two prefects and a burgomaster represented the towns. The peasants were not represented. The envoys announced they brought a directive from the hetman and the whole Host. They petitioned for the confirmation of the liberties given to Bogdan Khmelnitsky.

"The Zaporozhian Host has experienced frequent schisms" the petition read, "because after the death of Hetman Bogdan Khmelnitsky the hetmans diminished the liberties of the Host for the sake of honor and property. Even if there must be governors in Pereiaslav, Nezhin and Chernigov for defense from the enemy, according to Bogdan's articles, instead of defense they have brought us to greater destruction. The soldiers in our towns have plagued the people with frequent robberies, fires, murder and a variety of torments. Besides, they are unfamiliar with our ways and customs. Whenever one of them is seized for an evil deed and presented to a governor with a petition for justice, the governor drags out the affair. Such abuses provoked the outbreak of the present war.

"The great sovereign must remove his men from our towns and we ourselves will give quitrent to the treasury through our own officials, whom the Host will select. Until this happens the Ukraine will not be set right. These same governors, despite the established articles, infringe cossack rights and liberties and judge cossacks. This never before occurred in the Zaporozhian Host. When the Zaporozhian Host enjoys its own liberties there will be no treachery. The hetman and the whole Zaporozhian Host are troubled because your majesty the tsar agreed to yield the sovereign city Kiev to his majesty the Polish king. The Zaporozhian Host fought with Poland solely because the Poles turned the churches of God into Roman Catholic churches. Now in the current Sejm they have resolved to turn Orthodox churches into Catholic churches and to take the holy relics into Poland. All the members of the clergy and the entire Zaporozhian Host beg and pray, saying 'Have mercy, our great sovereign, God's anointed, do not hand your patrimony over to the Latin yoke!'"

The sovereign announced to them personally that he "ordered they be absolved of their guilt and permitted to receive his former generosity. Yet if ever again, forgetting the wrath of God and the favor of the great sovereign they engaged in treachery, or pestered others with and believed superstitious and quarrelsome words and letters, or fomented trouble of any kind and indulged in internecine strife, the great sovereign would not tolerate it. 'Begging mercy from Almighty God and the help of the Immaculate Mother of God,' the tsar said, 'and taking the holy and life-giving cross, and in all your zealous deeds giving witness to Almighty God, you must submit to the sovereign's person and cease being fractious.'"

ARCHPRIEST SIMEON ADAMOVICH WRITES TO TSAR

In the meantime information reached Moscow that only the cossack elders desired the removal of the Moscow governors. Also in January the already familiar Nezhin archpriest Simeon Adamovich, about whom Mnogogreshny had spoken so imprudently, dispatched a letter to the sovereign. The archpriest was aware he had been denounced to the tsar and accused of friendship and association with Methodios. Thus he began his letter with a justification.

"I do not ask mercy from you, great sovereign," he wrote. "As God is my witness, and all Little Russia, my soul is clean before God, before you great sovereign, and before all the people, of treachery and the bloodshed of innocent Christians. After my labors I did not at all wish to leave Moscow, knowing the inconstancy of my brothers, the Little Russians. Nonetheless your majesty the tsar ordered me to go to Little Russia to convey your sovereign favor and with documents to Archbishop Lazar Baranovich, to Hetman Demian Ignatovich Mnogogreshny and to Colonel Peter Roslavets. The [Novgorod-]Seversk hetman at first received me with love but then, according to the advice of the most holy Lazar, he grew angry and from November 27, 1668 to January 10, 1669 he harassed me with guards, with house arrest, and loyalty oaths. He would not allow me to journey either to Moscow, to Kiev, or to Nezhin. He insisted I accompany him everywhere. I wrote to the colonels and to the towns urging them to come under the authority of your high and powerful hand. I wrote also to Nezhin, to Governor Ivan Ivanovich Rzhevsky, urging him to convey all the news to you, great sovereign, and send his reply to me. With travelers whom I sent into Nezhin the governor sent messages to you, great sovereign. The moment the travelers came to me from Nezhin the hetman ordered them seized and imprisoned. I was to be sent from Berezna to Sosnitsa by night under guard. He also ordered all the messages to me read to him under threat of death and then burned. Had Governor Rzhevsky written the least little thing against him in these messages the hetman would have wished immediately to shoot me. As it was, he forbade me under pain of death to write anything to the governors or to Moscow. Then he dragged me with him to Novgorod-Seversk.

"The cossack elders gathered at Novgorod-Seversk from the regiments. According to the advice of Archbishop Lazar, Demian Ignatovich was made real [as opposed to acting] hetman of the three regiments, exactly as was done with the late Samko in Kozelets. Filipp Umanets Glukhovsky was made Nezhin colonel and Ostap Zolotarenko was dismissed because in Nezhin he had taken the oath to your majesty the tsar. There also, in Novgorod[-Seversk], the most holy archbishop persuaded the hetman to hold me under guard until Zabela and his comrades returned from Moscow. If your majesty the tsar permitted his soldiers to leave the towns in accord with the wishes of the archbishop and the hetman, I was to be allowed to live. If not, I was to be put to death or handed to the Tatars. I tearfully pleaded with the archbishop, not for my sake but for the favor of your majesty the tsar, to release me and allow me to go either to Moscow or to Nezhin. 'I would not do this for the earthly tsar,' the archbishop retorted, 'only for the heavenly tsar. Were it not for my protection the hetman would have put you to death long ago.'"

On the other hand, as Simeon Adamovich reported, "Vasily Mnogogreshny said to me 'My brother the hetman has done you no harm. The archbishop ordered you held under strong guard because he is vexed that you wish his majesty the tsar well and because you enjoy the sovereign's favor.' Vasily Mnogogreshny is loyal to you, great sovereign," Adamovich affirmed. "Many times he snarled against his brother, complaining that he is proud, he beats people, and does not wish truly to serve you, the great sovereign. Gvintovka is good as well. With my own ears I heard the archbishop say 'We must make sure the Muscovites do not set foot in Little Russia again. Should the sovereign not remove his soldiers from the towns the hetman himself will be finished, and the Moscow tsardom will be destroyed. Like fire it will ignite what lies under it, and it will burn itself out.'"

"Your majesty," Adamovich advised, "if you order your soldiers to leave Nezhin, Pereiaslav, Chernigov and Oster, do not think this will do any good. The people all will shout and weep, like the Israelites under the Egyptians,[8] saying they do not wish to live in slavery to the cossacks. Lifting up their hands, they pray to God that they may live as before under your sovereign power and authority. Everyone says that having lived for ten years under the authority of your illustrious majesty they never saw what they now see in one year under cossack rule. The current hetman, in the Severian territory, took for himself an immense tax in copper coinage.

From the peasants he took a ruble per vodka cauldron, a poltina[9] each from the cossacks, and from the priests (which never happened under Polish rule) a poltina per cauldron. From the cossacks and from the peasants alike he took two grivnas[10] for each unit of plowed land,[11] whether the land was plowed with horses or with oxen. For each unit of plowed land with grain mills he took five or six rubles and in addition a gold ducat[12] per wheel. At the fairs he collected ten altyns or two grivnas[13] per cart from both Little and Great Russians, which was unprecedented. If you do not believe this, seek out the people from Putivl, Severia and Rylsk. The cossacks no longer remain silent about him, nor do the peasants. They are arming themselves against him and they wish to resettle in the Holy Roman empire."[14]

"Oh! Oh! Oh! great sovereign," wrote Adamovich, "three times in secret conversations with the hetman I heard this from his own mouth. I admonished the hetman and reassured him in all ways of your majesty the tsar's mercy. He refuses to serve your majesty the tsar in any way. He maligns you, God's anointed, and your Orthodox tsardom too. I am ashamed to write it. Trust me as a priest, sovereign, he is a great enemy and harbors no good intentions towards you, your most illustrious majesty the tsar. Now the cossacks have broken into three factions. One faction supports this hetman, Mnogogreshny, another supports Doroshenko and a third supports Sukhovey. Nothing good will come from removing the governors and the soldiers from the towns.

"Now I would advise you to wait until the envoys of your most illustrious majesty the tsar are in Moscow. You should send three or four regiments with some intelligent governor from Sevsk to Glukhov, as if they were replacing those in Kiev. There Prince Romodanovsky's regiments should be invited into Gadiach. Then if your majesty the tsar settled soldiers in these two towns there would be nothing the cossacks could do! Oh their grief then, but they would concoct some fantastic story, pretending they had gained victory and conquest. Now the Host is divided, yet they petition for some privilege which never existed before, even when the whole Host was unified. Wise cossacks who remember their solemn oath, the burghers and all the tax-paying peasants speak loudly saying if you, great sovereign, permit your soldiers to leave the Little Russian towns they refuse to settle there. They will flee in different directions. Some will go to your majesty the tsar's border towns. Others will flee beyond the Dnieper to the towns of the Polish king."

Adamovich concluded with a recommendation. "Sovereign," he advised, "deign to detain Zabela and his comrades, whom the cossacks have sent to you from the hetman. Through these envoys conclude an agreement. If you do not do this and instead act as the archbishop and the hetman wish immediately they will turn to the Tatars, who are standing beyond the Dnieper with the kalgay.[15] Zabela and Gvintovka told me they do not want the sovereign's men to leave the towns. Order these two interrogated, sovereign, individually and in secret. If they fear God, let them say these things were not done on their advice, only on the advice of the archbishop and the hetman. I further beg your benevolence, great sovereign, and beg that you have mercy on me, your poor pilgrim, and not let my letter be made public. If it becomes public, I will be killed. Finally, for the sake of God, sovereign, forbid the men to leave the Little Russian towns. Better still, increase their number."

SHEREMETEV'S ENVOY REPORTS TO MOSCOW

On the heels of Simeon Adamovich's report, in the same month of January, the resident noble Vasily Ushakov arrived in Moscow. He had been sent by Sheremetev from Kiev to Mnogogreshny and Baranovich. Ushakov recounted his discussions with them. Invited by Sheremetev to consider the towns in the hands of traitors, Oster, Kozelets, Baryshpole and others, the hetman responded "I am waiting for the envoys of the great sovereign and for displays of sovereign favor. As soon as these towns witness the generosity of the great sovereign I think they will submit quickly to his authority."

"The great sovereign," Baranovich said, "must hasten to show favor to the hetman and to the whole Host and release their messengers without detaining them. If the messengers linger in Moscow nothing thoughtless should be done. Will his majesty the tsar surrender Kiev to the Polish king or not? When I was with Methodios in Moscow, the treaty articles were read to the whole community. In the articles it was decreed that Kiev would fall to the king's side. Yet as soon as we left the great sovereign's presence the opposite was reported about Kiev, that the sovereign in his mercy informed us that in no way would Kiev be surrendered. If his majesty the tsar surrenders Kiev to the Poles, the Little Russian towns on this side of the Dnieper will never be firmly under his authority.

"In all the Little Russian towns the clergy and the laity are very sorrowful about this. In the Kievan monasteries, in particular, the archimandrites, abbots and monastic elders lament and suffer great pain about the churches of God. They say that as soon as Kiev is surrendered to the king's side these churches immediately will be turned into Roman Catholic churches and the Union will be implemented. Moreover, it will vex the Poles that Methodios tore down the original stone Polish Catholic church in Kiev, wishing to build the Holy Wisdom monastery. Construction was never begun on the site, nevertheless the Roman Catholic church was destroyed. In retaliation the Poles will turn the Holy Wisdom monastery into a Catholic cloister. His majesty the tsar must stand firm for Kiev because it is the root of piety. Where there is the root, so also are the branches."[16]

In the course of discussion Mnogogreshny described his recent activities. "I heard that Doroshenko communicated with the great sovereign, indicating that he wished to be under the tsar's authority," Mnogogreshny remarked. "Don't believe it. These messages are lies. Doroshenko wishes to be sole hetman on both sides of the Dnieper. I will serve your majesty the tsar joyfully, in accord with my oath, to the end of my life. If you accept Doroshenko, he will murder me immediately. The great sovereign will derive no benefit from this."

Ushakov also reported on the situation in Kiev where allegedly everyone loved Metropolitan Joseph Tukalsky and wished he were metropolitan of Kiev as before. Further, the archimandrite of the Caves monastery [Innokenty Gizel] was offended. He served the great sovereign with great zeal. He helped the sovereign's soldiers with money and grain and stood firmly with the monastery's men against the traitors. Yet he still had not received any reward from the sovereign. All he received were inquiries about his health. Other monastery abbots who helped the soldiers with grain also were offended.

On January 24, 1669 the sovereign directed Boyar Bogdan Matveevich Khitrovo[17] to negotiate with Zabela and Gvintovka, the Little Russian emissaries. Khitrovo announced to them that matters must be decided in a council, to which Boyar Prince Grigory Grigorievich Romodanovsky, the table attendant Artamon Sergeevich Matveev[18] and the secretary Grigory Karpovich Bogdanov[19] would be sent. Khitrovo also announced that the sovereign ordered the Little Russian captives freed, 161 in all, and asked where it was best to convene the council. The envoys replied they could not say immediately. They would consider the issue. It would be better for the council to be near the Desna river. It should not be a black council [and include the rank-and-file cossacks] but should be limited to the colonels and elders because the countryside was devastated. If too many attended the horses could not be fed. In passing Khitrovo noted that the cossacks had selected Mnogogreshny as full hetman and indicated that the great sovereign would be pleased to confer upon him the mace and the banner.

The next day, January 25, the cossack emissaries were at the Crown Treasury with the conciliar noble Larion Dmitrievich Lopukhin[20] and the conciliar secretary Dementy Minich Bashmakov.[21] It was announced to them that the sovereign had released the 161 captives, and would release all the remaining captives if they provided a list. The messengers replied "We will provide a list at the council." "Give me written evidence against Bishop Methodios and the Nezhin archpriest," said Lopukhin. "Evidence was not sent with us," the envoys responded. "We will provide it at the council. We do know that Hetman Briukhovetsky's whole council of advisors definitely was with the bishop, and also with the Nezhin and Romanov archpriests."[22] "Who spoke these provocative words to you," asked Lopukhin, "saying they did not present your registers [the list of registered cossacks] to his majesty the tsar, and against whom did they speak?" "Briukhovetsky told us about this," responded the envoys. "His messengers, the standard bearer Popovich and the artillery clerk Mikifor, arriving from Moscow, told him that Boyar Ordin-Nashchokin would not present our registers to his majesty the tsar. Furthermore, he asserted that his majesty the tsar does not need Little Russia." "You yourselves must understand," said Lopukhin, "that this whole business is outrageous. Ivashka Briukhovetsky[23] purposely spread all these preposterous tales to make trouble."

The emissaries insisted that the council be held in Baturin. The sovereign decided it would be in Glukhov because of the availability of transport from the nearby towns for men, provisions and fodder for the horses. Further, the sovereign decided that it would be a black council.

MNOGOGRESHNY ELECTED HETMAN

On March 1, 1669 Romodanovsky and his comrades traveled to Glukhov. Lazar Baranovich arrived on the third. The same day the boyar called the council to his residence. Not many were present, only the delegates of the cossacks and the burghers. Romodanovsky announced that his majesty the tsar directed them to elect whomever they pleased as hetman, according to their rights and liberties. All answered that they favored Demian Ignatovich. Then the more difficult business began. They read the article stating that in Pereiaslav, Nezhin, Chernigov and Oster there were to be governors and soldiers. A shout was raised. "We petitioned for no governors on this side!"

"Yes, you petitioned about this," answered Romodanovsky, "but the great sovereign has ordered there be governors to assure a strong [Russian] presence and defense for you, the hetman, and all Little Russians. This is to assure safe travel to Kiev for everyone, and that the roads and river routes are clear for travelers and grain shipments. The governors and soldiers are not placed in the towns simply to collect taxes. You yourself, hetman, see that the inhabitants of the Little Russian towns are fickle. They believe all kinds of provocative seditious words and succumb to every temptation. Petrushka Doroshenko,[24] who calls himself hetman of the other side of the Dnieper, subjected himself to the Turkish sultan. Sending cossacks to this side, he tempts the local inhabitants to join in rebellion. Even now many of them support him. Pereiaslav, Nezhin and other towns are destroyed, their inhabitants dispersed, and everything is deserted. If none of the tsar's soldiers are there to defend these towns the returning inhabitants cannot build their homes and live [in safety]. Doroshenko immediately will seize these towns with his men. He will seize the road to Kiev and force you to subject yourselves to the Turk, as he himself has done." "In disputing this article," said Demian, "we mean no offense to you. Order the other articles be read, and we will discuss this one."

Then arguments began about Kiev, with requests made that it not be surrendered to the Poles. "You yourselves know," said Romodanovsky, "that on this side of the Dnieper the cossacks and many of the inhabitants broke away from his majesty the tsar and placed themselves under the authority of the Polish king by their own choice, before the Andrusovo negotiations. His majesty the tsar did not surrender these people. Rather it was agreed thus in the Treaty of Andrusovo in accord with their own actions."

"Indeed, we do know that local cossacks themselves submitted to the authority of the Polish king," the hetman replied. "We recognize that they were not surrendered by his majesty the tsar. If it has been established in meetings with the Polish commissioners that Kiev be returned, let it be according to the will of the great sovereign. Only do not permit the Poles to persecute the pious faith. Let his majesty the tsar permit the establishment of a metropolitanate in Pereiaslav." "No," objected Lazar Baranovich. "The metropolitanate must be in Chernigov. The town of Chernigov is more ancient than Pereiaslav and the principality too is older."[25]

The next day the quartermaster Peter Zabela, the aides-de-camp and the colonels of the Host came to the boyar. On behalf of the hetman they argued against governors in their towns. They presented a written petition regarding the articles. They requested that the tsar's governor, when he came to the town, bring the Host's artillery. They asked that there be thirty thousand registered cossacks, a five-year exemption from the tax and agreement that when there was insufficient money for the grants to the registered cossack soldiers, the tsar's treasury would pay. In addition they requested the hetman be permitted to live in Baturin. When Pereiaslav finally submitted to the sovereign's authority, he would live in Pereiaslav. They further asked that the governor be recalled within six months, or at most a year, when everything calmed down.

On March 5 there was another session. Romodanovsky began by announcing that the requests about the governors were unreasonable. "The governors," the hetman rejoined, "committed many insupportable offenses against the cossacks and the inhabitants. They interfered in our business and caused us losses. They beat the servicemen and dishonored the cossacks. They snarled at them and called them peasants. They stole their property and committed arson. In this matter, when the great sovereign relies on us we will serve loyally, without any hesitation and we will never betray him."

"Until now," Romodanovsky retorted, "there have been no petitions from the cossacks or the burghers against the governors and the soldiers. Henceforth in your laws and courts, both cossack and burgher, the sovereign will order the governors not to interfere, to allow you to judge your own disputes. Hitherto there have been no complaints of any kind. Were there complaints there would have been an inquiry and, in conformity with its outcome, punishment. Obviously this matter has been embellished. Do not even contemplate the removal of the soldiers from the towns. Have you given any thought to the kind of guarantee you would offer to assure no subsequent treachery?" The hetman and the cossack elders were silent.

"There have been treaties before," the boyar continued. "Cossacks affirmed these treaties before the Holy Gospel, pledging their own souls, and what happened? Did Ivashka Vygovsky, Yuraska Khmelnitsky, or Ivashka Briukhovetsky[26] observe them? Seeing such treachery from your side, what are we to believe? You undertake to defend the towns with your men, but this is impossible! First take Poltava, Mirgorod and the others from Doroshenko. In the remaining towns, were it not for the tsar's men, these too would have gone over to Doroshenko. There need be no more mention of this business!"

"For what reason," the archbishop then asked, "are we taxed? How can it be said that we petitioned the great sovereign about this? Now boyar, you say that you do not wish to negotiate about the removal of the soldiers. Then let it be written in the articles that later we may freely petition the sovereign about this." "We wish to speak with you only about what is written in the articles," countered the boyar. "In the evening we will consider this again," said the hetman, "but from the present discussion I myself recognize that we cannot be without governors and government soldiers in these towns."

On March 6, early in the morning, all convened and signed the articles in agreement with the will of the great sovereign. The articles stipulated that governors and soldiers would reside in the towns of Kiev, Pereiaslav, Nezhin, Chernigov and Oster. The governors would not supervise the inhabitants, only their own soldiers. Complaints about offenses committed by the soldiers would be judged by the governors. In such court cases respected, good and intelligent representatives from the Little Russian population would assist the governors. The tax would be collected as written in the articles of Bogdan Khmelnitsky. Thirty thousand men were to be registered cossacks and each would receive thirty Polish zlotys.[27] The hetman was to receive one thousand gold ducats per year, and the [general] quartermaster and the [general] chancellor a thousand Polish zlotys each. The [chief] justices of the Host were to receive three hundred zlotys, the court clerk one hundred, and the [general] standard bearer one hundred. The colonels were to receive one hundred efimoks,[28] the [general] aides-de-camp two hundred, and the captains one hundred.[29]

Old cossacks who had served for a long time would be included in the register. If there were too few of these old cossacks, burgher and peasant children would be accepted. Whatever already was granted to the nobles would be preserved. Henceforth the sovereign would grant this honor as a reward according to the petition of the hetman and the council of cossack elders. He would also grant charters to mills and villages as a reward to the hetman and cossack elders for military service.

The articles further stated that the great sovereign would order the hetman, the cossack elders and the whole Host to elect someone to reside in Moscow throughout the year. This official would write to the hetman about current matters and bring letters from the hetman to the chancellery officials, who then would relay them to the great sovereign. There would be no private messengers to the hetman from Moscow, nor would the hetman write to the great sovereign frequently, only in regard to the most important affairs, perhaps three or four times a year. Those travelling on such important business would be given twenty wagons and three couriers. This was because wagons invariably were lost, causing the cossacks and the burghers great hardship. Government soldiers would not be billeted in the cossacks' homes. Rather they would be billeted by the burghers and the peasants. Nor would soldiers call the cossacks traitors and peasants. Deserters would be returned.

In the event of a meeting with the Polish commissioners Little Russian representatives would be invited although their envoys would not sit with the ambassadors and the commissioners. This was to avoid disputes. When Little Russian affairs were discussed in these meetings the boyars would summon the Little Russian delegates and inform them about the matters being discussed. If the tsar's ambassadors and the Polish commissioners called them into a meeting to discuss the pious faith with them, or any other business, the discussion must proceed without disputes, in a quiet and polite fashion. (The cossacks did not agree at all to the stipulation that their envoys were not to sit with the ambassadors and the commissioners.)

If the hetman committed any offense, other than treason, he was not to be replaced without the decree of the great sovereign. Colonels from the Little Russian towns were to be named and a thousand registered cossacks would serve under them. In the event of trouble or treachery these colonels were responsible for suppressing the trouble and trying the instigators in accordance with their own cossack laws. The hetman was to live in Baturin.

After signing the articles the cossacks were directed to the square before the cathedral. Here Boyar Romodanovsky asked once again whom they wanted to be hetman. The cry rang out, "Demian Ignatov[ich Mnogogreshny]." Quartermaster Peter Zabela and the colonels brought Demian the mace.

"Although I do not wish to be hetman," said Mnogogreshny, "I cannot oppose the popular choice and I will serve the great sovereign loyally." "We too wish to serve loyally!" all shouted. The boyar handed the tsar's charters of confirmation to the new hetman and everyone entered the cathedral to take the oath.

On March 8 the sovereign's grants were distributed. The hetman received two timbers of sable pelts worth a hundred rubles per timber.[30]

The cossack elders received two pair of sable pelts each, the leading men in the regiments three pair each, and others one sable pelt apiece. Two timbers of sable pelts were sent to Lazar Baranovich. One timber was worth a hundred, the other fifty rubles.

PETITIONS TO MOSCOW

The division between the cossacks and the rest of the Little Russian population greatly assisted the Moscow government by enabling it to deny the demands of Mnogogreshny and Baranovich. This division clearly expressed itself in burgher petitions presented to the tsar. "Let there not be violence and taxes inflicted on Christians in the Little Russian towns, suburbs and villages by the cossacks," they read. "The inhabitants of Little Russia receive settlers [cossacks] from the other side of the Dnieper with the bread and salt of peace. In return the poor laity suffers great destruction and even bloodletting in their homes. Internecine strife and rebellions begin because these ravenous beasts are not satisfied with what they are given and forcefully take more from the burghers and the peasants.

"The civic affairs of the poor peasants must not fall under cossack power and authority. Let the cossacks enjoy their liberties, but they must leave the peasants alone. Nor should they interfere in town government or in the civil courts. None of the receipts for the great sovereign must be collected by the cossacks. Rather let the burghers and peasants collect them and give them to whomsoever his majesty the tsar designates, lest the burghers and the peasants be destroyed completely by the cossacks."

In April, following the council, the chief justice of the Host, Ivan Samoilov,[31] arrived in Moscow. He was sent by the new hetman and the whole Host bearing a petition. The first article demanded that Prince Romodanovsky and his army always defend the Ukraine, insofar as this had not been stated clearly in the tsar's directive. The petition also requested that all Little Russians exiled thanks to the calumny of Briukhovetsky and taken into captivity in the last war be returned to the fatherland. More important was another article. "If there is no collection of tax from the Little Russian towns," it read, "the annual grant should be paid to the Zaporozhian Host from the government treasury. At present all the Ukraine is ravaged and it will not recover soon. To all the towns, in accord with the sovereign's directive, an exemption has been granted for five years. According to this exemption tax will not be collected from anyone, as the mills are all destroyed." On all points agreement was reached, except the point calling for payment of the grant to the cossacks from the tsar's treasury. Joseph Tukalsky sent a request that the sovereign name him metropolitan of Kiev. Around the same time Archimandrite Gizel wrote supporting Tukalsky's request. The Moscow government responded that for several reasons Joseph could not be named metropolitan at this time. The negotiation between Russia and Poland in regard to Kiev still was not concluded. There would be a meeting, following which a ruling would be given. Then the tsar would issue a directive regarding the metropolitanate.

Neither the third outbreak of trouble in Little Russia, nor the third betrayal by the hetman succeeded in removing Little Russia from Muscovite control. The Turks and the Tatars did not support the rebellion of the barabasha (as the Crimeans then called the East Bank cossacks). The Poles, even had they wished to do so, could not act against Moscow nor could they help Moscow in the struggle with the cossacks. By the spring of 1668 both the tsar's emissary in Warsaw, Akinfov, and the Smolensk governor informed Moscow that in Poland and Lithuania there was great dissension and disorder. The Polish king was expected to abdicate and go to France.[32] Akinfov turned to the well-known Lithuanian referendary, Cyprian Paweł Brzostowski[33], with a question. "Who among the Polish and Lithuanian senators is strong, and from whom can we hope for service and zeal in the affairs of the great sovereign?"

"The Lithuanian chancellor, Krzysztof Pac, is very zealous towards his majesty the tsar," answered Brzostowski. "From the Polish king's men, Andrzej Olszowski, bishop of Chełm and vice-chancellor,[34] and Jan Rej, governor of Lublin, are ardent on behalf of the tsar. You must see them and assure them of his majesty the tsar's favor. In addition the king's chancellor, although he is not very enthusiastic, must not be crossed. You must see him and honor him also."

The same day Akinfov visited Olszowski and presented him with a timber of sable pelts. He also met with the king's chancellor and the governor of Lublin and assured them of his sovereign's favor, although he did not give them any gifts. To Pac he took sable pelts and a letter from Ordin-Nashchokin. Pac declared his desire to serve, remarking that when he left Moscow, he extolled Tsarevich Alexis Alekseevich to all as a man whose demeanor manifested wisdom, peace and a generous heart. He had worked to persuade everyone to look no further than the tsarevich for a sovereign. The Lithuanians were all inclined towards this idea, Pac reported, as were some although not all of the Poles. Those to whom the

French had presented great gifts were silent on the question of the future king yet were attracted to the French. The sovereign tsar should send plenipotentiary ambassadors to the next Sejm, Pac advised. At this Sejm the king was certain to renounce the crown and many would covet it, most of all the French. Pac indicated to the Russian government that powerful resources would be required to decide the election of the Polish king.

"Now his majesty the tsar should send an army against the cossacks. Do not let these regiments stray far from the border," he recommended. "Then the Turks and the French and other *schemers* will be cautious, thinking that since the Moscow government deals thus with the cossacks it will defend Poland as well. During the election in the Sejm those zealous to serve the interests of his majesty the tsar consequently will be more optimistic and bolder, knowing the sovereign's forces are on the border."

RELATIONS WITH POLAND AND SWEDEN

Meanwhile it was necessary to meet the obligation calling for plenipotentiaries of both Russia and Poland to meet in Courland. It was agreed that Swedish plenipotentiaries be invited also. After the Treaty of Kardis[35] the Swedes complained incessantly that not all captives were released by Russia and that Swedish merchants continued to suffer persecution on Russian territory. A new treaty concluded by the lord-in-waiting Vasily Semeonovich Volynsky with Swedish plenipotentiaries on the Pliusa river in 1666 did not end the complaints. In turn the Russian government complained about the persecution of Russian merchants in Swedish territory and about the inappropriate behavior of Swedish resident-agents in Moscow. "It is not proper that they reside in Moscow because they live by trade, seeking profits, and do not understand government affairs," the tsar wrote to the king.

In April 1668 a communiqué from the tsar arrived in Stockholm with an invitation for the king's plenipotentiaries to come to Courland for resolution of all trade difficulties. From the Russian side the head of the Chancellery for Foreign Affairs himself, Boyar Afanasy Lavrentievich Ordin-Nashchokin, keeper of the great sovereign's seals and the man in charge of important government foreign affairs, was sent to the meeting. On May 26 he left Moscow with great ceremony. In fulfillment of the words of the Gospel, "apart from me you can do nothing,"[36] the pious sovereign removed the icon of Christ Pantocrator from its abode and accompanied it in a procession from the Dormition cathedral, beyond the Tver gate, to the church of the Annunciation. Here, upon completion of a public service, the sovereign turned to the patriarchs[37] and begged them to pray that the mission be accomplished to the greater glory of the Holy Trinity, to the joy of Orthodox Christians and to the shame of the barbarian tribes. Then the sovereign announced to the patriarchs that since ancient times never was there a greater affair in Russia.

Nonetheless, Ordin-Nashchokin spent a year in Courland in vain. Neither the Swedish nor the Polish plenipotentiaries arrived. Queen Hedvig Eleonora of Sweden, writing in the name of her minor son, King Karl XI,[38] rebuked the tsar. "Your majesty arranged a meeting with the Polish king, neither announcing it to us nor showing us honor. This meeting is not necessary to our royal majesty because we settled the questions of free trade with you in the Treaties of Kardis and Pliusa, and with the Polish king in the Treaty of Oliwa.[39] We firmly support what was established by these treaties, without any curtailment. Therefore we do not deign to direct our ambassadors to this meeting. Should it be beneficial to your majesty the tsar to invite us as mediators for the conclusion of an eternal peace with Poland, we will be receptive and will be pleased to demonstrate every friendship."

A RUSSIAN CANDIDATE FOR THE POLISH THRONE

In August King Jan Kazimierz renounced the throne of Poland and the election of a new king ensued. The archbishop-primate, Hetman Pac and Referendary Brzostowski sent a message to Nashchokin announcing that Tsarevich Alexis Alekseevich was nominated as a candidate. They did not doubt the success of the affair, but wished to learn from Nashchokin whether the tsar agreed to send his son to Poland on their conditions.

"First of all," Nashchokin replied, "the agreement to meet in Courland must be fulfilled. God willing, during this meeting all confidential business relating to the eternal peace will be concluded. The Swedes have refused to attend the meeting. Clearly they are not happy to see a union between Moscow and Poland. In regard to the sovereign tsarevich, if he is to be the Polish king, who can oppose the righteous will of God? If He wishes this He will act in response to the petitions of those who believe in Him. First of all, we must confirm the eternal peace between the two great peoples. Then whether the sovereigns are native or foreign, they will live in unity with God-pleasing counsel."

Nashchokin explained the reasons stimulating him to decline the propositions for the election of the tsarevich as sovereign. "There is no need whatsoever to go to the Sejm," he asserted. "Eternal peace will not be concluded there, nor will the tsarevich be elected as king. They will only guarantee the original treaty. It is a terrible idea to enter the election. Think about how much Great Russia will have to give for the Polish throne. Were I to go to Poland as ambassador it would not be for the affirmation, rather for the destruction of the peace. Let others haggle over the crown of Poland like merchandise."

In October the courier Jan Gąsiewski arrived in Moscow bringing a communiqué from "the clerical and lay councils of both populations." He gave information about Jan Kazimierz's abdication and the original document of the Swedish king wherein he announced that he did not consider a meeting of plenipotentiaries of the three powers in Courland necessary because the Treaties of Oliwa and Kardis had resolved the trade issues adequately. "Thus," wrote the lords of the council, "it was not our fault that the meeting was not held, as we were prepared to send our commissioners." They agreed to another meeting at Andrusovo between Russian and Polish plenipotentiaries. The same Ordin-Nashchokin was named representative for the Russian side. Jan Gniński, governor of Chełm, was appointed to represent the Polish side.

At the meeting Nashchokin bluntly told the commissioners that the Poles had not upheld the peace agreements. In the war against the khan and Doroshenko they had not given the assistance agreed upon in the negotiations. As a result, Doroshenko was in possession of the tsar's towns. "In view of such confusion in the border regions," Nashchokin emphasized, "we must conclude a strong and eternal union to keep the Muslim at a distance."

"We cannot conclude an eternal peace now, during the years of truce," responded the governor of Chełm, "because then the conquered towns forever would remain in the possession of his majesty the tsar. We absolutely must set a date for the return of Kiev."

"If a date for the return of Kiev is set," Nashchokin rejoined, "we must also set a date for the return of the Ukrainian towns which Doroshenko now possesses. It is better to place all of this in the hands of God. Later the great sovereigns will correspond and decide about Kiev and the Ukrainian towns, in accord with common information and counsel."

The commissioners insisted a date be established. "First of all," reiterated Nashchokin, "we must agree about common action against the Muslim. If you do not agree, the tsardom of Moscow must seek the friendship of neighbors against whom you now demand an alliance." Finally, after long discussion, the commissioners of necessity were persuaded to lay aside their intransigent speeches and commit themselves to combining Polish and Russian forces against the Muslim. As December drew to a close, Nashchokin returned to Moscow.

ORDIN-NASHCHOKIN'S LAST SERVICE

By the spring of 1669 Ordin-Nashchokin was again on his way to a meeting, performing what would be his last service for the tsar. We have had many occasions to study the character of this renowned overseer of foreign affairs. We saw that Ordin-Nashchokin was one of the predecessors of Peter the Great, a man convinced of the superiority of the West, one who began to speak loudly about this superiority and to demand reform along Western lines. He paid dearly for his conviction when the admired West took his son from him.[40] His troubles were not limited to this. Recognizing the foreign as better, Nashchokin criticized his own as worse. When criticizing actions he inevitably criticized individuals, assuming the role of teacher. By so doing he asserted his own superiority. This was at a time when there were many powerful men who wished neither to recognize this superiority, nor to be students of Nashchokin.

We must admit that Nashchokin was none too tactful, for he bluntly claimed his own superiority and his right to teach. We cannot help but acknowledge that Nashchokin did not rise to his task very discreetly. He asserted his superiority and his fitness as teacher too brusquely. When anything was done in Moscow without advice from Afanasy Lavrentievich, or contrary to his advice, he never forgot it. He constantly repeated that all misfortune flowed from the fact that his opinion was not adopted and moreover was rejected simply from personal animosity. Oh, how he took advantage of this hatred and misused his relations with the tsar! Raised by the tsar from the common people and supported by him, he constantly appealed to the vanity of Alexis Mikhailovich. "You elevated me," he said, "it is shameful for you not to support me, to act contrary to my opinion, to give joy to my enemies who in acting against me act also against you." Thus preaching autocracy, Nashchokin directly sought to control the will of the autocrat. Tsar Alexis Mikhailovich could not but feel this, could not but be wearied by Nashchokin's incessant and unvarying complaints.

The Truce of Andrusovo, so desirable for all, particularly raised the status of Nashchokin. He was made a boyar and granted the wealthy district of Poret. He was made head of the Chancellery for Foreign Affairs with a grand new title. After this it is easy to understand why Afanasy Lavrentievich did not consider it necessary to change his behavior and the

tone of his speech. It is also easy to understand how he appeared to the
crown secretaries of the Chancellery for Foreign Affairs, men like Gerasim Semeonovich Dokhturov,[41] Lukian Timofeevich Golosov[42] and Efim
Rodionovich Yuriev,[43] who conducted business in the old manner when
Nashchokin wished to conduct it in a new way.

Nashchokin's opinion of the Chancellery for Foreign Affairs was
made clear to the tsar. "O, sovereign," he complained, "in Moscow government affairs are conducted carelessly. The Chancellery for Foreign
Affairs is the eye of all Great Russia. With an unwavering fear of God [its
personnel] are concerned at all times for the tsardom's highest honor and
well-being and for the business of the chancellery. At all hours the
chancellery officials discuss and advance your sovereign directives
regarding the peoples [of the world]. It is not proper for [the chancellery
secretaries] to isolate themselves as in a fortress, thinking solely of
personal profit. Sovereign, select and uncorrupted men must work to keep
a thoughtful eye on the realm's affairs, to expand the realm in all regions.
This, sovereign, is the only business of the Chancellery for Foreign Affairs. In this there is honor, and also baseness and meanness, in all
countries. Men from other chancelleries should not be used in the
Chancellery for Foreign Affairs, nor should the conciliar secretaries mix
great government affairs with minor matters, nor should they engage in
unsuitable talk with foreigners in Moscow."

Naturally, the chancellery officials who shouldered the burdens imposed by the exacting innovator did not speak well of him. They wished
to escape him and were ready weapons in the hands of Nashchokin's
enemies, particularly in his absence. Among the enemies of Nashchokin
was one of the tsar's closest advisors, Bogdan Matveevich Khitrovo. One
of the causes of the enmity was manifest. Nashchokin protected the
English, while Khitrovo protected the Dutch.

ORDIN-NASHCHOKIN CORRESPONDS WITH TSAR

While still travelling Nashchokin sent letters complaining to the sovereign. "My former colleagues, appointed to accompany me to the meeting,
have remained in Moscow to pursue their personal affairs. Now I am free,
spared the useless grief of having to listen to their complaints at being
forced to leave Moscow."

"Foreign affairs," Nashchokin lamented, "are founded on divine pre-
cepts. Peace is first among these [precepts], but then opposition appears
in the world. As you know, great sovereign, I am an orphan and hated. At

least now I do not have to witness my colleagues' woe and grief and can serve with a free mind, without much discussion. Be merciful, great sovereign. Pray do not take offense or force my colleagues from Moscow to join me. This, your great affair, will benefit the whole community. I, your slave, do not wish to be distracted from it by the grief and grumbling of others. I do not serve you because of a contract, or out of self-interest, great sovereign. I keep your most illustrious sovereign features in my thoughts and in my poor soul constantly, at every hour, along with those of the all-powerful miracle-working icon to assist and encourage me in [the task] of completing your urgent business, great sovereign. Never in my reports nor in my petitions about the insults I have suffered have I ever reproached my colleagues out of self-interest. It is a great responsibility before God and you, my sovereign, to safeguard the great affairs of the realm. I would resign owing to my great inadequacy, but do not ask me to do so. If I am unable to serve freely because of interference, and if my colleagues are afraid to voice their wishes in council, the disagreements would be detrimental to the entire realm."

The Polish commissioners became embroiled in the election of a king. At the beginning of May the tsar instructed Nashchokin to return to Moscow. "I have been ordered to see to government affairs," answered Nashchokin. "How can you ask this of me? I do not even know why I should wander from the embassy post to Moscow. In your sovereign instruction no reason is given. If I go to Smolensk for the icon of the Savior they will say that the embassy has been abandoned. Certainly I am not so bold as to leave the miracle-working icon in the embassy's headquarters in Mignovichi without your directive. Will the ambassadors wait for me while I am traveling to Moscow, or indeed am I to be removed from foreign affairs? All this talk and the contradictions in your affairs must cease."

Nashchokin suspected the snares of his enemies in this business. He surmised that the noble magnates and his colleagues in the Chancellery for Foreign Affairs had ensured he was not sent the necessary papers from the chancellery. They had written that he must go to Moscow without indicating the reason.

As was his habit, Afanasy Lavrentievich whined. "You would recall me, your slave, from an embassy the likes of which has never been seen before. Yes, and last winter I was cursed for nothing before the whole world! For your own well-being, great sovereign, look to chancellery disorder both for innumerable foreign misfortunes and every kind of insult. Order me, your loathsome slave, to abandon negotiations if I have angered you or proved inadequate defending you[r interests]. Some men of the council dislike me, therefore They also dislike these great government affairs. Rather than let the work I have done for the government be destroyed, cast me away! In the tsardom of Moscow, as in all countries, foreign affairs have been conducted in secret, closed councils from time immemorial. All business is conducted on the basis of reason and justice, and bribes are not accepted

Each and every day of my service I, your slave, weep because of my inadequacy. It is appropriate for privy boyars to be engaged in such affairs. They have great clans and many friends. They have the means to take part in these vast enterprises and yet still survive. The Chancellery for Foreign Affairs will not be cursed by anyone. I kiss the cross and give my oath to you, great sovereign, because owing to the insufficiency of my little mind I cannot stand alone."

Nashchokin's return to Moscow was not demanded again, but then misfortune struck from another side. A document arrived from Warsaw, from the lords in the council, dated April 20. "According to the Treaty of Andrusovo," the Polish lords wrote,"the surrender of Kiev was scheduled for the fifteenth of this month. From the document of his majesty the tsar it is clear that this surrender has been postponed until a commission meets in regard to the eternal peace. This is a clear infraction of the Treaty of Andrusovo. As the guardian and director of great foreign affairs you must work to assure that the Treaty of Andrusovo is not transgressed. We anticipate a satisfactory response." "It was made clear in the meetings," Nashchokin retorted, "who violated the Treaty of Andrusovo."

At the same time Nashchokin informed Moscow that fund must be established in Poland and Lithuania to ransom the burghers captured [by the Turks and Tatars]. Otherwise there would be large deficits and increasing intransigence on the side of the Polish commissioners. In addition, Nashchokin wrote that the Swedish document, written in a spirit hostile to Russia, which the Polish courier brought to Moscow, must be sent to Poland. "The document must be given to the Poles so that there will be no quarrels about it. It may be said in the Chancellery for Foreign Affairs that the document is needed as evidence against the Swedes but, as you can see, we must first make peace with the Poles. Then we can quarrel with the Swedes and establish their guilt. If the Chancellery for Foreign Affairs considers me audacious for assuring the Poles that this document would be returned, my audacity is for the glorification of the sovereign's name and for the maintenance of truth in all my affairs."

Nashchokin guessed correctly that articles of inquiry about his negotiations were being sent to him from Moscow. The articles of inquiry were
as follows.

Article 1. On what authority did you assure the Poles that the Swedish
document would be returned to them? When you were in Moscow you
said before the sovereign and the boyars that this document must be kept
firmly in our hands as evidence against the Swedes because such evidence
against the Swedes could not be bought for less than a thousand.
Nashchokin's Response. This document could be retained only until the
Poles asked for it. Once they requested it friendship demanded we return
the document inasmuch as they sent it to us in friendship. The evidence
will not disappear if the document is in the hands of a friend and ally.

Article 2. You wrote that we could receive Doroshenko, then you sent
articles stating that under no circumstances can he be received until the
negotiations in the meetings with the commissioners are concluded.
Response. This is the will of his majesty the tsar, and I gave my own word
on it. The eternal charter of the clerical estate [the Bible?] teaches that true
trust in the world is immortal. Without trust, the reception of Doroshenko
is always unpredictable, and there are many Doroshenkos. God helps
those who help themselves. My letter was sent to inform about the situation, in accordance with His holy will.

Article 3. In Nashchokin's opinion, the retention of Kiev must be accomplished through the vicar, Tukalsky. How?
Response. In reports about Article 21 in the Little Russian Chancellery it
is written in the original "When a gracious directive is sent from Moscow
responding to the petition of the Kievan clergy, as described in these
articles, a vicar will have to be named." The time now has expired.

Article 4. Let him clarify what was said in discussions in the Chancellery
for Foreign Affairs about the arrival of the current Crimean ambassador.
Response. We must negotiate firmly with the Crimean envoy so that in the
future general meeting, either in the Ukraine or in Valuiki, the sovereign's
ambassadors, Polish ambassadors and Crimean ambassadors will assemble to conclude peace by general consent.

Article 5. According to the reports left by Nashchokin in the Secret
Chancellery and the Chancellery for Foreign Affairs, Kiev cannot be
retained. In Article 16 it says "This does not pertain to Kiev." How does
he interpret this?
Response. These reports were left at the wish of the sovereign, and it will
be as God and the sovereign decree. The organization of the Eastern

church is laid out in the reports, according to the preferences of the clergy. *Article 6.* By what authority did Nashchokin give the letters of Innokenty Gizel to Stanisław Beniewski[44], and for what reason? *Response.* Who reported this? I will be happy to confront this person face to face for an account of this treachery. Beniewski is happy to quarrel over the fact that his words went to Gizel. Did my colleagues then see and hear my treachery and not admonish me and correct it? The arrangement [the offer of a confrontation] is rescinded because of such lying treachery. Such denunciation by confrontation would harm the Muscovite realm and proper justice. My colleagues would be happy to break me, the hated man who rooted out the thievery and lack of zeal in the Chancellery for Foreign Affairs. They would rejoice at my death. Then they could manage things as they did before. They could do as they wished with no interference. *Article 7.* When Nashchokin was traveling from Courland to Smolensk, among other things, why did he write without instructions to the Polish lords in the council about the surrender of Kiev to the Polish side according to the earlier treaty? By doing this he gave the Poles cause to demand the surrender of Kiev. Further, why did he detain the present Polish courier, not allowing him to come to Moscow, knowing about Article 20 of the Andrusovo treaty? *Response.* I wrote to the Commonwealth of Two Nations [Poland-Lithuania][45] so that the commissioners would be sent to the meeting before the time designated for the transfer of Kiev. This was not forgotten by the Poles. They did not need my letter to remind them. A courier was not sent to assure there would be no hindrance to the embassy's meetings. All this conforms to the translation of the pamphlet, the original of which was written to the Chancellery for Foreign Affairs. *Article 8.* The patriarch of Alexandria was told about the translation of the Little Russian clergy from the jurisdiction of the patriarch of Constantinople to that of Moscow. He wanted to write to the patriarch of Constantinople about this with a request, but said that without a council of all his clergy the patriarch of Constantinople dared not do this. Therefore he, the patriarch of Alexandria, could not write to a foreign eparchy and direct this be done.[46] *Response.* When something is not permitted by the original articles of the report, God will inform the great sovereign. My dispatch, along with many tiresome requests, raises the following questions. Why incur losses by retaining Kiev after the designated period? Why retain it? This is ridiculous. It is not my job to plead for eternal peace in the meetings without prior arrangement. Accomplish this with an exalted embassy composed of privy boyars. According to their own lofty and lordly agreement they will do as they wish, yet it will persuade no one because they are not bold.

Article 9. Why is the postal service not under oath? The documents are unsealed and Leonty Petrovich Marselis[47] said that they will remain unsealed. It is clear that information is copied in greater numbers than agreed. The gold pieces [spent on postage] provide evidence that more is sent through the post than is accounted for. Thomas Kelderman[48] did not petition to retain the postal service, and no one has heard a petition from him.

Response. Leonty Marselis must answer for himself as to how he receives [the post] and whether he took an oath to serve righteously. This is chancellery business. If the [officials of] the Chancellery for Foreign Affairs consider Marselis my friend they will be hateful to him and hinder the performance of his duties. It is better for me not to be a part of this. They will bid for him without me, and they will be kind to him. Until I die, for me there is but a single path. With God's help I will support and serve God's anointed one as if he were God himself, not fearing the powerful, and I will defend his son as well.

Article 10. The sovereign's communiqué was sent to Nashchokin, instructing that he return to Moscow, for the Crimean envoy had arrived on important business.

Response. I wrote about this directive in many reports. I asked what to do about the icon of the Savior and for what reason I was to come to Moscow, for the chancellery officials did not write to me about this. Life is not jolly in the embassy camp. In Lithuania there was great turmoil and argument as to whether the Muscovite army should be sent. All this has been held in check. To have followed the gracious instruction of his majesty the tsar would have taken me away from the embassy and my many tempestuous negotiations, which now are so difficult for the Chancellery for Foreign Affairs to hear described. I would be happy if the affairs of God and the sovereign were not cursed and if the Muscovite tsardom were not dishonored in other lands thanks to me.

Article 11. For himself, Matskeevich[49] spoke of no business other than bringing Doroshenko to submission. Now Doroshenko himself writes about this and is prepared to submit.

Response. Knowing Matskeevich, I wrote about his loyalty. Now God knows what you will hear about me in the chancellery and on the square. An innocent death sickens everyone and is to be avoided if possible. Just like my Lord, I have neither a fox's den, nor a bird's nest wherein to lay my sinful head,[50] but this is not necessary, for while He lived He did not grow tired of life even in misfortune.

Article 12. Nashchokin wrote on his own initiative to the Little Russian Chancellery about the Cherkassians, saying the chancellery was wrong to receive them. To what individual did he write this? Who received them incorrectly? What was correct, or incorrect about this reception?

Response. I turn to a righteous judge, to the merciful sovereign's heart, for a decision in this affair. No one lamented this, nor was it imagined by anyone, as the affair itself shows. Khmelnitsky's reception, after he turned away from the Turks, was stained with the blood of Poles and others spilled at Konotop, and it is the same now. Perhaps it is still not known that laymen went to Constantinople to the Turk with the blessing of the clergy to escape from what they call Polish persecution, just as Khmelnitsky formerly subjugated himself to the Turk. Moreover, this clerical approval of lay activity was not reported to the most holy patriarch in the Moscow tsardom. It is the same now.

Article 13. Why are the English and the Dutch ambassadors coming to Moscow now?

Response. They are coming to Moscow at the instigation of the Swedes. They seek to destroy what remains of the border towns with duties. What their governments desire, these envoys will extort. They recognize the weakness of the Chancellery for Foreign Affairs and will have everything their own way.

Article 14. Why was the Swedish resident-agent ordered to return to his own country?

Response. At his own request the Chancellery for Foreign Affairs intervened for this troublemaker in Moscow. He caused all kinds of trouble within the embassy. He sowed hatred and evil enmity among the chancellery officials. In this way he gained influence and mastery in the chancellery. Accomplishing all of this he went home, allowing Swedish friends to use his departure to inspire various fears, as is their practice in Moscow. The English ambassador threatened the Muscovite tsardom with the Swedes. This was passed on to the Swedish resident-agent by officials in the Chancellery for Foreign Affairs—an obvious manifestation of friendship to the Swede! Owing to this friendship the Swedish document was retained for the break with Poland, not for evidence against the Swedes. Fears have been sown in Moscow thanks to the bribery of the Swedes, but who will prove their guilt? The Lord God will support this affair of all

Christian peoples,[51] and his anointed will allow it to be saved from destruction. Soon he will allow me, Afonka,[52] to cast off this embassy and remain without assistants. Then I can work without interference, and everything will be done boldly, rather than in the old Muscovite fashion. Then everything will be settled in the eternal peace [with Poland], all will act in harmony according to their rights. No longer can I act in this affair with a dead heart. I am not accustomed to wasting my time.

In Moscow Leonty Marselis, the man Nashchokin had entrusted with the courier service, was attacked. Nashchokin praised the service of his favorite and in doing so did not pass up an opportunity to goad the chancellery. "On April 9," he wrote to the tsar, "Leonty Marselis visited me at the embassy's headquarters. He had gone to Wilno to arrange continuous government courier service with the local postmaster. This vital matter will assist the future unification of the country and will bring all kinds of benefits to the Muscovite tsardom. While in Wilno Leonty also investigated the printed trade statutes which regulate the collection of duties on every kind of merchandise. Given such close proximity, these are suitable [for use] in Moscow and in all Great Russia. Leonty brought these statutes to Moscow. There the boyars asked the leading merchants about the trade statutes. The merchants, cognizant of their own faults and desiring to further their own interests, wish to drive Marselis from your sovereign favor because he, having served in customs collections, wished to expose negligence by the heads of the chancellery and disagreed with the leading merchants. If only the issue could be discussed justly in the chancellery it would be seen that innumerable losses to your treasury are incurred!"

ORDIN-NASHCHOKIN CORRESPONDS WITH CHANCELLERY

While Ordin-Nashchokin corresponded with the Chancellery for Foreign Affairs which he headed a new king was elected in Warsaw, Prince Michał Korybut Wiśniowiecki, son of the notable Jarema, who had carried on such a bitter struggle with the cossacks.[53] From the town of Mignovichi Ordin-Nashchokin sent news to Moscow about the election of Wiśniowiecki, yet not a bit of news was sent to him from Moscow.

In the beginning of July he turned to the sovereign. "Foreigners," he wrote, "hear at your sovereign court that vociferous hostility towards me emanates from the Chancellery for Foreign Affairs and doubt that an eternal peace will be concluded. They are astonished that I am in charge of such important government business when I am so hated at court. The injustice against me is not exposed, nor are those who distract me from the embassy's business.

"You, sovereign, are an autocrat in full. It is known that in Moscow rulers are not elected by a Sejm," Nashchokin's missive continued, "and it is known that I am the beneficiary of your sovereign favor. The Swedish resident-agent hears much in Moscow and foments much secret bickering, as he has done in the past. An eternal peace with Poland cannot be concluded amid such strife among officials. The articles I requested in my report still have not been sent to me. It is unknown why the Swedish document requested in Poland has not been surrendered! The meetings continue yet I am a denounced and hated man and cannot carry on your sovereign affairs with my former confidence.

"Previously a colleague entrusted with a matter of state would not behave in such a fashion He would have been ashamed to denounce me in Moscow. This important business intended to allay Christian bloodshed cannot be conducted by such disgraceful and hateful men [as those in the Chancellery for Foreign Affairs]. Great sovereign, recall the many tears I shed before you. Whoever serves God and you steadfastly, without worldly concerns, is persecuted. It is clear to you, great sovereign, that I, your slave, serve you because of your infinite sovereign grace, not because I was chosen by a court camarilla, nor from a desire for worldly goods. Sovereign, for your favor I serve without wavering, not fearing the powerful, and I will die in righteousness. Should you, sovereign, no longer look upon me with favor, be it for lack of zeal in your service or any other reason, then explain [the reason] to me before I am punished, so that I may make expiation for my offense. Then others may be guided to act as boldly in government affairs as I have done, even without the protection of the powerful. Then whoever is selected for your affairs on the advice of the court camarilla will enjoy support. Opposing God's help, my enemies at court torment me with evil hatred, unable to prove to God and to you, great sovereign, that there is anything in my audacity which is harmful or which is not in the interest of the whole realm. I am accused of profiting from your sovereign affairs out of self-interest because the root of all evil is love of money.[54] My enemies complain about my conduct of affairs to foreigners, but as the apostle said "To all who work, much will be given.""[55]

Afanasy Lavrentievich passed up no opportunity to disparage the chancellery officials. A certain Greek petitioned the Chancellery for Foreign Affairs asking that officials in Minsk be instructed to allow his merchandise to pass without payment of customs duty. Nashchokin responded that this was not just. "I will not permit such an injustice to occur. The Chancellery for Foreign Affairs should not have given such a document to the petitioner. In Minsk your sovereign name will be excoriated by foreigners. The crown secretaries of the Chancellery for Foreign Affairs are neither poor, nor do they lack foreign transactions. They have not learned to hold government in high honor during treaty negotiations and those who live in Moscow fearlessly mix embassy matters with profits from the franchises for liquor and the custom duties from the territories."[56]

In Moscow Afanasy Lavrentievich was repaid in kind. Ivan Afanasievich Zheliabuzhsky,[57] a man Nashchokin disliked, was appointed to be his colleague. Nashchokin met Zheliabuzhsky with a question. "In the future, will you help me in the embassy's business?" he asked. "Announce your intentions now, because it will not be good to dismiss you later."

"It is not your business to interrogate me," retorted Zheliabuzhsky. "The Polish ambassadors have not written my name in their documents, so in the meeting I will rebuke them, and I will engage in embassy business, about which a directive will be sent."

Nashchokin sent a document to Moscow. "Great sovereign," he wrote, "such disagreement will destroy your affairs and God's! Evil reports are heard in Moscow from the Chancellery for Foreign Affairs and this is ruinous. Now the ambassadors are attacked with hostility and with unheard-of rebukes."

In his own justification Zheliabuzhsky wrote "I arrived in Mignovichi on the tenth of July. Boyar Afanasy Lavrentievich said nothing to me about government business until the twentieth. He receives letters from Poland through the post and neither calls me nor informs me about them. If he does summon me he says nothing about any business and only questions me as to what argument I used to convince the sovereign to send him Lutokhin as captain of the musketeers and why, after his letter, I came. He speaks as if he wrote to the great sovereign requesting that he not send me. He says he does not need me in the sovereign's affairs, as if I am up to mischief. He says I cannot be involved in the embassy's activities, because I will argue with the Polish commissioners. The boyar says he must accomplish everything through bows and petitions, lest the Polish commissioners be offended. He must pursue the commissioners with meekness for our own good (Kiev). Later he threatens and raises many questions. I am against his questions and make no secret of my arguments. Nonetheless, I tell no one anything and I have not disclosed any information, nor will I be a party to any mischief. I will participate in the embassy's business in meetings without opposition. Yet it is too much for me to bow and walk meekly behind the Polish commissioners. Now, thanks to the boyar's letter against me to the great sovereign, I cannot participate in affairs for fear that, suffering the hostility of Boyar Afanasy Lavrentievich in vain, I will incur the disfavor of the great sovereign and finally will be destroyed in Mignovichi."

Zheliabuzhsky was recalled to Moscow and the Swedish document was sent to Afanasy Lavrentievich, but this did not mollify him. He sent a new complaint to the sovereign against the chancellery crown secretaries, accusing them of sabotaging the eternal peace. He complained that the embassy instruction directing him to Courland was delayed by the chancellery crown secretaries. They rewrote the instruction and sent it to him by road, using a clerk as courier. After Nashchokin departed these same crown secretaries asked the sovereign whether they were still to refer to him, Nashchokin, as keeper of the tsar's great seal and guide of important foreign affairs of the realm. "The instruction and the articles for the peace decrees still have not been sent to me. In the Chancellery for Foreign Affairs am I really seen as blameworthy because I serve the great sovereign diligently? If the Chancellery for Foreign Affairs does not trust me, the interests of the crown will be harmed. In foreign realms I am recognized as responsible whereas in our own chancellery I am ignored."

ORDIN-NASHCHOKIN MEETS POLISH COMMISSIONERS

Beginning on September 25 Nashchokin embarked on meetings with the Polish commissioners, Jan Gniński, governor of Chełm, Mikołaj Tichanowiecki, governor of Mstislavl, and Paweł Brzostowski, the Lithuanian referendary. Nashchokin announced there must be mediators to help conclude the eternal peace. The commissioners declared the peace must be made without mediators. If the negotiations did not go smoothly they were willing to seek a resolution through mediators. Then they asked how the Ukrainians would be pacified and recovered from the authority of the Turks.

Nashchokin agreed this issue must be resolved first and argued that for the pacification of the Ukraine there must be meetings of ambassadors near Kiev, or representatives must be called from the Ukraine to Andrusovo. "No," objected the commissioners. "First an eternal peace must be concluded." "Eternal peace," Nashchokin insisted, "can be concluded only in accord with the conditions established by the Truce of Andrusovo." "Then why was Kiev not returned to us at the specified time?" asked the commissioners. "Because to occupy it you sent Colonel Jan Piwo with only a few men," was the reply. "It was scarcely possible for him to occupy such a fortress. This would have been tantamount to handing it over to the Muslims."

"Why were the tsar's regiments not united with ours between the Dnieper and the Dniester, as specified in the agreement?" the commissioners asked again. "Because the Tatars and Doroshenko prevented this," was the response. "Doroshenko crossed to the Putivl side and seized many cities, which he still holds. The king's regiments should have helped our regiments on the Putivl side." "Our regiments could not assist at that time," the commissioners rejoined, "because they were exhausted by the past war. This must be attributed to the will of God." "To pacify the Ukraine we must write," Nashchokin repeated. "Write what?" asked the ambassadors. "Let both sides write to the clergy and the laity requesting they send representatives to the current meeting, or send some other confirmation," suggested Nashchokin.

On October 19 these letters were dispatched. After this the commissioners again began to argue about Kiev. "We could not have surrendered Kiev to you," insisted Nashchokin. "There was trouble then in the Ukraine." The commissioners then discussed the eternal peace, demanding the return of everything obtained by the Treaty of Andrusovo. "There is nothing more to say about this," Nashchokin maintained. "Smolensk rightly belongs to us and will remain ours forever."

More than two months dragged on in these negotiations. In the ninth meeting, on November 29, the commissioners announced that they were instructed to confirm the agreement concerning the unification of the regiments. The agreement regarding eternal peace was set aside, though the commissioners stubbornly insisted that a date be set for the surrender of Kiev. This intransigence dragged the negotiations out to March 7, 1670, when the Poles finally ceased arguing about Kiev. They established that the original Treaty of Andrusovo would be preserved in every minute detail, including the agreement about the anti-Muslim alliance.

ORDIN-NASHCHOKIN'S DISMISSAL

Details about the further fate of Nashchokin are unknown to us. In January 1671, on the occasion of the tsar's wedding,[58] Boyar Afanasy Lavrentievich Ordin-Nashchokin was mentioned among the number of boyars attending the great sovereign. By February the name of the tsar's favorite, Artamon Sergeevich Matveev, appeared as the head of the Chancellery for Foreign Affairs. Nashchokin had left service and been tonsured under the name Antony in the Krypetsk monastery, about twelve versts from Pskov. In the court service registers the following information is preserved. "This same year (1671), the high ambassadors in Poland were Boyar Afanasy Lavrentievich Ordin-Nashchokin and Conciliar Noble Ivan Ivanovich Chaadaev. Afanasy Nashchokin was removed and in his place the sovereign sent the lord-in-waiting Vasily Semeonovich Volynsky." It is very possible that as a consequence of Chaadaev's appointment Nashchokin presented issues on which he and Chaadaev could not agree and Chaadaev refused to leave. The result of this disagreement may have been Nashchokin's final dismissal.

Even as the Chancellery of Foreign Affairs was changing its director relations with Poland assumed increased importance owing to Turkish affairs. In August 1670 the king's envoy, Jarema Komar [or Kamar], arrived in Moscow. He demanded that the tsar order his regiments to move into the Ukraine against the Turks and Tatars, who constantly threatened Poland. He demanded that help quickly be given to Belaia Tserkov, which was threatened by Doroshenko, who had broken off talks with the Polish commissioners in Ostrog.

He received this answer. "If the tsar's regiments appear in the Ukraine this will only anger the cossacks, particularly Doroshenko, who will not be appeased. On the contrary, in the movement of the tsar's and the king's regiments he will see a clear intent to destroy the Ukrainians and will call upon the Turkish army for protection. The tsar's troops in the Belgorod and the Sevsk regimental districts also protect the Ukraine. For both the great sovereigns it is better to lead the vacillating cossacks to obedience with graciousness rather than with harshness."

POLISH AMBASSADORS IN MOSCOW

In December 1671 there was a magnificent reception at the court of the great sovereign for the great plenipotentiary ambassadors of his majesty the Polish king, Jan Gniński and Paweł Brzostowski. Governor Gniński of Chełm waxed eloquent in a long speech before the tsar.

"He who carries out the affairs of God with a healthy eye and undarkened reason," declaimed Gniński, "he whose people are the jewel of the universe and the apple of heaven's eye, he who honors the sun in the East, the primal source of the Midians, Assyrians and Persians, and in the South and West, the Greek and Roman empires, the great wisdom, the power and the abundance of Egypt, the paradise of the promised land, its wealth and comfort, he who then sees these countries ground into dust and blood, without name and unwilling under a yoke and, what is worst, without the knowledge of God, he it is who must recognize that God decreed the return of all these peoples.

"God established and strengthened the people found in the possessions of the Polish king and in those of your majesty the tsar. He gave his majesty the king protection from the East and the West, having approved a firm alliance with his imperial majesty and with the whole house of Austria.[59] How great are the holdings of the house of Austria. Their domains extend from Africa to Sicily and they embrace America, rich with gold. The house of Austria defends Europe with its invincible scepter.

"Your majesty the tsar safeguards Europe from the other side. Within the boundaries of your holdings the Don, the Dvina and the Volga have their source. They grow and flow. You defeat the wild heirs of Batu and Tamerlane[60] and defend Europe, the zenith of the universe. You aspire to those countries watered by the Don river, since the universe also designates these unknown parts as Slavic. Most important of all, you mitigate the harshness of the North with your gracious governance. The eternal God placed both peoples, Polish and Russian, within the walls of Christianity. Anyone so audacious as to weaken or to divide them with disagreement or insincere friendship must answer before heaven."

The privy councillors Boyar Prince Yury Alekseevich Dolgoruky, Boyar Prince Dmitry Alekseevich Dolgoruky,[61] and Conciliar Noble Artamon Sergeevich Matveev were named for negotiations with the ambassadors. The ambassadors began with complaints against the cossacks of Severia. They entered the territories along the Sozh river in the governorship of Mstislavl and the district of Krichev, and were committing all kinds of deeds contrary to the peace decrees. "We have already notified Hetman Demian Mnogogreshny about this," the boyars answered.

Then the ambassadors introduced the most important business. "With great sorrow we announce that in the realm of his majesty the king there are some disturbances. Hetman Peter Doroshenko has betrayed us and foreign enemies attack the Polish crown. We request the great sovereign be so kind as to lend help with his soldiers in pacifying these disturbances, out of love for the king and in accord with the confirmed treaty."

Boyars. In the past year, when the high plenipotentiary ambassadors from both sides met, they wrote to the Ukraine, to the clergy and the laity, calling them to send their representatives to these meetings, that these representatives might hear and see that the ambassadors were negotiating solely about a Christian peace, and were doing nothing against the Ukrainian cities. Now Hetman Demian Ignatovich has sent the Kievan colonel, Konstantin Solonina, with comrades, honorable and reasonable men, to the great sovereign. If you ambassadors would permit these envoys to be present in the meeting hall for them to hear the discussion about the troubles the Severian cossacks have caused in Polish territories these envoys personally could present their justification to us. Let the envoys know that we are negotiating to achieve a brotherly friendship between the two great sovereigns and the pacification of both countries. Otherwise it will be just like before. There were no representatives from the Ukraine in Moscow during the confirmation of the Treaty of Andrusovo. Immediately afterwards Hetman Ivashka Briukhovetsky colluded with the king's hetman, Peter Doroshenko, to betray his majesty the tsar. As a result much innocent blood flowed.

Ambassadors. During our discussions it is not seemly for the hetman's envoys to be present because if it turns out that they oppose our pronouncements they will speak out about this immediately and rudely, in accordance with their own Ukrainian cossack ways. This would dishonor his majesty the king. Moreover, we do not have the king's instruction about this. Should the hetman's envoys have any concerns let them petition in the chancellery and you can inform us. Ukrainian representatives were not summoned during the Andrusovo meetings yet the Ukrainian people heard of the graciousness of both sovereigns. We do not need to call them to the present negotiations. The disobedient will be brought to obedience and they will be recovered from Turkish subjugation by the means described in the Moscow treaty, by common military action.

Boyars. There will be no dishonor to his majesty the king. Just permit them to be present to listen to the discussion. They will not interrupt the discussion, nor will they sit. They will stand like our other men and your nobles. Formerly the Ukrainian clergy, the metropolitan and two bishops sat in the Senate with the king himself and had a free voice. Not long ago the great crown hetman, Sobieski himself, negotiated with the Ukrainian cossacks. In Ostrog Stanisław Beniewski held a meeting with the cossacks and they negotiated according to Polish custom. Let it happen. Such an event is not new.

Ambassadors. In accord with the counsel of both great sovereigns there is no need to call the Ukrainians. They are not steadfast and never observe the rules. At the past meeting in Andrusovo Hetman Doroshenko wrote to us that he had petitioned about everything to his majesty the king during the election, and afterwards petitioned to serve under the authority of his majesty the tsar. It is dangerous for Hetman Demian's envoys to be present during our discussions. After learning about everything they will write to Hetman Demian and he will correspond with Doroshenko. During ambassadorial discussions only knowledgeable and loyal men need be present to know about government affairs. We consider Hetman Demian Mnogogreshny a subject of his majesty the tsar only for the duration of the truce years. When the truce years pass we can call him a subject of his majesty the king. Previously the metropolitan of Kiev and two prelates had a place in the Senate by the king's will, but this was a special matter. In these long discussions time will only be wasted and the negotiations will not be accomplished. May it please the great sovereign to be so gracious as to accept this decision.

NEGOTIATIONS

Important concerns were in hand to which it was difficult to hope for a rapid resolution. In January 1672 the ambassadors announced that only if another date for the surrender were designated could the king overlook with brotherly love the fact that Kiev was not surrendered on time. "In accordance with the obligations of the alliance," the ambassadors then asked, "what assistance would his majesty the tsar give his majesty the king against the Muslims?" They requested that the cossacks of Severia, who had crossed the borders of the governorship of Mstislavl and given aid to Doroshenko, be punished as enemies of both sovereigns. In addition, they demanded that those of the Roman faith living in the regions surrendered according to the Treaty of Andrusovo be allowed to conduct their own form of worship freely, and be permitted to receive chaplains in their homes or travel without hindrance across the border on pilgrimages. Further, they asked that nobles in these territories be allowed to transfer freely to the king's side. They complained that captured nobles and soldiers still were not released, nor had the relics, icons and church plate, and the records of the governorship of Kiev been handed over [to Polish officials]. They also requested the tsar to surrender Velizh to the governorship of Vitebsk, and Sebezh and Nevl to the governorship of Polotsk.

The boyars replied that a directive had been sent to Hetman Mnogo-greshny about the cossack raids. A copy of this instruction would be given to the ambassadors. The parties were supposed to have assembled at the border with boundary commissioners appointed by both sides, but no boundary commissioners appeared from the king's side. On the side of his majesty the tsar, no captives were being held. Only those who wished to do so remained. By contrast, on the king's side many captives still were being held. The boyars had not made a big issue of this to the ambassadors because this already had been discussed at length by both sides. From the Polish side not only were many omissions made in the tsar's title, books printed by the Polish sovereign and by his forebears also dishonored his majesty the tsar.

The alliance was infringed on the king's side. When the king's hetman, Doroshenko, waged war on the tsar's cities on the eastern side of the Dnieper with the Tatars the king sent no help. In Warsaw, in the king's palace, in the same chamber where ambassadors were received, the painting on the arch was offensive. On one side stood the king with his son and the lords of the council. On the other side the Polish hetman was pursuing Muscovite regiments and the tsar and the boyars were being taken into captivity in chains. The Poles speak about this with mockery, as if it were a victory, insulting the Muscovite tsardom and the Russian people. The body of Tsar Vasily Ivanovich Shuisky is now in Moscow[62] and it is not seemly to recall the past when doing so offends those who now live in peaceful relations. Out of brotherly love, his majesty the king should remove this *depiction* from his audience chamber.

To deflect the Muslim attack both great sovereigns need to write to the Christian rulers and the Turkish sultan. At this time his majesty the tsar cannot give military assistance and is unable to surrender Kiev because the king offered no assistance against Doroshenko and the Tatars. His majesty the tsar continues to help the king with Kalmyks, Nogay[63] and Don Cossack soldiers. Even now it is written in the broadsheets that the Turkish sultan suffers grievously. All the Christian sovereigns have concluded an alliance and wish to go to war against him. The broadsheets also claim that the Turkish sultan dispatched his army to the Black Sea. Then when he heard that the Russian army wanted to fight him there he ordered his army to return.

After this announcement the boyars gave the ambassadors a note about Doroshenko. "To the great sovereign," the note read, "Hetman Demian Ignatovich writes that Hetman Peter Doroshenko and the elders wrote to him from the Polish side asking that his majesty the tsar decree they be received under his authority because on the king's side the faith is persecuted. His majesty the king should permit his majesty the tsar to accept Doroshenko, thereby turning him from his Turkish allegiance. Should the king and the Commonwealth forbid us to receive Doroshenko, perhaps his majesty the tsar will receive him anyway. This is because the king in his document called him a subject of the Turkish sultan and wrote that he [Doroshenko] urged those on the eastern side of the Dnieper river to accept Turkish authority as well. Doroshenko writes otherwise, saying he subjugated himself to the Turkish sultan because of persecution of the faith. For these reasons his majesty the tsar may accept Doroshenko under his authority. In addition the Zaporozhians also beg to serve under the authority of his majesty the tsar. They do not want to be on the king's side because they have received no pay."

The ambassadors continued to demand that the Severian cossacks leave the governorships they occupied and the nobles whom they had despoiled receive compensation. Otherwise these nobles would disrupt the Sejm. They also demanded that the tsar provide the king with military aid against the Turks. The tsar, they argued, was obligated to do this, first because the Turks were preparing to make war on Poland in retaliation for its alliance with Moscow. Second, the tsar should help because when a neighbor's house is on fire the flames will spread to his own. "In Poland," the commissioners said, "there is an adage. Once a Rusyn[64] called a Pole for help against the Turks. The Pole refused and the Rusyn warned him 'I will subject myself to the rule of the Turk, and fight against the crown.'" Finally the ambassadors relentlessly continued to demand a date be set for the return of Kiev. "If we surrender Kiev to you," objected the boyars, "the Turks will enter the Ukraine and Kiev will become a nest for Turkish regiments."

In regard to Doroshenko the ambassadors declared "It is impossible and unseemly for his majesty the tsar to receive Doroshenko. Even were he to accept him things in the Ukraine would not be set to rights because Doroshenko himself has no claim to it [the hetmancy]. His majesty the king freely established Doroshenko as hetman and he is also at liberty to remove him, when he merits it. Since his majesty the king himself announced Doroshenko's treachery his majesty the tsar needs to provide assistance against him, not receive him. The Greek faith will not suffer persecution or curses. It is oppressed by Doroshenko, who pays the Muslim for his defense with Christian souls. He hands the entire church into eternal slavery and opens the gates to the establishment of mosques. If his majesty the tsar agrees to protect Doroshenko the Turks will not be placated. Rather they will flare up still more, for they will observe the domains of the tsar moving closer to Greece, which is under Turkish sovereignty.

"Were the king to allow his majesty the tsar to receive Doroshenko," the boyars argued, "great assistance and profit would accrue to the king and the Commonwealth of Poland and Lithuania against the Turks." "What benefit?" asked the ambassadors. "The sultan will be frightened," the boyars responded, "on finding that Doroshenko is a subject of the tsar and not of the king. He will think that we are all united against him and that the Wallachians, Moldavians and other people of the Greek faith will join us. Fearing this the sultan will not begin war. It will be as before when Sultan Bayezid II [reigned 1481-1512], learning of the alliance of Christian realms, immediately sent to the Polish king, Jan Olbracht [born 1459, reigned 1492-1501] requesting a truce, as related in the Stryjkowski chronicle."[65]

NEGOTIATIONS CONCLUDED

Finally, after lengthy disputes, agreement was reached on the following points. (1) Both great sovereigns are obliged to observe without violation the Andrusovo and Moscow decrees without diminution or contrary interpretation. (2) The sovereigns confirm the decrees of these past treaties and the present treaty with an oath before the Holy Gospel. (3) The difficulties appearing with regard to the fulfillment of several articles, for example, in regard to Kiev and the military assistance to be rendered to one another, is to be resolved by a commission which will meet in June 1674. (4) In the event of an attack by the Turkish sultan on Poland the tsar is to assist the king with Kalmyk and Nogay troops and soldiers from other hordes. These troops are to march overland and be supplemented with the Don Cossacks, who are to go by sea. In addition, the tsar is to send a directive to Zaporozhia for the local cossacks to go as quickly as possible to the sea in chaikas[66] in as large a force as possible. (5) The tsar is to send missives to the sultan and the khan discouraging them from going to war against Poland. (6) The tsar is to forbid the cossacks of Severia from helping the Muslims or Doroshenko. (7) The tsar is to allow those nobles who remain in the regions of Smolensk, Starodub and other places which have been annexed from Lithuania to return to the side of the king with their wives, children and property. (8) The people of the Roman faith who remain on the side of his majesty the tsar are permitted to cross the border to the closest Catholic churches for worship. Rus people[67] on the king's side are free to worship according to the Greek faith. (9) Burghers and merchants remaining on Muscovite territory will be released to the king's side once they have paid their debts, save for those who wish to remain. Further, burghers who live in the households of boyars or others are permitted to participate in the future commission. (10) Many parts of the holy cross were taken to Lublin. As many of these parts as can be located are to be returned. A search is to be made for the relics of St. Kallistratos[68] and the gold and silver church accoutrements and bells of the Smolensk cathedral. The items found are to be returned. His majesty the tsar is to circulate instructions to search for all books, plate, icons and church accoutrements and decorations. Whatever is found is to be returned to his majesty the king. (11) The Severian cossacks are to vacate the places occupied by them in the governorship of Mstislavl and the regions of Rechitsa and Mozyr without recompense for losses. (12) Two boundary commissioners are to be appointed in each governorship, region and district.

RUSSIAN MISSION TO THE TURKS

In fulfillment of the fifth article of the treaty in April 1672 the interpreter Vasily Aleksandrovich Daudov and the clerk Nikifor Dmitrievich Veniukov were sent to Sultan Mehmed IV with a document from the tsar. The sovereign wrote that Mehmed must refrain from war with Poland and prohibit the khan from attacking the king. Otherwise he, as a Christian sovereign celebrated by all surrounding Christian sovereigns, would make plans against the Turks and send instructions to the Don Cossacks to go to the Black Sea. He would send the Kalmyks, the Nogay and the Edisan Tatars overland. Besides this, he would rouse the neighboring Christian sovereigns and the Persian shah.

The grand vizier, answering for the sultan, excoriated the tsar for using impolite words, not proper to a sovereign, and ended his response saying "You may be friends or enemies to us. The path you choose makes no difference to us."

Returning to Moscow Daudov reported "In Moldavia and Wallachia the inhabitants say that were the Christians to gain even the smallest victory they too would act against the Turks." Then he reported something else. The Astrakhan and Kazan Tatars and the Bashkirs had gone to the sultan to request that he take these realms under his hand. They complained that the Muscovite people, hating their Muslim faith, beat many of them to death, relentlessly and unceasingly destroying them. The sultan told them to be patient a while longer and granted them caftans.

EVENTS IN THE CRIMEA

The threat gathered in the south. The peace agreements negotiated with regard to the Crimea were broken. On April 29, 1671 the captive boyar Vasily Borisovich Sheremetev[69] was summoned to the khan for release and was ordered to bow to the ground before Adil-Girey. The khan ordered the boyar be dressed in a sable coat and a gold caftan, and when Sheremetev left the palace they brought him an argamak[70] with full equestrian equipage. Then the khan sent him two caftans, one made of satin and another of wool, a hat and wool trousers. He sent a large coach with all the necessary equipment and six coachmen. Sheremetev left to travel from Bakhchisaray to Perekop, but fate harshly mocked this unhappy old man.

A courier arrived from Constantinople with a document from the sultan ordering that Khan Adil-Girey be replaced. The new khan, Selim-Girey, gave instructions not to release Sheremetev. The boyar was returned from Perekop to Bakhchisaray fettered in chains, together with the young Prince Andrei Romodanovsky and other noble captives. When the new khan arrived the chains were removed from Sheremetev and the bargaining commenced. An announcement was made to the boyar that Selim-Girey wished to live with the great sovereign in friendship and love, if only he would make up the arrears in tribute accumulated during the reign of Adil-Girey, because in these years the khan had not gone to war against Moscow. The boyar refused, saying he could not take responsibility for such a high matter himself. Then the khan's representatives turned to Romodanovsky and asked him to remit eighty thousand efimoks and sixty captured Tatars.

"My family will not give more than ten thousand rubles for me," answered Romodanovsky. "Why will they not give more?" asked the Tatars. "Your father is a boyar and rules the whole Ukraine. If he just goes with hat in hand he will collect more than a hundred thousand." "Even if the khan ordered me to be tortured, it could not be more than ten thousand rubles," Romodanovsky asserted. The sovereign, discovering that the captives again were being held, sent two hundred gold ducats to Sheremetev, and fifty each to the other noble captives, to Romodanovsky, Skuratov and Tolstoy.

"The privy councillors [of the new khan]," Sheremetev informed the tsar, "in their evil ways and unkindness to me, are not so well-meaning as their predecessors who were here during the reign of Khan Adil-Girey. Without ransom the khan will not release Prince Andrei and your nobles. The Tatars have set aside the earlier agreement with Adil-Girey as nothing, and they shout that according to their old customs and privileges the khan cannot take the captives[71] from them. These captives are given to them [as a reward] for service, for blood and for death in war, and they live by this. They have created many obstacles to your affairs, great sovereign, and there is great opposition from their people to my release. Those held captive by the best, the black Tatars [that is, the Tatar aristocracy], are taught the Tatar language and the Tatars insist that if I am released, afterwards there will be no ransom or exchange for them. Your sovereign letter told them there will be no ransom or exhange for them. Therefore they think they will attack in the Crimea."

"I, your poor and helpless slave," wrote Sheremetev, "who have long been a captive and who suffer from need, beg you to have mercy, great sovereign. Be gracious, righteous sovereign, and order such an injustice investigated. The Muslim council is like the cossack council, in that the khan and his privy councillors keep repeating something, but if the ordinary people of the yurts[72] do not wish to hear it they will have their way without restraint. Your envoys insisted to the khan and his councillors that according to the agreement with Adil-Girey the captives were to be released in exchange without ransom. Yet these same envoys, leaving the Crimea, took many captives with them whom they ransomed. For this reason too, the ordinary Tatars do not wish an exchange. They tell us there is no profit for them in exchange. The profit goes only to the khan. It is more profitable for them, they say, to release the captives ransomed by the envoys than to take ransom for them in Moscow. Be merciful, righteous sovereign, do not let us die a vain death, nor let our sinful bodies be eaten by dogs and beasts in a dishonorable place, nor let the bones of the abandoned be scattered. Order, sovereign, that there be an exchange on the Donets."

There was no exchange on the Donets and the captives remained as before in the Crimea. Soon their numbers increased as a consequence of the Turkish-Tatar war. Before we proceed to a description of this war we will return to Little Russia, which already had succeeded in changing the hetman.

III

DISTURBANCES PERSIST IN ZAPOROZHIA

ANXIETY ABOUT LITTLE RUSSIA

Trouble for the Moscow government in relation to Little Russia by no means ended with the successful conclusion of the Council of Glukhov. The new hetman, Demian Ignatovich Mnogogreshny, informed Moscow that on July 1, 1669 Sukhovey with the Zaporozhians and the Crimean nurredin sultan[1] were near Kanev, standing at Rassava. Sukhovey had a force of about three thousand Zaporozhians and there were a hundred thousand Tatars. In addition the cossack regiments of Uman, Korsun and Kalnik had turned to Sukhovey upon leaving Doroshenko. Moreover Doroshenko and Metropolitan Tukalsky had begged Yury Khmelnitsky to repudiate his monastic vows, for they wished to make him hetman. Only if Khmelnitsky were hetman could Doroshenko hope to save his life. If Sukhovey were elected hetman Doroshenko would not be allowed to live. Sukhovey would take revenge on him for drowning his people near Perevolochna.[2] On July 6 Doroshenko arrived in Kanev and distributed universals inviting the colonels to a council in Rassava.

In September a messenger from Lazar Baranovich appeared in Moscow announcing that Hetman Mnogogreshny was in Smelaia, between Putivl and Romny, accompanied by the tsar's troops, including about three hundred foot soldiers from Nezhin, and cossack regiments from Nezhin, Chernigov, Pereiaslav, Priluki and Starodub. Andrei Murashka was also with him. The hetman went to Smelaia against Grigory Gamaleia[3] and the horde because they were burning villages and hamlets in Little Russia, killing people and handing them over as captives to the Tatars. With Gamaleia were three regiments, the Mirgorod, Poltava and Lubny regiments. In addition, he had around three thousand Tatars. The hetman killed many Cherkassians and Tatars. On the other side, Doroshenko convened frequent meetings and many of the hordes joined him, including many Turks, Wallachians and Moldavians.

ARCHBISHOP LAZAR BARANOVICH WRITES TO MOSCOW

"I have written to your majesty the tsar many times and in many forms about military assistance," Baranovich wrote to the sovereign. "Now I write again at some length because Hetman Demian Ignatovich is troubling me with instructions and he himself is in Chernigov. When they brought the most holy father, Patriarch Paisios of Alexandria,[4] the hetman said 'Obeying your holiness, we kissed the cross and took an oath to his majesty the tsar in the hope that soldiers would be sent to help us. Now the horde attacks us and there is no help. If we are trampled by the horde this will open the gates into the Great Russian towns.' Be merciful, sovereign. Direct your boyar, Prince Grigory Grigorievich Romodanovsky, to hurry to help the Ukraine, for the hetman has come from Baturin."

Baranovich wrote even more strongly to Matveev. "The sovereign instructed Prince Grigory Grigorievich Romodanovsky to stand in Sevsk. What help does this offer to the hetman or to the Ukraine when these Muslim soldiers, along with the cossacks on both sides of the Dnieper, devastate the poor Ukraine at will, mocking both Hetman Demian Ignatovich and me? Had the sovereign's forces attacked at the beginning, immediately after the signing of the articles of Glukhov, as I advised your honor and as I wrote to his majesty the tsar, the Ukraine would have been pacified long ago. Even now it would not be difficult to accomplish this if help were sent rapidly to the hetman. The hetman is a valiant man and knows how to take action, if only he had the resources."

Baranovich also asked both the tsar and Matveev about his own affair, whether his book *Words of the Trumpets*[5] would be printed in Moscow, "so that soon I may be able to declaim in print in the sovereign city."

"According to our great sovereign directive," the tsar replied, "the boyar Prince Romodanovsky is ordered to go immediately to the Little Russian towns and is ordered to send in advance five hundred men, both mounted horsemen and infantry, to help the hetman. The book *Trumpets* has been submitted for examination. As soon as this is complete our decision will be announced."

The archbishop worried needlessly. Doroshenko, occupied with internecine strife in his own camp, could not be much of a threat to the East Bank. In Zaporozhia a new rival appeared to challenge him, Mikhail Stepanovich Khanenko,[6] whom the Polish government had named hetman of the West Bank and who was confirmed also in Uman[7] and in several other places. Sukhovey began to help Khanenko. Yury Khmelnitsky, throwing off the monastic robe, joined them. Khanenko wrote to

Mnogogreshny requesting his help against the common enemy Doroshenko, but Demian Ignatovich was told by Moscow not to interfere in this internecine strife. "I am prepared to fulfill the injunction of your majesty the tsar," answered Mnogogreshny. "Since they themselves have made the quarrels, let them straighten them out." The hetman understood the thinking of the tsar and calmed down.

ARCHBISHOP LAZAR CHAMPIONS THE TREATY OF GLUKHOV

As the only prelate on the East Bank since the removal of Methodios,[8] Lazar Baranovich now considered himself obliged to concern himself with the interests of Little Russia, and not to permit the infringement of the Treaty of Glukhov.[9] At the end of the year Abbot Jeremiah Shirkevich arrived in Moscow. He was sent by Baranovich to communicate a number of complaints. (1) In the Treaty of Glukhov it was established that at the first or second request of the hetman the sovereign's troops would go to the defense of the Ukraine. The hetman has been begging for troops all year and still has not received them. As a result there is much talk among the people. (2) In the Glukhov articles it was agreed that all prisoners sent to Moscow by Briukhovetsky as well as all cossacks taken in battle and village peasants were to be released. Now many Little Russians have gone to Great Russia to search for their relatives and returned empty handed. (3) Despite the Glukhov articles the army cannon and the town cannon taken by the governors still have not been returned. The cossacks are not pleased about this. (4) The church accoutrements and vessels have not been returned. (5) At Glukhov it was established that the commission would not proceed without cossack ambassadors. Now not only has the commission proceeded without cossack ambassadors but as is clear from the commission's letters to Doroshenko, it has been completed. This has incited great discontent. The archbishop petitions the sovereign to order the hetman's delegates attend the commission, if it still has not ended. This would soothe the troubled spirits of the Ukrainian inhabitants. (6) Plenipotentiary commissioners to the East Bank of the Dnieper directed messengers to the western hetman, Doroshenko, without informing the eastern hetman, who was enraged by this oversight. (7) These messengers from the commissioners caused great trouble. With their pamphlets they invited Little Russians of both sides of the Dnieper to delegate clerical and lay dignitaries to the council with petitions to the king about their needs. The Little Russians feared they would be given to the king by the commission.

"To show you our zeal," the tsar replied to Baranovich, "and to re-assure the hetman and the whole Host so they will be hopeful of our favor, I order that none of them, by the mercy of God, be removed from our power. You write about the Treaty of Glukhov, asserting that without cossack emissaries the commission must not proceed. The articles of Glukhov did provide for cossack emissaries at the commission, but the time for them has not yet arrived. It is written in the seventeenth article that if there are references by us, by the great sovereign, his royal highness or the Crimean khan, about the Zaporozhian Host, at this time cossack ambassadors will be present. When such discussions begin the hetman's emissaries will be called. You write that the commissioners' emissaries called Little Russians into the Sejm before the king whereas in the communication of the boyar Ordin-Nashchokin it is written 'Call people of both the clerical and lay ranks from the Ukraine for true information and spiritual discussion about a permanent settlement.' The communication also recommends you call Doroshenko to the commission, detaching him from the Muslim camp. The communication says nothing about sending Little Russian representatives to the king in the Sejm. Prisoners and captives who were found were sent back to the hetman. A list has been sent to you indicating precisely those who were returned. The governors wrote to us about the cannon, informing that they surrendered them to the hetman in accord with the Treaty of Glukhov. A list of items returned has been sent to you."

In the spring of 1671 the clerk Mikhail Savin came to Little Russia to search for a master vintner and a beekeeper, as well as a master gardener who could plant Kievan figs, pears, plums and nuts. On April 17, in Baturin, Savin was dining at the hetman's house. The colonels of the towns on the East Bank of the Dnieper were visiting the hetman to wish him joy on the holiday of the glorious resurrection of Christ [Easter]. Only the colonels of Poltava and Mirgorod were absent.

At dinner Mnogogreshny said to the colonels "I hear that the cossacks of all the towns entertain little love for me. If this is true, you should petition the great sovereign to call for the election of another hetman. I will cede the regalia of the Host to whomever you select, but insofar as it is in my power I will not step down as hetman until the headstrong cossacks are pacified. I swore an oath to the great sovereign to this effect. I am not like Ivashka Briukhovetsky, who took an oath to the great sovereign, like Judas to Christ, and then betrayed the great sovereign. I promised to die for the great sovereign so that after me glory would accrue to my family. No matter how much these headstrong cossacks twist and turn, they will get nowhere without the great sovereign."

At this point Colonel Rodion Dmitrashko-Raich of Pereiaslav struck the table, tearfully saying "We have had enough of electing these hetmans, on whose account Christian blood flows. We want only the great sovereign and we will subdue these headstrong cossacks."

The next day, April 18, the hetman with the colonels and the elders convened a meeting of the council of elders because they did not expect the year to pass without war. The colonels all took an oath and kissed the sovereign's banner, swearing they would not be seduced by the temptations of the enemy. They swore they would stand stubbornly against the enemy and obey the hetman in all. They told Savin that the colonels of Poltava and Mirgorod would not obey the hetman. Doroshenko was writing to them with threats seeking to ensure they not obey Hetman Demian, who in turn was writing to these colonels urging them not to succumb to Doroshenko's enticements. The people of Poltava and Mirgorod responded by locking themselves in their towns, refusing to listen to either. They also spoke poorly to Savin about other colonels. Colonels Dmitrashko-Raich of Pereiaslav and Peter Roslavets of Starodub had joined with Hetman Demian to serve the great sovereign loyally and with open hearts, but the colonels of other Ukrainian towns vacillated.

HETMAN MNOGOGRESHNY'S PRECARIOUS POSITION

The information aired at this council showed the position of the hetman in Little Russia to be precarious. Once again the hetman himself sent bad news about Zaporozhia. In July 1670 Mnogogreshny sent a missive to Matveev, "to his benefactor and gracious friend." The hetman complained that Khanenko and the Zaporozhians dispatched their own ambassadors to the great sovereign and in a document written to him, Demian, they had not called him hetman. "They intend to petition the sovereign," wrote Mnogogreshny, "to allow them to elect a hetman in Zaporozhia rather than in the towns. If his majesty the tsar allowed this, trouble would erupt again in the Ukraine because the Zaporozhians habitually drive people away."

From the standpoint of Moscow this was no time to establish a hetman in Zaporozhia. Razin[10] had aroused the eastern cossacks. In September the clerk Savin again visited Mnogogreshny in Baturin with a directive from the tsar instructing the hetman to select five or six hundred cossacks to be dispatched in regiments to Prince Romodanovsky to assist in the fight against Razin.

"According to the sovereign's instruction," Hetman Mnogogreshny responded, "I ordered universals be distributed in various towns, calling the cossack army to gather in Glukhov. I ordered an army of one thousand men to gather which will have as commander the general aide-de-camp Matvey Gvintovka.[11] I directed him to go with the army to Prince Grigory Grigorievich Romodanovsky. I then received information from Lubny and Mirgorod indicating that the Crimean khan was advancing with a large army, intending to make war against the other side of the Dnieper, against Doroshenko and the Polish towns. Yuraska[12] Khmelnitsky also is coming to this side with the kalgay sultan,[13] with an army of about sixty thousand soldiers. The Crimean khan wishes to make Yuraska hetman on both sides of the Dnieper.

"From Zaporozhia the cossacks wrote to Stenka Razin alleging that I, the hetman, was not in submission to the great sovereign. Stenka could go safely to the sovereign's towns located on the lower course of the river, thinking he had nothing to fear from me. Had I not received this news about the Tatars' arrival I would have sent my army with ten thousand men as the great sovereign directed. The great sovereign would be gracious to me were he to order infantry sent to Sevsk, say two to four thousand men either of regiments of the new formation[14] or of musketeers' regiments,[15] because I suspect there will be much trouble from our own people. Yuraska Khmelnitsky rides with the horde on this side and they have little love for me because I am not in their hands, do not enter into their evil schemes, and stop all their troublemaking. The captain of the Moscow musketeers is here with his regiment but I will not take him with me on campaign because he is needed here to protect my home."

At the same time our old acquaintance Archpriest Simeon Adamovich[16] and Captain Vasily Semeonov were in Moscow as messengers of Baranovich and Mnogogreshny. Through these couriers the hetman petitioned the great sovereign, observing that the Little Russian people were uneasy. They believed that since the tsar's ambassadors were having meetings with the king's commissioners they must have agreed to surrender Kiev and all the towns on this side of the Dnieper to the Poles. The brother of Colonel Peter Roslavets of Starodub, Ivan, was at the meetings and told the hetman about all the ambassadorial decisions. As a result the hetman and the elders were in great doubt, particularly because their own emissaries were not at the meeting. If now or at any time people from both sides of the Dnieper and the Zaporozhians were to petition the great sovereign, requesting a black council[17] be convened, the great sovereign should favor the hetman and not satisfy such a request. In this way between them the tsar and the hetman could ensure that internecine strife and bloodletting would not erupt as it had during Briukhovetsky's time. Mnogogreshny recommended that if Doroshenko were pressed by his enemies, Khanenko and Sukhovey, and fled to Kiev or to other towns on this side of the Dnieper or to settlements in the Ukraine, the great sovereign should order he not be received, lest internecine strife arise among them. If Doroshenko, Khanenko, Sukhovey or the colonel of Sumy, or any one else wrote to his majesty the tsar against him, Hetman Mnogogreshny, about any disloyalty the great sovereign should not permit this to be believed. If an enemy appeared on this side against the hetman the great sovereign should order he be defended with Muscovite troops. In dire necessity the hetman might be allowed to enter Great Russian towns with his household. Should this occur the great sovereign must assure that neither the governors nor the chancellery officials surrender him to his enemies. The great sovereign should reassure the hetman that Kiev and the towns on the eastern side of the Dnieper would never be ceded to the king.

Mnogogreshny thought that Sukhovey and Khanenko would force Doroshenko to flee. The opposite happened. Doroshenko defeated Sukhovey, Khanenko and Khmelnitsky. Moreover, he captured Khmelnitsky and sent him to the sultan. At first Khmelnichenko[18] was imprisoned in the Castle of the Seven Turrets[19] but then the sultan ordered him freed and granted him maintenance and a residence. A triumphant Doroshenko was considerably more dangerous for Mnogogreshny.

A CURSE AGAINST MNOGOGRESHNY

Strife between the hetmans was complicated still further by strife between the prelates. Joseph Tukalsky continued to agitate for the subordination of Kiev and all Little Russia to himself. Thus the political division of Little Russia into two parts, under the jurisdiction of two hetmans, also produced a church schism because Tukalsky was no less hostile to the hetman of the East Bank than Doroshenko. Moreover, if on the West Bank of the Dnieper on Doroshenko's side there was a pretender to the metropolitanate, on the East Bank of the Dnieper on Mnogogreshny's side there was also a prelate who coveted primacy within the Ukrainian Orthodox church, even at the price of Kiev being handed over to Poland.

Lazar Baranovich stood up for himself and also for his friend, Demian Ignatovich Mnogogreshny. "The most holy Joseph Tukalsky, metropolitan of Kiev," Baranovich wrote to the sovereign, "requested Demian Ignatovich to place the clergy of the East Bank in his jurisdiction and in obedience to him. I notified him that Demian Ignatovich could not allow this without the knowledge, will and directive of your majesty the tsar. What has happened?

"The Romanovsky priest (Roman Rakushka),[20] previously a cossack in Nezhin, stopped on this side of the Dnieper on his way to His Holiness Methodios, patriarch of Constantinople.[21] He was serving as a messenger from Metropolitan Tukalsky. With cunning he obtained a document pronouncing a curse against Hetman Demian Ignatovich, intending to use this document to intimidate, give offense and foment trouble on this side of the Ukraine. Although the hetman of your majesty the tsar is not under the jurisdiction of the patriarchal throne of Constantinople, we cannot ignore the name and power of the ecumenical patriarch. Demian Ignatovich and I are astonished that so frivolous a curse was imposed by the patriarch. This curse cannot but be viewed as an insult to your most exalted throne as well, because Demian Ignatovich is hetman of your Host.

"The hetman begs your majesty the tsar to petition the patriarch of Constantinople requesting a blessing for him and asking that henceforth the patriarch not issue such documents, not pronounce a curse so carelessly. It is more fitting to curse those who obtain such documents by treachery from the holy patriarch and those who dare insult the throne of your majesty the tsar. In this document containing the patriarchal curse Demian Ignatovich is not even called hetman. Rather he is called by the diminutive, Demko Ignatenko. There is no such person as Demko Ignatenko. The only hetman is Demian Ignatovich."

ARCHBISHOP LAZAR BARANOVICH'S PRETENSIONS

"Metropolitan Tukalsky wishes to rule the clergy on the East Bank of the Dnieper," Baranovich continued, "yet here the clergy and the laity all wish to be under my pastoral authority. I shall leave this to your majesty to decide. Should not all the clergy on this side of the Dnieper be in my charge, as the hetman is in charge of the laity? It is difficult for the clergy residing on your majesty the tsar's side of the river to transfer their allegiance to a metropolitan on the king's side. In this division every evil can proliferate. The metropolitan of Kiev, even as pastor of all Russia and exarch[22] of Constantinople, has not always had the clergy of this side in his charge since all obey their own particular pastors. The people of Chernigov look to the archbishop of Chernigov and the people of Pereiaslav look to the bishop of Pereiaslav. The metropolitan of Kiev also, sitting in his place in Kiev by the Holy Wisdom cathedral,[23] from earliest times was satisfied with just this side of the Dnieper. Now that he resides on this side of the Dnieper he should be satisfied with the local clergy. "I have written frequently and in many forms to your majesty the tsar about Kiev. Now I repeat that rumors are rampant here that the [peace] commission has ceded Kiev to the Poles, effective the last day of November of this present year. All Orthodox inhabitants of the Kievan monasteries weep about this and all Orthodox Little Russian people are in tumult. Oh most merciful, Orthodox tsar! Grieve for the blood and verity of your eternal patrimony because, being the blood of your majesty the tsar it is the blood of all Orthodox grand princes and tsars of Kiev. Do not allow your prize, the imperial diadem of this holy great city Kiev to slip from your sovereign Orthodox hands into those of the infidels, to the eternal humiliation and grief of all Orthodox Christian people."

Turning to another matter, Baranovich wrote "I will also be so bold as to recall the sovereign's word about the printing of my book, *Trumpets*.[24] A word can be perfected only by a deed. In this case I humbly beseech your most exalted majesty the tsar to allow your word to be perfected by the deed of printing the books, for the manuscript has been corrected and blessed by the holy Patriarch Joasaph."[25]

Archpriest Simeon also presented a copy of the patriarchal document containing the curse against Mnogogreshny. "Methodios, by the mercy of God archbishop of New Rome,[26] great patriarch," the document announced. "The honorable father Roman Rakushka-Romanovsky, archpriest of Braslavl, informed us that in the time of war and strife among people Demko Ignatenko seized the home of this cleric and plundered his property, taking four hundred eighth measures[27] of grain, six large kettles, four stallions, one hundred and fifty pigs, and two gold mounted sabers. If Demko Ignatenko returns all that he took to the archpriest, in full, without excuses, voluntarily, there will be a blessing. If he refuses to return this plunder he will be cut off from God, cursed and unforgiven, and his corpse will not be scattered until the Last Judgment. Stone, wood, iron, yes all will disintegrate and be scattered and will renew the earth but he, never. The earth will devour him, like Dathan and Abiram.[28] The wrath of

God will hang over his head. His property and his work will be cursed and never will he see happiness. His property will be scattered on the wind and nothing will be returned to his descendants. Yes, he himself will recognize that God is not with him and the holy angel of God will not be with him at the Last Judgment. He will be excommunicated from the church of Christ, and no one will allow him to enter the church. Neither will he be blessed nor enveloped in the divine incense. He will be refused the gift of God [the Eucharist] and no one will eat or drink or sit with him at table, or pardon him or ask after his health. When he dies, no one will bury his body on pain of our strict archiepiscopal curse. There will be on him the curse of the holy three hundred and eighteen God-inspired fathers of the Council of Nicea[29] until he returns all things taken from the father, Lord Roman."

TSAR RESPONDS TO ARCHBISHOP

On July 13 the archpriest and the captain were allowed into the presence of the great sovereign. They were honored with an audience on the porch before the entrance hall. In regard to the first issue, about Kiev, the sovereign himself announced to the messengers "Although in the Andrusovo articles reference was made to surrendering Kiev, now we cannot even think of surrendering Kiev to the king because the Poles have infringed several of the conditions. In the current commission the plenipotentiaries have not been authorized to say a word to the king's commissioners about the surrender of Kiev, and the Poles themselves have not even sought the eastern side of the Dnieper. The original decree about eternal peace has not been realized. If a treaty is drawn up the hetman immediately will be instructed to send his people to the commission, this in accord with the Glukhov articles."

In regard to the second issue, about a council, this answer was relayed. "Even were someone to petition about a black council[30] the great sovereign would not permit such a council. A black council is held for the election of a hetman, when a hetman dies or when the current hetman resigns. Further, the sovereign did not admit Doroshenko anywhere, but prohibited his reception."

In addition it was noted that the sovereign recognized the loyal service of Hetman Demian Ignatovich. Were anyone to write against the hetman the sovereign would not permit it to be believed. If absolutely necessary the tsar's governors would receive the hetman in the tsar's towns and not surrender him to his enemies.

In response to the petition of Baranovich it was stated that the sovereign had ordered the printing of *Trumpets* to begin immediately. Unfortunately there was no paper available, nor would it arrive from abroad until September 1. Concerning the complaint about the curse against the hetman, the tsar promised to send a reliable Greek to the patriarch of Constantinople to seek information. Finally, the Kiev region and Little Russia on the East Bank of the Dnieper were placed under the jurisdiction of Baranovich.

From Moscow, Archpriest Simeon wrote to the hetman. "His majesty the tsar manifests inexpressible charity towards your honor. There is no need to have the least doubt about his favor. Furthermore, quickly petition the sympathetic Lord Artamon Sergeevich (Matveev). He has perfect love towards your honor and, best of all, he is always by the tsar's throne. He grieves about the Zaporozhian Host and about all that relates to Little Russia, just as a mother grieves about her children. 'While I am alive,' he said to us, 'I will not change.' We have tarried here in accord with the good advice of Artamon Sergeevich, who wished us to be present at the release of the Zaporozhian Cossacks from the Lower Reaches.[31] Artamon Sergeevich is not ashamed of his charity. In the tsar's name he rebuked the Zaporozhians, asking why they named Khanenko as hetman in their writing, and why they honored the Severian hetman, yet did not honor the true hetman. The Zaporozhians gave their word that they would obey you."

A MUSCOVITE EMBASSY IN CONSTANTINOPLE

The translator Magnus Khristoforov was sent to Constantinople to petition the Byzantine patriarch about removing the curse from Mnogogreshny. He returned with curious news suggesting that the patriarch was in an extremely difficult position as a result of Doroshenko's submission to the sultan. In Jassy the tsar's messenger met with the renowned Pavel Ivanovich Teteria,[32] who had gone over to the sultan. In response to Khristoforov's question about what this meant Teteria answered that in Poland he was shown no honor whatsoever. Arriving in Constantinople,[33] Khristoforov was presented to the patriarch and gave him the tsar's document, in which Alexis Mikhailovich requested the curse be removed from Hetman Mnogogreshny.

"I do not recall the incident to which the tsar refers," responded the patriarch. "I will consult our registry books and will give you an answer tomorrow."

The next day Khristoforov was summoned to receive the answer to his question. "I have investigated this affair," the patriarch told him. "It was done arbitrarily. The Orthodox bishop of Lvov in the Polish kingdom died. Some Latin, by the name of Simeon, wanted the archiepiscopal throne and petitioned the Wallachian hospodar requesting he write to me about granting Simeon the position. The hospodar did write to me but I refused him, as I could not establish anyone in the episcopate without consulting all the Orthodox inhabitants of Lvov. Then this Latin found two banned metropolitans in the Wallachian land who consecrated him as bishop in the town of Suceava. They dispatched him to Lvov but the Orthodox people in Lvov would not allow him to assume the episcopal throne. Instead they selected a good and godly man for the post, the monk Joseph. They sent him to me and I established him as their bishop. The Latin Simeon then petitioned Doroshenko and Tukalsky, requesting they write to me on his behalf. They acceded to Simeon's request and wrote that this Simeon was a good man and a learned Orthodox Christian. Archpriest Roman Rakushka-Romanovsky of Braslavl came to me with their documents, to which I responded that a bishop already was established in Lvov, and nobody knows who consecrated Simeon. Then Roman went to the sultan and I received a communication from an official of Mustafa Pasha[34] informing me that the sultan wished me to fulfill Doroshenko's request. I did not obey. Then Roman went once again to the sultan and brought me a communication from the sultan himself, ordering me to fulfill Doroshenko's request immediately. There was nothing else I could do. I removed Bishop Joseph and blessed Simeon. At the same time Archpriest Roman petitioned me, writing that during the war Demian Ignatovich plundered his property and continued to hold it to this day. He said that I should place a curse on Demian for this act. He did not inform me that Demian was the hetman and a subject of his majesty the tsar. After consulting the whole church council I gave Roman a document recording the curse against Demian, in which it was written that if the situation really were as Roman asserted, Demian should be anathematized."

"Most holy patriarch," began Khristoforov, "be so kind as to give me a document absolving Hetman Demian Ignatovich, in accord with the request of his majesty the tsar. Then release me to return to his majesty the tsar with this document."

"I cannot do this," answered the patriarch. "Were it only myself who would suffer misfortune as the result of such an act I would accept such misfortune with joy, but I fear that it would bring misfortune to all Christendom. Were I to send a document of absolution to Demian Ignatovich he would boast about it. Doroshenko would learn what occurred and he would write to the sultan. Blood would flow as a result."

"You have nothing to fear," objected Khristoforov. "I will carry the document of absolution to his majesty the tsar. He will direct it be sent to the hetman and will instruct the hetman to keep it to himself, as something for his soul and not to be boasted about before the people."

"Look what was fabricated with the false document," the patriarch retorted. "It was as if I had written it to the great sovereign. The document was revealed to the vizier, who summoned me and desired it be destroyed and, if you please, good people defended me. Nonetheless, the affair cost me five hundred pelts." Finally the patriarch gave the document.

DOROSHENKO'S DECLARATION

In Constantinople the patriarch feared Doroshenko, as a vassal of the sultan. In Chigirin, Doroshenko convinced the Greek prelate that he had submitted to the Orthodox monarch. In the spring of 1671, while on his way to Moscow, the Greek prelate Manasios came to Doroshenko. "I dare not write to his majesty the tsar," Doroshenko told him. "Report to the great sovereign that we would be pleased to serve him but because of Polish oppression we are compelled at this time to subject ourselves to the Hagarites.[35] It would be well were the great sovereign to accept us under his rule for the sake of the holy Eastern church. It would be good if he supported us as he supports our brothers of the other side. If he does not wish to receive us, it would be beneficial if he would reconcile us with the Polish king. In [16]68 I came with the Tatars to the tsar's towns beyond the Dnieper in response to a request from Ivashka Briukhovetsky and some of the elders. At that time I did not allow the cossacks and the Tatars to do battle with the tsar's soldiers. I released to Moscow *many*(!)[36] of the sovereign's captured commanders and soldiers even though I suffered much grief from the Tatars for doing so. I did not incite, nor will I ever incite to rebellion, the colonels who subjected themselves to his majesty the tsar along with Demian Ignatovich. I did not release Zaporozhian messengers to the king to ensure that the hetman of that side remained friendly to me. Moreover, all the disputes which have arisen are caused by the Zaporozhians. The great sovereign must not believe anything they say. Should the sovereign send me his directive, I say that I will persuade even Stenka Razin to return to his former obedience to his majesty the tsar."

In Kanev, Tukalsky announced to Manasios that the moment the sovereign assured them that he would receive them as subjects he himself would go immediately to Moscow. At this time he dared neither to go to Moscow nor to write because his earlier letters ended in the hands of the Poles. In his communication to the tsar Doroshenko particularly excoriated the Zaporozhians. According to him, the Zaporozhians caused great trouble among Rus Christians during the time of Bogdan Khmelnitsky and the other hetmans. They murdered innumerable pious people, martyring them and causing much blood to flow.

"I myself," emphasized Doroshenko, "am a member of the Eastern church. I seek the welfare of the Russian churches.[37] Therefor, I would have you, Orthodox sovereign, as my leader."

WAR ON WEST BANK

In the summer of 1671 war broke out on the West Bank of the Dnieper. Doroshenko fought on one side with the Turks and the Tatars. The Poles fought on the other side, joined by Khanenko and Serko. They devastated the unhappy country. Nor was the East Bank of the Dnieper peaceful at this time.

At the end of 1671 Moscow received news that Hetman Mnogogreshny was seriously dissatisfied as a consequence of the indefinite border between Little Russia and Lithuania along the Sozh river. "If his majesty the tsar," the hetman told the clerk Savin, the tsar's messenger, "permits our land to be surrendered to the king piecemeal he might as well surrender us and everything, and the king will be happy! On this side we have an army of more than ten thousand. We will defend ourselves rather than give up our land," Mnogogreshny warned. "We do not act in passion, nor will we ever do so, but we will give up our lives for justice. Previously I anticipated greater benevolence from his majesty the tsar towards myself, but he allowed us to be surrendered against our will. The Poles plunder our merchants and hold them in prison. They pillage around Kiev with impunity. The great sovereign does nothing, nor does he defend us. Had we not defended ourselves the Poles would have taken us into captivity long ago. From Muscovites we have given up hope for anything in the way of defense."

The hetman spoke all of this in anger and immediately left with his men for the steppe. The local people told Savin "when the hetman is angry, or has any doubt, he goes to the steppe to meditate." Strong doubt really did possess the hetman. "I do not wish to retain my present rank," he said, "because I am very ill. Before I die, I wish to give up the hetmancy. Should I happen to die my wife, children and kin will be beggared because the cossacks have a custom that when a hetman dies all his property is dispersed. Yes, and this also happens among the cossacks when the hetman is near death, but does not die. When I lay ill the cossacks collected all my property to distribute among themselves."

HETMAN MNOGOGRESHNY'S COMPLAINTS

In January 1672, Lieutenant[38] Alexander Tikhonovich Taneev of the musketeers came to Demian in Baturin for a report about Polish affairs. "To be precise," the hetman told Taneev, "I said that the great sovereign was allowing our land to be given away piecemeal. I said this so that the great sovereign might allow us to drive the Poles beyond the Dnieper, not just beyond the Sozh. If they are only driven beyond the Sozh river they will intervene in the Little Russian towns, lands and holdings. They will claim many towns on this side of the Dnieper as their own. Their truth and constancy is well known to me. I know on which points they will insist and which points they will never honor."

At this time, Captain Grigory Neelov of the Moscow musketeers lived in Baturin with the hetman. He told Taneev much news. "The Nezhin archpriest Simeon Adamovich went to Novgorod-Seversk, to Archbishop Lazar Baranovich. Along the way he stopped in Baturin. He was with the hetman [Mnogogreshny], who said to him 'I heard that the sovereign ordered Colonel Konstantin Solonina of Kiev to take my place as hetman and to remove me.' The archpriest told the hetman not to believe these words. The sovereign had granted Mnogogreshny the hetmancy and would never change. At this the hetman grew angry and wished to cut off the archpriest's head with his own hands with the saber he had in the front room. The hetman poured all manner of abuse upon the archpriest, shouting 'You and the Muscovites are selling me out!' The archpriest was frightened. He did not remain at the hetman's house to meet Neelov, whom he ordered to avoid the hetman. He met Neelov secretly by the church and ordered him to take care that no evil occur in the Ukraine from these words."

Simeon Adamovich himself also described to Matveev his conversation with the hetman. "From the very beginning," he insisted, "with the help of God, I served the great sovereign loyally. Now too I serve with zeal, insofar as I can, although I cannot assuage the hetman's present insolent grief by any words or measures. Some troublemaker convinced the hetman that the great sovereign has made Konstantin Solonina the Zaporozhian hetman. He complained much about this. He lamented also that [the Polish Colonel Jan] Piwo and the Poles have devastated the monasteries and the monastery properties around Kiev. He asked where the border with the Poles is located. What do I know?

"He complained about Kiev and asked if the great sovereign would surrender the city. I swore to him, calling upon my soul and my holy order, that the great sovereign would not even think of such a thing. In response he harassed me and threatened me with execution, saying that if he heard anything unpleasant from Moscow he would order me killed in a ferocious fashion. I told him I was prepared to die for the truth and for the great sovereign. What he was told was false. I assured him continuously of the benevolence of the great sovereign. As I saw that his grief was inconsolable, after arriving from Baturin on February 1 and consulting with Conciliar Noble Ivan Ivanovich Rzhevsky I communicated this information to the great sovereign and to you, your grace, by rapid courier. For God's sake, take care. As soon as possible send some intelligent man from the great sovereign to the hetman with an official letter reassuring him. Write about Kiev and about the border. Assure him that Kiev will not be surrendered to the Poles and that there is no intention of installing Solonina as hetman. Reassure him, for the Lord's sake!" After receipt of the letter requested by the archpriest, he and a cossack,the general aide-de-camp Pavel Gribovich, were sent to Moscow as envoys from the hetman.

It is not really known whence came the rumors about replacing Mnogogreshny with Solonina in the Ukraine. We do know that in the Ukraine all kinds of rumors were readily believed. Hetman Demian's supporters were as worried as Demian himself. Colonel Matvey Gvintovka of the Nezhin Regiment came to Governor Rzhevsky to say that the tsar had ordered that the hetman and the whole council of elders be changed. Rzhevsky invited Gvintovka to dine with him. Gvintovka refused the invitation, saying "How can I visit you? What kind of people are you, that you act so capriciously?"

The old story about the cession of Kiev and all of Little Russia to the Polish king again made the rounds. "The sovereign has reconciled himself

with the king," Mnogogreshny told Neelov. "He has surrendered the city
of Kiev and all of us to the Poles. If this is done all of us, abandoning our
wives and children to the mercy of his majesty the tsar, will defend
ourselves to the death against the Poles. We will never surrender Kiev, the
Caves monastery and the Little Russian towns to the king's side. We will
never subject ourselves to the king. I heard this from Doroshenko, who in
turn heard it from the Polish ambassador."

When relating the rumor that he was to be replaced by Solonina
Hetman Demian drank without restraint and was angry for a long time. He
said nothing to Neelov, nor did he summon him. While drunk Hetman
Mnogogreshny cut Colonel Dmitrashko-Raich of Pereiaslav with his
saber so severely that the colonel took to his bed from the wound. Another
time, drinking to inebriation, he kicked Chief Justice Ivan Domontov,
slapped his cheeks and tried to cut him with his saber. Neelov snatched
the saber from the drunken hetman and for this Demian cursed him as a
Muscovite.

"When the hetman does not drink," Neelov told Taneev, "he has great
discernment. Now all the elders fear his glance and dare not speak about
affairs of any kind because the hetman has become unrestrainedly harsh
to them. The judges grieve much. They told me the hetman is now very
angry with all the elders. Someone breathes but a word and he goes after
him with his saber. He gives no one any quarter. He sacked Colonel Peter
Roslavets of Starodub and ordered his own brother, Savva Shumeiko, to
take Roslavets' place. Roslavets sits in Baturin under guard, though no
one knows why he is in prison and no one dares petition on his behalf. The
elders, the quartermaster Peter Zabela, the justices and Dmitrashko-Raich
serve the great sovereign loyally and communicate all the news to me. Yet
they fear to be seen with me by day because the hetman orders his men to
watch them constantly lest they meet with the Muscovites. They come to
me with news at night. I convinced them to take an oath and they kissed
the icon of the Savior, swearing to be steadfast under the sovereign's
jurisdiction.

"Once Hetman Mnogogreshny told me that if his majesty the tsar
permitted the hetman of the other side of the Dnieper, Peter Doroshenko,
to be taken under his hand, Doroshenko would be hetman on that side of
the Dnieper and he, Mnogogreshny, would be hetman on this side.
Doroshenko would protect that side of the Dnieper from unfriendly
people. This side of the Dnieper would be quiet and peaceful while on the
other side Doroshenko would assure there were no enemies."

Neelov also offered an explanation for the sudden change in Mnogo-greshny's attitude towards Doroshenko. According to Neelov, Hetman Mnogogreshny corresponded constantly and secretly with Doroshenko. At banquets he drank to Doroshenko's health and compelled Neelov to drink to it too. At a banquet given by Colonel Dmitrashko-Raich, Hetman Mnogogreshny told all the elders "See what high favor the great sovereign expresses towards me? Captain Grigory Neelov has been sent to me with a regiment of more than a thousand musketeers."

"Were it not for the tsar's benevolence, the zeal of our little father and the good offices of Artamon Sergeevich Matveev, who steadfastly seeks the sovereign's favor for the Ukraine," the council of elders replied, "and if the correspondence of Taneev were even a bit late, there would be great tragedy in the Ukraine. An angel must tell the great sovereign that in these evil hours, in this time of trouble and misfortune for us, he must send his ambassador. After the arrival of his ambassador all would go well for us as before and many innocent souls would be freed from anxiety."

Neelov concluded his report to Taneev, saying "If the hetman begins to drink as before, I fear disaster. I have the keys to the town. The hetman ordered me, nay, begged me to send those arriving from anywhere directly to him."

MOSCOW DISPATCHES ENVOY TO MNOGOGRESHNY

When the report of Simeon Adamovich was received in Moscow a translator from the Little Russian Chancellery,[39] Grigory Kolchitsky, galloped to Baturin with the tsar's official letter to the hetman.

"It was not our order," the sovereign wrote, "that Solonina be made hetman. We will never name a hetman without a petition from the whole Zaporozhian Host and without a cossack council, even at your death. Solonina has been detained in Moscow for negotiations with the Polish ambassadors." Listening to the official letter, Hetman Mnogogreshny said "In the letter it is written that it became known to the sovereign that I was in great doubt on account of Solonina. Does not the letter say who informed the sovereign about this?" "The great sovereign does not know this, nor do I," responded the messenger. "If rumors are being circulated by Little Russians, stop them in accordance with your law. If these rumors originate with Muscovite soldiers, write about this to the great sovereign."

"My servant heard in Kiev about the appointment of Solonina," said the hetman. "This servant told me that Solonina's wife distributed papers to the Kievan Regiment, directing it to prepare supplies for her husband's reception. I ordered her to come to Baturin for questioning." Solonina's wife came to Baturin with Kolchitsky and announced that she had heard nothing, nor had she given any orders. The hetman ordered she be released to return to Kiev.

The tsar's messenger also reassured the hetman in regard to Kiev, affirming that it would never be surrendered to the Poles. The hetman answered that he did not doubt this, then announced a new cause for dissatisfaction with Moscow. "What honor is there to me and the Host from the great sovereign?" Mnogogreshny demanded. "At the Council of Glukhov it was established that representatives of the Zaporozhian Host be present with a free voice during negotiations with the Poles. Now in Moscow our representatives are barred from the audience chamber. This is a great dishonor to the Zaporozhian Host and a great sorrow!" "After the negotiations," replied Kolchitsky, "we will inform Colonel Solonina and his comrades about everything, and letters will announce the results." "How can we believe this?" objected the hetman. "They show us what is written in Russian script.[40] In the letters they can write freely whatever they wish. Here we are in great doubt [about what is meant]." "They will show you what is written in Russian script, and also in Polish script," answered the ambassador, assuring the hetman that his service and zeal would not be forgotten by the great sovereign. "Had I suspected evil," responded the hetman, "I would not have uttered these words."

Kolchitsky was still in Baturin on February 20, 1672 when Neelov informed Governor Rzhevsky of Nezhin that Baturin was mutinous and he expected trouble. The Voroshilov Regiment[41] had arrived in Baturin and the cossacks of this regiment were billeted in the same homes where musketeers were quartered. The cossacks had spoken some rude words to the musketeers and there was trouble, as had happened before.

Rzhevsky himself wrote to Prince Grigory Afanasievich Kozlovsky, who had replaced Peter Vasilievich Sheremetev as governor of Kiev, saying he was informed by the son of Colonel Gvintovka of Nezhin that Hetman Demian had sent his brother Shumeiko's Starodub Regiment to Kiev and from Baturin he had sent the Voroshilov Regiment. In the same report Rzhevsky complained to Kozlovsky that Gvintovka was unkind to him, nor were the Nezhin inhabitants as friendly as earlier.

Isaac, a priest from Gogolev, came to Kiev and reported to the governor "I was in the Terekhtemirov monastery and heard from its abbot that Hetman Demian and the colonels of various towns on the Pereiaslav (the Eastern) side frequently correspond with Hetman Doroshenko, urging he prevent the sovereign from making peace with the Polish king. Further, if the sovereign returns Kiev to the Polish king, the colonels say that Hetman Doroshenko must unite everyone from both sides to stand and fight for Kiev against the Poles."

Taneev had just returned from Baturin, but he galloped there again. Listening to the conciliatory document from the tsar, the hetman remained silent for a long time. Then he spoke, saying "How can I, the leaders and the whole Zaporozhian Host not be afraid, seeing that the great sovereign is returning Kiev and this side of the Dnieper to the Poles in eternal insufferable bondage. It is a disgrace and a dishonor. He returns the churches of God secretly to the Union, to destruction and devastation. During the negotiations in Moscow he did not allow our envoys to sit in the negotiating chamber and freely voice their views. Rather he held them in Moscow like captives. He excuses himself, saying the king's ambassadors refused to hear or associate with our messengers, calling them their slaves. Yet it was the fault of the tsar's boyars, not of the king's ambassadors, that news of the return of Kiev and the Little Russian towns was kept from the Zaporozhian Host. This has dishonored the Zaporozhian Host forever. The Poles will laugh at us. In their chronicles they will write that Moscow did not allow cossacks in the delegation in order to spark a dispute. When someone is wounded on the brow, even if the wound heals, the scar remains until death. So too, we will never forget this dishonor for all eternity.

"The great sovereign did not take the city of Kiev and all the Little Russian towns with the sword. We submitted to the great sovereign voluntarily, for the one Orthodox faith. If the sovereign does not need Kiev and the Little Russian towns, or me and the whole Zaporozhian Host, and he is returning all this to the king, he should order his governors to leave the Little Russian towns. We will seek another sovereign. Briukhovetsky, witnessing the Muscovite injustices, suffered much. Ultimately he could not restrain himself. He stood his ground, accepting even death.

"I too, seeing great injustices, ordered that in Chernigov the citadel be partitioned from the lower town. God knows what will happen as a result. Yes, it is time for us to seek another sovereign, but not the king. We will all die, down to the very babes at the breast, rather than fall under the king's rule. The Poles want money from Moscow in order to go against Doroshenko, to subdue him and then take Kiev and the Little Russian towns. Rather than accept that we members of the Host on both sides of the Dnieper will unite with the Turkish regiments and the Tatars. We will attack the Polish forces. Even if we all die, we will not surrender Kiev and the Little Russian towns.

"Yes, and we will not wait. After Easter Sunday we will invade Polish territory and make war with a huge force. Warsaw and the Polish towns will not be able to hold out. They will surrender because in all the Polish towns there are many Orthodox people. Kamieniec-Podolski perhaps will resist, but not for long. Not one Pole will remain, unless of the Orthodox faith, and the people of the Commonwealth will fall under the power of the Turkish sultan. Moreover, what will happen to the Polish realm also will happen to another.

"The sovereign writes that copies of the negotiated articles will be sent with Colonel Solonina. Neither I, nor anyone in the Host, believe in these copies. We have not seen them with our own eyes, nor have we heard anything about them. I am sent so many letters from Moscow seeking to comfort me with paper and sweet words, but these letters convey nothing real and concrete. Extended negotiations are conducted with the Poles, but borders are not established. In the meantime Poles trickle into the Little Russian territories. Colonel Jan Piwo rampaged all around Kiev, killing people in the town quarters. The people of Gomel applied to the Zaporozhian Host for assistance and I had no choice but to receive them. The Host drives nobody away, and it is time for me to stand by my convictions.

"I wrote to his majesty the tsar about Doroshenko and the Zaporozhians. I was informed that Captain Mikhail Kolupaev of the Moscow musketeers soon would arrive with an answer, but this is not why Kolupaev was sent. I know why he comes. Well, so be it.[42] If you come to me again with injustice you will end up in the Crimea,[43] because you have acquired evil ways from the Poles. The Polish ambassadors, once they acquired money in Moscow, will return to their own territories, to Smolensk and to other local towns. Then our cossacks will divide this treasure with them. It would be good if the Polish ambassadors came to the Little Russian towns. Then we might achieve something."

Receiving such a reception Taneev hurried to Neelov, who confirmed that naturally Mnogogreshny had united with Doroshenko and was treating Neelov and his musketeers differently. The musketeer guards he placed were under strength. In addition, he ordered that the guards around the gates[44] be withdrawn. "The elders, the justices, the quartermaster Peter

Zabela and Colonel Rodion Dmitrashko-Raich loyally serve the sovereign and keep me well informed. They say that Demian has betrayed the sovereign. He has united with Doroshenko and bowed before the Turkish sultan. He gave Doroshenko twenty-four thousand efimoks to help his army. In all the regiments he has installed colonels from his own kinsmen, brothers, his in-laws[45] and friends. He wishes to do the same as Briukhovetsky. He brought his property from Baturin to the monastery of St. Nicholas of Krupitsk and from there he transported it to Sosnitsa. He ordered his brother Vasily to partition the upper town of Chernigov from the lower fortress, where there are soldiers of the tsar, and to make fieldworks. He also ordered Vasily to bring his property from Chernigov into Sednevo. Demian himself wishes to take his wife and children from Baturin to Lubny on March 15. Finally Mnogogreshny called the council of elders together announcing that the sovereign had written to him, ordering him to send all cossack elders to Moscow. From Moscow they would be dispersed to the Siberian towns for the rest of their lives."

COSSACK ELDERS DENOUNCE MNOGOGRESHNY

On the night of March 8 Taneev and Neelov went to Peter Zabela dressed in the homespun coats of musketeers and carrying bandoliers and poleaxes. In addition to Peter Zabela the justices Ivan Domontov and Ivan Samoilovich, as well as Colonel Rodion Dmitrashko-Raich, were there. When the cossack elders caught sight of the officials from Moscow they burst into tears and spoke their complaint. "Oh, our great misfortune, inconsolable grief, unquenchable tears! According to the devil's teaching, succumbing to the blandishments of Hetman Doroshenko, our hetman, forgetting the fear of God and His righteous judgment and forgetting the tsar's mercy and generosity, has betrayed the great sovereign. He has united with Doroshenko under the power of the Turkish sultan.

"The hetman sent his advisors, monks, to Doroshenko. Before the monks Doroshenko swore an oath to our hetman, and the monks in turn swore an oath to Doroshenko on behalf of our hetman. Then Doroshenko sent his messengers to Hetman Mnogogreshny with an icon of the Savior. In the presence of these messengers Mnogogreshny swore an oath to Doroshenko, and they in turn swore an oath to him on behalf of Doroshenko. After this oath was sworn the hetman sent a grant of twenty-four thousand efimoks to Doroshenko to aid the army.

"To us, the council of elders, Hetman Mnogogreshny has become unbearably harsh. He does not allow us to utter a single word. He beats and cuts us with his saber. He has assigned his own brothers, his in-laws, friends and cronies as colonels in all the regiments, and appointed them to the cossack council of elders. He talks as if he sent the Voroshilov Regiment to the Dnieper, in accord with the news received [about the activities of the Poles around Kiev, above p. 94]. In fact, he sent the regiment not to the Dnieper but to Lubny, to his son-in-law,[46] and ordered it to occupy the Chigirin road.

"In all the regiments he distributed universals asserting that the Tatars had gone to join Doroshenko. He ordered all the places to prepare for siege, precisely as did Briukhovetsky. His property was brought from Baturin to the monastery of St. Nicholas of Krupitsk, and from there it was transferred to Sosnitsa. He himself, with his wife and children, intends to go to Lubny on March 15, although he pretends he is going on pilgrimage to Kiev.

"He will take us, the cossack elders, with him. We fear that as soon as he leads us out of Baturin he will order us killed or drowned, or will disperse us among various prisons. Even more dangerous, when he leaves Baturin he will order peasants be set in force around the gates after he leaves. The musketeers will refuse to leave the gates and quarrels will begin. There will be much bloodshed and this will be a pretext for war. There are very few musketeers in Baturin. Those that are here are unfit and unreliable. Were he able to entice Neelov outside the town he would not be restrained, nor would he surrender him to the Crimean khan. For a long time he has wished to do evil to Neelov and the musketeers, but we have been careful. Perhaps he will release you. If he does, your documents will be examined in Krolevets and Glukhov.

"Bringing Stepan Grechany,[47] who was in Moscow with Colonel Solonina, into the room, he administered an oath to him. Grechany swore to be loyal to the hetman, who ordered him to write that he was never in Moscow at all, intending by this to turn the Ukraine against the sovereign. Once the hetman summoned all of us, saying 'For a long time his majesty the tsar has been writing to me, requesting that I send the elders to Moscow, whence he wishes to exile them to Siberia forever.'

"We do not believe what he says. Hetman Mnogogreshny embellishes everything with his evil fantasies. When he goes to Lubny and Sosnitsa he will gather all the elders and the clergy and he will read Stepan

Grechany's letter to them. He will tell them about the proposed exile of the whole council of elders to Siberia. 'You see how deceitful the Muscovites are?' he will say. 'What good can we expect from them?' Doroshenko sent a Tatar to the hetman in Lubny, and later the hetman himself was seen with him."

"The hetman called me one night," Dmitrashko-Raich declared, "and ordered me to kiss the icon of the Savior, swearing that I would be loyal to him and kill the sovereign's soldiers. After this he presented his own archer's bow to me. I do not stand by this oath for I was compelled to take it, fearing death."

The elders requested that Taneev inform Matveev about all of this, to be reported to the sovereign, lest he hand his patrimony over to a ravenous wolf for destruction. They requested the sovereign to order a group of about four or five hundred men, the most select cavalrymen, to be sent to Putivl quickly. They also begged the sovereign to send them a gracious and reassuring letter. They and Neelov would inform the soldiers so they could march quickly to Baturin. They could reach Konotop in a single night, but even before the soldiers arrived the elders would fetter the wolf and hand him over to Neelov. When the soldiers arrived they would take him with them to Putivl. Describing all of his treachery in writing, they would transport him to the great sovereign themselves. In the opinion of the elders all the misfortune came from his advisors, Archpriest Simeon Adamovich, the aide-de-camp Pavel Gribovich, Ataman Yeremey Andreev[48] of Baturin, and the mastermind, Colonel Matvey Gvintovka of Nezhin. "Archpriest Simeon is the biggest troublemaker of all," the elders charged. "The hetman sends him to Moscow to search for information. Wishing to please the hetman, the archpriest tells him things which never happened."

"I established the articles of Glukhov," said Zabela, "in which it is written that members of the clergy are not to be sent, nor are they to be received as part of the delegation. Specifically, Archpriest Simeon Adamovich of Nezhin is not to be sent. If God gives this evil henchman of Mnogogreshny into our hands, the great sovereign should reward us. He should appoint a Great Russian boyar as hetman, who will be steadfast and loyal. If the hetman is a Little Russian nothing good will ever come of it."

In the meantime Archpriest Simeon Adamovich and the aide-de-camp Gribovich, who according to the cossack elders were the instigators of all the evil, sent their own delegation to Moscow and transmitted Hetman Demian Ignatovich's message. The hetman asked about the boundary line between Little Russia and Lithuania. He also complained that the Polish ambassadors successfully barred cossack emissaries from the negotiations. "It is time for us to stop treating with the Polish lords. We sit on the same horses and carry the same weapons and the same sabers as they do. Let it be known that these are the sabers which freed us from slavery and heavy bondage and they have not rusted yet. We pray that his majesty the tsar no longer will allow the Polish lords to call us their slaves. We have been patient long enough! The Polish colonel Piwo has devastated Kievan farmsteads.[49] He has seized six men and it is not known where he has hidden them. We sent Colonel Ivan Lysenko, formerly of Chernigov, to Kiev and he requested Governor Prince Kozlovsky for help. "I cannot help you," responded the governor, "because I do not have a directive from his majesty the tsar permitting me to provoke the Poles." The emissaries were to give his majesty the tsar a list of the damage done by Piwo and ask whether the hetman and the army must remain longer in such confusion.

MNOGOGRESHNY IS SEIZED

The confusion ended. Zabela and his comrades fulfilled their promise. On the night of March 13 they seized Mnogogreshny and sent him to Moscow with General Chancellor Karp Mokrievich. Mnogogreshny's brothers, Vasily and Shumeiko, hearing of the hetman's fate, went into hiding. On April 6 the rector of the Kiev Brotherhood monastery,[50] Abbot Varlaam Yasinsky, came clandestinely to Prince Kozlovsky, the governor of Kiev, requesting an assurance of secrecy lest the Little Russian clergy and laity denounce him. The governor promised profound secrecy and Varlaam related his tale.

"Two monks came to me and showed me a safe-conduct document from Abbot Jeremiah Shirkevich of the Maksakov monastery," Varlaam said. "They said they came about their own affairs. I already had sent them from my cell when one of them returned and began to entreat me. 'Have mercy, father rector. Order that I be taken to the Kievan Caves monastery, so the people from Moscow and the cossacks and people of Kiev do not recognize me. I am the brother of Hetman Demian, Vasily Mnogogreshny! Now he is with me.'"

The governor immediately sent men to seize the fugitive in the Brotherhood monastery. He was brought to the governor's office where he was interrogated and then sent to Moscow.

News of these events had not reached Moscow when the hetman's messengers, Archpriest Simeon Adamovich and the aide-de-camp Pavel Gribovich, were released at the beginning of March. With them was sent Mikhail Kolupaev, the long-promised musketeer captain. On March 15 as Kolupaev approached Sevsk a musketeer from the governor galloped to meet him and gave him a letter in which the governor advised that a courier had come to him from Putivl with news. General Chancellor Karp Mokrievich and Colonels Roslavets and Dmitrashko-Raich were bringing Hetman Demian to Putivl in chains. They were taking him to the great sovereign, accused of treachery. Kolupaev responded to the governor saying that he must try to hold Archpriest Adamovich and his comrades in Sevsk by saying there was insufficient transport until the hetman's affair was explained. In the meantime, the governor should send quickly to Little Russia to learn about this affair.

This cunning plan failed. The governor announced to Adamovich that there was no transport but the next day the archpriest and his companions said they had collected transport and would go ahead alone.

"You cannot go alone," said Kolupaev. "We have only one document to the hetman for all of you." At this point Gribovich and his comrades began to shout and tried to storm out of the building. "We will go alone," they thundered. "We will not wait for you!" Kolupaev was compelled to explain to them that disturbing rumors had been received about the hetman and they must await genuine information. "We expect no mischief from the hetman," retorted the cossacks. "If he intended some villainy he would not have sent us to the great sovereign with the archpriest."

With these words Gribovich and his companions left, but Adamovich remained. He confided that the hetman had not been himself for some time. "The hetman ordered me to find out in Moscow whether Little Russia and Kiev truly would be surrendered to the king. Were this true, the hetman wished to send an army to occupy Gomel immediately. I asked him on whom he was counting, and he answered 'On this one, on that one, on Doroshenko. Briukhovetsky ignited a spark for justice. So be it. I too will set off such a spark. I will abandon Nezhin. There are few Muscovites in Pereiaslav. I will lay siege to Chernigov and I myself will go to Kaluga.'

"He sent six thousand thalers[51] to Zaporozhia to ensure the Zaporozhians would be obedient to him. Now there is a rumor that they are taking the hetman to Moscow in chains. There is no reason for me to go to Nezhin. I will petition the sovereign to allow me to live in Moscow." "Live in

Nezhin," advised Kolupaev, "and serve the great sovereign loyally as before." "As a result of Briukhovetsky's treachery I suffered greatly," responded Adamovich. "I lost my property. I kissed the icon of the Savior with Dmitrashko-Raich, swearing that if Hetman Demian takes the path of treachery we will all leave for Putivl."

On March 17 Karp Mokrievich and the colonels arrived in Sevsk with their prisoner. Two days later Kolupaev and Adamovich set off with them for Moscow. In Moscow the government was organizing. On March 17 soldiers were sent to various places to ferret out information. The soldiers were instructed to listen and to watch the cossacks and the burghers, to learn what they were thinking and saying about the capture of the hetman. They were told to find out what could be expected from the cossacks and burghers and whether they were loyal to the great sovereign. Upon their return, the reports of the [soldier-]messengers were unanimous.

"The cossacks, the burghers and all the rank-and-file were happy to be under the great sovereign," the messengers reported. "No one would stand up for the hetman. The rank-and-file also complained about the cossack elders, saying they oppressed them with labor services and collections. The rank-and-file cossacks complained that no hetman had ever *burdened* them as much as the present Hetman Demko, nor handed them over to the elders and their cronies in virtual slavery. Furthermore, they expected the same treatment from their elders. They praised the previous rule of the tsar's governor, when life was easier for them. The cossack elders, according to the rank-and-file, disliked the rule of the tsar's governor because they could not become lords. The cossack elders had led them into trouble against their will, frightening them with the Tatars. Now, no matter how terrified they were of the Tatars or the Poles, they did not believe the elders. Had they not feared the soldiers of the great sovereign they would have killed and plundered the whole council of elders. They were most dissatisfied with Colonel Matvey Gvintovka of Nezhin, with Vasily and Savva Mnogogreshny, with Colonel Konstantin Stryevsky[52] of Pereiaslav, with the Chernigov captains, Leonty Polubotok and Vasily Brukovsky, and with the former colonel, Rodion Dmitrashko-Raich. In addition, nothing good was said about Chief Justice Ivan Samoilov[ich] and General Chancellor Karp Mokrievich. They say that long ago the chancellor committed an act of treachery for the hetman, then when the tide turned and clear evidence emerged against the hetman Mokrievich spoke against him. Nonetheless, until clear evidence emerged against the hetman, the chancellor remained silent."

On March 25 the clerk Maksim Alekseev[53] went to Baturin, to the elders, with gracious words. On the road many Cherkassians[54] told him "We would like his majesty the tsar to send us his governors, so we can do without a hetman. He should also eliminate the whole council of elders. This would be better for us as there would be no more destruction or treachery by anyone. All the elders seek to enrich themselves in any way possible, coveting the rank of lord for themselves. They become perfidious and our leaders seek in vain for a safe path through the thicket of such treachery."

ACCUSATIONS AGAINST MNOGOGRESHNY

Two days after Alekseev's departure from Moscow, on March 28, General Chancellor Karp Mokrievich, Colonel Roslavets and Colonel Dmitrashko-Raich arrived there with their prisoner, Demian Ignatov[ich]. "On March 14," Mokrievich reported, "Demko gathered the whole council of elders and departed from Baturin with the elders and with Grigory Neelov. The hetman said he was leaving to fulfill a promise to pray in Kiev, but the Voroshilov Regiment stood in readiness at Ichnia. He also ordered the Wallachian Hussar Regiment, which was in Olshovka, to come to him. Having collected the whole army he wished to remain in Lubny a week or two to correspond with Doroshenko.

"Of course we elders realized Hetman Demko intended to betray the great sovereign. He wanted to beat us to death and to surrender Quartermaster Peter Zabela and Justice Ivan Domontov to Doroshenko as captives. We perceived that no good would come to Neelov and the musketeers either, because Demko told Neelov to his face that he would cut off his head, beard and all. Seeing all this, on the night of March 13 we entered the lower town and secretly placed musketeers around the hetman's courtyard as guards. Then we gathered with weapons and stealthily occupied his dwelling. At this time he was sleeping. Colonel Dmitrashko-Raich entered the bedroom first. In the dark he asked where Demko was. Demko awoke and defended himself but we all entered the bedroom and took him by force. We carried him into the courtyard to Grigory Neelov. Confronted by Grigory, Demko strained to reach his gun, wishing to fight us. I did not allow him to reach his gun, but shot him in the shoulder with a pistol. Demko sank to the ground from this wound. We chained him at this point and led him to the lower town.

"Before the whole council of elders," Mokrievich continued, "Demko said 'I will gather an army of about six thousand good cavalrymen and I will make war on the Great Russian towns. I do not need any more warriors than this, for the Crimean khan will help me in the spring, when the grass grows. Then I will seize Artem [Artamon Sergeevich Matveev] by the hair, and I know what I will do to him.'

"Demko was closely related to Doroshenko, both by blood and marriage," Mokrievich explained," because Doroshenko had betrothed his daughter to a blood relative of Demko, Mishka [Mikhail] Zinoviev, and the affinal relation went through Kunitsky.[55] Demko praised the Turkish sultan continuously, saying 'It is better for me to be under the Turks than under the Muscovite tsar.' He told the whole council of elders that Moscow was unjust. Together with the Poles Demko wished to cut all of us Little Russians down and lay waste the towns. He insinuated that the sovereign wanted the devastation of Little Russia and gave the Poles much money. 'With my courage,' he boasted, 'I will personally repulse the Muscovites, like Alexander of Macedon. Just as Alexander waged war against towns so too I, Demian, will devastate the Muscovite realm.'

"I told him to remember God and the oath he had sworn, and asked him why he was reneging on that oath. 'We have seen nothing evil,' I said, 'and we all live in freedom. Wait until Archpriest Simeon returns from Moscow.'

"Demian answered me, saying 'I know everything. There is no reason to wait! I do not wish to be under the tsar. Let whoever wants to come from Moscow. Yes! And let Baturin be filled with wealth. I need none of this!'"

The general chancellor also presented a formal written report. "The following improper words were spoken by the former hetman Demian against the high throne of his majesty the tsar. (1) During Lent, in his home, he spoke to the elders about the surveying, saying 'See what the tsar intends for us? He will surrender all of the Ukraine to the Poles, drawing the boundary from Kiev by the Desna river and the Seim up to Putivl.' (2) He said to us 'Verily I heard this from a captain living in Chernigov, who heard it from the tsar's council. This captain was ordered to tell us that there were five hundred peasant homesteads prepared for us in the tsar's settlement if we surrendered the cossack elders and the Ukrainians subordinate to them. When we replied, telling him to wait for the father, the archpriest, to see what bounty there would be from the sovereign he told us that our beards had grown but we had lost our wits.' (3) To Peter Zabela alone Hetman Demian said 'When the time is right we will have to seek another sovereign, for we can expect nothing good from Moscow.' (4) To Judge Samoilovich he said "Do you see what is being done? The

Poles are no friends of ours yet Moscow gave them money for an army of thirty thousand men. When it comes time to pay the Turk, the Muscovites will sell us out. We must give thought beforehand about finding a strong sovereign, as they did on the other side of the Dnieper.' (5) Last autumn, having sworn Andrei Murashka to secrecy, the hetman said to him 'What will I do to the Muscovites? You will see my saber covered in Muscovite blood. I will drive them back to their capital, if only you stand firmly by me.'" (6) Right before Shrovetide he said to Dmitrashko-Raich 'I have an order from the tsar himself to raze[56] Moscow.' (7) He said 'You do not know the Turkish sultan's opinion of the Muscovite tsar and the Polish king. He refused to permit the Polish king to be referred to as a proper king, but only as a kinglet.[57] He ordered the Muscovite tsar be told that he, the sultan, held him in the same respect he gave a Black Tatar.'[58] (8) All his words were offensive and terrible to recall. On hearing them, and now writing them, my whole body trembles."

Following this denunciation the council of elders sent another. This was the report of Captain Grigory Karpovich of Baturin, whom Mnogogreshny had sent to Tukalsky, accompanied by Tukalsky's messenger, Semeon Tikhy [or Tihkonov].

"When we arrived in Kanev," reported Grigory, "we visited the metropolitan. On the table before the metropolitan Semeon placed an icon which we brought from Baturin. The metropolitan kissed the icon and asked Semeon 'What good have you done there?' 'With your prayers, I accomplished everything for which I was sent,' responded Semeon. At this point Joseph Tukalsky approached me and taking me by my buttons said 'Not a moment too soon, lord captain. You must join your hetman. You yourself well know that he who has the khan on his side is lord. Both the Poles and the Muscovites know how numerous are the forces possessed by the sultan. Not only will they not come to attack us, they cannot even defend their own towns. They will be even more frightened when our hetmans abide together in unbreakable friendship.'"

"Were we to describe all the evidence of Demko's treachery," the elders wrote to the sovereign, "it would not fit on one sheet of paper, nor even on the hide of an ox." To add to this, Lazar Baranovich told Mikhail Fedorovich Samarin, the table attendant who was sent to him, "As soon as I found out that Demko was corresponding with Doroshenko I wrote to him, telling him to cease this correspondence and not to go to pray in the Kievan Caves monastery. After reading my missive he tossed it onto a table and told my messenger 'The archbishop should mind his own business.'"

INTERROGATION AND EXILE OF MNOGOGRESHNY

On April 14 the boyars and the councillors convened in the Chancellery for Foreign Affairs to question Demko Ignatov about his treason and about those who were his accomplices in this treachery.

"I did not intend to betray the great sovereign," Demian maintained. "I served him loyally and did not go beyond the Sozh river. I transferred the colonels in accordance with the advice of all in the council of elders. I wished to go to Kiev in response to a letter from the archimandrite of the Caves monastery informing me that the Poles were committing violence and pillaging there. I sent a message to Kiev, to Governor Prince Kozlovsky, asking that he defend the people of the Caves monastery from the Poles but General Chancellor Karp Mokrievich advised me to go to Kiev myself with the transport unit. I corresponded with Doroshenko about this lest he cause offense to anyone on this side of the Dnieper. I went to the Sozh in conformance with the counsel of the colonels and all the officers, and even more, in accordance with the advice of Chancellor Karp Mokrievich. I wished only to establish the border along the Sozh river."

"You wished to establish the boundary along the Sozh—good!" said the boyars. "But why did you seize Gomel, which is beyond the Sozh river?" "This was the will of the great sovereign," responded Demian. "Although Gomel is beyond the Sozh river, during the Polish war the inhabitants of Little Russia suffered great oppression from Gomel. Therefore I ordered it taken. Should there be another war with the Poles Gomel would provide great protection to the inhabitants of Little Russia because it overlooks the Sozh river itself."

"Why did you say to the tsar's messenger that, come what may, the sovereign already had given everything to the king, and more in a similar vein?" the boyars asked Demian. "I never said that," protested Mnogogreshny. The boyars called the messenger, who accused Demian to his face.[59] "I said this when I was drunk, in my delirium," Demian explained. The boyars asked about his words to Taneev. Demian refused to admit to them. "I said nothing of this," he said. "I told Chancellor Karp Mokrievich that the great sovereign gave us joy in his letter about Kiev. 'Don't believe everything you hear,' the chancellor replied. 'Listen to your own reason, lest the past be repeated. A document from the tsar was sent to

Briukhovetsky, reassuring the Zaporozhian Host. After this Prince Daniel Stepanovich Velikogo-Gagin was sent with an army and Zolotarenko, Samko and Silich were killed.'[60] Hearing such words from the chancellor, I began to doubt and to fear the tsar's army. In this I am guilty before the great sovereign, although I did not intend to betray him."

"Why then," the boyars asked, "did you not announce and condemn these words of the chancellor before the council of elders and the entire Host? Why did you not report them to his majesty the tsar? Furthermore, what kind of danger was there to you? Did you really not know that Prince Velikogo-Gagin did not kill Zolotarenko and Samko? Did you not know that he was at the council with the army because without the tsar's army you would have attacked the council?" "I am a simple and uneducated man," answered Demian. "On reflection, I chose not to write to his majesty the tsar, thinking that the chancellor spoke truthfully, warning me. I am guilty."

At this point in the interrogation a witness stood up. It was Archpriest Simeon, who once again happened to be in Moscow. "When I came to Moscow," he said, "I spoke to him more than once, reassuring him that he would be granted the tsar's mercy. I reminded him how Briukhovetsky betrayed his oath and what happened to him afterwards. At this he said to me 'As soon as you get to Moscow they will throw you into jail.'" Demian confessed.

"Why did you change your treatment of Neelov?" they asked the hetman. "Why did you order that the musketeer guards be decreased?" "I did not do so on my own initiative," answered Demian. "Here is what happened. Once I went into the church and asked, are there guards? I received the reply that two musketeer sergeants were standing guard, with about a hundred musketeers. I asked whether there was a shortage of supplies. I was told there was no shortage of supplies but there was disquiet among the guards. I discussed this with Captain Neelov and ordered that the guard be decreased by a few musketeers. I did not forbid anyone to converse with Neelov, nor did I order he be watched."

Responding to questions about relations with Doroshenko and about the change of cossack colonels, he answered "I did not send the monks to Doroshenko with treasonous messages. Rather, Doroshenko sent the cossack Senka[61] Tikhy to me because the Crimean Tatars on this side, in Lubny, had captured several Little Russians. Doroshenko soundly defeated these Tatars, rescued the captives and returned them to their homes. I did not send twenty-four thousand efimoks to Doroshenko. There was nothing for me to send because since I have been hetman I have never received even two thousand lion dollars[62] from the collection of dues. Moreover, I changed the colonels and other lower rank cossack officers according to the advice of the whole council of elders."

"Why did you tell the elders the tsar demanded they come to Moscow to be exiled to Siberia? Why did you order Grechany to write things which never happened? Did you compel Dmitrashko-Raich to swear on oath one night that he would support you? Did you send Abbot Shirkevich to Warsaw?" Demian denied all these charges.

Alexander Taneev confronted the accused hetman and asserted Demian's guilt according to his own list of accusations. As before, the accused denied all. Yet when Archpriest Simeon accused him, saying that he corresponded with Doroshenko, Mnogogreshny retorted "Before the great sovereign, I am guilty. I refuse to acknowledge the words of the archpriest."

The boyars questioned the hetman with great passion. They demanded that Demian confess, that he speak honestly about his treasonous correspondence with Doroshenko. Who knew about their confabulations and what was their substance? If he refused to speak, they would torture him.

Demian repeated that he had never contemplated treason. He corresponded with Doroshenko about love and friendship, to prevent Doroshenko from making war on the tsar's side of the Dnieper. Doroshenko did not incline him to the Turk. "My only sin is that I spoke angry words in a drunken delirium," he added.

"If you were not contemplating treason," said the boyars, "you would have sent all of Doroshenko's writings to the great sovereign." "I am a simple and uneducated man," Demian repeated. "All of this was presented to the chancellor of the Host. I directed that all letters be sent to his majesty the tsar, but the chancellor did not send them. Instead he conspired against me with the elders, seeking to alienate me from the mercy of his majesty the tsar and accuse me of treason. The elders always do this kind of thing when they wish to cause some trouble for the hetman. They lead him to this. I am a simple man and I corresponded with Doroshenko because of his flattery, but I did not think this was any kind of betrayal."

A new interrogation was carried out with torture. It elicited the same response. The hetman had not contemplated any kind of betrayal.

At this point Ataman Yeremey Andreev of Baturin spoke. "When Demko sent me to Doroshenko he directed me to say to him that they were trading two sheepskins for one. I asked him what this meant and he answered that Doroshenko would understand. He told me just to say the words." "I do not remember giving any such order," Demian answered. They took him to be tortured and gave him nineteen blows. "I talked about treachery, but I only talked," admitted Demian. "I did not correspond with Doroshenko about treachery. The words about sheepskins which I directed Yeremey to say meant that the Poles wished to take Kiev but his majesty the tsar did not wish to return it. If the Poles did not stop making trouble I wanted to have Gomel. No one knew about this treachery of mine. No one conspired with me. I thought this alone." At this time they also dealt with Matvey Gvintovka. They put his hands in a clamp and asked him about Demko's treason. Gvintovka replied that he knew nothing. He himself served loyally.

During the second application of torture Demian repeated the same words. They asked him about his relations with Tukalsky. "When Patriarch Paisios of Alexandria was returning from Moscow through the Little Russian towns," the hetman responded, "my brother Vaska[63] petitioned him and Archbishop Lazar Baranovich seeking absolution for the murder of his wife and permission to marry another. The patriarch and bishop gave him absolution and permission to marry, and also ordered him to give alms to the church. Vaska sent Archbishop Lazar and Metropolitan Tukalsky each a horse. The metropolitan wrote to me requesting he be allowed to take tribute from the churches in the Kiev region, but I refused him."

On May 6 Artamon Matveev and Conciliar Secretary Grigory Karpovich Bogdanov[64] questioned the hetman's brother Vasily Mnogogreshny, the aide-de-camp Pavel Gribovich and Doroshenko's messengers. Vasily Mnogogreshny asserted that he knew nothing. They showed Vasily his personal letter to Acting Colonel Leonty Polubotok in which he directed arrangements be made in regard to some Muscovite clerk. "Take this clerk from prison, give him alcohol and beat him about the stomach," Vasily had written. "Do not beat him with staves lest there be bruises. Do it by hand so that he will never forget. Be efficient in this so that the deed cannot be attributed to you. At night let the guards accuse him of trying to escape."

"I am guilty," Vasily admitted. "I wrote this document because the clerk insulted us. Before the start of the war with Briukhovetsky he said to the hetman himself 'We have worn Samko's caftans,[65] and we do not forswear to wear yours.'"

"If you were unaware of treachery on the part of your brother," asked Matveev, "and you yourself did not intend to commit treason, why did you abandon your position as colonel and flee Chernigov dressed in a monk's robe?"

"I am guilty of this," responded Vasily. "I fled for the following reason. Recently I had written to my brother reporting that the governor of Chernigov constantly demanded timber for construction in the town. He was repairing the town and preparing for battle in such a way that the soldiers began to fear us and fortified themselves for a siege. Moreover, the officers were said to be casting bullets. A Polish squire from Polotsk, an immigrant from the other side, told me that the soldiers were casting bullets, intending to go to war with the cossacks. I wrote to my brother about this and, in addition, sent the squire from Polotsk to report to him personally. My brother sent the young man Ivashka to me to say that I must not provoke any kind of dispute with the governor of Chernigov and the Muscovite soldiers. He, Demian, awaited the return of Archpriest Simeon and Mikhail Kolupaev from Moscow with a direct order for him. He expected that the Poles would cease their disputes and no longer make trouble for his majesty the tsar."

"In addition," Vasily said, "the young stripling Ivashka told me in confidence that a monk who had come from Moscow to Baturin told him that an order was given to seize Hetman Demian and send him to Moscow. The following day the lieutenant colonel came and sternly ordered me to report to the governor immediately. Perceiving that I was not invited in the customary manner, I was frightened. I guessed that things did not bode well for my brother, as the story of the monk suggested. Saddling my horse I rode towards the town, where I was met by many foot soldiers with guns and poleaxes. I was even more frightened and fled. I made my way to the monastery of the Virgin at Elets, and asked Archimandrite Galia-tovsky's[66] advice. I asked whether I should go to the governors or flee farther. 'Do as you wish,' the archimandrite said. 'Flee further, for you can do nothing here.' I traveled beyond the Desna river, to the monastery of St. Nicholas. Here I abandoned my horse, removed my cloak and dressed in a monk's robe. From the monastery of St. Nicholas I traveled to the Maksakov monastery, to Abbot Shirkevich. The abbot turned me over to an elder monk and one of his servants and ordered them to take me to Kiev by boat, by way of the Desna river."

Interrogated, Gribovich insisted he knew nothing save that Demian gave Doroshenko a loan of six thousand Polish zlotys. In regard to the dismissal of Colonel Dmitrashko-Raich he related what he knew. A rumor spread that Dmitrashko-Raich wished to transfer to the Poles or to Doroshenko. Demko sent one of his trusted men for him, but Dmitrashko-Raich refused to come. He locked himself in Baryshevka and told the hetman's messenger that just as Samko and Zolotarenko were destroyed, so they also wished to destroy him. Demian then took the tsar's soldiers and his own army and withdrew to Nezhin. Upon leaving Nezhin he met the Serbian metropolitan[67] and sent him to Baryshevka to persuade Dmitrashko-Raich to join him. A priest came from Baryshevka accompanied by Dmitrashko-Raich's wife to petition the hetman on behalf of the colonel. Demian reassured them and ordered Dmitrashko-Raich to visit him without fear. Yet as soon as Dmitrashko-Raich came to him in Basan the hetman ordered him put in chains, taken to Baturin and placed under guard. Then, after a request made by the Greek metropolitans, Hetman Demian freed Dmitrashko-Raich and ordered that he stay with him in Baturin. Konstantin Stryevsky[68] was sent in his place. The hetman replaced Colonel Peter Roslavets of Starodub in response to a petition from the cossacks and the rank-and-file because of the taxes. He replaced Roslavets in consultation with the council of elders and in his place sent his own brother, Shumeiko.

Vasily Mnogogreshny asserted that he intended to remain in the Kiev Brotherhood monastery. The elder of the Maksakov monastery contradicted this, saying that Vasily fought his way through to Tukalsky. Vasily Mnogogreshny was taken to be interrogated again. "Why did you conceal that you wished to go to Tukalsky?" he was asked. "I am guilty," Vasily responded. "I was frightened. I wished to flee to the metropolitan so he would protect me from Doroshenko without surrendering me to his majesty the tsar. To join them to go to war against the great sovereign was never my intention. Even had I wished to do this I could not have done so, because while I was in Zaporozhia I quarreled with the Zaporozhians. The general chancellor at Doroshenko's side, Mikhail Voikheevich, is my bitter enemy. I did not flee to wage war, only from great fear, in order to save my head. Abandoning everything, I wished to take monastic vows and be tonsured."[69]

On May 28 in the swamp behind the blacksmiths' forges, an executioner's block was erected for beheading Hetman Mnogogreshny and his brother Vasily. The offenders were brought out and their crimes were read to them, that is, all accusations against them were cited. "You Demko, were interrogated about everything. In all your treacherous words you were guilty. On May 20 the elders with all the Little Russian people sent a petition requesting you be executed in Moscow. They sent Captain Grigory Karpov[ich] of Baturin with the original denunciation. It is he who took the icon from you to Doroshenko and administered the oath in which you swore that you would serve the Turkish sultan. The boyars and the councillors, hearing your responses during the interrogation, sentenced you, Demko and Vaska, to be executed by cutting off your heads."

Demko and Vaska were placed on the block, but at the last moment a courier came running with the announcement that the great sovereign, responding to the supplication of his children, was moved to mercy. He decreed that Demko and Vaska not be executed but sent to the most remote Siberian towns for life. The boyars agreed to send to them their wives and children. The very same fate befell Colonel Matvey Gvintovka and the aide-de-camp Pavel Gribovich.

The next day the great sovereign relented, ordering that Demko be given fifteen rubles in alms, Vaska ten rubles and Gvintovka and Gribovich five rubles each. The Mnogogreshny brothers were given their belongings brought with them to Moscow, consisting of a few things of little value. The Mnogogreshny family consisted of the wife Nastasia, two sons, Peter and Ivan, a daughter Elena and a nephew, Mikhail Zinoviev. Two female servants accompanied them. Gvintovka was accompanied into exile by his wife Irina and two sons, Yefim and Fedor. It was ordered that the exiles be held in Tobolsk, fettered and under strong guard. From Tobolsk they were to be scattered among the various forts in cossack service as foot soldiers. The fate of the exiles was harsher following the escape of Gribovich. Then the order was given that Mnogogreshny and his companions, instead of being scattered among the various forts in cossack service, were to be held in chains in prison "because they forgot the fear of God and our sovereign's mercy," read the directive, "because their comrade Pashka Gribovich fled Siberia."

SERKO'S EXILE

In the meantime, on May 3, 1672, the old colonel of Chernigov, Ivan Lysenko, arrived in Moscow bringing a document. The cossack elders wrote that during the Easter holidays the colonels, captains and atamans were in Baturin and agreed that a cossack council be held in Konotop. This would not be far for Prince Romodanovsky and his colleagues to travel.

In addition they decided that the colonels, captains, military elders and the leading men should be at the council, but not the whole Host. This limitation was made to avoid riots erupting in the large crowds that a council of the whole Host entailed. The cossack elders also informed Moscow that Ivan Serko, separating from Mikhail Khanenko, hetman by the king's grace, was at the Poltava Regiment to sow rebellion among the people. Colonel Fedor Zhuchenko[70] seized Serko and sent him to Baturin. Finally, the elders petitioned that an order be given to Romodanovsky to defend them from the rebels.

Prince Romodanovsky and Conciliar Noble Ivan Rzhevsky were ordered to go to Konotop for the council to elect a hetman. At the beginning of June Romodanovsky informed the sovereign that there was dishonesty among the cossack elders in Baturin. Romodanovsky reported that the cossacks had set up camp near Baturin. On May 26 about four hundred of their men entered the town and approached the council of elders, saying "You have not told us where you have hidden the previous hetman and there is no other hetman. We have gathered near Baturin and waited a long time to elect a hetman. We have spent all our money on food. Come out of the town with the regalia, to the steppe for the council!"

The elders refused, fearing that once in the steppe the cossacks would kill them. The cossacks went to Neelov with the same demand. Neelov, recognizing a volatile situation, ordered the lower town shut and the cossacks not allowed to come further. In addition, information came to Moscow that the cossacks wished to elect Serko as hetman. The Muscovites sent this renowned Zaporozhian under guard to Moscow, and from there further, to Siberia.

A COSSACK COUNCIL AT KOZACHIA DUBROVA

Romodanovsky and Rzhevsky moved to Konotop. On July 15, about three versts from Kozachia Dubrova, the cossack elders met them, pleading that the great sovereign be gracious and order them to convene a council, not in Konotop but in Kozachia Dubrova, on the Krasena stream. The cossack Host was standing near Konotop and grass for the horses was trampled down for tens of versts around the town and further. "Fine," said the boyar, "we will convene a council in Kozachia Dubrova as you request."

Romodanovsky stood on one side of the Krasena stream, and the cossack elders stood on the other. The following day the cossack elders came to the boyar with a request not to delay the council. "According to the directive of the great sovereign," answered Romodanovsky, "we must wait for Archbishop Lazar Baranovich." "Can't we begin without the archbishop?" asked the elders. The boyar agreed discussions could begin and ordered the cossacks to gather to discuss the articles. The elders came to the officials' tent. Half of the cossacks who were with the elders were ordered to accompany the elders to the council. When the cossacks were gathered in and around the tent Romodanovsky announced that the sovereign graciously praised them for not participating in Demko's treachery and rewarded them with their earlier rights and liberties. He began to read the earlier articles of Glukhov and the new articles aloud and the cossack chancellor, Karp Mokrievich, read the articles, written in a notebook in his own *White Russian* script.[71]

Suddenly the reader fell silent. The tsar's courier, the resident noble Grigory Siniavin, entered the tent. "Boyar and Governor Prince Grigory Grigorievich!" he proclaimed to Romodanovsky. "I announce to you the joy of the great sovereign. On May 30, after the prayers of the holy father, God granted to his majesty the tsar a son, and to us, the subjects of the great sovereign, a tsarevich and grand prince Peter Alekseevich of all Great and Little and White Russia!"[72] The elders stood and congratulated the boyar.

The reading began again. Listening to the articles the elders and the cossacks said "We need all these articles except the twenty-second. This article calls for the appointment of a colonel for the free people with a thousand registered cossacks assigned to him to calm the headstrong in the event of rebelliousness and treason. Now we have petitioned the great sovereign to be so gracious as to forbid the hetman to be accompanied by a colonel and cossacks and to prohibit the colonels from having mercenary companies.[73] This is because the Little Russian people have suffered all kinds of damage and offense from such companies."

The boyar responded that the sovereign graciously ordered this article written according to their petition. In addition, the following articles were established. (1) The cossack elders and the whole Host petitioned that the hetman not be permitted to execute or dismiss anyone without a hearing of the case before the Host's court. This was to assure that they would not suffer the slavery and harshness from the new hetman they experienced from the traitor Demko. (2) The cossack elders and the whole Host petitioned that the hetman, unless directed by the great sovereign and the council of elders, not be permitted to communicate, either orally or in writing, about anything with other sovereigns, or with anyone, particularly not with Doroshenko. (3) If Little Russians really had settled along the Sozh river they must vacate the occupied lands and no longer move into the king's lands. Rather they must live with the king's subjects peacefully. (4) The Turkish sultan, because Doroshenko is his vassal, will make war on the king. If the sultan and Doroshenko attack Poland neither the hetman nor the cossack elders nor the any of the Zaporozhian Host will help Doroshenko. (5) The hetman, the cossack elders and the Host will not receive peasants or other people fleeing from Great Russia. Those whom they have received they will surrender.

The boyar then said "You sent Colonel Konstantin Solonina to Moscow to observe and listen to the negotiations between the tsar's boyars and the king's plenipotentiary ambassadors during discussions of Ukrainian affairs. The Polish ambassadors did not agree to allow your emissaries to listen to the negotiations, but everything that was said regarding Ukrainian affairs was read to Colonel Solonina. No longer should you send your emissaries to the ambassadorial meetings, as this is only a waste of time and complicates Polish affairs. When there is mention of your affairs, or any agreement is reached regarding them, the great sovereign will have you informed in writing." The elders submitted to the sovereign's will. "Now," said the boyar, "do you have any new articles you wish to propose?" "We have no articles of any kind," said the elders. "Then on June 17," Romodanovsky said, "be in the encampment by the official pavilion for the selection of a hetman."

THE ELECTION OF HETMAN SAMOILOVICH

On June 17, at the third hour in the morning,[74] Lazar Baranovich, archbishop of Chernigov, entered the encampment, followed by Captain Grigory Neelov of the Moscow musketeers. The general staff council and the military council of elders and the cossacks came, and before the elders they placed the sovereign's grant, the Host's regalia of the mace, standard, staff and kettledrums. The archbishop called for the new articles to be read to him. The boyar ordered them read. When the reading ended he announced they proceed with the selection of the hetman. Before the pavilion in the encampment they cleared a space. They placed an icon of the Savior on a lectern. They laid the mace on a table and placed the standard and the staff alongside. The boyar and the elders left the tent. The archbishop said a prayer before the icon. After the prayer, the boyar spoke. "The great sovereign," he said, "directed me to be present at the council for the selection of a hetman. You are to elect a hetman in accordance with your rights and liberties. His majesty the tsar made the selection of the hetman one of your military rights and liberties. He advises you select whomsoever you please as leader." Having spoken, the boyar left the table.

Speaking freely and quietly, they proclaimed Chief Justice Ivan Samoilovich hetman. Colonels Dmitrashko-Raich and Solonina took the successful candidate under the arms and lifted him onto the table. Quartermaster Zabela and other colonels brought him the mace, and unfurled the standard and the staff. "I do not wish to be hetman," began the new hetman, "but I cannot refuse the grant of his majesty the tsar, the mace and the banners. I proclaim that I will serve the great sovereign loyally and never with treachery, as earlier hetmans did." The elders, cossacks and burghers shouted that they were prepared to serve the great sovereign with the hetman. "Let Ivan take the mace and be hetman." Ivan took the mace, after which all moved into the tent. A prayer was offered and Lazar Baranovich administered the oath to the new hetman.

The new hetman, Ivan Samoilovich, was the son of a priest from the West Bank of the Dnieper. When the inhabitants of that side transferred in crowds to the East Bank because it was more peaceful, Samoilovich and his father also moved and settled in the town Stary Koliadin. The young Ivan Samoilovich was an educated man, intelligent, decent, sweet and obliging to all. Therefore he was soon established in Koliadin as scribe of the cossack company. He gained the favor of General Chancellor Stepan Grechany during the hetmancy of Briukhovetsky and was made a captain in Veprik. From captain he was made acting colonel in Chernigov at Grechany's personal request. Finally, at the Council of Glukhov, when Mnogogreshny was elected hetman, Samoilovich was made a chief justice of the Host.

Mnogogreshny's fall did not affect the peace in Little Russia. Serko's exile produced no repercussions in Zaporozhia. Here, at this time, a leader of a unique type appeared.

FALSE PROPHET APPEARS IN UKRAINE

In the autumn of 1672 the clerk Semeon Shchegolev brought to Zaporozhia five cannon, shot, powder and lead. Approaching the camp Shchegolev shot a volley from the cannon and from all the weapons, and was answered from the camp with the same. The priests ventured out to meet them with crosses. The Zaporozhians placed the tsar's gifts in the square and held a council. It was announced to Shchegolev that the leader of the camp was Field Ataman Nikita Vdovichenko, who had attacked Perekop without waiting for the tsar's cannon. The Zaporozhians announced they would accept the sovereign's letter with all joy, for the field ataman and Host were returning from Perekop.

On October 17 the army arrived from Perekop but without Vdovichenko. On October 19 a council was convened. As field ataman they elected Lukian Andreev and they read the document from the tsar, the king and the senators. When it was read, the new field ataman spoke.

"Brothers, soldiers, Dnieper sailors and seamen of the Zaporozhian Host! We hear, and with our own eyes we see the great mercy and the gifts of the great sovereign. With gracious words he permits us to rejoice. He ordered his emissary to ask about our health, and he sent cannon, cannonballs, gunpowder and shot. He has permitted Kalmyks, Don Cossacks and volunteers from the town to come to our aid in our struggle with the infidels. He also reassures us with chaikas,[75] grain supplies and provisions, as was only our right."

"We petitioned for the great mercy of his majesty the tsar!" shouted the council. "Of course this will be our right. We have had enough of being dragged hither and thither without a refuge. We served with the Tatars both after the treachery of Briukhovetsky and during Sukhovey's hetmancy.[76] The Crimean khan collected grain reserves from all of the Crimea and sent them to us in the camp. Now we would return his grain if we could, because we have been treated badly. The Tatars lead us by the neck and trade us like sheep. They sell us into slavery and confiscate all our goods and valuables. As long as the world lasts we will not stop going to the Dnieper, nor will we make peace with the Muslims."

The field ataman spoke again. "From now on," he said, "we promise, in God's name, to serve his majesty the tsar and his majesty the king loyally and without vacillation. Brothers! The Zaporozhian Host, the field atamans and the whole council! How is this my address to the thrones of both great sovereigns, to both Christian monarchs?" "Splendid, lord field ataman," replied the Host.

"To the Lord God and to the great sovereign," said the field ataman, "we offer our greatest praise!" In response the cannon and the weapons thundered. Then they went into the church for a service. Shchegolev discovered that until his arrival they had commemorated the Polish king first in the litanies.[77] He told the soldiers and the priests they must celebrate the tsar first and they obeyed him. Later Shchegolev invited the commander and the cossack elders to his hut and asked "Where is your chief, Vdovichenko, and whence did he come into Zaporozhia?"

"He came to Zaporozhia disguised as a beggar," was the reply. "He claimed to be an inhabitant of Kharkov, a holy man and prophet. The power to know the future he received from God. In this, the seventh year,[78] God ordered him to destroy the Crimea with the Zaporozhian Host and to take the golden gates[79] from Constantinople and place them in Kiev, in their original place. Prince Romodanovsky would not permit him to perform this feat and tortured him, but such annoyances did not affect him. "It is written that the son of a widow[80] will pacify all the land. Now God has sent him to the Zaporozhian Host. In the towns he ordered it be announced to all, right down to the infant at the breast, that he is precisely this man, so they would go with him to destroy the Crimea. It was said he would go to the Crimea, take five towns and winter there. The Muslims would not shoot at him it was said, because he would arrive at these towns unseen. The walls of the towns would fall by themselves and the gates spring open of their own accord. Consequently, Vdovichenko will be glorified in all the land. It was said he would take Perekop and fill the Zaporozhian Host with goods. Hearing these words many people abandoned their homes and, leaving the grain in the fields, followed Vdovichenko to Zaporozhia, to go with him to Perekop.

"Field Ataman Yevsevy Shashol refused to go, preferring to await the cannon from the great sovereign. The town people wished to kill Shashol, shouting they were not going for their cossack leaders, rather for the glory of Vdovichenko. The cossack soldiers in the camp were inclined to be persuaded by these words and gathered a council. They dismissed Shashol and elected Vdovichenko as their field ataman.

"When the army gathered near Perekop," the elders continued, "the cossacks asked Vdovichenko how many cannon they should take. 'I do not need cannon,' answered Vdovichenko. 'We will do fine without cannon. I heard that you sent to the tsar a petition about cannon. This is a useless petition, for you will gain little benefit. If you need cannon, take them to the closest and wealthiest Muslim town.' Several experienced people did not totally believe Vdovichenko and they took two cannon.

"In all about six thousand cavalrymen and about three thousand foot soldiers marched to Perekop. Vdovichenko himself marched to Perekop without rest. Many of the horses collapsed. Nearing the walls of Perekop he did not approach the town and did nothing. The cossack army, according to its custom, dug a ditch and moved up half the transport. Now the inhabitants of Perekop fired from cannon and muskets, killing and drowning our men. Vdovichenko took cover from the gunfire. The Host, seeing he was not the sort of man he pretended to be, retreated from Perekop. On the road they took the mace and standard from him and wanted to kill him but he hid."

Vdovichenko learned nothing from his experience at Perekop. He appeared in Baryshevka and began to preach the same message. Here he was seized and sent to the hetman who dispatched him to Romodanovsky.

IV

THE TURKS GO TO WAR. A PRETENDER IN ZAPOROZHIA

TURKS ATTACK POLAND

Even as a new hetman was established on the East Bank of the Dnieper a storm finally broke on the West Bank. This was a storm so long discussed, so long anticipated, so long the subject of gossip that it had ceased to excite fear. Doroshenko's alienation from Poland and his turn to the Turks exercised an important influence on the course of events. Seeking assistance against the Turks, a frightened Poland hurried to make peace with Moscow. Both realms were equally terrified of the Turks.

Jan Kazimierz did not wait for new misfortunes. In 1668 he renounced the throne. In view of the threat of a dangerous war it was expected that the Poles would elect as king a distinguished military leader, either a Pole or a foreigner. As if on purpose the Polish gentry elected instead a man from a noble but impoverished family. This was a man whose personal qualities made it unlikely that people would forget that he was not of royal blood. The gentry united could proclaim Wiśniowiecki[1] but could offer him little support against the magnates who opposed his election. These magnates formed a strong party and interfered with the king in everything. The great hetman and royal marshal Jan Sobieski,[2] a man whose talents and rank were obvious to all, was among those dissatisfied with the election.

Competing parties at the Polish court terrified one another with the Turks, yet gave no thought to defensive measures which the situation demanded. In fact, there was some justification for disregarding these fears. Five years had passed since Doroshenko switched his allegiance from Poland to Turkey yet the Turks made no preparations for war against

Poland. Initially Mehmed IV[3] was occupied with the Venetian war. The sultan was affected by the splendid conclusion of this war, the conquest of Candia in 1669.[4] Rumors circulated that he now had no interest in war, preferring to spend his time in the harem or hunting.

In the summer of 1671 the western Ukraine was troubled by war between the Poles and Doroshenko, assisted by the Tatars. Doroshenko attacked Uman but failed to take it. The town defended itself. Sobieski defeated Doroshenko's cossacks and Tatars at Braslavl and occupied several cities which recognized the power of the Chigirin hetman. This transitory success of Polish arms simply annoyed the sultan. It forced him to hurry preparations for a campaign against Poland, which his vassal Doroshenko had dared to attack.

BATTLE OF BATOG

In the spring of 1672 a Turkish army numbering more than three hundred thousand soldiers crossed the Dunay river.[5] An advance contingent consisting of forty thousand Tatars burst into Podolia and met the Poles on the banks of the Bug river, near Mount Batog. The Polish forces were under the leadership of Karol Stanisław Łużecki , castellan of Podlasie,[6] accompanied by Khanenko and his cossacks. In all there were no more than six thousand Poles and cossacks. Despite their small numbers Łu-żecki and his forces overwhelmed the Tatars, drowning them in the river.

Arrogant with success, Łużecki decided to pursue the Tatars beyond the river. Khanenko remonstrated in vain. Łużecki refused to listen. "At least allow me to remain as a guard on this bank," Khanenko said. "If you are successful on the other side you will have a witness of your remarkable deed. If things do not go smoothly we will hurry to share your fate."

Khanenko remained and quickly formed a camp for himself and his forces. Łużecki charged into the Bug river. He exhausted the horses and the firearms were damaged by dampness. With the handful of soldiers under his command he could not hold out on the opposite bank. Multitudes of Tatars pressed him from all sides, forcing him to turn back into the river. Łużecki scarcely saved himself. Many of his men were killed or captured. The fugitives found refuge in Khanenko's camp. As soon as the Poles had fled into the camp Khanenko began to retreat. Tatars pressed the rear and the sides of the retreating forces but the cossacks defended themselves with cannon and guns and the moving rampart and reached Ladyzhin. The Tatars laid siege to the town but failed to take it.

KAMIENIEC PODOLSKY FALLS TO TURKS

The town of Kamieniec suffered a different fate. In August the whole Turkish army invested it, led by the sultan himself. There were no more than fifteen hundred men defending this remarkable fortress. There was gunpowder but few cannoneers, and these of poor quality. It was rumored that for four hundred cannon there were only four cannoneers. Already exhausted by work on the fortifications, the besieged did not have a free minute for eating or sleeping. The Turks took the new castle and placed a mine on the face of the rock under the gates of the old castle. After this they mounted an attack but were repulsed with a loss of two hundred men.

Nonetheless the besieged saw they could not hold out for long and hung out the white flag. The combatants agreed upon the following conditions of surrender. (1) The safety of life and property was guaranteed. (2) Freedom to perform the liturgy was guaranteed. For this purpose, the Christians were to retain several churches. The remaining churches would be converted to mosques. (3) All were free either to leave the town with their property or to remain. (4) The soldiers were permitted to leave the town with their muskets, but without cannon and banners.

The conditions were accepted and the commander of the janissaries[7] entered the town, occupying it in the name of the sultan. The janissaries replaced the garrison. Three churches, one Russian, one Catholic and one Armenian, were left for the use of the inhabitants. The cathedral was turned into a mosque. In all the churches the Turks pulled down the crosses and dismounted the bells. Some of the gentry were seized for the sultan, some for the vizier and some for the pasha. With great ceremony Sultan Mehmed IV entered the conquered town, going directly to the chief mosque, formerly the cathedral. There before him the janissaries circumcised an eight-year-old Christian boy.

News of the fall of Kamieniec created a terrible impression in Moscow. This town was Poland's bulwark against the Turks in the south. Moscow had nothing to match it. Stories spread about terrors perpetrated by the Muslims in the vanquished town. It was said that the Turks destroyed both Orthodox and Catholic churches and turned them into mosques. Some claimed that the Turks carried icons away from the churches, stood them at the town gates and ordered Christians to file past and curse them. Those who refused were beaten to death. Rumor asserted that the vizier, the khan and Doroshenko bragged about attacking Kiev. Prince Grigory Afanasievich Kozlovsky, governor of Kiev, wrote that in Kiev, Pereiaslav and Oster there were few people. In Kiev work to repair the city defenses never ceased. Where the wall had crumbled trees were cut to strengthen it but it could not be reconstructed because the ground was sandy and there was no turf nearby. Tukalsky insistently wrote to Doroshenko seeking to persuade him to come to Kiev, reassuring him that the city had few defenders.

Doroshenko called himself a subject of the sultan and governor of Kiev. "For God's sake," Simeon Adamovich wrote to Artamon Sergeevich Matveev, "intercede for us before his most illustrious majesty the tsar. Do not fail! Increase the forces in Kiev, Pereiaslav, Nezhin and Chernigov! You know how fickle our people are. We will be in better condition when the number of the sovereign's troops is increased. Send a good man to Nezhin as governor, since Stepan Ivanovich Khrushchov is not fit to be governor. Send us someone like Ivan Ivanovich Rzhevsky and the people of Nezhin would be willing to die with him for the sake of the great sovereign."

MOSCOW RESPONDS TO TURKISH ATTACK

The tsar called the higher clergy, boyars and councillors to a council meeting. He informed them of the sultan's successes, announced his intention of going to defend Kiev, the Little Russian towns and the Severian Ukraine in the spring, and asked what should be done.

The council called for extraordinary collections from all service landholdings and patrimonial estates.[8] A poltina was to be collected from each peasant homestead and a tenth of their income from each townsman.[9] The sovereign announced his intention of going personally to Putivl at the head of all the forces. He also wrote to Hetman Samoilovich that the boyar, Governor Prince Yury Petrovich Trubetskoy, was assigned to Kiev with many soldiers. Table Attendant Prince Semeon Andreevich Khovansky was assigned to Chernigov, Prince Semeon Zvenigorodsky to Nezhin, and Prince Vladimir Andreevich Volkonsky to Pereiaslav. These men would leave Moscow quickly. If the sultan advanced on Kiev the great sovereign himself would go to face him. The order had been given to build quarters for the tsar in Putivl.

Everyone feared the spring although rumors offered some reassurance for the winter. The sultan had crossed over the Dunay river and gone into winter quarters, the khan retreated to the Crimea, and Doroshenko was in

Chigirin with only a few Tatars remaining. Still at Buczacz (in Galich) the Poles concluded a peace with the Turks, surrendering Podolia and the Ukraine and agreeing to pay the sultan twenty-two thousand ducats a year.[10] Thus the burden of any new Turkish war threatened to fall upon Moscow alone and the attention of the government turned south.

In December 1672 Ivan Samoilovich wrote to Matveev, his very gracious friend and benefactor. "My messenger told me that your grace now directs me to come to his most illustrious majesty the tsar," the hetman wrote. "Were I, the lowest slave, to receive such a directive from his majesty the tsar, in the name of Christ I would desire zealously to fulfill it, if only the time were convenient and unfriendly schemes did not estrange us. I pray humbly to receive information rapidly from your grace, my benefactor."

For some reason the hetman was not reassured by Karp Mokrievich, who also turned most humbly to Matveev. "I am ashamed to bedevil your grace with my frequent letters about my activities. I fear that my letters have not been received by you because at this time I still have not obtained the favor of the most illustrious lord hetman for my loyal, true and zealous service to the great sovereign. Not only do all recognize my loyal and zealous service, the hetman himself knows that I have worked loyally for his majesty the tsar, which I promise to do until the end of my life. Obediently I throw myself on your mercy. I humbly entreat you, my most gracious benefactor, to inform his majesty the tsar about my service with one of your most esteemed petitions, that I, a loyal subject and a tireless worker, will be in his favor just like others who have not performed the least service for the great sovereign, yet enjoy great favor, honor and profit."

SERKO IS LIBERATED

Simultaneously Mateev received a notice from Zaporozhia from Field Ataman Lukian Andreev. "To our most gracious benefactor I write about our patrimony Little Russia and about ourselves the Zaporozhian Host. To our most honorable mediator and most generous benefactor we send our deepest respect and we humbly pray you be gracious, like a father to his children, that by your merciful intercession the Kalmyks, the chaikas (boats) and the grain reserves are sent to us. Intercede so that Ivan Serko is released to us in the field, for there is no better soldier in the field nor a more avid persecutor of Muslims. He is a leader who will govern us well and fight as a terrible warrior against the Muslims. To the Muslims Ivan

Serko is a terrible scourge in the Crimea and a fortunate conquerer who has always defeated and routed them, freeing Christians from captivity. Hearing that he is not in the Zaporozhian Host, the Muslims will rejoice and conspire against us." The tsar replied that their requests would be met and the steppe warrior Serko released to them.

In fact, in March 1673 Serko was brought to Moscow and presented to the sovereign. First the tsar himself, then the patriarch and all the councillors, particularly Prince Yury Alekseevich Dolgoruky and Aratamon Sergeevich Matveev, firmly exhorted him to be loyal to the throne of his majesty the tsar. The patriarch threatened him with anathema and eternal damnation if he were not loyal and the cossacks were planning something evil. "I will release you," said the tsar, "in response to the pleas of our loyal subject Hetman Ivan Samoilovich and also because the tsar's word is absolute. I wrote to the Polish king and the Zaporozhians that I would release you."

SAMOILOVICH SENDS HIS SONS TO MOSCOW

Earlier it was noted that the tsar's government considered bringing the hetman to Moscow. Hetman Samoilovich let it be known that this would be difficult in the current circumstances. A compromise was devised. The hetman would remain in Little Russia and send security for his pledge of loyalty to the tsar.

At the end of 1672 Simeon Adamovich wrote to Matveev. "God witnesses my poor service and zeal towards his most illustrious majesty the tsar. Numerous hetmans, prelates and colonels gobble up as much of the state treasury as they can. They turn traitor and cause blood to flow. But I, a poor worm and no man,[11] continue as I began, laboring for God and the great sovereign. The current hetman, Ivan Samoilovich, relies absolutely on my counsel. I have convinced him, when our country is freed from hostile attack, to send his children to the great sovereign in my care at the first opportunity."

In March 1673 the archpriest arrived in Moscow with the hetman's two sons, Semeon and Grigory, accompanied by their *leader*, Vicar Isaac of the Baturin monastery, and their tutor, Pavel Yasilkovsky. Their sojourn in Moscow was intended to assure that their father, the hetman, remained true to his oath and served his majesty the tsar loyally. Samoilovich wrote that his sons must remain with the tsar until he himself came to Moscow. On behalf of Samoilovich Archpriest Simeon Adamovich petitioned the sovereign to order Prince Grigory Grigorievich Romodanovsky and

Hetman Samoilovich to march to the Crimea or against Doroshenko. In addition the petition requested that field artillery, powder and shot be sent for this campaign and that the sovereign send soldiers to the Little Russian towns.

On March 19 the hetman's messengers were summoned to view the cannon transported on a specially built structure from the St. Nicholas gates across the moat to the Savior gates. In addition to the Little Russians, merchants from various lands, Germans,[12] Greeks and Persians, were present. In the crowd clerks from the Chancellery for Foreign Affairs mingled secretly, listening to what the foreigners were saying. Archpriest Simeon said to the Cherkassians "The sovereign himself must be going on campaign against the Turkish sultan." All were amazed that the cannon were transported so efficiently and by means of such an ingenious structure. They praised the horses harnessed in pairs, noting their military build, and remarked that the great cannon would be very effective in war.

When the retinue of the lord-in-waiting Prince Ivan Petrovich Boriatinsky marched between the cannon the archpriest shrugged his shoulders, saying "Aye, truly divine mercy favors this campaign and this people. I expect their military activities will accomplish many good things because my experience suggests these people will go forth boldly and joyfully, anticipating victory. This is the divine will!"

The hetman's sons questioned the archpriest about everything. They counted the cannon, discussed which were larger and praised everything. The Greeks asserted that when the Turks took Candia,[13] and later Kamieniec, they had many cannon, only they were not as large. The sultan had some pieces two or three times larger than those now on display, but they were crudely made and unsuitable for war. The Germans also praised everything, saying that previously such devices could not be found in Moscow. Thus they concluded it was likely the tsar would emerge victorious over the Turks. "God will not abandon the tsar," they said, "because he is going to war in defense of the Christian faith." The Persians and the Armenians remarked that the shah had nothing like these cannon either and the Turks would never stand up to them.

The father archpriest was ecstatic about the reception in Moscow and wrote to the hetman. "The paternal graciousness of his majesty the tsar to your honor is beyond description. All your requests will be fulfilled. A stone palace is being sought to buy for your children. God sent your honor and your children a generous father in Lord Artamon. From him charity and intercession always can be expected when needed. He gave me his word that your children will be favored with many good things from his majesty the tsar. I cannot speak too highly of his majesty the tsar's generosity and Artamon Sergeevich's friendship and love." The archpriest was released to convey the tsar's response to the hetman's petition. In regard to the campaign in the Crimea the tsar decided to abandon this matter for a time. He ordered Prince Romodanovsky and Hetman Samoilovich to move to the Dnieper river and halt. Thence they were to send two reliable men with a message to Doroshenko referring to the petition he sent to the great sovereign requesting he be allowed to take an oath of allegiance. The great sovereign would permit this and send Doroshenko a gracious communiqué promising that the rights and liberties of the cossacks would not be infringed and the sovereign would defend Doroshenko from the Turks. Should Doroshenko then refuse to take an oath the messengers must warn him that the tsar's army would turn against him. If in defiance of Doroshenko the cossacks beyond the Dnieper signaled their desire to be subjects of the great sovereign, the messengers were to receive them, take their oath and in consultation with the whole Host establish a good and reliable hetman on that side. Then they must deal with Doroshenko. If the cossacks beyond the Dnieper requested Ivan Samoilovich be hetman on both sides of the Dnieper or asked for someone in particular from the East Bank as hetman, their desire was to be fulfilled.

NEWS FROM LEFT BANK

As previously noted, the sovereign promised to send a large army to Kiev with the boyar Prince Yury Petrovich Trubetskoy. In fact Trubetskoy moved into Little Russia at the beginning of 1673. The hetman and the cossack elders met him about ten versts from the Sosnitsa river. The hetman rode to the Sosnitsa, accompanying the boyar in a sleigh. On February 13 Trubetskoy entered Kiev.

The armies were to have gone on campaign, utilizing the last period before the spring thaw, calculated according to Moscow weather, but Romodanovsky informed the sovereign that this was impossible. "Here in the Ukraine," he wrote, "the snow in the fields is all churned up and the ice is melting. There is no way I can rush into a campaign. I don't have any troops."

In the midst of this, on the West Bank, as soon as news spread about the intended movements of the tsar's army people began to talk about becoming subjects of the great sovereign. Aide-de-Camp Yakov

Kondratievich Lizogub[14] corresponded from Kanev with Colonel Dmitrashko-Raich of Pereiaslav, promising to surrender Kanev as soon as the Russian army appeared beyond the Dnieper. "I would be happy," said Lizogub, "to cross the Dnieper to the side of his majesty the tsar with all my household and belongings, but I would lose my reputation. Here I am a prominent and distinguished man and everyone listens to me. It would be better for me to serve his majesty the tsar living here because all the people here, seeing the persecution from the Turks, curse Doroshenko and all of us and conceive all kinds of mischief."

"Doroshenko himself is sorry that he transferred his allegiance to the Turk," Lizogub asserted. "After Christmas he convened a council with all the elders. I heard that at the council Doroshenko announced that spring was coming and rumors were circulating that the tsar with all his forces would be in the Ukraine. 'So decide,' he said, 'with whom we will side.' The elders agreed they would neither leave the Turkish sultan nor anger him because in the current situation they had nowhere to turn but to him. The tsar could not accept them under his protection because of his treaty with the Polish king. None wished to be subject to the king. Having done much to offend him, the elders feared he would seek revenge. In addition, they said that from time immemorial they were never divided and now both sides wished to be together once again. The Turkish sultan would be in Kamieniec. He would see that the king was not fulfilling his treaty obligations nor had he ordered his soldiers to evacuate Belaia Tserkov.[15] The elders in the council argued that once we abandoned the Turk no one would come to our aid and the sultan would totally destroy us upon his arrival.

"When Doroshenko was campaigning with the Turks," Lizogub continued, "it was wise to honor him and he was called prince. At that time the cossacks were in dire straits. The Turks called cossacks pigs then and still do so. When they see a pig they call it a cossack. Now Turks are in Kamieniec, Mezhibozh, Bar, Yazlovets, Sniatin and Zhvanets. In all these towns they have destroyed the churches of God, turning some into barns and others into mosques, and melting down the bells for cannon. The inhabitants are subjected to great want, and the Turks take small children, marrying them by force. They do not allow the dead to be buried or infants to be baptized without a fee.

"The Turks forge chains unremittingly and send them to Kamieniec. They have raised two towers above [the town] and in addition buy cavalry equipment[16] at an expensive price. The reason for this is unknown. Let Hetman Ivan Samoilovich write to the great sovereign requesting soldiers.

Otherwise not a single town on the West Bank except Chigirin will remain standing. Would that the great sovereign had not surrendered us to the Polish king. The sovereign must occupy the Camp and Kodak[17] with his own army. If the Turks seize them it will be difficult for us here on the Poltava side." "I do not believe Lizogub," said Hetman Ivan Samoilovich. "All he says echoes Doroshenko's instructions. Moreover Lizogub has fields and cattle on this side, in the Pereiaslav Regiment. He is afraid I will take them from him. If Prince Grigory Grigorievich Romodanovsky and I cross the Dnieper they will not surrender honorably. Rather as soon as the Turkish sultan advances they will all disperse. Yury Khmelnitsky went to the Muslims and fled to Constantinople, but it will hardly benefit Doroshenko to go there from Kamieniec. In the long term it will not serve him. Do not inform Lizogub any more about our intentions. He will transmit everything to Doroshenko, who will think that we are sending dispatches about our plans to him because we fear the Turkish sultan and will incite the sultan and the khan to go to war." Dmitrashko-Raich thought differently. He praised Lizogub's loyalty and asserted that he was reliable.

KHANENKO PETITIONS TSAR
In April Khanenko sent a petition to Moscow. "Prostrating himself like a slave at the foot of the tsar's throne," it read, "Khanenko petitions to be received as a subject. As a hart longs for flowing streams, so longs his soul to find a place under the illustrious power of the one most holy monarch.[18] He, Khanenko, was subject to his royal highness the Polish king for many years. He spilled his blood to defend the Polish crown. For this neither he nor his troops received even the smallest reward. They only grew embittered by the senators' pride."

METROPOLITAN TUKALSKY'S POSITION
In relaying the story of the cossack council in Chigirin Lizogub let slip some curious news about Tukalsky. A burgher of Kiev, arriving from Cherkassy, said that during the council the metropolitan read a sermon in which he unequivocally reviled Doroshenko and other prominent people for serving the Turk, destroying churches and building mosques. After this the metropolitan advised the cossacks at the council to remain in an alliance with the Crimean khan alone and to separate from the Turks by whatever means necessary. Quartermaster Ivan Gulak responded to the

metropolitan, saying "Certainly father metropolitan you are interfering in our council. You should worry about your spiritual affairs and not meddle in our business. You have persuaded us already. You will not dissuade us so quickly."

ROMODANOVSKY AND SAMOILOVICH ENCOUNTER PROBLEMS

On April 17 Prince Romodanovsky advanced to Sumy with Hetman Samoilovich. It was decided that Romodanovsky and his soldiers would gather at Sudzha, the hetman in Baturin, and they would join forces between Glinsk and Lokhvitsa, by the Sula river. On May 22 the leaders united beyond Lokhvitsa by the Swan Lakes.[19] On June 1 they sent a detachment beyond the Dnieper to Kanev with a proposal to Doroshenko and Lizogub that they submit to the great sovereign.

Doroshenko, Lizogub and the people of Kanev rejected the proposal, saying they never wished to be subjects of the great sovereign. The detachment was returning across the Dnieper [to the West Bank] when between them and their goal a crowd of Tatars appeared on the East Bank. Romodanovsky sent the Kharkov colonel in pursuit. He was met by the Tatars near Kolomyk, fought for a whole day and barely escaped. This forced Romodanovsky and the hetman to leave Lubny and retreat to Belgorod. Romodanovsky and the hetman wrote to the tsar saying they could not cross the Dnieper since there was serious flooding on the river and Doroshenko had cut adrift all the boats.

"Putting this aside," responded the tsar, "were you ordered to go beyond the Dnieper? To be precise, you were ordered to halt at the Dnieper wherever suitable, construct a camp and then to send two reliable men to Doroshenko with gracious messages. You were not instructed to send a whole regiment. Further, receiving word of the Tatars, you were commanded not to retreat, rather to send part of your army against them." The tsar ended his message with the announcement that should the sultan, the khan or Doroshenko attack Poland he personally would sally forth on campaign. Samoilovich still tried to excuse himself for not crossing the Dnieper. The army was small, there were few supplies and Doroshenko spread rumors that the cossacks of the eastern and western side, uniting, would overcome the tsar's forces.

PUBLIC OPINION IN UKRAINE

In Little Russia people called for the tsar's troops although during the campaign in the country it was well known what accompanied the soldiers. Archimandrite Innokenty Gizel remarked "With very great charity, his majesty the tsar permitted his patrimony, the most glorious city Kiev, to be preserved. For this we rejoice. Yet God is witness to what the soldiers did along the road. Not only the newcomers, but also those who were here before, devastated the area surrounding the Kiev Caves monastery itself, seizing all the hay and driving off the horses and cattle of the homesteads. They also cut our forests, both coniferous and deciduous, and laid waste to them."

"Commanders and captains of the musketeers," Colonel Solonina complained, "who were traveling the road near Kiev seized many carts, of which more than half ended up scattered and lost. The musketeers beat anyone who went to search for their carts, tearing at their topknots,[20] and insulting them with all kinds of filthy words. They set fire to the poor people's homesteads and gardens, destroying them. They damaged all the hay, stole it or confiscated it violently. The poor people had never experienced such ravaging. I do not know how to describe it. Were these really Christians coming to the defense of Christians? The Tatars could not have done worse! Nothing that hostile people and Muslims do astonishes me."

Nor were Little Russians pleased with Trubetskoy himself or his colleagues. Prominent Little Russians complained that the boyar and the commanders were unapproachable and unkind to them. Trubetskoy prohibited his colonels from riding around from homestead to homestead [paying their respects].

This was not the case with the boyar Prince Grigory Grigorievich Romodanovsky, who received any Little Russians who came to him and treated everyone equally. For this reason all loved him. Wherever Trubetskoy and the army went in Little Russia they heard the same thing. "The great sovereign must send many people to Kiev and hold it for himself. If the Muslims attack Kiev we are all prepared to die for it. It is bad that the soldiers do not treat us properly and strut around arrogantly, yet even this does not distress us as much as the carts since many wish to leave by the Kiev and Pereiaslav roads."

Grumbling against the new hetman was also heard. Both prominent and humble people complained. "It was very difficult for us during the tenure of Demko," they protested, "but the difficulties continue even now. In the council the hetman was persuaded not to maintain volunteer regiments, nor collect taxes on cauldrons used for distilling alcohol and beer, nor on the mill wheels for grinding grain. This was done anyway,

just as in Demko's time. A little band of mercenaries[21] is gathered and
taxes are collected just as frequently as before."

The hetman, informed of these complaints, responded "I gathered the
mercenaries and ordered the taxes collected because right now I need
people to oppose the enemy. If all the soldiers from that side of the
Dnieper transferred to this side, I would receive and feed them. I do not
collect the taxes for myself but to support the military men who serve the
great sovereign without sparing themselves, leaving their homes and
belongings. It is common for soldiers to be hired to fight enemies and they
are given large payments. These people and their dependents are given
only supplies for themselves and their horses."

ATTACK ON AZOV

In August 1673, even as the campaign of the tsar's troops to the Dnieper
was ending unsuccessfully, activities began on the other side of the river,
near Azov. The commanders Ivan Savostianovich Bolshoy Khitrovo[22]
and Grigory Kasogov were directed to the Don with a force of eight
thousand soldiers and Don Cossacks. They approached the Kalanchinsky
towers.[23] Firing from cannon day and night they brought down the top and
middle of one of the towers and seized control of the aqueducts linking the
towers with Azov. The cavalry being inadequate, they failed to gain
control of the overland communication routes. All the people of Azov
came out to fight for the town but suffered defeat. The victors drove them
back more than a verst. There was no more shot, therefore the commanders and field atamans considered it impossible to attack the tower because
of the wide ramparts, deep moats and the thousand janissaries[24] who held
the castle.

Failing to take the tower, the commanders let the cossacks pass
through a navigation channel[25] to the sea in twenty-two rafts for action on
the Turkish and Crimean shores. The Don Cossack Host[26] wrote to
Matveev informing him that about forty thousand infantrymen and
twenty thousand cavalrymen would be needed should the great sovereign
order an attack on Azov. With such a force an attempt could be made to
take Azov. With anything smaller an attack was impossible for the place
was large. The Kalanchinsky towers were ten times stronger than Azov.
They could not be taken. To send men and spend money in the effort
would be a waste.

A PRETENDER[27] IN ZAPOROZHIA

While the Muscovite soldiers and cossacks were preoccupied with Azov a curious incident took place in their rear. Khitrovo reported that on the Don there was much brigandage, perpetrated by an old comrade of Stenka Razin named Ivan Miiuska, around whom had gathered more than two hundred men. Travel across the steppe now was difficult and much brigandage could be anticipated since Razin's followers, leaving Astrakhan and the fortified lines, were settled in the towns along the upper Don.

At Khitrovo's insistence the Don Cossacks sent a detachment against Miiuska on the northern Donets. Miiuska, warned of this initiative, crossed the estuary of the Chernaia Kalitva tributary. Much brigandage ensued both upstream and downstream. Traders and servicemen could not travel. Rumor had it that in the spring Miiuska would move to the Volga where, like Razin, he would be joined by many outlaws from the Don and the smaller towns upstream. The cossacks sent by the governor of Voronezh failed to find any trace of Miiuska. He was destined to emerge elsewhere.

At the beginning of winter Hetman Samoilovich announced a man had appeared in Zaporozhia who was well-made and slender with a long face that was neither ruddy nor brown, but somewhat swarthy. It was difficult to tell his age from his face. The cossacks guessed he was about fifteen. He was quiet and had two standards, painted with eagles and curved sabers. Eight men, apparently from the Don, were with the young man. He wore a green caftan lined with fox and under this a shorter caftan of crimson nankeen.[28] He called himself Tsarevich Simeon Alekseevich. His guide, a cossack called Ivan Miiuska, told the Zaporozhian judge that on his right shoulder and on his hand this tsarevich had marks which looked like a tsar's diadem.

News arrived in Zaporozhia that Serko was approaching. The tsarevich, unfurling the standards, granted Serko an audience. Serko sat the tsarevich next to himself and said "I heard from my deputy you call yourself the son of some tsar. You are very young. Speak truly, fearing God. Tell me, are you the son of our great sovereign Alexis Mikhailovich, or of some other ruler who is subject to him? We do not want to be deceived by you, as others in the Host have been deceived by swindlers." The young man stood, removed his hat and spoke in a tearful voice. "Do not be afraid of me. As the righteous God is my witness, I am the son of your sovereign."

Hearing this Serko and all the cossacks removed their hats, bowed to the ground and began to treat him to drinks. They asked the impostor if he would write to Hetman Samoilovich himself and to their little father,[29] the great sovereign. "I am conveying oral instructions to the lord hetman," he replied, "but it is difficult to write to the little father and be assured that my message will not fall into the hands of the boyars. I very much fear this, and there is no man to be found to give my message into the hands of the little father himself. Further, field ataman, be merciful and do not talk about me to any Russians. I was exiled to the Solovetsk island,[30] just like Stenka Razin, and I went to him secretly and lived with him until he was seized.[31] Then I moved to the Caspian Sea[32] with some cossacks, and from there I moved to the Don. I was not known to the Host there. Only one cossack chieftain knew about me."

The guide Miiuska told Serko that the tsarevich really did have a mark on his body that looked like a tsar's diadem. The tsarevich's intention was to slip secretly into Kiev and from there go to the Polish king.

On December 14 Captain Vasily Chaduev of the musketeers and the clerk Semeon Shchegolev were dispatched to Hetman Samoilovich and to Serko in the cossack camp for the pretender. "I have already written to Zaporozhia," Samoilovich told them, "directing them to send the impostor and his comrades to me. I do not think Serko will oppose me, but I fear that nobody in Zaporozhia will deliver anyone up. It is said that the Host is free. Whoever wishes comes and goes freely."

On the road, in the small town of Kereberda, the Zaporozhian Cossack Maksimka Shcherbak encountered the Muscovite messengers. "You know Shcherbak of the Don," said he, "and he knows why you were sent to Zaporozhia. You have come in vain and you will leave empty handed. The true tsarevich Simeon Alekseevich now has declared himself in Zaporozhia. I know all about this. The tsarevich struck his grandfather, Boyar Ilia Danilovich Miloslavsky[33] with a plate. For this reason he fled, but his fame spread all over Moscow. This is the truth. I was in Moscow at the time, sitting in prison and I was freed thanks to the petition of Demian Mnogogreshny. I have been in the Don and in Zaporozhia. I left Zaporozhia last week." "This man is a thief, a swindler, a pretender and a deceiver," said the messengers. In response to this Shcherbak spat in their eyes and said "Shut your mouth, or you will be struck down by a filthy death."

Samoilovich's messengers met Chaduev and Shchegolev who were riding to Zaporozhia. "When the Zaporozhians," they declared, "heard

the hetman's letter about the pretender they laughed and made many
unseemly and rude remarks about the hetman and the boyar. They call the
pretender tsarevich, as Serko ordered. The hetman was not notified. The
pretender wrote to him, sealing it with his seal which is like that of his
majesty the tsar. The Zaporozhians made him this seal from efimoks and
a taffeta banner with a double-headed eagle and also gave him good
clothing.

"On our departure the pretender addresed the council. He disparaged
the hetman, saying 'Your hetman is stupid for describing me as a fraud.
Were you not such sweet souls I would order you hanged. If the hetman
desires to know who I am, let the quartermaster Peter Zabela and Judge
Ivan Domontovich come and see. The boyars will send many prominent
people in the name of his majesty the tsar with decrees about my extradi-
tion, but I will not come [to Moscow] for three years. I will go to the sea
and to the Crimea, but whoever is sent [after me] will not wander in vain.'"

In Kishenka the Muscovite emissaries found Vasily Mnogogreshny's
retainer Luchka and Mereshka, a comrade of the pretender. Both warned
Chaduev and Shchegolev not to go to Zaporozhia under any circumstances. They would be intercepted and hanged as soon as they reached
Kodak. The cossacks were not even thinking of handing over the pretender. "I lived with him for a long time," Luchka said, "and I saw on his
shoulders red birthmarks: a tsar's diadem, a two-headed eagle, and a
moon with stars."

Ignat Ogloblia arrived in Kishenka sent by Serko as a messenger to
Hetman Samoilovich. He said that Serko wished to kill Chaduev because
of the pretender and called him a son of a bitch. Hearing all this news
Chaduev and Shchegolev took measures to assure their personal safety.
Shcherbak, Luchka, Mereshka and Ogloblia were sent to the hetman in
Kanev, to be held there by the hetman until their return.

TSAR'S EMISSARIES AND THE PRETENDER

On March 1, 1674 the tsar's emissaries arrived in Zaporozhia from
Kishenka. On March 9 they entered the Camp. Field Ataman Serko and
the Zaporozhian delegation rode out of the town for the meeting. Chaduev
and Shchegolev were established outside the town in a Greek hut on the
banks of the Chertomlik river. The next day the emissaries were summoned to the ataman's hut. There they found Serko, the cossack judge,
scribe and unit atamans and prominent cossack councillors.

"On what business of the great sovereign were you sent?" asked Serko. "Did we hear correctly that you have come for the tsarevich?" "This is not a tsarevich," retorted Chaduev. "This is a thief, a swindler, a pretender, an obvious deceiver and apostate, a disciple of Stenka Razin." "Not true," argued the Zaporozhians. "This is the genuine Tsarevich Simeon Alekseevich and he wishes to see you." "We were sent to seize this thief and pretender," replied Chaduev, "not to meet with him." "We will show him to you in the council," said Serko. "You will speak with him and, recognizing him, will know that you must bow to him in the proper manner."

After this exchange Serko, the judge, scribe and the village atamans drank with the pretender for almost the whole day. Serko, becoming drunk, seemed to sleep. About two hours before dusk the pretender belted on a saber and left his hut, accompanied by Judge Stepan Bely, the scribe Andrei Yakovlev, the aides-de-camp and about three hundred cossacks. All were drunk. They approached the hut where the tsar's emissaries were staying and shouted to Shchegolev "Come out! The tsarevich calls you!" Shchegolev did not appear but Chaduev went to the vestibule and opening the door, asked "Who asks for Shchegolev, and why?" In response, the pretender called "Come out to me!"

Chaduev. What kind of a man are you?

Pretender. I am Tsarevich Simeon Alekseevich.

Chaduev. Recall the great and awesome name! You call yourself the son of a monarch greater and more glorious than man has ever imagined. You are not permitted to present yourself as a tsarevich-sovereign either in the steppe or in the grasslands. You are Satan, an apostate. You are the son and pupil of Stenka Razin, a thief, a swindler and a fake.

Pretender. Fat bellies, traitors! See how our slaves insult us! I'll fix you!

Waving his saber he ran up to the doors against Chaduev, who grabbed an arquebus, wishing to kill him. The cossack scribe seized the pretender crosswise and shoved him behind a grain barrel. He then accompanied him into the town. The cossacks remained and attacked the hut, using logs as battering rams. Others chopped at the roof and cursed, shouting "You, you old codger, wanted to shoot the little sovereign."[34]

At this point Chaduev with his arquebus, Shchegolev with a saber and the musketeers with their muskets bade one another goodbye and settled in, expecting to die, but the affair did not come to bloodshed. The ambassadors waved the sovereign's communiqué and shouted "Wait until the council. There you will hear the great sovereign's notice."

The cossacks shouted to the judge and the aides-de-camp "Set a guard over them so they do not leave. The Muscovites know how to escape." Then one after another the cossacks dispersed. In their place appeared Colonel Alexis Belitsky, accompanied by cossacks with muskets, shot and powder. The came up to the very doors of the hut, prepared to do battle.

In the evening Serko sent a judge, a scribe, an aide-de-camp and a village ataman to the envoys with a message. "You have done badly in trying to shoot the little sovereign in the midst of the Host. On March 12 there will be a council and the little sovereign will be in attendance. The fact that you wished to shoot him is now known to all and if the Host is ordered to do something to you, it will explode like poppy seed set afire. As soon as you enter the council, you must try to petition him and bow down to the ground." "The evil conduct of disloyal servitors is not pleasing to God," Chaduev responded. "You call yourselves loyal servitors of his majesty the tsar, you beg for and receive his charity, yet you surrender his ambassadors to death, believing some unknown fraud! We were not sent to you with death, rather with rejoicing and the announcement of his majesty the tsar's most gracious favor to you."

On March 12 the council convened. The tsar's agents were called to the council, but their knives were taken from them and they were followed by guards with muskets. The pretender stood in the church and looked out the window at the council. Serko, hearing the tsar's notice, his directive and the hetman's missive, said to the Zaporozhians "My brothers, valiant atamans, members of the Zaporozhian Host of the lower Dnieper, both old and young! In the past we had good young men in the Zaporozhian Host who never would have surrendered anyone, and neither will we surrender this young man!" "We will not surrender him, lord field ataman!" thundered the mob. "My dear brothers!" Serko continued. "If we surrender him Moscow will drag all of us away one by one. Moreover, he is neither a thief, nor a swindler. He is the true tsarevich. He sits like a bird in a cage. He is guilty of no crime against anyone."

"Let them look this swindler in the eye themselves!" cried the cossacks. "They will find out what sort of a swindler he is! They go on about the seal and about a letter. The tsarevich himself says the boyars wrote all this and sent it without the order of the great sovereign. They will continue to send more until they are drowned or their hands and feet are chopped off."

Serko spoke again. "Take care my brothers," he cautioned. "The hetman has many of our men, and these others, Chaduev and Shchegolev, were sent to the hetman for their freedom. While they are in our hands we will keep them alive, or release one of them, in return for the release of some of our men. They are under strong guard and they will not leave. Let us send to Doroshenko and ask him to surrender the Host's regalia to us in the encampment. Yes, let him come to us. He will listen to me because he is my godfather. Thanks to him the Host's regalia were not handed over to Romodanovsky. What right does Romodanovsky have to the Host's regalia? When he killed Yuraska Khmelnitsky and took the military regalia he did not surrender them to us. He will do the same again if Doroshenko gives him the regalia." "Let us send word, lord field ataman," thundered the crowd again. "Order that letters be written to Doroshenko."

At this point Serko ordered Chaduev and Shchegolev to leave the council, but the cossacks raised a racket. "Show them the tsarevich so they will act according to his will. If they do not do so, kill them!" Serko again sought to calm the crowd. "He is the little sovereign. Why do you drag him out for the council? When the time is right they will see him and act according to his will without the council. For now, release them."

In the evening the judge, scribe and aide-de-camp went to the envoys saying "The tsarevich is most grieved that he has not been called to meet you in the council. He wishes to meet you, and the field ataman wishes to bring him and you to his own hut." "We were sent from his majesty the tsar to the Zaporozhian Host to seize the pretender, not to converse with him," the envoys answered. "If the field ataman brings him to his hut with a saber and he decides to make mischief, then what happens? Now, as before, we will not risk our necks."

On March 13 Serko gathered the village atamans and prominent cossacks in his hut. He summoned the ambassadors and said "You have stolen much in Zaporozhia and you wished to raise your hand against a great man, to kill the little sovereign. It is proper that you should die. God has sent to us from heaven a most precious pearl, a sparkling gem. Never before has this happened in Zaporozhia. He says that he was driven from Moscow in the following fashion. Once he was with his grandfather, Boyar Ilia Danilovich Miloslavsky, and the boyar was speaking with a foreign ambassador about business. The tsarevich interrupted the conversation and the boyar impolitely waved him aside with his hand.

"The tsarevich, returning to his own chamber, said to his mother, Tsaritsa Maria Ilinichna, 'If I were tsar, even if only for three days, I would hang all the malignant boyars.' 'Whom would you hang?' asked the tsaritsa. 'First of all, Boyar Ilia Danilovich,' retorted the tsarevich. The tsaritsa flung a knife at his foot. The knife found its target and the tsarevich fell ill from the wound. The tsaritsa ordered the crown agent Mikhail Savostianov to poison him, but the agent poisoned one of the choirboys instead. Removing the choirboy's clothing he laid it on a table, and dressed the dead choirboy in the tsarevich's garments. For three days he cared for the tsarevich secretly. Then he hired two poor monks, one without hands and the other with only one eye, gave them one hundred gold ducats, and they carried the tsarevich from the town on a small cart under matting. They handed the tsarevich over to a peasant from the town quarter and the peasant carried him to the Archangel wharf."

"The tsarevich wandered for a long time," Serko continued, "and finally he came to the Don. He was with Stenka Razin at sea. Not revealing his identity, he served as a cook, calling himself Matiushka.[35] Before Stenka was seized the tsarevich told him his story under oath. After Stenka, an emissary of his majesty the tsar from the treasury was at the Don. He showed favor to the tsarevich, who sent a letter with him. The boyars did not allow this letter to reach his majesty the tsar. When the time comes he will send a letter to his majesty the tsar with a man who will deliver it personally to him."

"I gave little credence to this tale," continued Serko, "but recently during Lent he fasted. I ordered his priest to witness his confession, under oath, and if it was genuine, to say so. He said under oath that he spoke truly and took communion. So now, whatever anyone says or writes, we believe him." At this point Serko crossed himself, saying "He is the true tsarevich! Would we give him up to Providence when he has just asked us for a list of what is needed for the Host? We will take three thousand or more crimson clothes, at ten arshin[36] per man per year, as well as great reserves of money, lead shot and powder. We will also have a master gunner able to fire with this ammunition, and reeds[37] and chaikas. The tsarevich says and we ourselves well know why we and the Don Cossacks do not receive the sovereign's grant, cannon and other military supplies and chaikas. His majesty the tsar is magnanimous to us. He promises much, the boyars do not even give a little. His majesty the tsar ordered woven cloth sent to us, we received only about one and a half ells[38] per man."

"Enough of this talk," Chaduev retorted. "Hand over the pretender and send him to the great sovereign with a hundred or more of your own men. They will all be given grants, and in addition cloth, cannon, shot, a master gunner, cannonballs, lead, reeds and chaikas will be sent to you in the encampment."

"Even if we sent a thousand men with him," Serko replied, "the cossacks would seize him on the road so that he would not reach his majesty the tsar. If the gentry or commanders with soldiers are sent for him, they will not surrender him. Moscow calls all of us thieves and swindlers, as if we did not know who is who and what is what. Should the sovereign, in conformance with the boyars' advice, communicate with Hetman Samoilovich and order him not to permit grain and food supplies to pass through to us in Zaporozhia because we refused to surrender the tsarevich, we will be without grain again just as when Demko Mnogogreshny refused to permit grain to pass. Then we will seek another sovereign for ourselves. The Crimean burghers will give us grain for our own sake because in the time of Sukhovey's hetmancy they gave us all kinds of grain from Perekop.

"Moreover, the Crimean khan knows about the tsarevich. He sent a messenger to find out about him and we told him that we have such a man in the camp. The Turkish sultan absolutely wishes to campaign this spring near Kiev and beyond. Let the rulers correspond with each other. We will find our own place. Whoever is stronger will be our sovereign. We pity Pashka Gribovich. If Pashka were with us now I would look across the steppe and find out what it is like in Siberia, and you would learn what kind of a front-line soldier Serko is.[39]

"What kind of a peasant have they placed in the hetmancy?" Serko continued. "He destroys his own but cannot destroy anything else. He fished and dragged along the Dnieper. Then, accomplishing nothing, he turned back. Now we have four hetmans, Samoilovich, Sukhovey, Khanenko and Doroshenko. None of them do any good. They sit at home quarreling among themselves over the hetmancy, over property, over mills, and they spill Christian blood. It would be well if the Crimea destroyed them and ended the war. At the council, when Romodanovsky gave the hetmancy to Samoilovich, the Host asked me and wanted to give me the hetmancy.

"Romodanovsky did not heed the Host's wishes and long ago sent me to the precipice. I hear that many towns on this side of the Dnieper and also Yakov Lizogub have joined your hetman. Praise God! Lizogub has been licking someone's boots, but the boots he licks will be hot in the heels. I would not act in this fashion. I did not lick anyone's boots even when the

Host wished to make me hetman. Were I hetman for one year and if the Muscovite turncoat, that priest's son Hetman Samoilovich, gave me four regiments, Poltava, Mirgorod, Priluki and Lubny, I would know how to use them. The Crimea would be totally destroyed."

"Now Prince Romodanovsy and the hetman have many troops," declared the ambassadors. "Go to them and act together with them." "They will not deceive me as before," Serko rejoined. "Earlier Romodanovsky described the sovereign's benevolence to me. Believing him, I went to him and he sold me for two thousand gold ducats." "Who gave these ducats for you?" asked the ambassadors. "His majesty the tsar, feeling magnanimous towards me, ordered Romodanovsky to give them."

On March 17, before the church service, Serko sent a priest and eleven of the village atamans to examine the tsarevich. They found neither diadem, nor eagle, nor moon, nor stars. All they found were eight white spots on the pretender's chest, extending from one shoulder to the other, made by the prodding of a finger, and on the right shoulder a mark from herpes that was wide and white. The pretender told them that his mama Tsaritsa Maria knew about these marks. In addition he said that now, except for the crown agent Mikhail Savostianov, no one would recognize him and he would believe no one save the crown agent, who was writing to the tsar. After this Serko and all the cossacks were even more convinced that this was the true tsarevich.

On the same day it was announced to the Muscovite envoys that they would be released to return to the tsar. They would be accompanied by cossacks who could hear about this man themselves from the mouth of his majesty the tsar, return to the encampment and report what they had heard. Then they could reach their own conclusions.

The same old story! The Zaporozhian field ataman's heart was broken. Why had they not selected him as hetman, he who for so long was a supporter of Doroshenko? He feigned belief in the pretender. The cossack had his say, "Let the sovereigns argue it out among themselves, we will give our support to the strongest."

The fate of Zaporozhia was sealed by these words insofar as whoever finally emerged as strongest no longer would wish to tolerate people who roamed from sovereign to sovereign, biding their time until it was decided which was the strongest. It offended Serko that the hetman, the priest's son Samoilovich, was successful on the western side of the Dnieper.

DOROSHENKO NEGOTIATES WITH MOSCOW

In fact, at the beginning of 1674 a long conceived plan to bring the tsar's weapons to the West Bank was brought to fruition. Samoilovich received a directive from Moscow to unite with Romodanovsky and to move against Doroshenko although the fruitless negotations about his subjection to Moscow continued. Doroshenko and Tukalsky had sent the monk Serapion to Moscow with a proposal for submission, including the conditions under which Doroshenko was willing to bow to the great sovereign. Doroshenko demanded that Kiev be surrendered to the cossacks and the tsar remove his men from the town. In return the cossacks would permit the tsar to occupy a fortress with his troops in any other town that he pleased. Should the tsar not agree Serapion was instructed to ask for reassurance that Kiev would not be surrendered to the Poles.

Doroshenko also demanded a single hetman for both sides of the Dnieper who would control the army and foreign affairs. This single hetman would rule like a sovereign, just as was now the case beyond the Dnieper, and all would obey him. Traditionally the hetman from the Ukraine did not recognize his majesty the tsar as hereditary sovereign. Thus the hetman must be confirmed for life. In particular the cossack liberties need be confirmed in their entirety. Further, the tsar must not tolerate the insubordination of some Ukrainians, as recently happened under several hetmans. "Where a household has many heads," the proposal asserted, "there is no order, particularly when there is neither agreement nor obedience." Therefore the sovereign must order the Zaporozhians to obey the hetman.

In regard to the Polish boundaries it was proposed that three former districts,[40] Kiev, Braslavl and Chernigov, be included in the Ukraine. The tsar must defend the Ukraine and wage an aggressive war against the Muslims. The issue closest to Doroshenko's heart was that of the double hetmancy. "I never will concede this," said Doroshenko. "It is an impossible situation and unheard of in the Ukraine that there is a hetman on that side of the Dnieper. Not only will I not agree to such a thing, neither will anyone on this side who is under my leadership. With two hetmans we will never accomplish anything. Witness the example of Poland and Lithuania. The relationship is poisoned by constant jealousy and what good is ever accomplished there?

"I do not boast, but who is Lord Samoilovich? Can he trace his cossack lineage from his great-grandfathers and his grandfathers, as I can? Does he know Zaporozhia, its tributaries, the sea straits, its rivers and the sea itself? Has he participated in many wars? When did he ever smooth out difficulties? When he had business with the monarch did he fight or did he negotiate, that now he is in a position to serve his majesty the tsar? If he points at himself, suggesting that he knows all and can do good, I will give way to him and bow low to him because he will have released me from a heavy burden. Was he not once in the Host, and not that long ago, as a cossack? Was he a colonel for a long time? Did he move up the ranks of our elders from small to great?

"More than once he inflicted filthy tricks on me! He takes cossacks from our side and himself rides on cossack horses stolen from our side. Someone who served by me stole and then fled to the other side and Samoilovich did not order the thief surrendered. He made Rodion Dmitrashko-Raich a steward to spite me. Let his majesty the tsar judge. How can we agree after this? How can he help me in need? Is it a good thing to have two hetmans constantly quarreling, to have one hetman playing filthy tricks on the other, letting Poland perish because of their disagreements? Besides this, one side of the Ukraine is not defended from the Turks, nor is it defended from the [Tatar] Horde.

"This business does not concern me. I have no children. I will take two or three thousand foot soldiers to the steppe and live there. This affair concerns all people who could be destroyed by my conduct. If his majesty the tsar makes me hetman of both sides I will try to serve well. If his majesty the tsar listens to Samoilovich, no good will come of it. More than a few can be found who reign when it is peaceful but who do not stand up for the general Christian good. It is understandable that the Nezhin priest Simeon Adamovich does not agree to the unification of the Ukraine under my hetmancy. Then the clergy would have to fear the supervision of a pastor. Now they do whatever they wish."

Samoilovich repaid Doroshenko in the same coin. He wrote to Moscow that Doroshenko and Tukalsky thought only about how to seize both sides of the Dnieper with the help of the Turks. Samoilovich claimed that he wanted no relations whatsoever with Doroshenko, who wounded him in the most un-Christian manner by sending arsonists to the East Bank to burn whole towns. The tsar calmed Hetman Samoilovich, reassuring him that Doroshenko would be accepted as a subject of the tsar only under the condition that he remain as hetman on the West Bank only.

In reality the tsar sent word to Doroshenko saying "His majesty the tsar is amazed that he, Hetman Peter Doroshenko, excoriates Hetman Ivan

Samoilovich for low origins and speaks as if he knew nothing of the conduct of the Zaporozhian Host. He, Doroshenko, need recall previous hetmans, save Bogdan Khmelnitsky, and ask himself whether Samko, Tsytsura,[41] Bezpaly, Barabash, Pushkarenko, Zolotarenko, or Briukhovetsky were of noble family or educated people. They were selected by free voices according to the laws of the Zaporozhian Host because the sovereign did not forbid the Zaporozhian Host to elect their hetmans."It is no reproach to Ivan Samoilovich that he did not negotiate with the monarchs. He could not do this because he was under the jurisdiction of his majesty the tsar. It is known to the whole world how Doroshenko with his treaties pacified the Zaporozhian Host whereas Hetman Ivan Samoilovich and the entire Zaporozhian Host on the East Bank lived in peace. In Poland and Lithauania, from earliest times, great hetmans and field atamans disagreed among themselves. It was God's will that this happened, and it is not meet to cite this as an example." In addition, it was ordered that Doroshenko be told that at present he could not become hetman of both sides. In the spring if the troops of both sides, going to the steppe, wished to have him as the only hetman in accordance with their cossack rights, his majesty the tsar would confirm it.

Doroshenko, forever referring to cossack rights and liberties, refused to recognize the chief cossack right, the right to elect a hetman, fearing this could be used to his detriment. "There is no chance of that," Doroshenko responded, "because certain people will not allow this. I would exhaust myself pursuing unrealistic possibilities. Who then would defend me from the Turks and Tatars? Given the unfriendly attitude of Lord Samoilovich, I see no reason to expect help from him. I am told that it is difficult for his majesty the tsar to replace Samoilovich, who received the regalia through his majesty's charity. The tsar passed over others who were deserving without consulting our brother cossacks. The cossacks were compelled to accept him as hetman because Prince Romodanovsky supported him. Then as now, if his majesty the tsar desires something, it is done. Well, things will be just fine when the Host remains divided under two mutually hostile hetmans! I want one thing, he wants another. Can anything good come of this?"

It is understandable that Samoilovich could not relax, knowing the character and pretensions of the Chigirin hetman, Doroshenko. Yet he was even more afraid of Mnogogreshny's friends. "Mnogogreshny and his advisors go where they wish. It is understood they are planning something," wrote the hetman to the Chigirin colonel, Vasily Dunin-Borkovsky. "Gribovich is already beyond the rapids. We saw him with our own eyes, and who knows where the Mnogogreshny brothers are? God knows what will come of this! Stenka was not too clever either, and see what misfortune he caused! There is no need to accept the truth of this information on faith. More than once we heard with our own ears that they wanted to pitch their camp near Moscow itself. So, it happens, clearly they lie."

SAMOILOVICH OPPOSES RECEPTION OF DOROSHENKO

Samoilovich was just as unhappy as Doroshenko about the division of the hetmanate. "If both hetmans send their deputies against their own enemies, how will the boyar who comes with government soldiers and officials know which hetman to oblige?" Samoilovich asked the tsar's ambassador Leonty Bukhvostov. "During the time of Polish dominion there were never two hetmans. When Bogdan Khmelnitsky petitioned for another hetman it was because he wished to give the hetmancy to one of his own kin. Moreover, at that time there were many soldiers on both sides, now on that side there are few. As before, Doroshenko wants to be acclaimed on this side and take it away from me. If his majesty the tsar wishes to receive Doroshenko to avert a Turkish war he should know this will not avert war. Once he receives Doroshenko he must defend him from his enemies and station soldiers in the towns, in Chigirin, in Kanev, in Uman and in Cherkassy, because the Turkish sultan will go to war against Doroshenko to avenge his treachery.

"Moreover, as soon as Doroshenko becomes a subject of the great sovereign he constantly will send to Moscow begging for assistance and other things, and his messengers will pass through our towns. These emissaries will always plague us. They will beg, or seize things violently and cause weeds of every kind to sprout among the populace.[42] We will be subjugated to them.

"Doroshenko reproaches me for being of lowly origin. Let him but look in a mirror honestly and he will see that not only is my birth equal to his, it is even more honorable. I was brought up by my parents. God and honorable people are witness to this. Coming of age I did not remain idle, immediately I occupied myself with military affairs, rising through the various ranks. After I served as colonel I was made chief justice, a post which demands fullest humanity, namely the fear of God and discernment.

"Doroshenko also rails against Father Simeon Adamovich. God help us! If only there were more like the father archpriest. Metropolitan Tukalsky ruined Vygovsky. When King Jan Kazimierz was besieging Sevsk and Glukhov he persuaded Vygovsky to rise up against his majesty the king. Vygovsky obeyed him and wrote to Serko and to Sulimka[43] telling them to gather the Zaporozhian Host and come to him because he wished to intercept the king by the Dnieper. The letter fell into the hands of Teteria who, together with the Polish colonel Sebastian Machowski, murdered Vygovsky and sent Tukalsky into captivity in Marienburg.[44] Tukalsky also ruined Briukhovetsky, tempting him with the mace on both sides of the Dnieper. In the beginning Demko Mnogogreshny did not speak indecent words against the sovereign and against the council. As soon as he began corresponding with the metropolitan and Doroshenko he was carried away with pride and began to speak and write abusive things against the sovereign and the realm. Doroshenko destroyed Stepan Opara,[45] who was elected hetman by the troops after Teteria, and made himself hetman forcibly, with the help of the Tatar Horde, not by free election."

ROMODANOVSKY AND SAMOILOVICH CROSS TO WEST BANK

In order to bring the affair to a conclusion and either subjugate Doroshenko unconditionally to the will of the great sovereign or drive him from the hetmanate, Samoilovich and Romodanovsky had to move beyond the Dnieper. Matveev received a letter from Archpriest Simeon Adamovich. "In all affairs," it read, "Hetman Ivan Samoilovich places himself totally in the hands of God, the hands of the tsar and in your hands, my benefactor, and will do nothing without the directive of the tsar and your counsel. Now, in accord with the sovereign's order, he has prepared the regiments for the campaign. On the road he learned that Prince Trubetskoy promised Doroshenko the hetmancy on both sides and undertook to convene a general council[46] attended by the cossacks of both sides. The hetman wrote with his own hand to me about this, how he set out on campaign and we had made such an agreement with him. If something grieves him he writes to me and I relay this to you, my gracious benefactor. Under God and his majesty the tsar we now have no defender but your grace. Do not reject us from the sphere of your benevolence. You began as our benefactor. Let it be so to the end."

In the meantime a courier rushed to Kiev with an order to Trubetskoy not to correspond with Doroshenko about becoming a subject of the tsar.

If Doroshenko wrote asking about this Trubetskoy was to reply that this affair was the responsibility of Romodanovsky and Samoilovich, and he must discuss it with them. On December 31 Samoilovich *hurried* from Baturin. On January 8, 1674 he reached Gadiach. Romodanovsky arrived there on January 12. On January 14, having discussed everything, both military commanders accompanied by about eighty thousand soldiers between them moved forward to the Dnieper. Even though Doroshenko "entrusted himself to the paternal charity of his most high, grand vizier," the Turks did not defend him at this time. On January 27 the town of Krylov surrendered. On January 31 Peter Dmitrievich Skuratov, a comrade of Romodanovsky, approached Chigirin with Russian and cossack regiments. He burned the town quarters,[47] attacked a number of Doroshenko's men and pursued them to the town wall. On February 4 Romodanovsky and Samoilovich occupied Cherkassy. On February 9 Romodanovsky and Samoilovich were just approaching Kanev where Doroshenko's general aide-de-camp Yakov Lizogub was stationed, when Colonel Ivan Gursky of Kanev appeared with all the elders in the camp, approached the united military leaders and petitioned to be accepted as subjects of his majesty the tsar. All the people of Kanev were brought to swear an oath of fealty.

When news reached Moscow about the outbreak of hostilities beyond the Dnieper, the taking of Cherkassy and Skuratov's march to besiege Chigirin, Captain Kolobov[48] of the Moscow musketeers was sent quickly to the commander and the hetman. He was to ask after their health, praise their service and then ask "Why did the boyar and hetman not accompany the soldiers to Chigirin? Why did they send only Skuratov and the cossack colonels? Why did they burn homes around the town containing various supplies and provisions. Moreover, not taking any action against Chigirin itself, they turned back when it would have been useful to construct fortifications on the outskirts of the town and elsewhere and actively besiege Doroshenko in Chigirin. Had this been done all the regiments, seeing Doroshenko under siege, would have surrendered. In Cherkassy and in other places around Chigirin the great sovereign ordered a very strong blockade to bar grain from the town and the besieged from leaving. Should many regiments from this side surrender a council must be convened. The colonels, commanders and cossacks were to be told to elect another hetman in place of Doroshenko, a good, available and, most particularly, a loyal man. Khanenko was to be summoned to become a subject of the tsar."

"We did not go to Chigirin with all our forces," responded Romo-danovsky and the hetman, "because there were more than ten thousand soldiers there with Doroshenko, in addition to the settlers, whom they drove in from the surrounding areas for defense. There were also more than two hundred cannon and ample food reserves. Moreover, the Chigirin citadel is located in an ideal defensive position, as everyone who has been there knows. It cannot be assaulted from any direction, nor can trenches be dug in winter. To maintain a lengthy siege without fodder for the horses posed difficulties for the troops, and there was nowhere to take the horses [for fodder] nearby. The troops, standing and growing weary, would have had to retreat in shame. Everything is going well now."

Romodanovsky and the hetman did not consider it necessary to remain on the West Bank and moved to Pereiaslav with the bulk of the force. This decision they justified with the fact that from February 5 to February 15 roads were impassable owing to heavy rains and there was no snow on either side of the Dnieper, making it impossible to travel by sleigh. Moreover, horses were collapsing from lack of fodder and the soldiers constantly deserted. The hetman repeatedly and rather tiresomely told Kolobov that the great sovereign must dismiss the cossack regiments because no one had ever seen or heard of such onerous service.

Despite the withdrawal of the chief leaders the campaign on the West Bank was successful. On March 2 the Muscovite colonel Tseev[49] and a force of lancers, cavalrymen, dragoons and soldiers, accompanied by the general aide-de-camp Ivan Lysenko, clashed with Doroshenko's brother Grigory and a force of Tatars about fifteen versts from Lysenka and routed them. The defeated [fled and] locked themselves up in Lysenka, where they were seized with the help of the townsmen. Grigory Doroshenko was taken into captivity. Hearing about this defeat, Grigory Gameleia and Andrei Doroshenko rushed from Korsun to Chigirin. Leaving several colonels in Korsun, including those of the Korsun, Braslavl, Uman, Kalnik and Podolsk regiments, they petitioned the great sovereign to accept them as subjects.

KHANENKO WRITES TO PRINCE TRUBETSKOY

On March 4 Khanenko wrote the following letter to Governor Prince Yury Petrovich Trubetskoy of Kiev. "Humbly I pray you petition his majesty the tsar to favor me with his munificence like a generous father.

Faithfully and righteously I served the king and the Polish Common-wealth. Without misgiving I left my wife and children in Poland. Without reward I spilled my own blood. Yet now I am compelled to flee from here because of the enmity and insupportable malice of Hetman Jan Sobiesksi who without cause ordered my eldest son tortured and killed and now plots against my life. I promise to subject myself to his majesty the tsar." Khanenko did not limit himself simply to a written announcement. With regiments consisting of two thousand cossacks he presented himself to Romodanovsky and Samoilovich.

SAMOILOVICH ELECTED HETMAN OF BOTH BANKS

On March 17, the tsar's name-day,[50] a cossack council convened in Pereiaslav. The colonels of the East Bank gathered, including the colonels Konstantin Solonina of Kiev,[51] Rodion Dmitrashko-Raich of Pereiaslav, Filipp Umanets of Nezhin, Peter Roslavets of Starodub, Vasily Dunin-Borkovsky of Chernigov, Lazar Gorlenko of Priluki, and Ivan Serbin of Lubny. Those attending the council from the West Bank [from Doro-shenko's general staff] included the aide-de-camp Yakov Lizogub, the quartermaster Ivan Gulak and Chief Justice Yakov Petrov,[52] as well as the colonels Ivan Gursky of Kanev, Mikhail Solovey of Korsun, Stepan Butenko of Belaia Tserkov, Grigory Belogrud of Uman, Stepan Shcherbina of Targovitsa, Pavel Lisitsa of Braslavl, and Migalevsky[53] of Povolochie.

Before the commencement of the council Khanenko with all of his comrades laid down the military standards, the mace and the staff, received from the king. Romodanovsky announced that as soon as the Host of the West Bank committed itself to eternal submission to the great sovereign, according to the tsar's directive they might select for themselves a hetman for their side.

The cossack elders and the Host responded that they did not wish to have many hetmans. Many hetmans had caused them destruction. They requested the great sovereign decree but one hetman for both sides of the Dnieper, Ivan Samoilovich.

Samoilovich demurred, but a shout was raised that he was the favored candidate. The elders seized him, set him on the bench and covered him with the standard, tearing the hetman's garments. The existing council of elders was confirmed and requested that Hetman Samoilovich live in Chigirin or Kanev. If he could not reside on the West Bank, at least let him live in Pereiaslav. Then they beseeched the great sovereign to post his soldiers in Chigirin and Kanev. Khanenko was made colonel of the Uman Regiment.

DOROSHENKO PETITIONS TO BECOME SUBJECT OF TSAR

After the council everyone went to Prince Romodanovsky's abode to dine. All gave assurances to serve the great sovereign wholeheartedly and prevail over the Muslims. At dinner the same day they reported to the prince that a messenger had arrived from Doroshenko. The new hetman of both sides of the Dnieper, Ivan Samoilovich, did not foresee that this messenger from Doroshenko ultimately would be his successor. The messenger was General Chancellor Ivan Stepanovich Mazepa.[54]

Mazepa made a humble speech before the prince. "Kissing the icon of the Savior and the most holy Mother of God, Doroshenko promised he would subject himself to the tsar with the whole Zaporozhian Host of that side. May the great sovereign be generous and order him received, and may Boyar Prince Grigory Grigorievich [Romodanovsky] receive him on peril of his soul, that no misfortune befall him."

"Tell Peter Doroshenko," responded the boyar, "to come to me in the regiment without misgivings, trusting in the mercy of the great sovereign." At this time also news spread that in Chigirin Joseph Tukalsky had gone blind.

MOSCOW AND ZAPOROZHIAN PRETENDER

Moscow rejoiced at the news from Pereiaslav but it disturbed those in Zaporozhia with their own tsarevich. An order had been sent to Romodanovsky that should the pretender from the cossack camp go anywhere for plunder the prince, in consultation with Hetman Samoilovich, must send Muscovite and Little Russian soldiers against him. On May 1 the Zaporozhian messenger Prokopy Semeonov appeared in Moscow with his comrades and presented a message. "To the annointed by God, the most merciful light and spirit of our most illustrious majesty the tsar from his loyal servants of the Zaporozhian Host, from the Dnieper cossacks and the nomadic cossacks, the leaders and the population, from those living in the meadows, in the fields, in the glades and in all the nooks and crannies of the Dnieper, the steppe and the seas." Serko announced in the letter that a young man came to him calling himself Tsarevich Simeon. He recounted the pretender's story about his wanderings, omitting his acquaintance with Razin, and in conclusion wrote "We keep him with us because he calls himself the son of our majesty the tsar. We are guarding him and he will not be allowed to leave us. Be gracious to our messenger and let us hear from our majesty the tsar whether this is true or not." The messengers also presented a letter to the tsar from his imaginary son. "Your son, the pious Tsarevich Simeon Alekseevich, who has been praised with your most illustrious majesty the tsar, I petition you, my little father, against the conciliar boyars. They wished to kill me but were not successful because at that time I [fled] with your prayers, my little father. I am now living in glorious Zaporozhia with the Zaporozhian Host, with loyal servants of your most illustrious majesty the tsar. My little father, when you see me with your own eyes then truly you will understand. When I stand before your majesty and fall at your feet, then verily you will recognize that the all-powerful God knows all. I wanted to come to you my little father, but feared trouble along the road. The Host serves you loyally, my little father. Look with favor upon the Host's petition concerning plans for the best campaign against the Muslims. Not only will the cossacks of the steppe prevail over the Muslims and repel the enemy. They will cross the water and invade the Muslim's territory and attain a notable victory over them. In addition, prostrating myself at your feet, my little father, I petition and complain against Semeon Shchegolev and Vasily Chaduev who, without the order of your majesty the tsar, following their own evil inclinations, wished to shoot me with an arquebus."

"This letter," the tsar responded to Serko, "to us, our majesty the tsar, is not and never was necessary. You scorned our inexhaustible benevolence and our promise and gave the seal and the banner to this thief and pretender. Before the arrival of Chaduev you did not inform us about him. You sent a priest and cossack nobles to question this pretender without our order. You corresponded with Doroshenko without our directive. Our son, the Tsarevich Simeon, died on June 18, 1669. His remains were buried in the church of Michael the Archangel in our presence and in the presence of Patriarch Paisios of Alexandria and Patriarch Joasaph of Moscow.[55] You, the field ataman, must remember your promise and send the pretender and the cossack Miiuska to us in chains under the very strongest guard. Until you send them your messengers will be detained in Moscow. We will send chaikas and arquebuses. Woolen cloth and gold already have been sent. Until you send the impostor to Moscow these supplies will be held in Sevsk."

SERKO SENDS PRETENDER TO MOSCOW

On August 12, 1674 Serko informed Romodanovsky that he had dispatched the impostor to the great sovereign. "We held the man who calls himself the son of your majesty under strong guard," Serko wrote in his official letter. "We gave honor not to him but to your most illustrious majesty the tsar, to our light and breath, because he called himself your offspring. Now, as a loyal servant, I send him to your majesty. I wish to fulfill my promise and truly serve you until the last days of my life. I corresponded with Doroshenko, wishing to persuade him to enter the service of your majesty the tsar. Be merciful, great sovereign. Grant us various supplies in abundance, as you did on the Don. We asked Hetman Ivan Samoilovich to give us the ferry at Perevoloka, but this he did not do. We did not request this ferry to collect needed supplies, as others are doing now. We requested it for the defense of the Christian faith. Your officials do not report to your majesty all that they requisition from Christians in the Ukraine, and they give us not even one ferry."

THE END OF THE PRETENDER

On September 17 a whole company of Moscow musketeers, led by Captain Yanov, stood by the earthen wall opposite the Smolensk gates. They took the thief and pretender, set him on the same wagon on which Stenka Razin was transported, and chained his hands to a rack behind his neck. Completing this ceremony, they carried him along Tver Street to the city hall. On the same day, all the boyars, lords-in-waiting and councillors collected in the city hall for an interrogation.

"I am of Polish birth, of the Wiśniowiecki clan. My father was called Jarema and they call me Semeon. My father lived in Warsaw. Foreigners kidnapped me near Warsaw, on the Vistula river, and sold me to a merchant of Glukhov who in turn sold me to a Lithuanian. I lived in Glukhov for about five weeks and then fled with comrades. We proceeded to Kharkov and Chuguev and from there to the Donets, whence I made my way to the Don. From the Don I proceeded with Miiuska to Zaporozhia. I wanted to go to Kiev or to Poland but Miiuska told me that I should call myself the tsarevich. I could not call myself such an awesome and great name, but Miiuska threatened to kill me and I called myself so from terror. Even more than Miiuska, Serko compelled me to assume this awesome name. Gathering a force, they intended to go to war against the Muscovite realm and kill the boyars. I did not know Stenka Razin. I only found out about him when the cossacks brought him to the Don in chains." They hung him in the torture chamber and he said "I am the son of a peasant. My father lived in Warsaw. He was a burgher, a subject of Prince Dymitr Wiśniowiecki. He came to live in Warsaw from Lokhvitsa. They called him Ivan Andreev, but his nickname was the Sparrow. They named me Semeon. Miiuska, who was by birth a Ukrainian,[56] taught me thievery. We wanted to collect a force, call the Crimean horde, invade Muscovite territory and kill boyars." Tortured with fire he repeated the same thing.

On the same day the great sovereign directed, and the Holy Patriarch Joachim, the boyars, lords-in-waiting and councillors passed sentence. The impostor and pretender was to be executed in the same fashion as Stenka Razin. The sentence was carried out the same day. The pretender was executed on Red Square by being broken on the wheel. The next day his body was carried to the marsh and he was placed alongside Stenka Razin. The sovereign favored Field Ataman Ivan Serko and ordered he be sent two timbers of sable pelts,[57] valued at fifty rubles per timber. In addition, he was given two suits of clothing, valued at seven rubles per suit.

Serko presented a petition, saying "I have grown old in military service and nowhere can I live freely with my wife and children. I do not wish to receive charity from anyone but his majesty the tsar. If the great sovereign would but favor me and order I be given the town of Kereberda near the Dnieper in the territory of the Poltava Regiment." The town was given to the field ataman and the ferry at Perevoloka was given to the soldiers.

V

DOROSHENKO BROUGHT TO HEEL

DOROSHENKO REJECTS SUBMISSION TO TSAR

The situation was pacified with respect to Serko. It was still necessary to deal with Doroshenko who had no intention of traveling to Pereiaslav and surrendering himself to Romodanovsky and the hated Samoilovich, who was now hetman on both sides of the Dnieper.

As early as May 5, 1674 an official letter in the name of the tsar was sent from Moscow to Doroshenko. "We have been informed that owing to hostile and provocative letters you are no longer inclined to place yourself under the protection of our high hand. Your mind is filled with doubts, you vacillate and are confused. You constantly correspond with the Turkish sultan and the Crimean khan. We, the great sovereign, trust in the Lord God and in the most holy Mother of God, just as did our forefathers, and our father. We, the great sovereign, live and reign and the destiny of the realm resides in that trust.

"If as a result of your calumny the Muslims attack and something happens to the holy churches of God and the monasteries, how will you answer God at the Last Judgment? Remember the previous hetmans who did not keep their promises, Vygovsky and others! Where are their wives and children? Are they not orphans living in poverty? Recalling this, you should place yourself under the protection of our high hand in submission without procrastination, not fearing our wrath. We will support you and all your kin with our bounty."

The musketeer hundredman Elizar Terpigorev, a messenger from Romodanovsky, arrived in Chigirin on May 25. "Become a subject of the great sovereign," the hundredman told Doroshenko. "Come to Pereiaslav and take the oath before the boyar governor. If you do not wish to come yourself, send your father-in-law Pavel Yanenko, or your brother Andrei, or some other cossack nobles as hostages and the boyar will send the captain of the Moscow musketeers to you for negotiations."

"I cannot do any of this now," answered Doroshenko, "because I am a subject of the Turkish sultan. The sabers of the sultan, the khan and the king hang over my neck. Previously I wished to be a subject of his majesty the tsar, but the elders and colonels decided to become subjects of the sultan. Now the elders and the colonels have transferred their allegiance and become subjects of the great sovereign, but this is temporary. They did this only for sable pelts with no intention of remaining loyal forever. Later they will turn traitor. Should the boyar and the hetman come to Chigirin I would be happy to give them my support if only they will wait for the Tatars [to join me]. In fact even without this, I have Tatars [at my command]."

TATARS COME TO DOROSHENKO'S AID

Terpigorev was detained. This is explained by the fact that about four thousand Tatars came to assist Doroshenko. In the month of May, together with the Chigirin cossacks, they laid siege to Cherkassy where the Muscovite governor, Ivan Ivanovich Verderevsky, resided. The besieged repulsed the enemy and drove him to an area about fifteen versts from the Tiasmin river. Doroshenko's brother Andrei, accompanied by cossacks, Serdeniats and *Cheremis*[1] took the villages of Orlovka and Balakleia by deception, announcing himself as a subject of the tsar. The inhabitants were led into captivity by the Tatars. The eyes of some of the elders were gouged out with an auger and others were hanged.

DOROSHENKO'S BROTHER DEFEATED AND HIS EMISSARY SEIZED

In Smelaia the inhabitants were not deceived. They routed Andrei and drove him to Chigirin. On receipt of this news Romodanovsky and Samoilovich sent the cavalry colonel Moisey Beklemishev and the cossack colonel Dmitrashko-Raich of Pereiaslav with five cossack regiments. On June 9, by the Tashlyk stream between the settlements of Smelaia and Balakleia, Beklemishev and Dmitrashko-Raich confronted the enemy and routed him. Many murzas[2] lay dead on the field and Andrei Doroshenko left the battlefield wounded. To receive new assistance from the Tatars and the Turks more quickly Doroshenko sent our old friend Ivan Mazepa to the sultan with fifteen captives, cossacks from the East Bank, as a gift.

Serko seized Mazepa once again and detained him, sending documents to Samoilovich, who forwarded them to Moscow. "Evidently," Samoilovich wrote, "Serko did this to advertise his former loyal service and make amends for his indiscretion."

Serko did even more. In accord with Romodanovsky's first demand Serko sent him Mazepa himself, at the same time writing to Samoilovich politely requesting in the name of the whole Host that they not send him anywhere. Samoilovich gave his word and asked the tsar to permit Mazepa's return. Despite this, Mazepa reproached Hetman Samoilovich, accusing him of sending people to prison.

IVAN MAZEPA

We became acquainted with Mazepa in passing when he travelled to Pereiaslav as a messenger from Doroshenko, whom he served as general chancellor. Beyond this, we have some information about his earlier life. Mazepa was born a cossack. He was ennobled by King Jan Kazimierz and served him during his reign as gentleman of the bedchamber. Rumor said he left Poland for the following reason.

Mazepa had property in Volhynia adjoining the property of a Polish magnate, Lord Falibowski.[3] Servants reported to Falibowski that his neighbor Mazepa frequently dropped by in his absence and was very graciously received by the mistress of the house, with whom he also constantly corresponded. Once the lord departed on a long journey. His servant overtook him on the road, carrying a letter from his wife to Mazepa, inviting him to visit because her husband was not at home. Falibowski ordered the servant to go to Mazepa, deliver the letter and request a rapid reply. The servant was ordered to bring the reply to Falibowski. The messenger soon returned with Mazepa's note, saying he would come right away. Falibowski took the letter and waited on the road. Mazepa appeared on the road and seeing Falibowski greeted him. Greeting Mazepa in turn, Falibowski asked Mazepa where he was going. Mazepa invented some fictitious destination. At that point, Falibowski grabbed Mazepa by the neck, shouting "And what is this? Whose note is this?" Mazepa's heart stood still. He begged forgiveness, saying it was the first time he had gone to Falibowski's house in his absence.

"Servant!" cried Falibowski, "How many times has this lord been at my house when I have not been there?" "As many times as I have hairs on my head," the servant replied. Mazepa was forced to own up to everything but the confession did not help. Falibowski ordered the sinner stripped naked and then tied to his own horse with his face toward the tail. Irritated by blows of a knout and frightened by gunshot exploding over its head, the horse took off for home at top speed, tearing through thickets in the forest, and stopped directly in front of the gates of Mazepa's home. A servant came out and saw a monster! Fleeing back inside, he called the whole household. Only then did he recognize his own master.

This incident occurred in 1663. The same year Mazepa received an important commission. He was to go to Hetman Teteria[4] and from there, according to the advice of the hetman, go either to Samko[5] in Pereiaslav to negotiate his submission to the Polish king, or to Zaporozhia and persuade the local cossacks also to abandon their loyalty to Moscow. We do not know how this commission was fulfilled. In all probability, not wanting to return to Poland, where even before his encounter with Falibowski he was unpopular because he was a cossack, Mazepa remained with the cossacks of the West Bank where he served until he was appointed general chancellor thanks to his talents and education.

MAZEPA'S TESTIMONY IN MOSCOW

Now Mazepa appeared in Moscow as a prisoner, rather than in Constantinople. His fate was by no means guaranteed by Samoilovich's request. Mazepa was brought to the Chancellery for Little Russia to be questioned before its head, Artamon Sergeevich Matveev. Mazepa hastened to win the favor of the tsar's favorite with a long, detailed answer. It was known that he had come to Pereiaslav with a promise of submission from Doroshenko, then he detoured to the Crimea to convince the khan to attack the sovereign's frontiers. Mazepa began his story with his journey to Pereiaslav.

"The elders of the town of Lysenka sent to Doroshenko," Mazepa related, "announcing that they had become subjects of his majesty the tsar. They said he should come to them in the council in Korsun, bringing with him the mace and the staff, that he too might become a subject of the tsar. Doroshenko sent me to this council of elders with a formal reply. He also sent a note with me to Prince Grigory Grigorievich Romodanovsky. When he gave these to me, he ordered me to take an oath that I would remain in Korsun with my wife, and while at the council I speak to the boyar and the council of elders in accordance with his direction. He instructed me to tell the council of elders that if they could secure for him the hetmancy on that side of the Dnieper he was prepared to become a subject of the sovereign. If they did not make him hetman the sovereign's nobles must take an oath, swearing they would do nothing evil to him.

"When I arrived in Pereiaslav I found a council had convened on the very same day of my arrival.[6] I gave one of Doroshenko's missives to the boyar Prince Romodanovsky and the other to the council of elders. The prince and the hetman wrote to Doroshenko, sending the document with me, saying he might come to them without fear. He replied that they should send an honorable man to Cherkassy and he would send his own people as hostages. The boyar sent the captain of the Moscow musketeers to Cherkassy. Then Doroshenko called a council in Chigirin and asked 'Should we send hostages to Cherkassy, or not?' It was decided to send them, then news came from Krylov that Serko's messengers were on the way. The hostages were detained until it was discovered what the Zaporozhians had to say.

"The messengers announced that Doroshenko had not surrendered the mace and the staff in Pereiaslav and that he himself was not to come because there must be a hetman on the West Bank as before. They also announced that the Zaporozhians wished to unite with him and with the Crimean khan to act together, as they had during the time of Bogdan Khmelnitsky. The Zaporozhians had written to the khan requesting he reconcile Serko with Doroshenko, and send Doroshenko to Zaporozhia for confirmation of the hetmancy and of the union. Doroshenko did not go to Zaporozhia, fearing the tsar's soldiers. Instead he sent a cossack to take the oath in his place.

"I begged Doroshenko to permit me to visit my wife in Korsun. 'You wish to betray me!' Doroshenko cried. 'Obviously Romodanovsky has seduced you with sable pelts! During the time of Metropolitan Tukalsky I was ordered to swear an oath that henceforth I would serve Tukalsky. At the same time, in Pereiaslav evil rumors were circulating about him. I swore the oath and five days later Tukalsky sent me to the Turkish vizier with documents.'"

Serving the great sovereign, Mazepa announced "Doroshenko's resident-agent in Constantinople, Poryvay, wrote that of course the Crimean khan would agree to this. He would reconcile the Poles with the Turks and turn the army against the Muscovite realm."

Mazepa also reported something about the pretender Simeon who was with him in Zaporozhia. "Serko called him the real tsarevich and told me that the tsarevich asked him for one or two hundred soldiers, wanting to go with them to Chertomlik island.[7] From there he intended to write to the Don, to the rank-and-file cossacks, telling them to destroy all the elders in the Don and rally to him. When the rank-and-file supported him he would collect people in the towns and advance on Moscow. 'Why do you need to collect an army?' Serko asked him. 'If you wish to go to Moscow, I will let you go with provisions.'

"'I cannot go to Moscow,' the pretender replied. 'The boyars will kill me.' From this time on Serko ordered he be watched to make sure he did not leave the Camp. As the tsar's emissaries were leaving Serko's camp the pseudo-tsarevich, taking a horse, chased after them and wished to cut them down. Informed of this, Serko immediately sent cossacks after the impostor to prevent him from killing the emissaries."

Mazepa was an inexhaustible source of important information. "Sobieski has a strong and sincere friendship with Doroshenko," he asserted. "Orekhovsky[8] went to Chigirin to convince Doroshenko that he must leave the protection of the Turks and turn to the Commonwealth in submission.

Orekhovsky also presented the conditions under which this submission must be accomplished. (1) There must be a commission about the damages the Uniates did to the Orthodox churches in Poland and Lithuania. (2) The borders of the Zaporozhian Host shall extend to the provinces of Kiev and Braslavl. The inhabitants of these provinces must determine the form of compensation from the Zaporozhian Host. (3) Polish quarter troops[9] shall never be stationed in the Ukraine. Only the Zaporozhian Host can summon them. (4) Doroshenko must send the Turkish standards to Warsaw. If for any reason he cannot do this, let him send his brother with other cossacks as hostages, in return for which Sobieski promised to remove his commandant from Belaia Tserkov. In addition it was proposed among the conditions there be no reference to, nor a request made to the Commonwealth for such liberties as the cossacks enjoyed on the East Bank under Moscow.

"What kind of liberties were these?" the document asked, according to Mazepa. "Look at what the population suffers under the Muscovite governors! The present hetman was selected, not according to the rights and liberties of the Host but under the threat of poleaxes and muskets. His children were held as hostages. The hetman's power was torn from his hands. He could not even punish guilty cossacks, instead had to send them to Moscow as prisoners. In the end, Mnogogreshny was disgraced!

"Sobieski suggested to Doroshenko means of defending himself from the tsar's armies. He should send a proposal for submission to Warsaw. Then he, Sobieski, immediately would write a document to the tsar asking him to prohibit his soldiers from attacking any subject of the Commonwealth.

"The Poles," continued Mazepa, "asked the khan and Doroshenko to persuade the sultan to make peace with Poland and make war against the

Muscovite tsardom. 'What reasonable people these Poles are!' said the Turks. 'Rather than dining with them in Cracow, now we will sup with them in Kiev!' Doroshenko's resident in Constantinople wrote to the hetman advising him not to be distressed at losing the Ukraine, for it would not be difficult to take it back. The Ukraine was nothing in comparison with Crete and Kamieniec Podolsky. In this current war the sultan desires to release Khmelnitsky from captivity and keep him in reserve. Should Doroshenko turn traitor, he will establish Khmelnitsky in his place."

Mazepa also described in detail Doroshenko's resources in Chigirin. In total, including the inhabitants of Chigirin, he had about five thousand men. He also had about two hundred cannon, large and small, in both towns, with a large reserve of munitions and supplies. The townsmen's grain reserves were sufficient for a year, although the soldiers had no reserves whatsoever and salt was in short supply. According to Mazepa, Doroshenko said secretly that when he heard of a Muscovite campaign he would flee from Chigirin to the Turkish sultan. Now he was maintaining the siege, perhaps waiting for a communication either from the Turkish sultan or Sobieski about assistance. More than half the inhabitants of Chigirin had no love for Doroshenko, whom they wanted to submit to his majesty the tsar. His kin and friends agreed. Cossack Captain Blokh secretly sought to persuade the cossack cavalrymen to unite with the tsar's army. Doroshenko and the council of elders talked among themselves, saying that if the tsar's army beseiged Chigirin it would be better to negotiate with Prince Romodanovsky than with their own cossacks.

Mazepa made an excellent impression in Moscow. He was granted an audience with the tsar, given the tsar's bounty and permitted to leave without hindrance. He was sent with an official letter of invitation to Doroshenko and the townsmen of Chigirin, but it was not intended that Ivan Stepanovich remain in Chigirin. Rather he was to return to the regiment, to Romodanovsky and the hetman, who were ordered to guard him so that he would not go anywhere.

THE TSAR REFUSES TO RELEASE SAMOILOVICH'S SONS

Sending Mazepa to Moscow, Samoilovich petitioned the sovereign to release his sons to him. The reply was negative. "Your children reside with his majesty the tsar in the greatest munificence, which will never be revoked. In view of the current troubles in the Ukraine they cannot be released to you lest the disobedient Ukrainian people think the hetman's

sons were released from Moscow as a result of having fallen out of favor."
The grounds for refusal were not very skillfully conceived, but the
example of the four hetmans had made Moscow suspicious.

ROMODANOVSKY AND SAMOILOVICH ATTACK CHIGIRIN
In the midst of all this military activities continued on the western side of
the Dnieper. On June 23 Romodanovsky and Samoilovich approached
Chigirin. They built entrenchments and began a continuous artillery
barrage of the town. Many homes were destroyed and many cossacks and
citizens were killed and wounded. Tukalsky's home too was destroyed by
grenades. The metropolitan moved to the upper town and there fell ill
from terror. The Crimean khan sent his physician to attend him.

At the end of July the Muscovite army under the leadership of Colonel
Sasov, head of the cavalry and lancer units, and other leading officers, and
the Little Russians under the leadership of the standard-bearer Leonty
Polubotok and Colonel Dunin-Borkovsky of Chigirin, were dispatched to
Chigirin from the Crimean side. About two versts from the town the
hetman's brother met them. Andrei Doroshenko was defeated and the
victors pursued him to the town walls. There they destroyed all the grain
in the environs of Chigirin, losing only six men killed and one ensign[10]
taken prisoner.

SULTAN AND KHAN MOUNT NEW OFFENSIVE
Even as this victory was being won news arrived that the Crimean khan
had crossed the Dnieper downstream from Soroki. There a bridge had
been constructed across the river to allow the passage of the sultan himself and the whole Turkish army. The army intended to move to Uman and
from there directly to Kiev.

On August 6 a Turkish detachment appeared near Ladyzhin. The
Greek Anastas Dmitriev, well-known for his partisan actions against the
Tatars and the Turks, was standing here. A merchant, he was leader of a
motley band of volunteer cossacks, Poles and Wallachians. Colonel
Andrei Murashka and [Captain?] Savva[11] barricaded themselves in Ladyzhin with Anastas. There were about two thousand five hundred soldiers
and about twenty thousand burghers with their wives and children.
Among the burghers perhaps four thousand were fighting men. They had
one cannon in poor condition, the ramparts were in disrepair and there
were no reserve supplies at all. Eighty Turkish cannon began to thunder

against the town. Murashka with the archpriest and the captain fled the town, taking refuge in the enemy camp. The defenders of Ladyzhin elected Anastas colonel and vowed to fight to the death. After repelling five attacks the people of Ladyzhin surrendered in despair and were taken prisoner. Anastas, in disguise, was mistaken for a simple peasant and later gained his freedom. Murashka was overcome with repentance. He began to curse, calling the vizier and the sultan petty thieves. He damned Mohammed and was beheaded.

From Ladyzhin the Turks moved to Uman, where the people surrendered. The Turks left a garrison in that town and moved further along the Kiev road. The people of Uman, irritated by the violence of the Turkish garrison, slaughtered it and barricaded themselves inside the town. The vizier and the khan, hearing about this, returned and blew up Uman with underground mines. From the other side, Tatars arrived to relieve Chigirin on August 9, 1674. As soon as they appeared outside the town Romodanovsky and Samoilovich retreated to Cherkassy, arriving on August 12.

The next day the khan came to Cherkassy with Doroshenko. Battle raged from the second hour of the day[12] until evening. The commanders reported that the tsar's soldiers killed many Tatars and cossacks and the transport arrived intact. Deserters from enemy regiments reported that the khan and Doroshenko crossed to the East Bank of the Dnieper and the Turkish vizier was coming directly to Cherkassy from Ladyzhin.

RUSSIAN ARMY RETREATS TO EAST BANK

At this news Romodanovsky and Samoilovich burned Cherkassy, which previously had been left to its inhabitants. They crossed to the East Bank and halted opposite Kanev. At the same time Tatars appeared from the direction of Azov. They advanced to the steppe towns, Zmeev and Merekhva, taking many of the inhabitants captive. Colonel Grigory Donets of Kharkov went on the attack. He overtook the Tatars beyond Torets, on the Bychok stream, routed them and freed all the prisoners. He seized a Tatar murza and a distinguished Turk.

The terror aroused by the Turkish and Tatar campaign in the Ukraine was not protracted. By the beginning of September the Turks were on the road home. The khan and Doroshenko accompanied the sultan to the Dniester river and then turned back. At first it appeared they intended to cross over to the eastern side of the Dnieper, but at this point they were exhausted. They were defeated and on October 8 the khan departed for the Crimea.

HETMAN OPPOSES UNITING RUSSIAN AND POLISH FORCES

Official communications were sent to Romodanovsky and Samoilovich from Poland attempting to convince them to join with the king's army and confront the enemy. Such plans were far from the thoughts of the commander and the hetman. The clerk Semeon Shchegolev was sent to the hetman, who told him "The Poles write to me and to Prince Grigory Grigorievich Romodanovsky saying now we should join them and act against the enemy. They are a cunning people! When the enemy has retreated and nothing is heard of him they write about unifying the armies. This obviously is chicanery because they are constantly engaged in secret negotiations with the sultan and the khan. Let the following questions be raised. Who will go to war? Against whom will they stand? To what town will they go? There is no point in going to Wallachia and Moldavia which are already devastated by the Turks. If they wish to move to Moldavia and Wallachia, let them. These regions are closer to them. Perhaps the plan is to occupy Chigirin? What do they intend to feed themselves and their horses? Near Chigirin and other steppe towns, since there is arable land, there are peasants. Why did the Poles allow the sultan, the vizier and the khan to pass through them and attack the boyar and me? Why did they not attack them from the rear?

"Indeed I know about their deceitful conduct. The Turkish and Crimean soldiers are in the Ukraine not only because of Doroshenko. The Poles themselves would have been very happy to snatch both sides of the Dnieper and Kiev from the hands of his majesty the tsar. It is obvious that they surrendered the Ukraine in the following fashion. The kalgay,[13] the Crimean sultan, remained in the territory of Wallachia all last winter, constantly corresponding with Sobieski. Until they came to an agreement no one dared enter the Ukraine. When an agreement was concluded stipulating that the sultan, the vizier and their khan would not go to war against the Poles and not engage in plundering they opened the road into the Ukraine and Kiev to the enemy. Then the Turks and the Tatars entered the Ukraine and did whatever they wished.

"Hearing about their evil conduct," Samoilovich continued, "I considered all kinds of ways to break up their evil caucus and alliance, and the Lord God gave me the answer. When Grishka[14] Doroshenko was taken in battle I took from him eight blank pieces of paper to be written upon in the hand of Doroshenko and stamped with the military seal. I gave Doroshenko these pieces of paper and ordered him to write in his own name to the elders and the people in the town. On one page I ordered him to write in the Polish language in the name of Doroshenko to the Crimean kalgay saying that Sobieski, by his own sly stratagems, had made himself Polish king and the khan should beware of the king's cunning.

"At this time there was a Polish commandant in Mezhibozh. I ordered Colonel Dmitrashko-Raich to give the note to the commandant, as if it was intercepted on the road, and the commandant transmitted it to the king. When the boyar and I retreated from Chigirin the khan and Doroshenko pressed us hard. Then suddenly a courier arrived from the sultan ordering the khan and Doroshenko, abandoning all, to march to Uman because the Poles were breaking the conditions of the treaty. While waiting for the khan the sultan took Uman, then would go no further, and forbade the khan to go to our side [the West Bank] of the Dnieper.

"After this a Pole, Colonel Lazicki,[15] came to us and said that an enemy, Doroshenko, had written to the Crimean kalgay asserting that the king gained his throne by plotting. Heretofore the king was perfectly gracious to Doroshenko, looking after him in everything. The colonel told us that now that this had happened, it was out of their hands. In this fashion the last Turkish and Crimean war was averted by my service, thanks to these messages which I sent to the commandant of Mezhibozh. Now Doroshenko, having heard that the king is angry with him, begs pardon and promises to serve him to ensure the king will restrain himself. In the meantime he will send for the Crimean khan just as earlier he swore to submit to his majesty the tsar and then sent for the sultan, the vizier and the khan.

"Field Ataman Serko still receives him despite all his evil," Samoilovich complained. "Doroshenko convened a council and Metropolitan Tukalsky was present. 'No one loves us and we cannot live here,' the metropolitan said. 'We will go to the sultan and petition that he give us a place. He can make you hospodar of the Wallachians, and I will be there too.' They decided on this, packed their belongings in trunks and live in a state of readiness, waiting to see what the future will bring."

The movement of the Polish army and its occupation of several towns on the West Bank agitated the eastern side of the Dnieper, again bringing rumors that the tsar intended to cede Kiev and the East Bank to the king. It was necessary to write assurances that the sovereign did not intend to surrender Kiev and the East Bank to Poland. In fact he did not even intend to surrender the West Bank. Samoilovich rejoiced at these assurances yet did not cease stirring suspicions in Moscow about Polish designs on Little Russia. Rumors circulated among the populace that the Poles certainly would cross to the East Bank. From the other side rumors spread that the tsar himself would come to Little Russia with his army. Some rejoiced in anticipation of the tsar's arrival, others said the tsar would march to Putivl merely to destroy the Ukraine in alliance with the king. The tsar would come from Putivl, and the king from Kiev. The sovereign wrote to Romodanovsky that if there were really no enemies in the Ukraine he could withdraw to the Muscovite borders and disperse the soldiers. Samoilovich could go to Baturin but the young Prince Mikhail Grigorievich Romodanovsky[16] must remain in Pereiaslav with the detachment of Muscovite soldiers. It had reserve supplies and therefore could continue to serve. Similarly, Samoilovich must leave a detachment of cossacks in Pereiaslav after assigning them an acting hetman.

ROMODANOVSKY REPORTS TO TSAR

Romodanovsky responded to this directive with a curious epistle. "The soldiers of the Sevsk and Belgorod regiments, after continuous campaigns for a year and a half, are impoverished, naked and hungry," he wrote. "They have no supplies at all and their horses have collapsed. Many have deserted in desperation and the flow of deserters continues. The few who now remain have no provisions and cannot serve any longer. Owing to poverty and a shortage of people I cannot leave my little son Mishka.[17] Now we are together, sovereign, and we live in great want. My poor thin little villagers [on my estates in Russia] have been destroyed totally without me because I have served you in the Ukraine constantly for twenty-two years. Even my little son Mishka has served for six years without release. My other little son, Andriushka, spilled his youthful blood for you and now languishes in agonizing want in Crimean captivity. Fettered, his life has been a torture for seven years."[18] The tsar ordered the father to go to Kursk, and the son be given leave to go to Moscow for a wedding.[19]

The hetman returned on leave to Baturin where his enemies did not give him a moment of peace. Once again the old rumors circulated that the sovereign wished to return Demian Ignatovich Mnogogreshny from exile and place part of the Host under his command. At the beginning of 1675 the tsar had to reassure Samoilovich with one of his official documents that this would never happen and order that sowers of tares be executed.

ARCHBISHOP BARANOVICH DENOUNCES SIMEON ADAMOVICH

In the meantime Lazar Baranovich denounced Archpriest Simeon Adamovich. By September of 1674 the crown agent Leonty Bukhvostov was in Little Russia to announce to the most eminent local people news of the birth of Tsarevna Feodora Alekseevna.[20] First he presented himself to Lazar Baranovich who said to him "When you go to Moscow let it be known that Archpriest Simeon Adamovich of Nezhin is engaged in sly and duplicitous affairs. He secretly corresponds with the Turkish sultan and Doroshenko. In his missives he praises the sultan, saying he can defend Doroshenko with his soldiers stationed in distant countries while his majesty the tsar, with soldiers stationed only five hundred versts away, cannot defend the inhabitants on either side of the Dnieper. By such means the archpriest tempts the Little Russians into evil. I have his letters in hand. I will not send them with anyone. I myself would like to come to Moscow soon, although the hetman begs me not to go. As soon as I am in Moscow I will report to the great sovereign about these letters and other affairs."

Understandably, in Moscow there could be only amazement when the archpriest arrived on the business of the archbishop, bringing with him Baranovich's book, *Trumpets*. Baranovich requested that the treasury purchase all the books. He was told that while the sovereign praised the book *Trumpets* he would not direct the treasury to buy the books and distribute them to the monasteries against their will. Instead, the tsar ordered the books sold at their proper value. "In the Russian tsardom all kinds of books are sold by the Printing Office." Baranovich was told, "No one is given books against their will, nor are they sent to monasteries." Baranovich was asked how he wished the government to organize the sale of his book.

In April 1675, according to the directive of the great sovereign, Boyar Artamon Sergeevich Matveev ordered one hundred and two bound copies of *Spiritual Trumpets*,[21] printed in Kiev, be distributed to burghers with kiosks [in Moscow]. The books were valued at two and one half rubles per book, a total of two hundred and fifty-five rubles. The order was given to sell these books with great zeal and fairly at a realistic price. The books were to be distributed to the burghers with a receipt. They were to be distributed only to the very best people, people who were trustworthy, not to carousers. The money was to be collected in this same month of April, without arrears. This then is what was meant when it was said the books were not to be forced on anyone! Baranovich asked that he be allowed to establish a printing office in Chernigov.[22] The request was approved. He requested that he be sent cloth and fox pelts. The cloth and fox pelts were dispatched. The tsar reassured Baranovich and the hetman that he would never surrender Kiev to the Poles. The hetman swore he would never become a subject of the king, but denounced the Zaporozhian field ataman, Serko, as not of the same mind. When the king entered the western Ukraine there would be vacillation within the encampment. "We will stay and sacrifice our lives for the sovereign in whose realm we were born," Serko had said. "If the Host does not wish to go to the king as the sovereign of their own forefathers then I, Serko, will go even with only a tenth of the horses, to make obeisance to my sovereign." Someone spreading gossip was seized in Nezhin, sent to the hetman and executed by him as a *sower of tares* on account of loose talk about treachery in the eastern Ukraine. These events supported the distrust of the Muscovite governors and encouraged their unfortunate habit of calling Little Russians traitors.

Archimandrite Mikhail Lezhaisky[23] of the Savior monastery in Novgorod-Seversk wrote to Matveev. "I do not know why the governors in the borderlands call our Ukrainian people traitors. Please be forewarned! Let the governors be careful to assure that such measures and such untrustworthy information does not embitter the Little Russian soldiers. Take care lest a small spark ignites a huge conflagration." As a consequence an order was distributed to the governors along the border very firmly directing that Little Russians not be called traitors and that Russians live with Little Russians in unity and amity. The directive further stated that henceforth harsh punishment without mercy awaited those who indulged in such unseemly and insulting speech. Samoilovich incessantly denounced Serko, claiming that he wished to go to Astrakhan and to the Siberian lands in the hope that the Kalmyks could be attracted to his cause.

HETMAN SAMOILOVICH DENOUNCES SERKO

On August 23 the hetman wrote to Matveev. "God sees my conscience," he maintained, "and knows that I do not denounce Field Ataman Ivan Serko from hatred of any kind. During Lent a Zaporozhian chancellor was with me and he secretly revealed to me Serko's intrigues, tearfully begging this be kept secret for the time being. Serko constantly tells the leading cossacks in Zaporozhia that as their ancestors did not serve the Muscovite sovereign they too should not serve him. Rather they should support the sovereign of their grandfathers.[24] He says that if he is given no help he himself will go to his majesty the Polish king, even if he goes with only a dozen men. He maintains that the oath he took in Moscow was not taken voluntarily and therefore he regards it as nothing. Further he maintains that even though the Muscovites freed him from Siberia he didn't ask them to do this.[25] He could have escaped himself in some other way.

"The same chancellor said that Serko sent him to his majesty the tsar with the pretender, directing him to petition about the little town of Kereberda, saying 'I just hope they do not suspect my intentions and will give me the town! Then I could take my wife from the Settlement Ukraine Regiment,[26] and I would know what to do!' This little town is convenient to him for his evil plans because it is located on the bank of the Dnieper river above all the towns of the Poltava Regiment. All those who live in these areas are from the West Bank. When Briukhovetsky turned traitor Serko incited several of the towns near him to rebel and settled the inhabitants in Kereberda, a place previously uninhabited. Now the Zaporozhians have dispatched their emissaries to the great sovereign, but have not written a single word to us. The tsar's order that the Zaporozhians inform us of things for which they wish to petition has come to nothing. Now thanks to their idleness about a hundred and fifty of these Zaporozhians have been dispersed by force. Travelling along the road they cause great disorder in the towns. This has happened before. Under Briukhovetsky this cossack rabble was allowed to taunt noble people with their sins and shame. No longer will we tolerate them, nor permit them to scorn us."

HETMAN COMPLAINS ABOUT SIMEON ADAMOVICH

Samoilovich quarreled with the archpriest Father Simeon Adamovich. "I communicate to your grace my grief and sorrow which my friend Simeon, archpriest of Nezhin, has caused me," he wrote to Romodnovsky. "When he travelled to Moscow with the archbishop's books I did not charge him with any business because thanks to the charity of the great sovereign all information and orders reach us without him. Yet there, in Moscow, he announced impossible things about us to highly-placed people. He himself is not reliable. It is high time he is stopped from doing this. I have here several trustworthy witnesses who say he has given them hope in a peculiar form. Whatever ranks they want allegedly will be given to them in Moscow, where he is not refused anything. He has misled good people with his fantasies."

SERKO CORRESPONDS WITH MOSCOW

In May Zaporozhian messengers appeared in Moscow with a communication from Serko. The field ataman wrote that the Polish king had called them to serve him but they could not move without the tsar's order. He requested that Hetman Samoilovich go together with them to the Crimea. There they would dissuade the khan from assisting the sultan. He complained that they had not received the ferry at Perevoloka and asked that the seals of the Host earlier held by Khanenko be given to Zaporozhia.

Samoilovich's information did have an impact in Moscow. Serko was told not to go to the Polish king. He should march alone, with his own Zaporozhians, to the sea. The seals could not be given to Zaporozhia because they were entrusted to Khanenko by King Michał [Korybut],[27] and Khanenko had surrendered them to Hetman Samoilovich. In regard to the ferry, an order was sent to the hetman. The substance of this order was that the hetman was to act as he saw fit. The Zaporozhians' journey was to be paid for by the treasury, just as it paid for earlier travels of the Crimeans. About a hundred and fifty men started on the expedition but since Samoilovich did not permit them all to pass, only forty-one arrived. The tsar sent an order to Zaporozhia that henceforth no more than ten men could be sent. If more were dispatched they must support themselves at their own expense.

In June Samoilovich let it be known that Zawisza,[28] the king's emissary, had arrived in Zaporozhia. Serko took this as an excuse to appear out of the steppe with a large detachment of soldiers, as if this were necessary to accompany the ambassador. The Zaporozhians, suspecting that Serko intended to go directly to the king, remained in the steppe. They elected another council of elders and returned to the encampment while Serko, with only three hundred devoted followers, departed with Zawisza. As it turned out, he went to the Crimean yurts[29] for booty and returned with captive-informants[30] to Zaporozhia.

TROUBLE IN KANEV

In this same period the tsar was disturbed by troubles in Kanev, a town important because of its proximity to Chigirin. In March 1675 the governor

of Kanev, Prince Mikhail Ivanovich Volkonsky, wrote to Prince Romodanovsky saying that there were only two companies of Muscovite
musketeers in Kanev, and these were not up to strength. Many fled the
musketeer captains, Alexander Karandeev and Maksim Lupandin, having suffered unbearable beatings. There remained only sixteen hundred
men. Volkonsky complained that the captains did not obey him, refusing
him everything he asked.

The captains described things differently. In their version money was
sent to Kanev to purchase grain for the musketeers. Volkonsky bought no
grain, nor did he give the money to the musketeers. As a result the musketeers starved and deserted. The governor summoned the town prefects
and the burgomasters and in front of them castigated the captains, calling
them traitors and accusing them of wishing to join Doroshenko. The
sergeants, corporals and rank-and-file musketeers confirmed the account
of the captains, sending Romodanovsky a complaint that the governor
withheld their salaries. The tsar ordered a letter sent to Volkonsky with the
threat that should this happen again he would face harsh punishment.

Volkonsky responded to this with a new complaint against the musketeer captains. "These captains possess their own keys to the town gates
and they open the gates without informing me," he protested. "On March
7 I was in church. When I went home after the service Karandeev and
Lupandin were waiting for me in the vestibule and insulted me with rude
and inappropriate words, threatening to beat me. They commanded their
orderlies to seize my regimental clerk.[31] They beat him with truncheons
and held him prisoner. In terror I sit in my home behind locked doors."

The quarrel between the governor and the musketeer captains was resolved. Karandeev and Lupandin promised to obey the governor. Nonetheless, it was not long before Volkonsky came into conflict with others
more powerful than the musketeer captains. On June 14 a spy seized on
the square was brought to the governor in the assembly house. After being
tortured with fire three times the spy announced "Doroshenko sent me
with a note to the local colonel, Ivan Gursky.[32] The colonel took the note
from me and placed it in his shirt. Then he shouted to his servant to give
me bread and take me to his mother's home, where I could live for the
present."

They took the colonel's servant for a confrontation with his accuser,
the spy. At first the servant refused to speak but under torture he admitted
that all the accusations of the spy were justified. Colonel Gursky refused

to speak and the governor handed him over to the custody of the musketeer captains, Karandeev and Lupandin. The governor immediately reported this incident to the sovereign, asking for instructions. The governor's report did not arrive in Moscow until June 25. On June 27 the tsar responded to Volkonsky, directing that he order the hetman to take Gursky, his servant and the spy from Kanev to his own quarters in Baturin for a proper investigation. The three must be judged according to the law of the Host. This answer must have taken at least ten days to reach Kanev. In the interim, news about events in Kanev stimulated strong dissatisfaction in Baturin.

The governor had surrendered the colonel under guard! The hetman wrote to Matveev asserting that Gursky was a good man and a loyal servitor of the tsar. He was not guilty of anything. He also stated that Doroshenko's army wished to cross over into Kanev and submit to the tsar. Now recognizing that there was some kind of trouble in Kanev, this was postponed. "For this reason, lord boyar," he wrote, "I beg your favor. Be so good as to intervene as a special mediator for Little Russian so that the great sovereign honors the liberties of our Host and his own decrees. Should the great sovereign not extend his grace to me and to the Zaporozhian Host by ordering the governor changed quickly, Kanev will be desolated, as it would have been long ago had not Mus-keteer Captains Karandeev and Lupandin held fast. It is very offensive to me and to the entire Host to speak as if I were a traitor to his majesty the tsar."

During the sojourn of the tsar's emissary in Baturin Gursky's wife, the quartermaster and the field ataman arrived there. "Without our colonel we are like small children without their mother," they said. "The enemy is near Kanev and soon will appear. What will we do without our colonel? Doroshenko's cossacks curse and shame us. 'Submit yourselves to the tsar, submit yourselves to the tsar!' they say. 'The tsar's bounty is favorable for you!' We would have dispersed long ago, had the musketeer captains not held fast.' The captains told the governor not to intervene in such matters. He should give orders only to the tsar's soldiers in the town. The colonel should be sent to the hetman, but the governor calls him and the captains traitors.

In Moscow it was considered necessary to conciliate the hetman. Volkonsky was replaced. "To large extent you have caused this by your own folly," the tsar's order to him on this occasion stated. "Forgetting our order, you infringed on their rights and liberties. For this we have ordered you confined to quarters for one day. When you arrive in Moscow our further decree will be communicated to you."

DISCUSSIONS ABOUT NEW CAMPAIGN ON WEST BANK

In 1675 the arrival of spring turned thoughts to a renewal of military activities. On April 26 the sovereign sent Romodanovsky and Samoilovich instructions to gather with the Belgorod and Sevsk regiments and the cossacks and to move to those places on the Dnieper river where it could be crossed conveniently. Arriving at the Dnieper they were to write to the Polish and Lithuanian hetmans to agree among themselves to which nearby places on the Dnieper they would march. When the Poles arrived they were to agree with them about a rendezvous along the following lines.

The two armies would unite on the other side of the Dnieper, near Korostyshev, or Motovilovka, or near Pavoloch because these localities were wooded and much forage was available. They should name the precise time and place for the rendezvous, specifying that the force include all Polish and Lithuanian forces, with infantry and artillery. Hostages must be given from both sides if necessary. Should the Turks and Tatars choose not go to war this year the armies of the two monarchs would not join. In that case, only a few Turks and Tatars were to remain with Doroshenko.

The tsar's armies would not move beyond Pavoloch, nor were they to be sent to its approaches, except for volunteer troops. When they met the enemy the king's armies must be allowed to give battle first. The tsar's armies must not march ahead, neither in advance, nor in retreat. Rather they must stand together as one and not abandon one another when in need. The tsar's forces were not to be restricted in regard to horse fodder or any supplies. The armies must remain unified until the enemy retreated. Further, agreement must be sought to extend the original peace for another ten years so the enemy, seeing the inclination of both sovereigns to live in brotherly accord, would abandon his intentions. In gratitude for the joint activities of the armies the king must be asked to cede in perpetuity all the conquered places.

Further, the Poles must recognize Hetman Samoilovich and not dishonor or reproach the Zaporozhian Host in any way. Were the king's hetmans to make a treaty with the sultan and the khan it must include an article stating that the latter's soldiers must not enter the tsar's borderlands with Turkey and the Crimea. In addition should the Turks and Tatars violate such a treaty their majesties the tsar and the king would march against them together.

On May 29 in Sumy Hetman Samoilovich with the council of elders responded [to the sovereign's directive] in the presence of Prince Romodanovsky and the tsar's emissary, the crown agent Semeon Yerofeevich Almazov. "There are many reasons that make it dangerous for us to unite all our forces with the Poles. Last winter, when the king was in the Ukraine and Sultan Haji-Girey[33] stood not far from there with six thousand soldiers, the Poles engaged in no battle of any significance with this horde. Rather they corresponded with the sultan and Doroshenko about peace. Rumors spread that the king was in the Ukraine not to repel the Turks but to seize the Ukraine and Kiev itself by one means or another. For this reason not only do we refuse to join the Polish forces, we even refuse to correspond with them on even the smallest matters. We have but one defender, the Orthodox monarch, his majesty the tsar.

"If the tsar wishes to assist the Poles he can send some Muscovite and cossack forces, but not all of them. It would be terrible to hand them as hostages to the Poles. In past years they gave the Turks hostages from Lvov, including members of the clergy, the gentry and the burghers, all distinguished men. The Turks did not honor their word and killed them after a time. Yes, for these reasons we cannot unite with the Poles. The Poles are an arrogant people. They will dishonor us and call us their subjects. Then the cossacks will stand firm for their rights and quarrels will erupt. Should the enemy appear at Kiev with all his forces we and the boyar will repel him, insofar as the merciful God lends help. This will be of great assistance to the king. Nonetheless, we refuse to join with the Poles because this leads only to violent quarrels."

"The Poles talk much about unification of the armies," said General Chancellor Savva Prokopov,[34] "but they do so with guile in their hearts. It is impossible to believe them. This past winter Senators Stanisław Jan Jabłonowski and Mikołaj Hieronim Sieniawski[35] came to Kiev to learn about the army and the city fortifications and any other news from Moscow. They presented themselves as simple members of the Polish gentry, as if they visited to make purchases. Thus they announced their intentions."

Romodanovsky and Samoilovich spoke in unison."If the great sovereign instructs us to march to the Crimea we hope to wreak great destruction there." Aide-de-Camp Yakov Lizogub, who previously followed Doroshenko, told Almazov "The vizier had a secret meeting with Doroshenko with only three present, Doroshenko, the vizier and I. 'We wish to take Kiev and Zaporozhia,' said the vizier. When the discussions ended Doroshenko said to me as he was leaving the tent, 'Did you hear what the vizier said? They will sell our hides!' Weeping he continued, 'God forbid that their plans be successful!'"

At the end of July, in response to news from the Ukraine, the tsar ordered Romodanovsky to move from Kursk to Sudzha and to dispatch capable people to the other side of the Dnieper to gather authentic information. He was to write to the king's hetman, Prince Dymitr Wisniowiecki, [informing him] that if the Polish and Lithuanian soldiers were not united and in agreement the tsar's soldiers would not join the king's hetman only.

At the beginning of August another order was received. Romodanovsky was to move from Sudzha and Samoilovich from Baturin to meet at the Dnieper with good men and cross by detachments. Samoilovich declared to the tsar's messenger that he was prepared to obey the order of the great sovereign, but first it was necessary to drive the Tatars away. There was no need to join with the Poles. "I, the hetman, and our whole Host prefer to die rather than to live dishonored and enslaved by the Poles. If the boyar and I cross the Dnieper this is tantamount to abandoning ourselves to the Poles. They have only to say that the Muscovite infantry is capable of holding the towns and against our will they will force us to seek out the khan in the open steppe and to try to recover Kamieniec Podolsky. They will call us peasants and claim us as their subjects, they will beat us with axes, demand provisions from us and berate us.

"If you call us up in the autumn, you must feed us. Moreover, now the cossacks are not allowing the Poles to pass and they are fighting the Turks and Tatars. What good can be expected? The cossacks will fight. We cannot unite with the Poles for a single moment! It is highly offensive to the Poles that on this side Little Russian people live under the rule of the tsar with many liberties, in peace and plenitude. The Poles constantly seek a ruse so they can take this side into their own hands, destroy it and ruin the people. In particular, the king's hetman Prince Dymitr Wiśniowiecki is striving for this because his family had property on this side.[36] Neither I nor the Host need the Polish and Lithuanian armies to come to the Dnieper. Rather it is essential that not a single Pole appear in these areas. The worth of their oath is well-known. After swearing an oath they surrendered Boyar Vasily Borisovich Sheremetev into Crimean captivity! Now they have abandoned their king in the Ukraine and scattered to their homes!"

RUSSIAN ARMY CAMPAIGNS ALONE

The unification of Russian and Polish soldiers was decisively rejected. At the beginning of autumn a separate movement of the Russian armies began. Romodanovsky and Samoilovich met by the Obechevskaia marsh, between the Galitsiia river and Priluki, about five versts from Monastyrishche and fifty versts from the Dnieper. From there they moved to Yagotin on September 11, where they camped until September 16. An inadequate supply of horse fodder and a *lack of firewood* compelled them to move closer to the Dnieper. On September 18 they came up to the river. They camped about ten versts from Kanev and sent a detachment of Muscovite soldiers to the other side of the river under the command of Major General Frants Vulf,[37] accompanied by cossack soldiers under the command of the general aide-de-camp Lysenko.

DOROSHENKO'S POSITION BECOMES UNTENABLE

Hearing about the approach of this army two of Doroshenko's regiments, composed of mercenary infantrymen,[38] abandoned the towns of Korsun, Bogoslavl, Cherkassy, Moshny and others and left for Chigirin. The inhabitants also abandoned their towns, villages and hamlets and crossed over to the eastern side of the river. This movement inspired great fear in Doroshenko. He begged in vain for assistance from the Turks and Tatars, who themselves were engaged in war with the Poles.

Although Romodanovsky and the hetman departed without launching anything of significance, the boyar going to Kursk and the hetman to Baturin, Doroshenko's position did not improve. He was becoming the target of burgeoning hatred because ultimately submission to the sultan turned out to have some very dire consequences in the Ukraine. Chigirin, as an eyewitness reported, was turned into a slave market. Everywhere on the streets Tatars displayed and sold captives,[39] even under the very windows of Doroshenko's home. If one of the people of Chigirin wished to buy the freedom of a countryman, for the sake of Christian charity, he attracted suspicion as one hostile to the guardians of the Ukraine, the Turks and the Tatars.

In the towns there was no limit to oppression from voracious Tatars. Curses against Doroshenko were on all lips. He might have been able to ignore these curses save for the fact that in Chigirin there was little grain because for two years none was sown. Only those who could buy grain secretly from the other side could feed themselves. In such dire circumstances Doroshenko decided to turn to Serko. "Was it possible to hold out in some way with the help of Zaporozhia? Could favorable conditions be obtained from the tsar? Could he remain hetman?"

At the end of September Serko informed Moscow of his loyal service. In accord with the tsar's order Prince Kaspulat Mutsalovich Cherkassky, Table Attendant Ivan Yurievich Leontiev, Musketeer Captain Lukoshkin, the murza Mazin with some Kalmyks, and Ataman Frol Minaev with some Don Cossacks had arrived in Zaporozhia. Serko joined them and on September 17 all participated in an attack against the Crimean camps. Beyond Perekop they destroyed a Tatar outpost, fell on the settlements, took many captives and freed many Christian souls. All returned safe and sound from the campaign.

Along with his report Serko presented a petition. "For a long time," he wrote, "I have campaigned against the enemy without sparing myself. Now I am weary from the administrative burden and from the frequent campaigns and I am disabled from wounds. My wife and children wander in the small Ukrainian town of Merekhva without shelter, my horses and livestock have been destroyed by Tatars and I, Ivan, am no longer fit for service in the field. There is no one to look after and comfort this old man. Merciful sovereign! Command me, your slave, to live in a small hut with my wife and children so that living apart I will not be utterly destroyed and die from old age without shelter. Command that I be given your charter so that living in my little hut no one will persecute me."

"The time has not yet come," the tsar replied, "for you to live at home with your wife and children. When that time comes, when hostilities are ended and peace reigns, we will reward you. We will permit you to live at home and will reassure you with our charter."

SERKO SEEKS TO MEDIATE FOR DOROSHENKO

Shortly after October 15, 1675 the field ataman announced another of his services. "Peter Doroshenko, hetman of the Zaporozhian Host, for many years intending to subject himself to the most illustrious throne of your majesty the tsar, could not do so because of the many obstacles erected by jealous people. Now, wishing to accomplish his intention, he has written to the Host of the lower rapids,[40] asking that we go to him for this good cause. After a general council of the Host we decided to visit him. As soon as we arrived in Chigirin with the Zaporozhian Host of the lower rapids and with part of the Don Cossack Host, Doroshenko immediately took an oath on the Holy Gospels in the presence of the clergy, all comrades both old and young, all of his own soldiers and the people of the community. He swore eternal submission to your majesty the tsar. In turn, we swore an oath to him that he would be received by your majesty the tsar with paternal graciousness. He would retain in their entirety, without harm to health, honor and chattels, all the towns, all his comrades and soldiers, the grants and military seals, without suffering vengeance for past crimes from any enemies, be they Tatars, Turks or Poles. As soldiers of his majesty the tsar, they would be defended. All desolated places on this (the western) side of the Dnieper would be resettled and comforted and assured of their liberties just as those on the other (the eastern) side of the Dnieper."

MOSCOW REJECTS SERKO'S MEDIATION

This Zaporozhian initiative infringed the order established at the last Council of Pereiaslav and greatly displeased Moscow. "You did this contrary to our instruction," the tsar replied to the field ataman, "and without informing Prince Romodanovsky and Hetman Samoilovich. We sent you no instruction about this. The order concerning Doroshenko's submission was sent to Prince Romodanovsky and Hetman Samoilovich. In the future, neither you nor the Zaporozhian Host of the lower rapids are to correspond with Doroshenko or interfere in this matter. Nor should you quarrel with Hetman Ivan Samoilovich. We know that you took the hetman's regalia from Doroshenko, which we gave to the previous hetman. You took the mace, staff and standard and carried them to Zaporozhia, and now you have the regalia. You must send these items immediately to Prince Romodanovsky and the hetman because hetmans in Zaporozhia have never had regalia before."

Serko continued to give orders. Passing over Samoilovich, hetman of both sides of the Dnieper, he distributed directives to the colonels. "I proclaim that *Hetman* Peter Doroshenko has broken from the Turkish sultan and the Crimean khan and has submitted himself to the high and powerful hand of his majesty the tsar. Therefore kindly cease internecine strife between Christian people and order others, of whom there are many, to cease, for this is not good for common Christian affairs. As we are all created by the one God, we must live in a fashion that pleases God and is praiseworthy before the people, so God will turn his wrath on the Muslims. Order all people to refrain from going to the other side of the Dnieper and to commit no offense of any kind." Again the tsar had to remind the field ataman that these matters were entrusted to Prince Romodanovsky and Hetman Samoilovich.

It is easy to understand how these events must have disturbed Samoilovich. He turned to Matveev, "to his benevolent patron." "More than once," wrote Samoilovich, "I was warned by good people to take into account Ivan Serko's unreliability and intrigues. I have already written to you, gracious boyar, how he petitioned the tsar for several cossack regiments under the pretense of making war in the Crimea. Then he petitioned to be allowed to remove his wife from the towns of Settlement Ukraine. Shortly thereafter he petitioned to include the town of Kereberda in the Poltava regimental district. At the same time he revealed a secret to his secretary, saying 'If only I could get into that corner, I would know what to do! I worry about only one thing, how I can collect an army, go to the town [of Kereberda] and start trouble there.'

"Doroshenko, seeing that he is not hetman over anyone (because from the Dniester to the Dnieper rivers there is not a human soul anywhere except where a Polish fort stands) summoned Serko to Chigirin. On October 10 he met Serko with the clergy, after a consensus was reached that the people wished to live under the tsar's rule. There is manifest duplicity here, as someone close to him informed us. He is receiving no assistance from the Turks or the Tatars, and the Poles are here as guests. Moreover, we are not far away. So look at him! To survive the winter somehow, receive food from our side and attract followers again, he spreads these rumors about becoming a subject of the tsar. Being particularly envious of our Ukraine, which lives in peace, Doroshenko and his followers agitate to make trouble here. During the past year, 1674, Serko impeded our good work. Now Ivan Stepanovich Mazepa and Vasily Leontievich Kochubey, both of whom were previously with Doroshenko, are with me. They report that Serko sent a message to Doroshenko saying 'If Moscow attacks you the Zaporozhian Host will assist you. Do not under any circumstances give the regalia to Moscow.'"

To Romodanovsky, Samoilovich wrote "Consider, my patron, these tangled affairs! They will do nothing for us but to some Frol or Miiuska, to some pretender from the Don who was brought to Serko, they swear some kind of oath! What kind of conscience does Doroshenko have? Ten times he has sworn an oath to us and ten times he lied! We found out, my patron, that they have taken counsel among themselves. They will try to petition his majesty the tsar through their emissaries. If he allows them to convene a black council they will pull this bank of the Ukraine into it. They will start trouble here but not submit to us."

Romodanovsky was as offended as the hetman by Doroshenko's action. Before October 12 Doroshenko informed him of the oath he had taken before Serko and Frol Minaev, and requested that good people be sent to Chigirin "for genuine discussions."

"When we stood by the Dnieper," Romodnovsky retorted, "you did not fulfill your promises according to my letter and your own dispatches. You did not come to us at our camp for the oath of allegiance. Now you request we send nobles to you for discussions. This astonishes me! When I and the loyal, steadfast subject of his majesty the tsar, hetman of both sides of the Dnieper, Ivan Samoilovich, zealously desired you to take the oath and to be reassured by the sovereign's bounty, you refused to do so *because of the difficulties* of your own customs. How can I send noblemen to you for discussions now? If in truth you have submitted to his majesty the tsar come to me and to Hetman Ivan Samoilovich and take the oath of allegiance before us."

Samoilovich's denunciation produced great dismay in Moscow. The tsar wrote to Romodanovsky and the hetman. "Now, as before, we put you in charge of the Doroshenko affair. Use your own judgment, but ensure the problem is resolved by spring and is not allowed to spread."

Finally, a communication from the tsar was dispatched to Chigirin. "The gracious word of his majesty the tsar to Peter Doroshenko. In truth we did not honor your promise, given before Ivan Serko and Frol Minaev, because they came to you in Chigirin without our instruction. These affairs of ours were not delegated to them and this important matter they could not witness. You, Peter, go to Boyar Prince Romodanovsky and Hetman Ivan Samoilovich and receive the oath of allegiance. If you do not go, we will order the boyar and the hetman to take action against you."

"I never begged to come to you before," Doroshenko replied to Romodanovsky. "The previous discussions were always about my safety. Now, having taken an oath to the great sovereign, we prepared an embassy to his majesty the tsar and informed your grace and Hetman Samoilovich about this. The hetman did not respond, while at his order the cossacks beyond the Dnieper plundered a Chigirin village above the Tiasmin river, a Pereiaslav colonel ruined many people near Cherkassy, and along the banks of the Dnieper a strong guard was established with the hetman's order not to allow my envoys to pass. I most humbly beg that you end this war with us as we are already subjects of the same sovereign, and send from there [the Dnieper] a good man to ensure the safety of our envoys. When this man comes to us we will release the envoys and the Turkish officials[41] to his majesty the tsar."

Doroshenko's emissary, falling at Romodanvosky's feet, begged "Let Doroshenko acquire the generous favor of the tsar through no one else, only through the benefaction of his excellence the boyar, so he will be safe and secure."

Receiving this letter from Doroshenko, Romodanovsky quickly dispatched a crown secretary to Samoilovich with an order to halt all hostile actions against Doroshenko and to send Colonel Vestov with two hundred foot soldiers to Chigirin to receive the envoys and the Turkish officials.

To Doroshenko himself Romodanovsky wrote "As a friend and well-wisher, zealously desiring your welfare and that you receive the tsar's favor, I advise your grace to meet me in Kursk with Colonel Vestov without any delay. From Kursk we will go to the great sovereign. If this is done I will show you great honor and convey you from Kursk with my own son, Prince Mikhail."

Doroshenko had no intention of ending this affair so quickly. At the end of December the Chigirin ataman, Ivan Senkeevich, arrived in Moscow on behalf of Doroshenko. "Peter Doroshenko directed me to petition," Senkeevich announced, "that his majesty the tsar reward Peter and the whole embassy and order a gracious instruction be prepared to reassure and give joy with his benevolent document. Thereby Peter, his kin and the whole embassy would fall under the high hand of his majesty the tsar in eternal subjection, their health and belongings and liberties irrevocably guaranteed. Doroshenko will serve the great sovereign and wish him every prosperity and, without desiring the hetman's regalia, be prepared to die if only he receives the sovereign's solicitude and favor.

"When Boyar Prince Romodanovsky and Hetman Ivan Samoilovich stood by the Dnieper river Doroshenko did not meet them to take the oath. Fearing for his health, and wishing to assure that those hostile to him on the West Bank of the Dnieper would not cross to the eastern side and do unto him as they had done to Samko and Briukhovetsky, he did not go to Boyar Prince Romodanovsky and Hetman Samoilovich to take the oath of allegiance when they were at the Dnieper river. Instead Doroshenko wrote to Zaporozhia, to the field ataman Ivan Serko, to come to Chigirin for a council and to act as witness when Doroshenko took the oath of allegiance to his majesty the tsar. When Serko arrived the oath was administered and the Host's regalia were handed to him. At this time Serko and the whole Host led Doroshenko to sign himself as hetman, pending the confirmation of the great sovereign.

"Doroshenko and the Turkish officials were subjects of the Turkish sultan and he accepted this [status] at a general council of all the elders. When in the course of time he receives both the document of the gracious sovereign and the document of reassurance from the Polish king, he will assemble the elders and ask which sovereign they choose. The elders wished the protection of the Turks and the Crimeans, yet when the sultan and the khan came to the Ukraine for their defense they destroyed the towns, killed many innocent people and seized others for slaves. At the same time his counsellors, laying the blame on Doroshenko and wishing the hetmancy for themselves, crossed to the East Bank along with the inhabitants of the area. Doroshenko, remembering the tsar's gracious missives and encountering no interference from anyones, broke away from the sultan and the Turkish officials and turned to the great sovereign through his father-in-law and his brother Andrei. The moment he receives full assurance through these emissaries he will come quickly to Moscow without any excuses. With him now are the towns of the Chigirin Regiment, Krylov, Voronovka, Buzhin, Borovitsa, Subbotovo, Medvedovka, Zhabotin, Cherkassy and Belozerie."

Senkeevich presented a document from the hetman. In it Doroshenko compared himself with the crippled invalid in the Gospel who had no one to lead him to the healing font. "I have no one," wrote Doroshenko, "to save me from this evil sickness, from the Muslim's yoke, to lead me to the healing font of the protection of your most powerful majesty the tsar. Be merciful, great sovereign tsar! Do not reject me and deny me the sight of your illustrious face. Be merciful! As the heavenly tsar Christ told the crippled invalid to rise, take up his bed and walk, order me to leave the shameful bed of the Muslim's yoke!"[42]

"All that has happened in the past shall be forgotten," responded the tsar. "Without any doubt whatsoever, come to this side of the Dnieper to Prince Romodanovsky and Hetman Ivan Samoilovich and take the oath of allegiance before them. If you wish to come to us in Moscow with your kinfolk you will receive our great benevolence and reward, and we will direct you be given leave to go to the Little Russian towns as before. We will permit you to live in whatever town you wish, without any offense or reproach."

For Hetman Ivan Samoilovich this was an unwanted guest. The hetman did not believe that Doroshenko would decide to come to the East Bank as a private person. He feared all kinds of trouble from Doroshenko and Serko, the calling of a council and his own overthrow. He sent a dispatch to Zaporozhia with a rebuke, asking how Ivan Serko and his comrades could go to Chigirin and there confirm Doroshenko in the hetmancy without the knowledge of the hetman and all the members of the Zaporozhian Host stationed in towns. Then he asked how they dared distribute dispatches to the colonels urging them to abandon their hostility to Doroshenko.

"Blood has already flowed for almost thirty years for our sins," Hetman Samoilovich wrote. "Every one of the good young men, fearing God and loving justice, knows that the West Bank was ruined thanks to Doroshenko, who brought misfortune on himself from all sides by subjecting himself to the Turkish sultan, under whom he lost the last of his people. When he saw there were few left, to remain hetman for a time he involved you in his schism. I exhort you! There is no need to summon a council in any of our towns, for his majesty the tsar will gain nothing. Already there have been two councils in four years."

To Almazov, the tsar's envoy, the hetman said "Serko and Doroshenko have a long-standing friendship and have sworn to one another to seek their common good. Now Serko will support Doroshenko. Were it not for Serko, Doroshenko would have come to Prince Romodanovsky or to me long ago."

In January 1676 noble emissaries arrived in Moscow as Doroshenko promised. These were Doroshenko's father-in-law, Pavel (Yanenko-) Khmelnitsky,[43] with his comrades and emissaries from Zaporozhia. They brought the Turkish officials, the staff and two taffeta standards. Asked why they came, the emissaries announced "Peter Doroshenko directed us to ask clemency from the great sovereign. He requests that his majesty the tsar forgive his faults and permit him to be taken under his high hand, retaining his original rank of hetman and the original regalia of the Host. In return he, Doroshenko, will serve forever, not sparing his health. Of course, the great sovereign shall decide about the hetman's rank.

"Peter Doroshenko further petitions the great sovereign to grant permission to him, his kin and the whole community to live as before on the other side of the Dnieper in his old settlements, with his possessions and liberties, just as the Little Russian inhabitants live in all peace and liberty on this side of the Dnieper, so that the churches of God on the other side are preserved from ruin and on this side all strife between households is prevented.

"Rumors circulate among us that we will be forced to desert our homes, burn the towns and move to this side. Peter Doroshenko petitions the tsar to do as he requests so that we will be defended from the Turkish sultan, the Crimean khan and the Polish king, the churches of God on the other side of the Dnieper will not be desolated, and the two sides of the river will not be separated. As soon as we return to Doroshenko with a gracious instruction in response to this petition he will come himself to petition the great sovereign. Until that time he will not come to Moscow or to the regiment to meet the boyar and hetman."

In response the emissaries were told they would be released to the custody of Prince Romodanovsky and Hetman Samoilovich and detained until Doroshenko crossed to this side of the river and took the oath of allegiance to the great sovereign. At the same time, Romodanovsky and the hetman were informed that "Considering the local situation if it is more appropriate to release Pavel Yanenko[-Khmelnitsky] and his comrades to Doroshenko in Chigirin, then do so. Act according to your own judgment guided by the Lord God, so that Doroshenko is absolutely reassured and crosses to this side of the Dnieper."

Further, an order was given regarding Doroshenko's petition that was presented by the emissaries. "The tsar graciously gives praise for your choosing to be subject to the tsar and for the delivery of the Turkish officials," the decree stated. "The oath of allegiance administered by Serko is not valid. The oath must be taken before Prince Romodanovsky and Hetman Samoilovich. All of your earlier crimes are forgiven. There is to be one hetman for both sides of the river, Ivan Samoilovich. The sovereign grants the town of Chigirin with all its settlements to Peter Doroshenko and the whole community. For the defense of Chigirin and Kanev government soldiers will be sent once Doroshenko takes the oath before the boyar and the hetman, promising for all eternity to be a subject of the tsar. Doroshenko may live where he wishes. He will not be persecuted in any way. Doroshenko's brother Grigory will be freed and sent to the boyar and the hetman."

EVENTS ON DON

In the areas of the Ukraine near the Dnieper affairs began to take a favorable turn for Moscow. In another borderland, near the other cossack river, the Don, this was not the case. The year 1674 passed uneventfully. Prince Peter Ivanovich Khovansky, the new governor who replaced Ivan Savostianovich Khitrovo (the elder), arrived at the Don late. He went to inspect the place on the Miius river where a fort was to be built and found it was impossible to build anything there. The governor's report to the tsar was filled with news about government soldiers deserting.

In the summer of 1675 the sovereign sent an order to the Don instructing them to go to the cossack navigation channel,[44] excavate there and construct a fort. Khovansky discussed the order secretly with Ataman Kornil Yakovlev, who gathered a circle[45] in Cherkassk to announce the order. The cossacks retorted they could not excavate the channel, build a fort and, when the time came, sit out a siege with so few men. With these words the circle dispersed with a shout. The field ataman called them back to the circle and for the last time asked "Tell me in one word. Will you excavate the channel and build a fort or not? Do this so that I may write truthfully to the great sovereign."

The cossacks wished to leave the circle without committing themselves to anything definite. Ataman Kornil Yakovlev began to shout and threaten saying they must resolve the issue before leaving the circle, striking two or three cossacks with his staff. The cossacks raised a shout, threw themselves on the ataman and beat him. They wished to beat one of the elders, Rodion Kaluzhanin, to death but he fled waving a knife and hid with Khovansky in the new fort, where the tsar's soldiers were stationed.

Three days later Khovansky proceeded to Cherkassk, taking Rodion with him. After the church service the governor sought to convince the cossacks to abandon their disobedience and take counsel with the elders. The cossacks pardoned Rodion and allowed him to live in Cherkassk as before, but Kornil Yakovlev was removed from the post of ataman and replaced by Mikhailo Samarenin.[46]

After electing a new ataman the cossacks gathered in a circle and discussed whether they should go to the navigation channel and see whether they could dredge and build a fort. Khovansky proceeded to the channel, taking about four thousand government soldiers with him. Ataman Mikhailo Samarenin visited the channel also, taking about three thousand cossacks. They examined the site and found that it was possible to build two forts along the channel, but a third fort could not be built on the shoreline facing Azov because the land would not bear the weight of a stone structure. "We will build the forts," Khovansky told the cossacks. "You will man them and receive a stipend from the sovereign."

"Even if the sovereign granted us a stipend of a hundred rubles we would refuse to man the forts," the cossacks replied. "We would be happy to die for the sake of the sovereign, even without the forts, but thirteen thousand soldiers are needed to man these forts, and in total we have only about six thousand cossacks on the whole river."

Having examined the navigation channel, they all returned to Cherkassk. The cossacks began to talk among themselves, saying they should put to sea for action against enemies and take booty for themselves. About three thousand of these cossacks gathered and sent a messenger to Khovansky requesting government soldiers to assist them. The governor himself came to escort them to the channel with four thousand soldiers.

As the party approached the navigation channel, arriving at the same place they had reconnoitered earlier, they found observation towers and entrenchments constructed along the other side of the channel, near Azov, manned by soldiers from Azov with cannon. Bullets and cannon balls began to whistle. The Russians dug trenches on their side and bombarded the enemy across the river for five days and nights. They killed many and took three prisoners alive. With this they were satisfied. The cossacks, discovering there were warships moored near Azov, grew frightened. They did not put to sea. Instead they all returned to Cherkassk.

When news of these events reached Moscow an angry missive from the sovereign was dispatched to Khovansky on the Don. "The cossacks act, forgetting the fear of God and in contempt of our grant," wrote the tsar. "In Moscow Ataman Rodion Kaluzhanin petitioned in the name of the whole Host asking that we order the cossacks and our soldiers to dredge the channel and build three forts along it. He said that the cossacks were prepared to man these forts if given a grant of ten rubles per man. Further he said that these forts could hold not only Azov under siege, but Constantinople itself. Now the cossacks have refused you everything and have dishonored their own elders! We will forgive them in accordance with the request of our sons, the tsareviches, only if they go quickly to the channel and build the forts. If they do not do this they will not receive our grant and we will forbid our towns to permit supplies to pass through to them, on pain of death."

The letter was read to the cossacks in a circle. In response they raised a clamor. Abusing Khovansky because the letter was sent in response to his letter, they refused to go to the channel. To mitigate the refusal in some way the field ataman and the elders announced to Khovansky they could not come to any decision without convening a council which would include the cossacks from the forts of the upper Don.

There was another reason for the clamor among the cossacks. The tsar demanded the notorious thief Senka Buianko[47] be surrendered. Kornil Yakovlev and other good cossacks agreed to surrender Buianko then other cossacks shouted at Kornil "You have acquired the habit of carting us off to Moscow, like slaves from Azov. Be careful or you will suffer the same fate as Razin.[48] If Buianko is surrendered, we can expect dispatches from Moscow until the last cossack is gone!"

Rodion Kaluzhanin stepped forward in the circle and spoke, saying "You scorn the command of the great sovereign because of one man. Do you recall what you said, laying in the reeds under the watch tower? You said a fort must be built on the channel, that the fort would be besieged in place of Azov and the cossacks would have a free path to the sea. In accordance with these your own words I informed the great sovereign when I was in Moscow, but now you have become fickle in everything."

Frol Minaev supported Rodion, confirming his words. A shout was raised against both of them. "You both gain by this. You collect your reward[49] [from the tsar] and destroy the Don. You, Frol, are to be congratulated! You play one side off against the other!"[50] Only one voice was silent, the voice of Ataman Mikhailo Samarenin. It is unlikely he could have said anything to calm the cossacks! From this time forth the cossacks treated the tsar's soldiers badly, cursed them as butchers, fought with the musketeers, plundered them and refused them justice.

As usual messengers had to be elected in the winter camp to be sent to Moscow. They elected Kornil Yakovlev and other cossacks who were distinguished by their zeal toward the sovereign. Kornil said he would not go to the winter camp. "I went to Moscow before and I reported to the great sovereign about our service. Now what can I tell him? That you are completely disobedient to him?"

The cossacks raised a great commotion. "If you do not go," they shouted, "we will fetter you together with the outcast Rodion and do the same to you as you did to Razin."[51] After these threats Kornil could no longer refuse. "Look," the cossacks shouted at him, "go to Moscow and don't say much of anything. Say only that they should remove their soldiers. We have enough soldiers without them!"

It was reported to Khovansky that in all the barracks in all the forts the cossacks were gathering to attack the government soldiers. These cossacks wished to kill the Muscovite musketeers and give free rein to the town musketeers. "There are only a few Muscovite musketeers," the cossacks were reported as saying, "and the borderland musketeers will not fight against us. If the sovereign sends a large army to the Don we will make peace with Azov and raise the Crimea. We will kill the elders who did not support Razin and who are well-disposed towards the sovereign so they will not carry the news to Moscow."

It was reported further that the soldiers who deserted the regiments were being persuaded by the cossacks to remain with them. There would be many of these deserters in the spring and they would remain on the Don. In all the forts the cossacks allowed rumors to circulate that the musketeers would not go to Moscow for anything. According to the rumors Boyar Matveev had ordered that, for each of his own men [killed], two companies of musketeers must be cut down.

When they heard on the Don that Khovansky had dispatched this news to Moscow the council of elders came to him with explanations. "We heard," they said, "that some drunken cossacks in the upper forts began to agitate and babble inappropriate words and that you, prince, wrote about this to the sovereign. We reassure you that the cossacks in the lower forts do not and have not entertained any malicious intentions. They serve the sovereign in accordance with their oath of allegiance and will continue to serve his heirs. If the drunken cossacks in the upper forts have rebelled we will seek out these bandits and punish them without mercy."

APPENDIX

COSSACK RANKS IN THE HETMANATE

The Cossack Hetmanate, founded in the middle of the seventeenth century, was organized hierarchically. Although later assimilated, influenced and ultimately abolished by Moscow its institutions originated independently. Therefore cossack ranks did not correlate to those used in the various Russian services in the second half of the century. With few exceptions, cossack ranks in this volume have been translated in accordance with George Gajecky, *The Cossack Administration of the Hetmanate*, 2 vols. (Cambridge, Mass., 1978). The brief description of the organization of the hetmanate offered here is based on Gajecky's much more detailed description.

At the center of the hetmanate were the hetman and the officers of the general staff. The hetman was the chief officer of the organization, and institutionally above the general staff. Originally he was elected by all cossacks at a general council. By the time of events in this volume the hetman elected required the approval of the Russian government.

The general staff consisted of seven to nine members who in this period either were elected at a general council or appointed by the hetman. The general quartermaster (generalnyi oboznyi) was second in command within the hetmanate, after the hetman, and acted as head of the general staff council. He was responsible for artillery and military supplies, and possibly for the maintenances of fortresses within the hetmanate. He served as acting hetman when the need arose.

Two general judges (generalni suddi) headed the general court of the hetmanate, hearing appeals as well as cases of the first instance. Generally one judge, assisted by a legal scribe, heard a case, although when important cases were being tried, other members of the general staff council could serve on the bench of the court as well. Further, the general judges could be sent by the hetman to adjudicate disputes within the regiments, or appointed to serve as envoys on foreign missions.

A general chancellor (generalnyi pysar) managed the hetman's chancellery and supervised his correspondence. The general chancellor also directed the diplomatic affairs of the hetmanate, supervised the archives and served as "keeper of the keys" with the authority to sign the hetman's decrees in his absence. It was not unusual for a general chancellor to act as confidante of the hetman, and to attend to his personal affairs.

The office of general treasurer (generalnyi pidskarbii) was instituted during the time of Bogdan Khmelnitsky, but did not become a part of the general staff until 1728. For obvious reasons the hetmans preferred to control the treasury themselves. In the period covered by this volume only one general treasurer served for a very brief time. Roman Rakushka-Romanovsky held the post from 1663 to 1668.

Two general aides-de-camp (generalni osauly) were appointed to the general staff council. Their primary function was military. They sometimes served as acting hetman when the occasion arose. With respect to the general staff they served as envoys and were responsible for the internal security of the hetmanate. They also commanded the mercenary troops that in the period covered by this volume served the hetman, and were available for *ad hoc* assignments.

Finally there was a general flag bearer (generalnyi khorunzhyi) and a general standard bearer (generalnyi bunchuzhnyi). These were the lowest ranking officers of the general staff. The general flag bearer carried the great military banner at the election of a new hetman, or when launching a campaign. He also might serve as an envoy, or carry out special assignments for the hetman. For the majority of the period covered by this volume the general standard bearer was an officer of the hetman's court. He became a member of the general staff only in 1675. The general standard bearer displayed the horsetail standard of the hetman (the bunchuk) during ceremonies and on campaign. He was available also for special tasks assigned by the hetman.

The hetmanate was divided into territorial units called regiments, and these were further subdivided into companies. The number of regiments and companies during this period fluctuated and their boundaries were fluid. The offices within a regiment paralleled those within the general staff. Each regiment was led by a colonel (polkovnik) elected by the cossacks of the regiment and ratified by the hetman. The colonel was the chief military officer of a regiment. He was also the chief civil official responsible for implementing the orders of the hetman, as well as for the collection of taxes, tolls and duties, providing police protection, maintaining roads, bridges and fortifications, etc. In addition, a regimental colonel was a member of the general council of officers that met regularly and advised the hetman.

The regimental quartermaster (polkovyi oboznyi) was responsible for a regiment's artillery, munitions and supplies, and for maintaining the fortifications in the territory. Two regimental justices (polkovi suddi) administered justice in the territory, although the right to impose the death penalty was reserved to the regimental colonel. The regimental chancellor (polkovyi pysar) supervised the administration of a regiment's chancellery. Generally he came from the general chancellery where he had served time learning his business as a scrivener or clerk (pidysok). Among his myriad duties was keeping the register of cossacks current. Two aides-de-camp (osauly) served as administrative assistants to the colonel, commanded detachments during campaigns, and sometimes served as acting colonels when the need arose. There was also a regimental flag bearer (khorunzhyi).

Companies were ruled by captains (sotnyky). A captain had a small staff, including a scribe, an aide-de-camp, a flag bearer, and several camp atamans (kurinni otamany). The latter commanded cossacks in outlying villages or settlements; these camps or settlements were the smallest territorial units within the hetmanate. The captain like the colonel was chief military and civil officer in his territory. He also served on the regimental council (Polkova Rada), which convened when occasion demanded.

NOTES

Additional information on personalities and topics found in the text and notes is available in Joseph L. Wieczynski, et al., eds., *The Modern Encyclopedia of Russian, Soviet and Eurasian History* (MERSH, formerly *The Modern Encyclopedia of Russian and Soviet History*); Harry B. Weber, et al., eds., *The Modern Encyclopedia of East Slavic, Baltic and Eurasian Literatures* (MESBEL, formerly *The Modern Encyclopedia of Russian and Soviet Literatures, Including Non-Russian and Emigré Literatures*); Paul D. Steeves, ed., *The Modern Encyclopedia of Religions in Russia and Eurasia* (MERRE, formerly *The Modern Encyclopedia of Religions in Russia and the Soviet Union*); and David R. Jones, ed., *The Military Encyclopedia of Russia and Eurasia* (MERE, formerly *The Military-Naval Encyclopedia of Russia and the Soviet Union*) all published by Academic International Press.

PREFACE and INTRODUCTION

1. There is no biography of Soloviev in English. In Russian, see Sergei M. Soloviev, *Moi zapiski dlia detei moikh* (My Notes for My Children). Ed. by Nadezhda Zilper (Newtonville, Mass., 1980) and V.E. Illeritskii, *Sergei Mikhailovich Soloviev* (Moscow, 1980). For an assessment of Soloviev's place in Russian historiography, see Anatole G. Mazour, *Modern Russian Historiography. A Revised Edition* (Westwood, Conn., 1975), pp. 113-119.

2. A bogatyr is a hero in Russian epics and folklore, an individual of truly Herculean proportions and superhuman capacities.

3. See C. Bickford O'Brien, *Muscovy and the Ukraine from the Pereiaslavl Agreement to the Truce of Andrusovo, 1654-1667* (Berkeley, 1963), Chapter 6, and for a summary of the terms of the agreement of Andrusovo, pp. 115-119; A.N. Kopylov, "Andrusovo, Armistice of" in Vol. 1, pp. 226-227 of *The Modern Encyclopedia of Russian, Soviet and Eurasian History* (Academic International Press: Gulf Breeze, Fla., 1976-), hereafter MERSH, and *Supplement,* hereafter SMERSH. For extracts from these treaties in English, see George Vernadsky, ed., Sergei G. Pushkarev, comp., *A Source Book for Russian History from Early Times to 1917,* Vol. 3. *Early Times to the Late Seventeenth Century* (New Haven, Conn., 1972), pp. 304-306.

4. In the seventeenth century the Sejm, or Diet, consisted of the House of Delegates and the Senate. Along with the king these comprised the three component estates of the Rzeczpospolita obojga narodów (The Commonwealth of Two Nations) created by the amalgamation of the kingdom of Poland and the grand duchy of Lithuania at the Union of Lublin in 1569. Every landholding

noble in the realm was entitled to participate in the provincial bodies, or dietines and through them to elect representatives to the House of Delegates in the National Diets, which by law was convened at least every two years. Senators to the upper house were appointed to a life term by the king from among the wealthiest and most powerful nobles, or magnates, in the realm. The Jagiellonian dynasty died out in 1572 and thereafter the kings of the Commonwealth were elected. In effect the nobility controlled the Commonwealth, and the nobility were incessantly, and often violently, in conflict among themselves and with other orders, such as the burghers. Moreover, political disagreement and conflict were inextricably intertwined with religious disagreement and conflict among Roman Catholics, Orthodox, Protestants and Uniates, conflicts which sharpened in the course of the seventeenth century. "The Commonwealth was," as Frank Sysyn describes it, "a heterogeneous state and society held together mainly by a patriotic nobility that was able to manage the rest of the population." Throughout the seventeenth century the ties that bound grew increasingly frayed. See Frank E. Sysyn, *Between Poland and the Ukraine. The Dilemma of Adam Kysil, 1600-1653* (Cambridge, Mass., 1985), pp. 9-20 and *passim;* Norman Davies, *God's Playground. A History of Poland,* Vol. 1. *The Origins to 1795* (Oxford, 1981), pp. 321-372 and *passim.*

    5. There is a dearth of recent literature on the hetmanate in English or other western languages. I have made extensive use of George Gajecky, *The Cossack Administration of the Hetmanate,* 2 vols. (Cambridge, Mass., 1978). This is an excellent resource for identifying individual cossack officers and following their careers, and a foundation for further research on the cossack administration. For recent literature in languages other than English, see Mykola Zharkykh, *Bibliohrafiia staroi Ukrainy, 1240-1800 gg.* (Bibliography of Old Ukraine, 1240-1800) (Kiev 1998).

    6. Institutionally the metropolitanate of Kiev was under the jurisdiction of the patriarch of Constantinople. In support of its efforts to assimilate the Ukraine the Moscow government worked to gain control of the metropolitanate of Kiev, and thus control of the Ukrainian Orthodox church, by transferring it to the jurisdiction of the patriarch of Moscow and all Russia. In the Treaty of Pereiaslav concluded between Moscow and Hetman Bogdan Khmelnitsky in 1654, an article was included allegedly asserting that the metropolitan of Kiev and all the clergy would be under the authority of the patriarch of Moscow, with the understanding that he would not interfere in the rights of the Ukrainian clergy. This controversial article was included in a later version of the 1654 agreement signed in 1659 at Gadiach, and became a bone of contention and a focal point for power struggles within the Ukraine as well as a source of friction between the Moscow government and the patriarch of Constantinople. See John Basarab, *Pereiaslav 1654. A Historiographical Study* (Edmonton, 1982), pp. 9-10, and Appendix 1, article 18, p. 234; Appendix 3, article 6, p. 242; Appendix 4, article 8, p. 247.

    In 1659 Moscow appointed Archbishop Lazar Baranovich of Chernigov locum tenens or vicar (acting metropolitan until a permanent one was selected) of the Kievan metropolitanate, despite the fact that Metropolitan Dionysios Balaban of Kiev who held the post through Constantinople was still alive, though residing on the Right Bank. In 1661, annoyed with Baranovich for not showing sufficient zeal in pursuing Moscow's interests, the Moscow government appointed Bishop Methodios of Mstislavl (the archpriest Maksim Filimonovich or Filimonov, who took the name Methodios when tonsured in 1661) vicar of Kiev in Baranovich's place. In response the patriarch of Constantinople acted on a request by Metropolitan Balaban and Hetman Yury Bogdanovich Khmelnitsky and excommunicated Methodios in 1662. Initially Bishop Methodios's appointment was accepted in Kiev. By the time Metropolitan Balaban died on May 10, 1663 Methodios's activities had eroded his support and the Kievan clergy were petitioning for his removal. See Ivan Wlasowsky, *Outline History of the Ukrainian Orthodox Church*, Vol. 2. Trans. by Mykola Haydak and Rev. Frank Estocin, ed. by Ivan Korowytsky (New York, 1979), pp. 132-134; Vitalii Einghorn, *Ocherki iz istorii Malorossii v XVII v. Snosheniia malorossiiskago dukhovenstva s moskovskim pravitelstvom v tsarstvovanie Alekseia Mikhailovicha* (Essays on the History of Little Russia in the Seventeenth Century. The Relations of the Little Russian Clergy with the Moscow Government During the Reign of Alexis Mikhailovich) (Moscow, 1899), Chapter 3.

7. The Eternal Peace was signed by Russia and the Polish Commonwealth on May 6, 1686 and ratified by both powers by the end of the year. Five years earlier, on January 13, 1681, a twenty-year truce was signed by Russia, the Ottoman Turks and the Crimean khanate at Bakhchisaray recognizing Russian claims to Left Bank Ukraine and authority over the Zaporozhian Cossacks.

8. N.I. Kostomarov, *Istoricheskye monografii i issledovaniia* (Historical Monographs and Studies), 21 vols. (St. Petersburg, 1903-1906), and see G. Karpov, *Kostomarov kak istorik Malorosii* (Kostomarov as an Historian of Little Russia/Ukraine) (Moscow, 1871); Mykhailo S. Hrushevsky, *History of Ukraine-Rus'*, 10 vols. in 11 books (Lviv, 1898-1931; reprint Kiev, 1991-1997) is currently being translated and edited by the Canadian Institute of Ukrainian Studies at the University of Alberta, under the direction of Frank E. Sysyn. Volumes 1 and 7 have been published by the University of Toronto Press, and others are in process. An edited one-volume edition of Hrushevsky's work is *A History of the Ukraine*. Ed. by O.J. Frederickson, with a preface by George Vernadsky (New Haven, Conn., 1942. Reprint Archon Books, 1970). It does not, and perhaps could not do justice to his accomplishment. Hrushevsky's work is Ukrainocentric in response to the Russo-centric orientation of Soloviev and other contemporaries, but in the breadth of its conception and the resources used it owes much to Soloviev's approach.

9. Some but by no means all of this material has been published in document collections. See *Akty, otnosiashchiesia k istorii Iuzhnoi i Zapadnoi Rossii, sobrannye i izdannye Arkheograficheskoiu komissieiu* (Acts Relating to the History of Southern and Western Russia, Collected and Published by the Archeographical Commission), 15 Vols. in 13 (St. Petersburg, 1862-1892); D.I.

Bantysh-Kamenskii, *Istochniki malorossiiskoi istorii* (Sources of Little Russian History) (Moscow 1858); *Sobrannie gosudarstvennykh gramot i dogorov, khraniashchikhsia v Gosudarstvennoi kollegii inostrannykh del* (Collection of State Documents and Treaties, Preserved in the State College of Foreign Affairs), 4 Vols. (Moscow, 1826); *Akty Istoricheskie, sobrannye i izdannye Arkheograficheskoiu komissieiu* (Historical Acts, Collected and Published by the Archeographical Commission), 5 Vols. (St. Petersburg, 1841-1842); *Dopolneniia k Aktam Istoricheskim, sobrannye i izdannye Arkheograficheskoiu komissieiu* (Supplements to the Historical Acts, Collected and Published by the Archeographical Commission), 12 Vols. (St. Petersburg, 1846-1872); *Pamiatniki diplomaticheskikh snoshenii drevnei Rossii s derzhavami inostrannymi* (Memorials of the Diplomatic Relations of Ancient Russia with Foreign Powers), 10 Vols. (St. Petersburg, 1851-1871).

10. *Letopis' sobytii v Iugo-Zapadnoi Rossii v XVII veke, izdannaia Vremennoiu Komissieiu dlia razbora drevnikh aktov* (Chronicle of Events in Southwestern Russia in the Seventeenth Century, Published by the Temporary Commission for the Sorting of Ancient Acts), Vol. 2. *Samoil Velichko* (Kiev, 1851).

11. *Reszty rekopismu Jana Chryzostoma na goslawcach Paska* (The Writings of Jan Chryzostom Pasek). Ed. by S.A. Lachowicza (Wilno, 1843). This has been translated into English and edited by Catherine S. Leach, as *Memoirs of the Polish Baroque. The Writings of Jan Chryzostom Pasek, a Squire of the Commonwealth of Poland and Lithuania* (Berkeley, Cal., 1976) and is cited in the notes below. See Leach's preface, pp. xv-xxiii, for a discussion of the manuscript, as well as Lachowicza's edition.

12. Soloviev used this in a Russian translation, published in *Chteniia v Obshchestve istorii i drevnostei rossiiskikh* (Readings in the Society of History and Russian Antiquities), 1 (1846).

13. Zharkykh, *Bibliohrafiia* and Note 5 above.

14. For institutions in the West supporting the study of Ukrainian language, culture and history, a useful web site is located at http://www.brama.com/diaspora/edu.html.

CHAPTER I

1. The Thirteen Years War, or the Russo-Polish War of 1654-1667, was a series of conflicts between Russia and Poland-Lithuania centered in the Ukraine. The conflict ended with the signing of the Treaty of Andrusovo, the terms of which favored Moscow (see Introduction, p. xiii). The Thirteen Years War marked a change in the balance of power in Eastern Europe. Poland-Lithuania entered a period of decline and Russia moved to the fore as a major European power. See Bickford O'Brien, *Muscovy and the Ukraine*; also the entry by Chester Dunning, MERSH, Vol. 32, pp. 138-144.

2. Nikon (1605-1681), born Nikita Minich Minin, was consecrated patriarch of Moscow and All Russia on July 25, 1652. He was selected to implement a broad-ranging program of church reform, and undoubtedly enjoyed the firm support of Tsar Alexis Mikhailovich. Patriarch Nikon's approach to reform immediately generated opposition from other clergy close to the court and equally interested in church reform. Faced with this opposition and the increasing coolness of the tsar towards himself and his activities, Nikon abandoned the patriarchal throne on July 10, 1658. Nikon's unprecedented action threw the Russian church into disarray and it remained without an effective head for nine years. The Church Council of 1666/1667 deposed Nikon and exiled him to the Ferapont monastery. At the same time it affirmed the program of church reform and branded his opposition as heretics. In the following decades opposition to the program of church reform continued, burgeoning into the movement popularly known as Old Belief. For translated sources relating to this "Nikon Affair," see William Palmer, *The Patriarch and the Tsar*, 6 vols. (London, 1871-1876). For interpretations perhaps the most accessible treatment in English remains S.M. Soloviev's, in Volume 21 of this series. For other works in English see the relevant sections in Philip Longworth, *Alexis Tsar of All the Russias* (London, 1984), Joseph T. Fuhrmann, *Tsar Alexis. His Reign and His Russia* (Academic International Press, 1981), N. Lupinin, *Religious Revolt in the XVIIth Century. The Schism of the Russian Church* (Princeton, 1984). For Nikon's career see the entry by Edward Orchard, MERSH, Vol. 25, pp. 4-10. The two eastern patriarchs referred to by Soloviev were Patriarch Paisios of Alexandria and Patriarch Makarios of Antioch.

3. Karp Mokrievich, or Karpo Mokriievych was general chancellor of the hetmanate from 1669 to 1672, and later served as a judge in the Chernigov Regiment (1688-1690). In 1667 he was probably a clerk or notary in the general military chancellery of the hetmanate. See Gajecky, *Cossack Administration*, Vol. 1, p. 77; Vol. 2, p. 665. Here Soloviev refers to him as Karp Mokrievich whereas in Chapter III and other places Soloviev calls him Karp Mokriev, or Karp Ivanovich Mokriev. In the interests of consistency and clarity I have used Karp Mokrievich throughout.

4. Ivan Martynovich Briukhovetsky was hetman on the Left Bank of the Ukraine from 1663 to 1668. In the following pages Soloviev relates the problems leading to Briukhovetsky's downfall. For his earlier career, see Volume 20 of this series.

5. In the seventeenth century the principalities of Wallachia and Moldavia, located in the Balkans on territory north of the Danube and south of the Pruth rivers, now incorporated in Rumania, were subject to the Ottoman empire. Hospodar, a word meaning "lord", was the title of dignity given by the Ottoman Porte to the governors appointed to Wallachia and Moldavia. The sultan at this time was Mehmed IV (1648-1687).

6. The town of Targovitsa is on the Syniukha river, approximately forty-five kilometers southeast of Uman and quite close to the territories and influence of

the Crimean khanate. Between 1664 and 1676 a Cossack regiment was attached to Targovitsa and this regiment remained consistently loyal to the hetman on the Right Bank of the Ukraine, Peter Doroshenko (hetman 1665-1676). See Gajecky, *Cossack Administration*, Vol. 2, pp. 642, 654. The Crimean khan at the time was Adil-Girey (1666-1671).

The notion that silver rather than copper money would attract popular support was not ill-founded. Copper was, and was perceived as being less valuable than silver. When the tsar's government, chronically short of money, sought to solve its fiscal difficulties by debasing the currency, replacing silver coinage with copper, it stimulated inflation and popular discontent and often led to rioting. Patrick Gordon, an immigrant Scottish soldier who sought to make his fortune in the service of the Russian tsar, complained upon his arrival in 1661 that the worst thing about Russian service was that "the pay was small, and in base copper coin, which passed at four to one of silver." In July 1662 this same Patrick Gordon witnessed and described the so-called Copper Riot, writing that "about 4 or 5000 men without arms, only some had clubs and sticks, ...pretended a redress as to the copper money, salt and other diverse things, papers having been to that purpose placked on in diverse places of the city [Moscow], and a writer reading a paper before the *Zemsky Dvor* [City Hall], containing their grievances, with the names of some persons whom they deemed guilty of abuses, inviting all to go to the tsar and seek redress and the heads of the evil counsellors...." The riot was brutally suppressed with hundreds tortured and executed and more exiled to Siberia. The Copper Riot of 1662 had not been forgotten by government officials in 1667. See Paul Dukes, *The Making of Russian Absolutism, 1613-1801* (London, 1982), pp. 31-32.

Despite his disappointment with the wages Patrick Gordon remained and served the tsar for thirty-eight years, from 1661 to 1699. His diary and letters offer a unique perspective on Muscovite life in that period. The original of the diary is in Moscow, in the Central State Military-Historical Archive (fond 846, op. 15, ed. khr. 1-7). Some of the letters are in London, in the British Library (Manuscripts, Add. 41842). Some of this material has been published. See P. Gordon, *Passages from the Diary of General Patrick Gordon of Auchleuchries, A.D. 1635-A.D. 1699* (Aberdeen, 1859); S. Konovalov, ed., "Sixteen Further Letters of General Patrick Gordon," *Oxford Slavonic Papers*, 13 (1967), pp. 72-95; M.A. Obolenski and M.C. Posselt, eds., *Tagebuch des Generals Patrick Gordon, während seiner Kriegsdienste unter den Schweden und Polen vom Jahre 1655 bis 1661, und seines Aufenthaltes in Russland vom Jahre 1661 bis 1699*. 3 volumes (Moscow and Leipzig, 1849).

7. Throughout the 1650s and 1660s Russia engaged in a complex series of military campaigns, interspersed with negotiations, against Poland and Sweden in efforts to regain territories in the Ukraine, White Russia and the Baltic region, lost as a result of the Time of Troubles. This protracted struggle drained the Russian treasury with little result. In these struggles the cossack hetmanate played an important and inconsistent role. At the battle of Konotop, June 28, 1659,

Russian forces led by Prince Semeon Romanovich Pozharsky and Prince Semeon Petrovich Lvov were annihilated by cossack forces led by Hetman Ivan Astafievich Vygovsky (1657-1659) assisted by the forces of the Crimean khan. Both Pozharsky and Lvov were taken captive, handed over to the Crimean khan and died in captivity. Konotop was a fortress-town situated on the Yezych river, about seventy-five kilometers northeast of Nezhin. For Soloviev's account of these events, see Vol. 20 of this series.

8. See above, Preface and Introduction, Note 6. At a cossack council held in Nezhin in 1663 to elect a new hetman Bishop Methodios, Moscow's appointment as vicar of Kiev, supported the successful candidature of Ivan Martynovich Briukhovetsky. Despite the support, on assuming the post Briukhovetsky moved to diminish the power and influence of the clergy in general and of Bishop Methodios in particular. Thus he proposed that the Kievan see be filled by a Great Russian appointed by Moscow. Rumors of Briukhovetsky's action spread throughout Kiev, causing considerable anger, and Briukhovetsky wavered. In March 1666 a delegation from the now alienated Bishop Methodios and the Kievan clergy, headed by Melety Dzik, abbot of the Kiev St. Cyril monastery, traveled to Moscow to petition to be allowed to elect a metropolitan for the see of Kiev. About the same time Bishop Methodios and Archbishop Lazar Baranovich arrived in Moscow to attend the Church Council of 1666/1667, convened to resolve the Nikon affair. As this passage suggests, the issue of the Kievan see still was not resolved in 1667. Here Hetman Briukhovetsky, who was also in Moscow with Colonel Matvey Gvintovka of the Nezhin Regiment, is arguing for his own solution, one which could only further agitate the clergy in Kiev.

9. Bogdan Mikhailovich Khmelnitsky (c. 1595-1657) was hetman from January 1648 to August 6, 1657. He led the cossacks of Polish Ukraine in rebellion in 1648, a part of the wave of rebellions that marked the year in Europe. This phase of turmoil ended with the Treaty of Pereiaslav in 1654. See Mykhailo Hrushevsky, *History of Ukraine-Rus'*, Vol. III, Parts 2, 3, Vol. IX, Parts 1, 2 (Toronto, forthcoming); G. Vernadsky, *Bohdan, Hetman of Ukraine* (New Haven, 1941); and Sysyn, *Between Poland and Ukraine*, Chapter 6 and *passim.*

10. Grigory or Grishka Guliantisky, as colonel of the Nezhin Regiment, led his cossacks in a heroic three-month defense of Konotop in 1659 (see Note 7, above), engaging the whole Russian force and contributing greatly to the cossack victory in that battle. Gajecky, *Cossack Administration*, Vol. I, pp. 127, 131.

11. The articles referred to here are known as the "1665 Moscow Articles." These articles represented the agreement reached in September 1665 when Hetman Briukhovetsky and his entourage were received in Moscow. They consisted of ten proposals from the hetman and cossack officers, officially confirmed by the tsar. In effect the articles instituted further restrictions of cossack rights and liberties and contributed to further discontent in the Ukraine. See Basarab, *Pereiaslav 1654*, p. 16.

12. "To lay down the mace" was to abdicate the post of hetman and hold a new election.

13. Matvey Gvintovka freed himself from suspicion and became general aide-de-camp first to Hetman Briukhovetsky, and later to Hetman Mnogogreshny. Gajecky, *Cossack Administration*, Vol. 1, p. 132.

14. For Treaty of Andrusovo, see Introduction, p. xiii.

15. Koidak, or Kodak was a fortified settlement in Zaporozhia. Kremenchug, or Kremenchuk was a port on the Dnieper river.

16. The Sheremetev family was one of the most important families in Russia during the time of Tsar Alexis Mikhailovich, many of its members holding the highest rank of boyar. Soloviev asserts that the position of the Sheremetev family was acquired through talent. Two Sheremetevs, Vasily Borisovich and his son, the Peter Vasilievich named here, served as governors of Kiev. Soloviev describes Peter Vasilievich Sheremetev as "a man of great abilities, but boastful, extremely greedy for military glory, and unbearably proud and arrogant." See Vol. 23 of this series, pp. 144-145.

17. Bishop Methodios was appointed by the Moscow government as vicar of Kiev in 1661, and served until 1668. See Preface and Introduction, Note 6.

18. In July 1666 building tensions in Pereiaslav exploded. Cossacks attacked the Pereiaslav Regiment led by Colonel Daniil Yermelenko, in the Bagushko suburb, killing the colonel. The mob then proceeded to Pereiaslav proper, killing Muscovite soldiers stationed there and burning the citadel. The causes of the rebellion were multiple. Yermelenko was an appointee of Hetman Briukhovetsky, who was not popular in Pereiaslav. His close relations with Moscow aroused suspicion. His actions in relation to the struggle over the Kievan metropolitanate were opposed. Moreover, his rapacious collection of taxes, duties and dues angered both cossacks and burghers alike. Although Bishop Methodios was in Moscow when the trouble erupted, he actively fanned the flames of discontent in Pereiaslav in the months preceding his departure. The rebellion was decisively repressed by the joint action of Hetman Briukhovetsky and Moscow's governor in Kiev, Boyar Peter Vasilievich Sheremetev. Military repression did little to increase the popularity either of Briukhovetsky or the Russians in the Ukraine. For these events, see Volume 20 of this series and Bickford O'Brien, *Muscovy and the Ukraine*, pp. 103-107.

19. Chief Justice (eneral'nyi or general'nyi sud'ia). There were two chief justices attached to the general staff of the hetmanate. They were appointed by the hetman, generally from among the junior ranks of those serving on the general staff or from among former colonels. Loyalty to the reigning hetman was more important than legal experience. Chief justices frequently served as advisors to the hetman and sometimes as acting hetmans when the need arose. Gajecky, *Cossack Administration*, Vol. 2, pp. 659-660.

20. Camp (Sech) refers both to the Zaporozhian military community in the Ukraine in this period and to their headquarters. Here the reference is to the headquarters of the Zaporozhian Cossacks, located on one of the islands beyond the rapids (za porozh'e), in the lower Dnieper river. For the history of the Camp and a bibliography see Edward Sokol, "Sech'," MERSH, Vol. 33, pp. 161-168.

21. The Russian word is kuren and was used to designate both the military camp as well as the local subdivision, or platoon, of the Camp occupying the camp. Each kuren numbered a few hundred men and was headed by an elected field ataman, or koshevoi.

22. A verst is a unit of measure, equal to 3,500 English feet or 1.06 kilometers.

23. This refers to Matthew 7:9. "Or what man of you, if his son asks him for bread, will give him a stone?" This and all following biblical references are cited from Herbert G. May and Bruce M. Metzger, eds., *The Oxford Annotated Bible. The Holy Bible. Revised Standard Version containing the Old and New Testaments* (Oxford, 1962).

24. According to Gajecky, *Cossack Administration*, Vol. 1, p. 364, it was Ivan Donets rather than Fedor who was aide-de-camp of the Gadiach Regiment in 1667.

25. Trinity Sunday (Troitsyn den') or Pentecost (Piatdesiatnitsa) is a movable feast in the Orthodox church. It occurs on the seventh Sunday after Easter and celebrates the descent of the Holy Spirit upon the disciples. See Grigory Diachenko, ed., *Polnyi tserkovno-slavianskii slovar (s viaeseniem v nego vazhneishikh drevne-russkikh slov i vyrazhenii)* (Complete Church-Slavic Dictionary [With Clarification in It of the Most Important Early Russian Words and Expressions]) (Moscow Patriarchate, 1993), p. 734. This differs from the custom in the Western Christian churches, which do not equate the two feasts, and celebrate Pentecost, or Whitsunday, a week before Trinity Sunday.

26. Cossacks listed on the rolls, registered cossacks, were exempt from paying taxes and providing labor to the government and received a subsidy for their military service. Thus it was of considerable import whether one were listed among the cossacks, or among other tax-paying groups of the population.

27. The term used is moskali (pl.), a pejorative form for Muscovites, and Muscovite soldiers. See Vladimir Dal', *Tolkovyi slovar' zhivago Velikoruskago iazyka* (An Interpretative Dictionary of the Living Great Russian Language), 4 vols. (St. Petersburg and Moscow, 1880. Reprinted Moscow, 1981), Vol. 2, p. 349.

28. An old Russian unit of money, equal to two copecks. See Dal', *Tolkovyi slovar'*. Vol. 4, p. 618.

29. An old Russian unit of money. The relative value is not precise. Probably it was equivalent to a shag, or grosha. See Dal', *Tolkovyi slovar'*. Vol. 4, p. 602.

30. The Kievan Caves monastery, founded probably in the early eleventh century, was not the first monastic community in Rus but undoubtedly it was the most important for the later development of Christianity among the East Slavs. Already by the end of the eleventh century its reputation and prestige was established, growing in succeeding centuries as its influence spread. See Nikolai Dejevsky, "Kievan Caves Monastery," MERSH, Vol. 16, pp. 220-223; R. Casey, "Early Russian Monasticism," *Orientalia Christiana Periodica*, 19 (1953), pp. 372-343; A.P. Vlasto, *The Entry of the Slavs into Christendom* (Cambridge, 1970), pp. 301-307. The Patericon of the monastery is *The 'Paterik' of the Kievan*

Caves Monastery. Trans. by Muriel Heppell (Cambridge, Mass., 1989). Innokenty Gizel (c. 1600-1683) served as archimandrite of the monastery from 1656 until his death. He was an active participant in Ukrainian intellectual and political life, and a prolific writer whose works exerted considerable influence both in the Ukraine, Belorussia and Russia. There is no substantive work on Innokenty Gizel in English, but see MERSH, Vol. 12, pp. 184-185.

31. Jan III Sobieski (1629-1696) was born in Olesko, near Lvov. He was the second son of the nobleman Jakub Sobieski, governor-general of Ruthenia, and his equally noble wife, Maria Daniłowicz. The death of his elder brother made him heir, and a very well-connected and wealthy heir in the Polish Commonwealth. Despite the numerous opportunities open to him he chose a military career, joining the army in 1648. He was promoted rapidly and achieved the supreme military honor in 1668, the baton of the grand hetman of the crown. In 1674, following the death of King Michał Korybut Wiśniowiecki (born 1640, reigned 1669-1673), he was elected king with very little opposition. He was not crowned until 1676 owing to war between Turks and Tatars. At his coronation Sejm the participants engaged in a violent discussion of religious questions. A resolution was adopted which demanded that the Orthodox church's relations with Constantinople cease and forbade Orthodox Christians to leave the country. Davies, *God's Playground*, Vol. 2, pp. 473-474.

32. Belaia Tserkov, in Ukrainian Bila Tserkva, is a town located on the Right Bank of the Dnieper and was the center of one of the core regiments of the hetmanate in this area. The Treaty of Andrusovo (see Introduction, p. xiii) institutionalized the division of the Ukraine into Right Bank and Left Bank, and effectively Belaia Tserkov and the other Right Bank territories and regiments were lost to the hetmanate. Hetman Peter Doroshenko, hetman on the Right Bank 1665-1676, attempted to reunite the hetmanate under his rule and eliminate Polish control on the Right Bank through an alliance with the Ottoman Porte. This attempt was unsuccessful and introduced a period marked by the decimation of the population in endless warfare and the desolation of the whole region. The correspondence related by Soloviev in this passage is one of the numerous attempts to win Doroshenko away from the Ottoman Porte. For an overview, see Orest Subtelny, *Ukraine. A History*, 2nd ed. (Toronto, 1994), pp. 138-157; Magocsi, *A History of Ukraine*, pp. 217-228.

33. The union of the Orthodox church and the Roman Catholic church in the Polish-Lithuanian Commonwealth was accomplished formally at a church council in Brest in 1596. In discussions and negotiations before the council between Orthodox and Catholic bishops and Polish officials, the Orthodox bishops agreed to bring their church into a union with Rome, accepting the authority of the Pope, in return for a guarantee that the Orthodox liturgy and rites, as well as other customs such as the right of priests to marry, would be respected. The union was approved at Brest in the face of massive opposition. The result was not the union of two churches into one, rather the creation of a third church, the Uniate church or Greek Catholic church as it later came to be called, and

continued religious turmoil in the Ukraine. See Oscar Halecki, *From Florence to Brest (1439-1596)* (Rome, 1958); T. Hunczak, "The Politics of Religion. The Union of Brest 1596," *Ukrainskyi Istoryk,* 2-4 (1972), pp. 97-106.

34. A universal was an official document of the Ukrainian hetman, equivalent to the Russian gramota. See Sergei G. Pushkarev, comp., George Vernadsky and Ralph T. Fisher, Jr., eds., *Dictionary of Russian Historical Terms From the Eleventh Century to 1917* (New Haven, Conn., 1970), p. 169.

35. Joseph Neliubovich-Tukalsky was an active participant in ecclesiastical and secular politics in the Ukraine. Metropolitan Dionysios Balaban of Kiev installed him as bishop of Mstislavl. When Metropolitan Dionysios died in 1663 Tukalsky was selected as his successor by a clerical and lay faction in the electoral synod. Bishop Anthony Vynnetsky was selected by a second faction comprised of bishops and representatives of the hetman. King Jan Kazimierz confirmed both candidates, thus further confusing ecclesiastical administration and exacerbating political struggles. Metropolitan Joseph Tukalsky, metropolitanate 1663-1675, claimed jurisdiction over the Right Bank of the Ukraine, White Russia and Lithuania, and coveted jurisdiction over the Left Bank of the Ukraine as well.

36. Yury Bogdanovich Khmelnitsky (1641-1685) was the youngest son of Bogdan Mikhailovich Khmelnitsky. He was elected hetman in 1659 but failed in efforts to unite the Ukraine. He abdicated in 1663 and became a monk, taking the name Gedeon. Time dimmed his religious zeal and in 1677 he again claimed the rank of hetman on the Right Bank, with the support of the Turks. He was executed by the Turks in 1685. See Volume 20 of this series.

37. Afanasy Lavrentievich Ordin-Nashchokin (c. 1605-1680) was among the "new men" who came to the fore during the reign of Tsar Alexis Mikhailovich, men who gained positions of power and influence based on their talent and education, although not from families which traditionally had held rank in the Council. Serving effectively in various government posts, in 1667 he was rewarded with the post of head of the important and influential Chancellery of Foreign Affairs. In that position he successfully negotiated the Treaty of Andrusovo. His active efforts to reform the Chancellery of Foreign Affairs and his firm support for an alliance with Poland brought him into conflict with other influential men at the Moscow court, including Bogdan Matveevich Khitrovo, another of the "new men" who supported a northern foreign policy. Ordin-Nashchokin's preference for a Polish alliance, coupled with his general lack of knowledge of Ukrainian affairs, made him no friend of the cossacks. In 1671 Ordin-Nashchokin was removed from his post and took monastic vows. See pp. 55-71, below, for Soloviev's description of Ordin-Nashchokin's difficulties. See also the article by E. Chistiakova, MERSH, Vol. 26, pp. 72-73; Robert O. Crummey, *Aristocrats and Servitors. The Boyar Elite in Russia, 1613-1689* (Princeton, N.J., 1983), pp. 100-101, 151, 156, 160-161; Hans-Joachim Torke, "The Unloved Alliance" in Peter J. Potichnyj, Marc Raeff, Jaroslaw Pelenski, Gleb Żekulin, eds., *Ukraine and Russia in Their Historical Encounter* (Edmonton, 1992), pp. 38-66.

38. In 1673 Vasily Mikhailovich Tiapkin was serving the tsar as Russian resident in Warsaw.

39. Ivan Vygovsky was elected hetman in August 1657 following the death of Bogdan Khmelnitsky, and served until 1659. Angered by Russian interference in Ukrainian affairs, he supported close relations with the Poles and broke off relations with Moscow. On September 16, 1658 Vygovsky and the Poles signed a treaty at Gadiach with the intention of establishing an "eternal and unbroken peace between the Ukrainians and the Polish." The treaty recognized the Ukraine as a co-equal "Ruthenian Principality" and ostensibly guaranteed full rights and freedom for the Orthodox church in the Ukraine. The Treaty of Gadiach was rejected in Warsaw owing to the opposition of conservative Polish factions. After Gadiach, Russia offered support to pro-Russian cossacks even more blatantly and in November 1658 supported the election of Mikita Bezpaly as new hetman. Relations between Vygovsky and the Russians deteriorated and on April 29,1659 a Russian army suffered a catastrophic defeat at the battle of Konotop, where it was lured into a trap by Vygovsky and destroyed by his forces. Vygovsky's pro-Polish policies were equally displeasing to many cossacks on the Right Bank and Zaporozhia who opposed the Polish alliance and rejected the agreement made at Gadiach. In September 1659 he was compelled to flee the Right Bank and a cossack assembly convened at Belaia Tserkov deposed him as hetman. He was replaced in the post by the youngest son of Bogdan Khmelnitsky, Yury. See Basarab, *Pereiaslav 1654*, pp. 11-14 and 23-24, Note 12, and for an English translation of the Treaty of Gadiach, Appendix 4, pp. 245-24; article by Lindsey A.J. Hughes, MERSH, Vol. 43, pp. 123-125; Bickford O'Brien, *Between Musvcovy and the Ukraine*, pp. 47-61.

40. One person who opposed Vygovsky as well as his Polish policy was Colonel Martyn Pushkar (or Pushkarenko) of the Poltava Regiment. Pushkar commanded this regiment throughout Bogdan Khmelnitsky's reign as hetman, then in 1658 led a bloody rebellion opposing Vygovsky's agreement with the Poles, a rebellion actively supported by Muscovite agents. Vygovsky subdued the revolt and Pushkar was killed. The Pushkar rebellion marked the beginning of the destructive civil wars of the period know as "The Ruin." MERSH, Vol. 30, p. 94; Gajecky, *Cossack Administration*, Vol. 2, p. 514; Magocsi, *A History of Ukraine*, p. 220; and for Vygovsky's narration of events, see Basarab, *Pereiaslav 1654*, Appendix 6, pp. 259-264.

41. Mikita Bezpaly was the Russian-sponsored candidate for hetman in November 1658. The situation changed rapidly in the Ukraine in these years. When Yury Khmelnitsky was selected as hetman at the assembly of cossacks at Belaia Tserkov, replacing the deposed Ivan Vygovsky, the Russian government changed course and offered its support to Khmelnitsky in October 1659. Later, in 1666, Bezpaly served as colonel of the Gadiach Regiment. See Basarab, *Pereiaslav 1654*, pp. 13-14; MERSH, Vol. 4, p. 84; Gajecky, *Cossack Administration*, Vol. 1, pp. 355-357, and Note 39, above.

42. Yakov Barabash was Zaporozhian field ataman in 1657 and 1658, and a member of the pro-Russian faction among the Zaporozhian Cossacks, centered in the Camp. With the encouragement and support of Moscow he participated along with Martyn Pushkar in the so-called Pushkar rebellion. In June 1658, when two opposing cossack armies fought a bloody battle near Poltava, Barabash was captured and later executed. On page 19 of Soloviev's text Bishop Methodios maintains that the Muscovites sent Barabash to the Poles as a gift, presumably to be executed by them, but I have not found confirmation of this. MERSH, Vol. 3, p. 85; Magocsi, *A History of Ukraine*, p. 220, and Note 40, above.

43. Soloviev probably refers here to Ivan Serko, colonel of the Kalnik Regiment in 1658 and 1659. This regiment was located along the western boundary of the hetmanate, with headquarters either at Kalnik on the Kalnivka river about 175 kilometers from Kiev, or Vynnytsia on the Bug river 205 kilometers southwest of Kiev, and was involved in the strife of the period. As field ataman Colonel Serko led several notable sorties against the Crimean Tatars. MERSH, Vol. 35, p. 149; Gajecky, *Cossack Administration*, Vol. 2, pp. 600, 602-603, 701.

44. For the Treaty of Gadiach, see Note 39 above and article by V.A. Golobutskii, MERSH, Vol. 12, p. 50.

45. The Wiśniowiecki family (Lords of Cherry Village) were princes of the eastern lands. One of the most powerful and influential families in the Ukraine, they traced their origins back to Gediminas and Riurik, the legendary founders of the Lithuanian and Rus dynasties respectively. In the territorial divisions between the Commonwealth and Russia, culminating with the Treaty of Andrusovo, they lost much land in the territories which came under Russian jurisdiction, primarily around Smolensk and in Volhynia. Prince Jarema Wiśniowiecki was a leading opponent of Bogdan Khmelnitsky. His son Michał Korybut was elected to the throne of the Polish Commonwealth but the reign of four years (1669-1673) was remarkably forgettable. Davies, *God's Playground*, Vol. 1, pp. 153, 177, 362, 447, 470-472.

46. Pushkarenko is another form of Martyn Pushkar's family name. For Pushkar and his rebellion, see Note 40, above.

47. Ivan Iskra was another member of the Poltava Regiment during "the Ruin." In 1649 and 1652 he served as acting colonel of the regiment. From 1696 to 1700 he served as colonel in his own right. He was executed by Peter I in 1708, ironically for his participation in a conspiracy to betray Ivan Mazepa's plans to the tsar. MERSH, Vol. 15, p. 14; Gajecky, *Cossack Administration*, Vol. 2, pp. 514-515, 519. For Ivan Mazepa, see below, pp. 160-164, and Chapter IV, Note 54.

48. Yakim Samko was a brother-in-law of Bogdan Khmelnitsky. He was appointed acting hetman on the Left Bank by Yury Khmelnitsky from 1660 to 1663, while Khmelnitsky and the cossacks were campaigning with the Russian army. The campaign against Poland was a failure and the Russians were defeated,

whereupon Khmelnitsky defected to the Poles. Samko remained loyal to Moscow and continued to defend the Left Bank against Khmelnitsky. Moscow did not recognize his assistance and Samko was never confirmed as hetman by the tsar. Samko was a contender for the position of hetman at the full cossack council of 1663, competing against Vasyl (or Vasiuto) Zolotarenko and Ivan Briukhovetsky. Briukhovetsky emerged victorious and both Samko and Zolotarenko were put to death. Gajecky, *Cossack Administration*, Vol. 1, pp. 127, 292.

49. Vasyl (Vasiuto) Zolotarenko was the younger brother of another brother-in-law of Bogdan Khmelnitsky. He served as acting colonel of the Nezhin Regiment from 1654 to 1655, and as colonel from 1655 to 1656 and 1659 to 1663. He too was a contender for the position of hetman at the full cossack council of 1663, and was executed by Ivan Briukhovetsky, the victor of the contest. He was replaced by Matvey Gvintovka as colonel of the Nezhin Regiment. MERSH, Vol. 46, p. 118; Gajecky, *Cossack Administration,* Vol. 1, pp. 127, 130-132.

50. Anikii (Ioanikii) Silich was colonel of the Chernigov Regiment (1657-1663). He too was involved in the struggle over the position of hetman in 1663, and was executed by the victorious Briukhovetsky at the conclusion of the full cossack council of that year. Gajecky, *Cossack Administration*, Vol. 1, pp. 70-71.

51. The phrase in Russian is "tsarskogo prestola nizhaishaia podnozhka," literally the lowest step (or footboard) of the tsar's throne.

52. Stepan, perhaps better know by the diminutive Stenka, Razin was commander of a group of Don Cossacks who first attracted attention for raids in Persia, along the Caspian coast and the lower Volga river. In the spring of 1670 his activities grew more ambitious and he and his band moved up the Volga, proclaiming freedom from government officials and the landholding nobility. Soldiers, peasants and townsmen welcomed Razin and his cossacks, supporting and assisting in the murder of leading people. By the time Razin reached Simbirsk his forces grew perhaps to two hundred thousand men. Regular Russian regiments ultimately put Razin's unorganized and poorly disciplined followers to flight. Razin himself was seized by cossack authorities and handed over to Russian officials in the spring of 1671 and he was publicly and gruesomely executed. See Paul Avrich, *Russian Rebels* (New York, 1972), pp. 50-132, for a colorful recounting of the Razin rebellion; Philip Longworth, *The Cossacks* (London, 1969), pp. 124-153; James G. Hart, "Razin, Stepan Timofeevich" MERSH, Vol. 52, pp. 56-62; S. Konovalov, "Ludwig Fabritsius's Account of the Razin Rebellion," *Oxford Slavonic Papers,* 6 (1955), pp. 72-101; *idem,* "Razin's Execution. Two Contemporary Documents," *Oxford Slavonic Papers,* 12 (1965), pp. 94-98. For a thoughtful analysis of the nature of the uprising consult Michael Khodarkovsky, "The Stepan Razin Uprising. Was it a 'Peasant War'?" *Jahrbücher für Geschichte Osteuropas,* 42 (1994), pp. 1-19. For diminutives and their uses, see below, Chapter I, Note 92.

53. In the Russian Orthodox church a lavra was a coenobitic monastery of the highest rank. Today there are four monasteries recognized as lavras by the

Russian church: the Holy Trinity-St. Sergius monastery near Moscow, the Caves monastery in Kiev, the Alexander Nevsky in St. Petersburg, and the Pochaev monastery in Volhynia.

54. In this passage Methodios uses a simile of a small strip of skin, a small piece of Little Russian territory, versus the whole hide, or all of Little Russia. Unfortunately, a literal translation does not work well in English.

55. Vasily Dvoretsky served several terms as colonel or acting colonel of the Kiev Regiment between 1653 and 1668. The Dvoretskys were an important family among the cossack élite. Along with the Solonina family the Dvoretsky family controlled the Oster company of cossacks throughout most of its existence. The Oster company was centered on the city of Oster on the left bank of the Desna river, about fifty-two kilometers north of Kiev. Until 1667 it was attached to the Pereiaslav Regiment but then was transferred to the Kiev Regiment. Gajecky, *Cossack Administration*, Vol. 1, pp. 204-206, 239.

56. This is rendered as "Sheremet" in the two cases indicated in the text, probably in error.

57. For Yakov Barabash, see above Note 42. I can find no evidence to support Methodios' assertion here.

58. Ivan Samoilovich served as hetman from 1672 to 1687. Before his appointment as hetman he served as colonel of the Chernigov Regiment (acting colonel in 1665; full colonel, 1668-1669) and as chief justice on the general staff of the hetmanate (1669-1672). See the article by Hughes, MERSH, Vol. 33, pp. 76-79; Gajecky, *Cossack Administration*, Vol. 1, p. 71, Vol. 2, pp. 664, 661 and *passim*.

59. Soloviev identified the colonel of Pereiaslav in 1668 as Dmitry Raicha. In other parts of the text Soloviev refers to this individual by different variations on "Dmitry" and "Raicha" and combinations thereof. The colonel of Pereiaslav from 1666 to 1671 was Rodion Dmitrashko-Raich, a Serbian mercenary appointed to the position by Hetman Briukhovetsky following a rebellion in the regiment. The name has been rendered uniformly as Dmitrashko-Raich throughout the translated text. Gajecky, *Cossack Administration*, Vol. 1, p. 293.

60. Kissing the cross was a means of affirming an oath, one which made the breaking of the oath a mortal sin, thus bringing the procedure into the jurisdiction of the church. For cross-kissing and its effectiveness or lack thereof in early Russia see Horace W. Dewey and Anne M. Kleimola, "Promise and Perfidy in Old Russian Cross-Kissing," *Canadian-American Slavic Studies,* 9 (1975), pp. 156-167.

61. Maslenitsa or Butter Week. A week of festivities on the eve of Lent corresponding to Shrovetide in the West. In the Orthodox church it is forbidden to eat meat during this week but cheese, butter and fish are permitted.

62. The term translated here as "town council" is ratusha. This is a Russian form of the Polish ratusz, which in turn is a Polonized form of the German Rathaus, or council house. In central Russia the term came into use by the end of the seventeenth century. The Ukraine, with its close links to Poland, adopted the term earlier. See MERSH, Vol. 30, pp. 201-202.

63. Chancellery for Kiev is the translated term for Kievskii prikaz as given in the text. The prikaz or chancellery system was a system of Muscovite administration which evolved organically over the centuries as need arose. The Little Russian Chancellery (Malorossiiskii prikaz) was instituted in Moscow in 1662 for the governance of the Left Bank Ukraine, and was subordinate to the Chancellery of Foreign Affairs (Posol'skii prikaz). There was no actual Chancellery for Kiev. This term is used because the term prikaz is found in Soloviev's text. The Little Russian Chancellery did maintain offices (prikaznye izby) in the important cities and towns, such as Kiev, Chernigov, Nezhin, etc. For an introduction in English to the Russian chancellery system in the seventeenth century, see Bořivoj Plavšic, "Seventeenth-Century Chancelleries and Their Staffs" in *Russian Officialdom. The Bureaucratization of Russian Society from the Seventeenth to the Twentieth Century*. Ed. by Walter M. Pintner and Don K. Rowney (Chapel Hill, N.C., 1980), pp. 19-45.

64. The term translated here as councillor is raitze, from ratusha. See Note 62, above.

65. Dishonor here translates beschest'e. In Russia in the seventeenth century and earlier the honor of a family and of individuals within families determined social rank and status as well as service rank and thus potential emoluments and less tangible rewards. Dishonor was a serious affair and one ajudicated in the courts. For a thoughtful analysis of the role and significance of honor in early modern Russia, see Nancy Shields Kollmann, *By Honor Bound. State and Society in Early Modern Russia* (Ithaca, N.Y., 1999).

66. Lazar Baranovich was active in the political struggles in the Ukraine, both secular and ecclesiastical, in the second half of the seventeenth century. Sometimes supporting and sometimes opposing Moscow, Baranovich always looked out for his own interests. From 1650 to 1656 he was rector of the Kiev Academy and abbot of the Brotherhood monastery in Kiev. In 1657 he was made archbishop of Chernigov and Novgorod-Seversk. From 1659 to 1661 he served as vicar of the metropolitanate of Kiev, appointed by Moscow. He played an important role in the eucharistic controversy of the late 1680s and in the machinations over the subordination of the Kievan metropolitanate to the Moscow patriarch during the tenure of Patriarch Joachim. He was a prolific writer of religious and polemical tracts. The full corpus of his writing has yet to be established. There is no substantive work on Lazar Baranovich in English, but see MERSH, Vol. 3, p. 96.

67. Black Forest refers to the heavily forested region at the foot of the Carpathian mountains, along the Transylvanian border, which may be considered an extension or a part of the famous Swabian Black Forest.

68. This phrase echoes Matthew 15:8. "You hypocrites! Well did Isaiah prophesy of you, when he said: 'This people honors me with their lips, but their heart is far from me.'"

69. Ivan Afanasievich Zheliabuzhsky (1638-after 1709). Zheliabuzhsky's family had served the Russian government since the end of the sixteenth century,

when his grandfather immigrated from Poland. Ivan Afanasievich worked his way up the ranks through service primarily on foreign missions. In 1667, recently returned from an embassy in Vienna, he was dispatched to Kiev. In 1674 he was named a stolnik (table attendant) and in 1676 dumnyi dvorianin (conciliar noble), thus entering the Duma or Council. For his assignment as aide to Ordin-Nashchokin in negotiations with the Poles to complete the Treaty of Andrusovo and transmute it into an eternal peace between Russia and Poland, see below, pp. 68-69. See also the article by Orchard, MERSH, Vol. 46, pp. 37-38 and H.J. Torke's introduction to *Zapiski russkikh liudei* (Notes on Russian People) (St. Petersburg, 1841, reprinted in the Russian Memoir Series, No. 27, Newtonville, Mass., 1980), pp. 6-7.

70. The Russian term used here is nemets, a term which can mean "German," understood broadly as Northern European, or even more broadly as "foreigner." The name of the nemets in question here, Yagan Gults (Johann Schultz ?), suggests the colonel was, in fact, of Northern European origin. In the second half of the seventeenth century, in conjunction with reforms intended to modernize the Russian military, foreign mercenary officers frequently served in the Russian army. See John Keep, *Soldiers of the Tsar. Army and Society in Russia, 1462-1874* (Oxford, 1985), pp. 53-54, and pp. 80-92 for the new-style regiments; Richard Hellie, *Enserfment and Military Change in Muscovy* (Chicago, 1971), pp. 181-234 and *passim*.

71. An old Russian unit of money. Two hundred dengas equaled one ruble.

72. The Don Cossacks were another cossack host, centered on the lower Don river, to the east of the Zaporozhian Cossack Host. See the article by Edward D. Sokol, MERSH, Vol. 9, pp. 218-221.

73. Patriarch Nikon was removed from the post of patriarch of Moscow and all Russia by a church council in 1666/1667. See Note 2, above.

74. The reference here is to the wide-ranging program of church reform, energetically directed by Patriarch Nikon until his downfall. These reforms did not support the Union, permit Roman Catholic priests to marry, or include a change of alphabets from Cyrillic to Latin letters, as asserted here. As pointed out above, Note 2, the dénouement of the Nikon affair did not bring a halt to reform, nor to the opposition to those reforms. By the 1660s opponents of the reforms were branding them as latinstvo, asserting that the Russian church was falling under the influence of the "Latin heresy," that is, of being influenced by the Roman Catholic church. The charge resonated in the Ukraine which had a long history of struggle against persecution by Roman Catholics and against the imposition of Church Union. For the Union see Note 33, above. For these disputes over reform as they unfolded to the end of the seventeenth century in Moscow, see Cathy Jean Potter, "The Russian Church and the Politics of Reform in the Second Half of the Seventeenth Century" (Ph.D. diss., Yale University, 1993), Volume 2.

75. Briukhovetsky refers here to the towns on the Right Bank of the Ukraine, ceded to Poland in the recently concluded Andrusovo truce. For a list of these

towns see the extracts from the Treaty of Andrusovo in Vernadsky, *Source Book*, Vol. 1, pp. 305-306.

76. Golut'by, in Ukrainian golytba, or "naked ones," were the unregistered cossacks without a secure source of income.

77. For Ivan Samoilovich, see Note 58, above.

78. The Crimean khan in 1668 was Adil-Girey (reigned 1666-1671).

79. Sotniki, or cossack captains, headed the companies or platoons which composed the cossack regiments. Gajecky, *Cossack Administration*, Vol. 1, p. 10.

80. Michał Pacs (1624-1682) was a member of an important Lithuanian family. Michał was Lithuanian hetman, his brother Bonifacy was an important military leader, and another brother, Krzysztof, served as chancellor. Other members of the extended family distinguished themselves as officers in the army, as governors of provinces and as prelates.

81. Cherkasy or Cherkassians was a Muscovite name for the Ukrainians, in common use in the sixteenth and seventeenth centuries. See Pushkarev, *Dictionary*, p. 7.

82. Prince Grigory Grigorievich Romodanovsky (died 1682). The son of the boyar Prince Grigory Petrovich Romodanovsky, Prince Grigory rose through the ranks, becoming a lord-in-waiting in 1656 primarily thanks to his military service in the Ukraine. On May 15, 1682 he was killed by musketeers in the rebellion which marked the death of Tsar Fedor Alekseevich and the struggle over succession. His son Andrei was a prisoner of the Tatars from 1668 to 1681 (text, pp. 79-80). See the article by Hughes, MERSH, Vol. 31, pp. 156-158.

83. Lavrinko is not identified by Gajecky, *Cossack Administration*. He is described as a pisar'. In the hetmanate, at the company level, this would best be translated as scribe. At the regimental or general staff level this was an important post, translated as chancellor. In view of the importance of the mission Lavrinko may well have been Briukhovetsky's general chancellor. Because this is not certain I have used the lower rank, scribe.

84. Among the Crimean Tatars a bey was the leader of a clan. The bey was selected by the clan, and among other responsibilities assumed command of whatever military force the clan provided for the Tatar army. See Alan Fisher, *The Crimean Tatars* (Palo Alto, Cal., 1978), pp. 21-23.

85. Chetvert', or quarter, as a measure of grain was equal to approximately eight bushels or 57.5 kilograms.

86. Novoe mesto, or new town, indicates a new area, generally a commercial suburb, which sprang up on the outskirts or outside the walls, if present, of the original old town.

87. Here Soloviev identifies this individual, the colonel of the Starodub regiment, as Peter Roslovchenko. In other places he uses Peter Roslavets, Roslavets (Roslovchenko) or Roslovchenko (Roslavets). According to Gajecky, *Cossack Administration*, Vol. 1, pp. 14, 15-19, 53-54, the name is Roslavets, and I have

used that form throughout. The Roslavets family was an important one, controlling the Pochep company throughout its existence. In 1663 the Pochep company was transferred to the Starodub Regiment. Peter Roslavets apparently began his career in the Pochep company, serving as captain from 1653 to 1657. In 1659 he became acting colonel of the Starodub Regiment, and was raised to full colonel in 1663 only to be replaced almost immediately by an appointee of Hetman Briukhovetsky. From 1668 to 1672 he served his second tenure as colonel of Starodub, then was sacked by Hetman Demian Ignatovich Mnogogreshny in favor of the hetman's brother (see text, p. 97). Returning to the post after a few months in 1673, he retained it until arrested by Hetman Ivan Samoilovich in 1676 for attempting to detach the Starodub Regiment from the hetmanate and join it to Russia.

88. See Preface and Introduction, Note 6.

89. The reference here is to the battle at Khotin in 1621. The Commonwealth, assisted by the Zaporozhian Cossacks defeated the Ottoman Turks, thus redeeming an earlier catastrophic defeat at Cecora (Tsetsora) in 1620. Both these encounters were part of the sporadic conflict on the southern frontier which characterized relations between the Commonwealth and the Ottoman Turks, as well as between Moscow and the Ottoman Turks, in the seventeenth century.

90. I am uncertain of the meaning here. The Russian is podushchenie vsegdashnee ot varvar imeiut.

91. Matthew 9:20-22. "And behold, a woman who had suffered from a hemorrhage for twelve years came up behind him and touched the fringe of his garment; for she said to herself, 'If I only touch his garment, I shall be made well.' Jesus turned, and seeing her he said, 'Take heart, daughter; your faith has made you well.'"

92. Ivashka is a diminutive of Ivan. The Slavic languages are rich in diminutives, particularly of personal names, and diminutives of diminutives. Among family and friends such diminutives manifest affection. In formal official contexts the diminutive can serve to indicate relative rank. For example in petitions to the tsar in the early modern period protocol demanded that even the most illustrious boyars use the diminutive of their given name, generally coupled with the designation, "your slave." See for example *The Travels of Olearius in Seventeenth-Century Russia.* Ed. and trans. by Samuel H. Baron (Palo Alto, Cal., 1967), p. 147. Historians have argued that this protocol was a part of the "facade of autocracy," a practice aimed at maintaining harmony, consensus and political stability. See Nancy Shields Kollman, *Kinship and Politics. The Making of the Muscovite Political System, 1345-1547* (Palo Alto, Cal., 1987) and Marshall Poe, "What Did Russians Mean When They Called Themselves 'Slaves of the Tsar'?" *Slavic Review,* 57, No. 3 (Fall 1998), pp. 585-608, a detailed and sensitive analysis of meaning as it evolved. Diminutives also are used in an intentionally insulting and derogatory fashion, as here.

CHAPTER II

1. Mikhail Doroshenko was killed in a campaign in the Crimea in 1628. Earlier he participated in more successful campaigns in the Crimea. The Zaporozhian Cossacks' depredations in the Crimea in the mid-1620s threatened the stability of the area and led to conflict between the cossacks and the Poles in 1625. The Poles were victorious. In the disarray of their defeat the cossacks elected Mikhail Doroshenko hetman to negotiate a peace. See Volume 18 of this series.

2. General cossack councils had the right to elect, or dismiss hetmans. In theory all cossacks enjoyed the right to participate in the general councils. During "The Ruin," general councils were very influential, and included clergy, townsmen and peasants. These are the black councils, so called because they included the common, or "black people" (chernye liudi). The most famous full or black council was the one held in 1663 when there were a number of contenders for hetman. Ultimately Briukhovetsky was elected. The black council of 1663 served as the subject of an historical novel by the noted Ukrainian author, Panteleimon Kulish. See above, Chapter I, Notes 48-50. Magocsi, A History of Ukraine, p. 236.

3. Ivan Dmitrievich Serko (died 1680) was a member of the Kalnyk-Vynnitsia Regiment and colonel of the Kalnyk Regiment in 1658-1659. Colonel Serko, as field ataman of the Zaporozhian Cossacks, led several daring and devastating raids against the Crimean Tatars. See above, Chapter I, Note 43.

4. The Priluki colonel was probably Ivan Shcherbyna-Koshovyi. According to Oleksander Lazarevs'kyi, Opisanie staroi Malorossii (Description of Old Little Russia), Volume III. Polk Prilutskii (The Priluki Regiment) (Kiev, 1902), pp. 9-10, Shcherbyna-Kosovyi was appointed colonel by Doroshenko in December 1668. Mykola Kostomarov, Ruina (The Ruin) in Sobranie sochinenii (Collected Works). New Series, Vol. 6 (The Hague, 1967), p. 152, argues for a date of April 1669. In this period, as Soloviev's narrative shows, Peter Doroshenko, Demian Mnogogreshny and Peter Sukhovey or Sukhoveenko all claimed the hetmancy, contending for the loyalty and support of different regiments and appointing their own colonels when the situation permitted.

5. Rodion Dmitrashko-Raich was a Serbian mercenary and a colonel of the Braslavl Regiment in 1666 when the cossacks of the Pereiaslav Regiment rebelled and killed their colonel, Daniil Yermolenko. Hetman Briukhovetsky crushed the rebellion and appointed Rodion Dmitrashko-Raich as colonel of the Pereiaslav Regiment. He served in this position from 1666 to 1671, and again from 1672 to 1674. Gajecky, Cossack Administration, Vol. 1, pp. 293-294; Vol. 2, pp. 580, 584. See above, Chapter I, Note 59.

6. Vasko is a diminutive of Vasily, thus the reference is to Vasily Dvoretsky, who periodically served as colonel or acting colonel of the Kiev Regiment between 1653 and 1658. See Chapter I, Note 55.

7. Jeremiah Shirkevich was abbot of the Boris and Gleb monastery in Chernigov until 1664, when he was transferred as abott to the Maksakov monastery of the Transfiguration of the Savior. He appears below, Chapter III, p. 83, again representing Lazar Baranovich on a mission to Moscow in 1669. See Pavel Stroev, *Spiski ierarkhov i nastoiatelei monastyrei rossiiskiia tserkvi* (Lists of Prelates and Heads of Monasteries of the Russian Church) (St. Petersburg, 1877), pp. 518, 529.

8. For the bondage of the Israelites in Egypt, and their deliverance through God's agent, Moses, see the Book of Exodus.

9. A unit of Old Russian money. One poltina equaled fifty copecks, or one-half a ruble.

10. A unit of Old Russian money. One grivna equaled twenty Muscovite dengas. One hundred grivnas equaled one ruble, ten copecks.

11. The term used here is sokha, literally a wooden plough. Here it refers to a unit of land which varied considerably in size according to the quality of land, the region and the time period, and as the passage indicates, whether the land was worked with horses or oxen. Roughly, it was equivalent to eight hundred chetverts of good quality land, one thousand two hundred chetverts of medium quality land, and one thousand eight hundred chetverts of poor quality land. As a surface measure, a chetvert was equivalent to about 1.35 acres. See Dal', *Tolkovyi slovar'*, Vol. 4, pp. 283-284.

12. A unit of money. One ducat (chervonnye zolotye) was equal to approximately three rubles.

13. Units of money. One altyn was equal to three copecks, one grivna to ten copecks.

14. It is not totally clear where precisely these unhappy people wished to settle in the Holy Roman empire. Geographically, the closest possibility would have been Transylvania, but in the Treaty of Vasvar (1664) Emperor Leopold I (reigned 1658-1705) recognized the claims of the Ottoman Turks to suzerainty over this long disputed region. The more distant but more likely goal was Transcarpathia, on the western slope of the Carpathian mountains. This area was long among the Habsburg holdings and by the late eighteenth century boasted a significant Ruthenian population, evidence of earlier migration.

15. In the Crimean khanate the khan, chosen from the Girey clan, appointed two officials, the kalgay sultan and the nurredin sultan, both "deputy sultans," also chosen from members of the Girey clan. In theory both these officers were considered heirs to the throne, the kalgay sultan first in line and the nurredin sultan second. In practice, they rarely succeeded. Fisher, *Crimean Tatars*, pp. 18-19.

16. Romans 11:16. "If the dough offered as first fruits is holy, so is the whole lump; and if the root is holy, so are the branches."

17. Bogdan Matveevich Khitrovo (1615-1680) entered the boyar council in 1647, probably with the patronage of the favorite of Tsar Alexis Mikhailovich,

B.I. Morozov. Before 1647 he completed several diplomatic and military missions. Beginning in 1649 he held a number of chancellery posts, none of which really suggest his influence as a favorite of the tsar. He was an enemy of Patriarch Nikon, opposed generally to the policies of Artamon Sergeevich Matveev, and also to those of Afanasy Lavrentievich Ordin-Nashchokin. See Crummey, *Boyars and Servitors*, pp. 52, 57, 60, 99, 101-102, 105-106, 160, 188, 231 (Note 85), 245 (Note 77).

18. Artamon Sergeevich Matveev (1625-1682) began his service career as a page at court and worked his way up, and into the favor of Tsar Alexis Mikhailovich, through the successful completion of a series of military and diplomatic missions. His reputation as a "westernizer" may have assisted him in attracting the favorable attention of the tsar. In 1669 he was a stolnik (table attendant) and in the following year he entered the Boyar Duma as an okol'nichii (lord-in-waiting). In 1671 his ward, Natalia Naryshkina, became Tsar Alexis Mikhailovich's second wife and Matveev's career flourished. He held many important positions, including head of the Chancellery of Foreign Affairs and head of the Chancellery of the Apothecary (responsible for the health of the tsar's family). In 1675 he attained the highest rank of boyar in the Duma. The tsar's death in 1676 and the subsequent ascendancy of the Miloslavsky family, relatives of the tsar's first wife, led to Matveev's disgrace and exile. He returned to Moscow and to power in 1682, following the death of Tsar Fedor Alekseevich, only to be killed by a rioting mob. See Hughes, "Matveev, Artamon Sergeevich" MERSH, Vol. 21, pp. 142-144.

19. Grigory Karpovich Bogdanov was a career chancellery official. Among other assignments he accompanied Afanasy Ordin-Nashchokin to Poland in 1663-1664, was present at the conclusion of the Andrusovo treaty and served as a secretary in the Little Russian Chancellery from 1668-1669 to 1675-1676. In the last capacity his journey to Little Russia for the selection of a hetman is noted here by Soloviev. Several years later, on December 1, 1671, he was made a dumnyi d'iak (conciliar secretary). This is probably the same G.K. Bogdanov who fell afoul of the musketeers in the troubles of 1682. The musketeers demanded he be executed but he escaped with exile. His career is summarized in S.B. Veselovskii, *D'iaki i pod'iachie XV-XVII vv.* (Secretaries and Undersecretaries from the Fifteenth through the Seventeenth Centuries) (Moscow, 1975), pp. 56-57.

20. Larion, or Illarion Dmitrievich Lopukhin first appears in the sources in 1610-1611 as a zhilets (resident noble). He enjoyed a long and by all indications successful career in the tsar's service. In the 1630s he served as a guard for various embassies visiting Moscow. He also served for a time as captain of the musketeers. By the end of the 1640s he was a secretary in the Chancellery for Kazan and in 1650/51 he was sent to Zaporozhia, to Hetman Bogdan Khmelnitsky. In that same year he was made a conciliar secretary and posted again to the Chancellery for Kazan, where he served for ten years. In 1659, as part of an embassy to Zaporozhia, he was present at Yury Khmelnitsky's selection as

hetman. After a brief and temporary posting to the Novgorod Chancellery he was returned to the Chancellery for Kazan. In 1667 he was promoted to conciliar noble (dumnyi dvorianin) in the same chancellery. In 1676 he was still living and serving in the Khlebnyi prikaz (Grain Chancellery). Veselovskii, *D'iaki,* pp. 299-300.

21. Dementy Minich Bashmakov also served in the chancellery system in a variety of capacities and departments. His career spanned more than forty years. He is first recorded as an under secretary participating in a survey of crown lands in the Novgorod region in 1644-1645. After serving in several chancelleries, in 1663 he was promoted to conciliar secretary . His promotion to conciliar noble came in 1688. See MERSH, Vol. 3, p. 149; Veselovskii, *D'iaki,* pp. 45-46.

22. The phrase translated here as "with the Nezhin and Romanovka archpriests" is a direct and literal translation of "s nezhinskim i romanovskim protopopami." This does not make sense. No archpriest from Romanov, a town on the Right Bank, appears in the narrative of these events. It is probable that the reference is to Roman Onisimovich Rakushka-Romanovsky (1623?-1703), a cossack elder, who served in different posts in the hetmanate from 1654 to 1668, including the post of general treasurer from 1663 to 1668 and several stints as acting colonel of the Nezhin Regiment. He was associated with the rebellion of Hetman Briukhovetsky and had to flee to the town of Braslavl on the Right Bank. There he became a priest. See the unsigned article in MERSH, Vol. 30, p. 177, and Chapter III, Note 20, below.

23. Ivashka is a diminutive of Ivan. See Chapter I, Note 92.

24. Petrushka is a diminutive of Peter, intended to denigrate Doroshenko and his claims. See Chapter I, Note 92.

25. In terms of settled locations it is debatable whether Chernigov or Pereiaslav is older. Both originated as local centers of tribal unions and developed into administrative centers during the rise of Kiev under the Rus. Which of the towns is older in regard to ecclesiastical administration is also debatable. Some scholars have argued that Pereiaslav preceded Kiev as the seat of the first metropolitan, which if true would certainly give it precedence over Chernigov. Unfortunately no scholarly consensus has emerged. What perhaps can be agreed upon is that Archbishop Lazar Baranovich's concern in this argument is with ecclesiastical political goals rather than historical veracity.

26. Ivashka is a diminutive of Ivan, Yuraska of Yury or Yuras. See Chapter I, Note 92.

27. A Polish or Lithuanian zloty was a large silver coin of the sixteenth and seventeenth centuries equal to twenty-four grosha or twenty copecks. See Pushkarev, *Dictionary,* p. 193.

28. Efimok was the Russian term for Joachimsthaler. These were large silver coins minted in Bohemia and frequently used in other European countries, including Russia. In Moscow, for a short time in the mid-seventeenth century, efimoks were stamped over with the emblem of the Russian realm and called efimki s priznakami (efimoks with marks). At mid-century the tsar's treasury

accepted one efimok as the equivalent of fifty copecks. A efimok with marks was valued at sixty-four copecks. See Pushkarev, *Dictionary,* p. 18.

29. Owing to the fact that the different ranks were paid in different coinage and to Soloviev's failure to identify which officers were attached to the general staff of the hetmanate and which to the regiments, the compensation described here does not appear to be in proportion to rank. In fact, if a rough translation is made of the different coins to relative copeck equivalencies, and a separation is made between officers of the general staff and those of the regiments, compensation correctly follows rank. Thus of those attached to the general staff of the hetmanate the hetman received 30,000 copecks, the general chancellor 20,000 copecks, the general aides-de-camp 10,000 copecks each, and the chief justices 6,000 copecks. The two lowest ranks of the general staff, the court clerk and the standard bearer received roughly 2,000 copecks each. The colonels and captains, the highest ranks in the regiments, outranked the court clerk and the standard bearer on the general staff. Each received approximately 5,000 copecks. The rank and file cossacks received about 600 copecks each.

30. Furs were measured in timbers, with each timber containing forty pelts.

31. Ivan Samoilov (or Samoilovich) was a member and later colonel (1668-1669) of the Chernigov Regiment. He was made chief justice of the general staff of the hetmanate in 1669 and served in that capacity until 1672. In 1672 he was elected hetman. See text, pp. 120-121.

32. The monarchy in the Commonwealth was an elective office, thus Jan Kazimierz's renunciation of the throne necessitated an election (see Preface and Introduction, Note 4). This opened the door for a Russian candidate, a possibility which offered some potential advantages for the Moscow government. Other realms and dynasties entertained the same idea. Through his wife Marie Louise Gonzaga or Queen Ludwika Maria as she was known in Poland Jan Kazimierz had strong connections to the French King Louis XIV and a considerable amount of French money flowed into the Commonwealth to influence Polish politics. The well-financed French candidate for the now vacant throne was Henri Bourbon, son of the Prince de Condé. In addition, Lorraine, Prussia and Austria all supported aspirants and there were several local contestants as well. Michał Korybut (Wiśniowiecki), a local candidate, prevailed (see Chapter I, Note 45). For a very lively contemporary account of these "elections" see *Memoirs of the Polish Baroque. The Writings of Jan Chryzostom Pasek, a Squire of the Commonwealth of Poland and Lithuania.* Ed. and trans. by Catherine S. Leach (Berkeley, Cal., 1976), pp. 171-176, 205-216 and *passim.*

33. In the government of Poland-Lithuania the referendary (referendarz) was an important position, ranking just below the grand secretary. Brzostowski died in 1688.

34. Andrzej Olszowski (1621-1677) was bishop of Chełm and vice-chancellor of Crown Poland. A powerful individual, he played an important role in this election and was largely responsible for the victory of Michał Korybut (see Chapter I, Note 43). This increased Olszowski's power but did not make him popular among his peers.

35. The Treaty of Kardis (or Cardis) of 1661 concluded the Russo-Swedish war of 1656-1658. The treaty restored the boundaries fixed in 1617 by the Treaty of Stolbovo and required Russia to cede some territories in Estonia and Livonia. The treaty also established conditions of trade along the borders. In English, see MERSH, Vol. 6, p. 107 and Volume 20 of this series. See also V.V. Pokhlebkin, *Vneshniaia politika Rusi, Rossii i SSSR za 1000 let* (The International Politics of Rus', Russia and the USSR for 1000 Years), Vol. II, Book 1 (Moscow 1995), pp. 212-214, for a concise, yet complete summary in Russian.

36. John 15:5. "I am the vine, you are the branches. He who abides in me, and I in him, he it is that bears much fruit, for apart from me you can do nothing."

37. The eastern patriarchs who participated in the church councils of 1666-1667 were still in Moscow in 1668. See Chapter I, Note 2, above.

38. Hedvig Eleonora (1636-1715) was the daughter of Duke Friedrich III of Holstein Gottorp and Maria Elisabeth of Saxony. In 1654 she married King Karl X Gustav of Sweden and was crowned queen. Widowed in 1660, she served on the regency council for her son, King Karl XI (born 1656, reigned 1660-1697), who came of age in 1672 and assumed the reins of power in his own right. Queen Hedvig Eleonora outlived her son, and served on the regency council for her grandson, King Karl XII.

39. For Treaty of Kardis, see above Note 35. The Treaty of Oliwa, signed May 2-3, 1660, at the Oliwa monastery, now a suburb of Gdańsk, ended the First Northern War (1654-1660) between Poland and Sweden over a dispute about succession to the Swedish throne. The end of this war allowed Poland to turn full attention to the east, to territorial disputes with the Moscow government. See George J. Lerski, ed., *Historical Dictionary of Poland, 966-1945* (Westport, Conn., 1996), p. 402. The Treaty of Pliusa (1666) supplemented the Treaty of Kardis. See MERSH, Vol. 28, pp. 137-138 and Pokhlebkin, *Vneshniaia politika*, Vol. II, Book 1, pp. 217-218.

40. Voin Afanasievich Ordin-Nashchokin fled to the West in 1660, although he later returned to Russia. See Volume 20 of this series and Longworth, *Alexis,* pp. 138-139.

41. Gerasim Semeonovich Dokhturov's grandfather, Cyril, came to Moscow from Constantinople to serve as a physician to Tsar Fedor Ivanovich. His father, Semeon Kirillovich, served for over thirty years in different chancelleries. Starting as an undersecretary in 1613, he was promoted to crown secretary in 1631. When he retired in 1649 he was given a pension and inscribed in the lists of the select Moscow gentry. Gerasim, thanks to the elevation of his father, began his career in the chancelleries as a secretary in 1647, and was promoted to conciliar secretary in 1666-1667. Veselovskii, *D'iaki,* pp. 158-160.

42. Lukian Timofeevich Golosov appears to have been a second generation servitor in the chancellery system. He began his career as an undersecretary in the Chancellery of Military Tenures around 1644-1645 and was promoted to conciliar secretary in 1666-1667. In 1682 he was made a conciliar noble. Veselovskii, *D'iaki,* pp. 123-124.

43. Efim Rodionovich Yuriev began his career as an undersecretary in the Chancellery for Foreign Affairs at the end of 1648, and worked in various capacities in that chancellery throughout his career. In 1655-1656 he was promoted to crown secretary. He died in 1672-1673. Veselovskii, *D'iaki,* pp. 593-594.

44. Stanisław Beniewski was the Polish castellan of the Volyn district and a Polish ambassador to Russia.

45. Rzeczpospolita, the Commonwealth or Republic of Two Nations, created by the Union of Lublin (1569) in which the kingdom of Poland and the grand duchy of Lithuania were combined into a single realm through a real union and the Ukrainian lands of Lithuania were ceded to Poland. See Davies, *God's Playground,* Vol. I, pp. 152-155, and Preface and Introduction, Note 4.

46. The metropolitanate of Kiev was under the jurisdiction of the patriarch of Constantinople. According to canon law a change in jurisdiction could not be implemented without the approval of a full church council. Patriarch Paisios of Alexandria, still in Moscow following the Church Council of 1666-1667, was correct in his assertion that he had no authority to write to the patriarch of Constantinople in regard to such a matter, as well as in his explanation that the patriarch of Constantinople alone had no authority to effect such a change. On the other hand, insofar as the intent was to elevate the power of the patriarch of Moscow at the expense of that of the patriarch of Constantinople, there were also strong political reasons for Patriarch Paisios to do all in his power to avoid writing such a letter. For the correspondence see *Ikon* (Icon) in *Arkhiv iugozapadnoi Rossii* (Archive of Southwestern Russia), Vol. 5 (Kiev, 1872).

47. Peter Gavrilovich Marselis (died 1672) was a Danish merchant and manufacturer in Russia whose father already was established in Moscow. He received important charters from the Russian government allowing him to organize iron works on the rivers Vaga, Kostroma and Sheksna in 1644. In 1665 he was allowed to exploit the sources of copper ore in the Olonets district. In 1642-1643 he traveled to Denmark on a diplomatic assignment for the Russian government. At the direction of Ordin-Nashchokin, Marselis and his son Leonty Petrovich, referred to here, organized a temporary postal system between Moscow and Wilno. See V.S. Rumiantseva, "Marselis, Petr Gavrilovich," MERSH, Vol. 21, p. 110. Those interested in this extended and important family may consult E. Amburger, *Die Familie Marselis* (The Marselis Family) (Giessen, 1957) .

48. The phrase is " i v zolotykh ulika est'," literally "there is evidence in gold pieces." Thomas Kellerman (or Kelderman) was the son of Heinrich (Andrei) Kellerman. Both were English merchants living in Moscow and serving the tsar. Both performed diplomatic missions for the Russian government, one or the other travelling to England, Holland, Venice and the Holy Roman empire at the tsar's behest. Like native merchants they also served as factors for the tsar, engaging in trade on his behalf and apparently making a good profit for him. In

reward for service they were named gosti, the highest rank of merchant in Muscovy and one which bestowed lucrative privileges. See Samuel H. Baron, "Who Were the *Gosti?*" *California Slavic Studies,* 7 (1973), pp. 19-20.

49. Matskeevich was a courier sent by Doroshenko to Moscow. I have been unable to locate more information about him and thus assume he was a rank-and-file cossack.

50. Matthew 8:20. "And Jesus said to him, 'Foxes have holes, and birds of the air have nests; but the Son of man has nowhere to lay his head.'"

51. "The Christian affair" was the desired alliance of the Catholic and Orthodox powers against the Ottoman Turks promoted as a holy crusade by the papacy. In the end differences of interest proved stronger than Christian sympathy. There appears to have been a serious split within the Russian elite on the question of foreign policy, one group including Ordin-Nashchokin favoring a southern orientation in foreign policy, and another group including Khitrovo favoring a northern orientation in foreign policy. This may have been a relevant issue in the fall of Patriarch Nikon. Further, Paul Bushkovitch argues convincingly that a northern versus a southern cultural preference, with ramifications for foreign policy, was also an important issue in the Alexis Petrovich affair. See Paul Bushkovitch, "Power and the Historian. The Case of Tsarevich Aleksei Petrovich, 1716-1718 and N.G. Ustrialov, 1845-1859," *Proceedings of the American Philosophical Society,* 1/2 (June 1997), pp. 177-198.

52. Afonka is a diminutive of Afanasy, used by Ordin-Nashchokin, rather insincerely one would think, to signify his humility. This form of self-reference was required by the protocol of the day when addressing the tsar. See Chapter I, Note 92.

53. See above, Chapter I, Note 45.

54. 1 Timothy 6:10. "For the love of money is the root of all evils."

55. I have been unable to locate the phrase in the gospels "To all who work much will be given." Perhaps it is a paraphrase of 2 Corinthians 9:6: "he who sows sparingly will also reap sparingly, and he who sows bountifully will also reap bountifully." Or perhaps Luke 19:26, "I tell you, that to everyone that has will more be given; but from him that has not, even what he has will be taken away."

56. The phrase is s chetvertnymi i s kabatskimi otkupami. In the sixteenth and seventeenth centuries a chetvert' or chet' (literally quarter) was one of four (later five) financial departments that collected taxes from certain regions or territories to pay salaries to military serviceman. A sixth chetvert', the Novaia or New chetvert', collected revenues from the sales of alcohol and from customs duties. Given the context, the reference here is probably to the Novaia chetvert'. See Pushkarev, *Dictionary,* pp. 7-8.

57. See above, Chapter I, Note 69.

58. Soloviev refers here to Tsar Alexis Mikhailovich's second marriage to the young Natalia Kirillovna Naryshkina, the ward of Artamon Sergeevich Matveev.

59. His imperial majesty is Holy Roman Emperor Leopold I (Habsburg), born 1640, reigned 1658-1705. The "house of Austria" refers to the Habsburgs, including the Spanish line with its American possessions, as Jan Gniński recalls in his declamation. King Carlos II of Spain (reigned 1665-1700) was the last Habsburg to sit on the Spanish throne.

60. Batu was the son of Juchi, eldest son of Genghis Khan. Juchi predeceased his father, whereupon Batu inherited control of Juchi's appanage which faced Europe and comprised the attacking wing of the Mongol empire. It was Batu who, at least nominally, led the campaign which swept through the steppes south of the Russian principalities and overwhelmed the Kama Bulgars and the Kipchaks. In 1238 the Mongol forces turned north, overpowering the fragmented forces of the Russian princes, sacking Riazan, Kolomna, Moscow, Vladimir, Suzdal, Yaroslavl and Tver. Novgorod in the north appears to have been spared only by a thaw. The following year the southern Rus regions were taken. Chernigov was sacked, Kiev was captured and destroyed and Galicia was devastated. This marked the beginning of the so-called Mongol Yoke. About a century and a half after the conquest of the Russian lands Tokhtamysh, a descendant of Batu, was swept aside by another conquerer from the East, the Turk Tamerlane or Timur lenk (the Lame). Formerly allies, Tokhtamysh and Tamerlane disagreed over the possession of Azerbaijan. In 1391 Tamerlane defeated Tokhtamysh near present-day Orenburg. Tokhtamysh fled and his army was destroyed. Tokhtamysh's revival by 1395 incited another campaign. Tamerlane and his feared warriors raged as far north as the Russian town of Yelets in the upper Don Basin. Tamerlane did not attack Russia proper, but turned south. In 1396 his armies ravaged the southern regions, devastating the Kuban and the Caucasus and destroying the trade between the Genoese colonies of the Crimea and Central Asia. By "the wild heirs" of these two conquerors, who had left such an indelible impression, were meant nomadic groups such as the Crimean Tatars, the Kalmyks, the Nogay, which had emerged out of the fragmentation of the empires of these conquerers. A good introduction to the steppe empires is René Grousset, *The Empire of the Steppes. A History of Central Asia.* Trans. by Naomi Walford, (New Brunswick, N.J., 1970), pp. 254, 264-268, 409-465, and *passim.* For Soloviev's interpretation of the Mongol period in Rus, see Volume 4 of this series. For some translated Russian sources describing and lamenting the Mongol conquest, see *Medieval Russia's Epics, Chronicles, and Tales.* Ed. and trans. by Serge A. Zenkovsky, 2nd ed. (New York, 1974), pp. 193-223.

61. The Dolgoruky (or Dolgorukov) family was an eminent and princely one in Muscovy, able to trace its lineage back to Riurik. Princes Yury and Dmitry were sons of Prince Alexis Grigorievich. Both enjoyed long and distinguished service careers, although Yury was the more prominent of the brothers. Both attained the rank of boyar, Yury in 1648 and Dmitry in 1671. Yury participated in the sessions which generated the Ulozhenie or Law Code of 1649 and in subsequent years was personally close to Tsar Alexis Mikhailovich and thus influential in important political events of the time. Dmitry's first wife was a

cousin of Tsar Alexis's first wife, Tsaritsa Maria Ilynichna Miloslavskaia. His daughter Daria married Hetman Ivan Martynovich Briukhovetsky.

62. Tsar Vasily Ivanovich Shuisky was crowned tsar in 1606 during the Time of Troubles, following the murder of the First False Dmitry. In July 1610 he fell from power, was handed over to the Poles who were in Moscow at the time, and died a prisoner in Warsaw in September 1612. The return of his remains to Moscow was one of the conditions of the Truce of Polianovka. His reburial in the Archangel cathedral in the Kremlin on June 11, 1635 indicates that following these tumultuous events his brief reign was legitimated. For these events, see Volume 16 of this series, pp. 240-242. See also Chester Dunning, "Shuiskii, Vasilii Ivanovich" in MERSH, Vol. 35, pp. 61-67.

63. The Kalmyks and Nogay and others, such as the Crimean Tatars and Edisans, were nomadic tribal communities formed out of the fragmentation of the Golden Horde. This was a long process, the endpoint probably occurring in 1500 when the Crimean Tatars decisively defeated the khan of the Golden Horde. See Michael Khodarkovsky, *Where Two Worlds Met. The Russian State and the Kalmyk Nomads, 1600-1771* (Ithaca, NY., 1992) for a careful analysis of the evolution of the Kalmyk nomads in their interaction with the Russian government. For the Crimean Tatars, see Alan Fisher, *The Crimean Tatars*, pp. 1-50, for their history up to the time of Catherine II.

64. Rusyn was a term East Slavs living outside the boundaries of the Muscovite realm called themselves.

65. The Stryjkowski chronicle has not been translated into English, which is unfortunate. For a scholarly edition, see Maciej Stryjkowski (1547-c. 1582), *Kronika polska, litewska, zmódzka i wszystkiej Rusi Macieja Stryjkowskiego* (Chronicle of Poland, Lithuania, Samogitia, Lithuania and all Rus by Matthew Stryjkowski) (Warsaw 1980).

66. A chaika (literally a seagull) was the name given to a flat-bottomed boat commonly used by the cossacks for transport or war on the lower reaches of the Dnieper river and on the Black Sea. According to Guillaume Le Vasseur, Sieur de Beauplan, the boats were about sixty feet long, ten to twelve feet wide, and twelve feet deep, with no keel. Rather they were built on the hull of another boat. The boats were equipped with two rudders, one at each end, to avoid the need to turn the boat around when retreat was required. The boats had no decks. Inside the hulls bundles of reeds about the width of a barrel were attached, joined together end to end, extending the whole length of the boat. These reeds served to keep the boats from sinking when filled with water. See Guillaume Le Vasseur, Sieur de Beauplan, *A Description of Ukraine*. Introduction, Translation and Notes by Andrew B. Pernal and Dennis F. Essar (Cambridge, Mass., 1993), pp. 63-64, for a description and sketch.

67. Soloviev uses the phrase, russkim liudiam, translated as Rus people.

68. St. Kallistratos (Greek church), Callistratus (Western church) was one of the early martyrs for the faith, dying c. A.D. 304. A native of Chalcedon and a soldier in a cohort quartered at Byzantium on the opposite side of the Bosphorus,

he was charged before his officers with being a Christian by some of his fellow soldiers. He boldly confessed his faith and was beaten, then sewn up in a sack and thrown into the Bosphorus. The sack allegedly burst on touching the water and when Kallistratos emerged two dolphins bore him on their backs to the shore. The saint's life tells us that this miracle converted forty-nine soldiers. Further miracles worked by the saint converted a hundred and thirty-five more soldiers. The saint and the converts were imprisoned and put to death. The feast day of St. Kallistratos is celebrated on September 27 according to the Greek and Russian calendars. He does not appear to be celebrated in the Western calendar.

69. Vasily Borisovich Sheremetev commanded the Russian army at the battle of Chudnovo on September 17, 1660. The Russian forces were routed by the Poles under the commanders Stanisław Potocki and Jerzy Lubomirski, Sheremetev was captured and spent the next twenty years in Crimean captivity. For the Sheremetev family, see above, Chapter I, Note 16.

70. The word argamak is of Central Asian origin and means Arabian horse. In the first half of the seventeenth century their value ranged from 10 rubles to 100 rubles, with a median value of 36.25 rubles. They appear to have been used primarily for riding, but sometimes for military purposes. See Richard Hellie, *The Economy and Material Culture of Russia, 1600-1725* (Chicago, 1999), pp. 39, 43.

71. Yasyr' is a word of Turkic (Kirgiz) origin meaning captive or slave.

72. A yurt is a dwelling, a circular domed tent, usually of skins stretched over a frame, used by the nomads of the steppe. Yurt also signified the territory to which a nomadic Tatar tribe had grazing rights.

CHAPTER III

1. See Chapter II, Note 15.

2. This may refer to the incident described above in Chapter II, p. 39, where the Priluki colonel (Chapter II, Note 4) who remained loyal to Doroshenko slaughtered a delegation of Tatars sent to him by Sukhovey, or it may refer to an incident which occurred in 1663 during the chaos of the Ruin described in Vol. 11, Chapter II, pp. 121-122 in the Mysl' edition of Soloviev's work.

3. In 1669 Grigory Gamaleia was serving his second of three terms as colonel of the Lubny Regiment. During his first tenure as colonel of this regiment (1664-1666) he encountered difficulties with Briukhovetsky and was arrested. Clearing his name, he was appointed colonel again in 1668, but in 1669 joined Doroshenko. From 1671 to 1673 he was colonel of the Pavoloch Regiment, returning to the Lubny Regiment as colonel only in 1687. According to Gajecky he also served for a time as acting hetman, but the dates are not indicated. See above, Chapter I, p. 30, where Soloviev identifies Gamaleia as an emissary of Hetman Briukhovetsky to the sultan in April 1668, and Gajecky, *Cossack Administration*, Vol. 2, p. 400, 620, 622.

4. Patriarch Paisios of Alexandria was traveling home at this time, through the Ukraine, following the church councils of 1666-1667.

5. Lazar Baranovich was a prolific writer, producing many religious tracts, both polemical and doctrinal, as well as sermons, letters, etc. The work mentioned here, *Trub sloves* (Words of the Trumpets), was completed in 1667 but his request to the press of the Caves monastery in Kiev was refused owing to a shortage of paper and materials. Baranovich petitioned Moscow to print his work from 1669 to 1671. Finally, Baranovich was informed that Moscow could not print the work but the tsar did suggest he print it himself, and provided paper sufficient for the task. Only in 1674 was Baranovich successful in persuading the press of the Caves monastery to print *Words of the Trumpets*. See S. A. Klepikov, "Izdaniia Novgorod-Severskoi tipografii i lozhnochernigovskie izdaniia 1674-1679 godov" (Publications of the Novgorod-Seversk Printing Office and Pseudo-Chernigov Publications 1674-1679) in *Kniga. Issledovaniia i materialy. Sbornik VIII* (The Book. Research and Materials. Collection VIII) (Moscow, 1963), pp. 255-278.

6. Mikhail Khanenko was colonel of the Uman Regiment from 1656 to 1660, and again from 1664 to 1669. In 1669, with the support of the Poles, he proclaimed himself hetman, thus splitting the Uman Regiment. It was only in August 1674 that Uman fell to Doroshenko's Turkish allies. See MERSH, Vol. 16, pp. 123-124 and Gajecky, *Cossack Administration,* Vol. 2, pp. 623-624, 626, 654.

7. Uman lies on the Umanka river, about two hundred kilometers southwest of Kiev. The cossack regiment was organized in 1648 by Demian Gandza, and protected the southwestern border of the hetmanate. In 1669 Colonel Khanenko of this regiment proclaimed himself hetman. See Note 6, above.

8. For Bishop Methodios's disgrace, see text Chapter I, pp. 36-38.

9. For the Council of Glukhov and its results, see text, Chapter II, pp. 48-53.

10. For Stepan (diminutive, Stenka) Razin, see Chapter I, Note 52.

11. See Chapter 1, Note 13. Gvintovka was arrested by Hetman Briukhovetsky in 1667 under suspicion of conspiracy. As this appointment indicates, Gvintovka managed to free himself from suspicion, later gaining the confidence of Hetman Mnogogreshny.

12. A diminutive intended to convey insult as it is used here. The given name is Yury or Yuras, the diminutive Yuraska. See above Chapter I, Note 92.

13. A kalgay sultan was a deputy sultan. See above, Chapter II, Note 15.

14. Soldatskie polki or infantry regiments of the new formation. Military reforms in Russia in the seventeenth century led to the creation of regiments formed and trained on West European models, and often led and trained by foreigners. In addition to infantry regiments, cavalry regiments (reitarskie polki) and dragoon regiments (dragunskie polki) were formed. See Pushkarev, *Dictionary,* p. 137. For Muscovite military and the process of reform see Keep, *Soldiers of the Tsar,* and Hellie, *Enserfment and Military Change.*

15. Streletskie prikazy or musketeers' regiments. The musketeers regiments were the first permanent, regular regiments of the armed forces in Muscovy,

organized in the middle of the sixteenth century. In the sixteenth century the musketeers were a relatively small force, augmenting the noble cavalry, but in the seventeenth century their numbers grew. In the middle of the seventeenth century in Moscow alone there were more than twenty regiments of musketeers, each regiment numbering between 800 and 1,000 men. If in the first half of the seventeenth century the musketeers were the best foot soldiers in Russia, by the end of the century they were more remarkable for their participation in palace coups. Following a riot of the Moscow musketeers in 1698 Peter I executed more than one thousand alleged rebel musketeers and disbanded the regiments. See Pushkarev, *Dictionary*, pp. 149-150, also Keep, *Soldiers of the Tsar*, and Hellie, *Enserfment and Military Change*.

16. Simeon Adamovich, archpriest of Nezhin, was at one time a friend and follower of Archbishop Methodios, but later split with him. His activities are described above in Chapters I and II.

17. A black council, or a general council. See above, Chapter II, Note 2.

18. Khmelnichenko is a diminutive of Khmelnitsky and is intended to be derogatory. See above, Chapter I, Note 92.

19. The Castle of the Seven Turrets in Constantinople was a part of the fortifications surrounding the city. It was built by Sultan Mehmed II in 1457-1458, and incorporated the famed Golden Gate of Constantinople.

20. This is Roman Onisimovich Rakushka-Romanovsky (1623?-1703). The surname also appears as Rakushchenko or Rakusha in historical sources, as here. He has been identified as the author of the Letopis' Samovidtsa (Chronicle of an Eye-Witness). A cossack elder, he served in different posts in the hetmanate from 1654 to 1668. He was associated with the rebellion of Hetman Briukhovetsky and thus had to flee to the town of Braslavl on the Right Bank. There he became a priest. From 1676 to his death in 1703 he lived in Starodub, serving as priest of the church of St. Nicholas. See MERSH, Vol. 30, p. 177, and Chapter II, Note 22.

21. Patriarch Methodios III of Constantinople is mentioned in passing by Sir Steven Runciman, *The Great Church in Captivity. A Study of the Patriarchate of Constantinople from the Eve of the Turkish Conquest to the Greek War of Independence* (Cambridge, 1968), pp. 233, 250. There is a paucity of accessible information about the Constantinople patriarchate in this period. Deno John Geanokopolos, *A Short History of the Ecumenical Patriarchate of Constantinople (330-1990). "First among Equals" in the Eastern Orthodox Church* (Brookline, Mass., 1990) offers a good overview but by its nature cannot give information about specific patriarchs.

22. The term exarch can refer to several different secular or ecclesiastical functionaries depending on the time and the place. In this instance it denotes the representative of the patriarch of Constantinople in the Ukrainian territories, which administratively were directly dependent on the patriarch.

23. The Holy Wisdom cathedral was begun by Grand Prince Yaroslav in 1037 in front of Kiev's main central square. Modelled after the Byzantine cross-in-square church plan, the cathedral was a five-aisle building with thirteen domes.

The original mosaic and fresco decoration was completed by the time of the cathedral's first consecration in 1046 and included portraits of the founder and his family, as well as scenes from the life of St. George, Yaroslav's patron saint. The cathedral was greatly enlarged and modified in the seventeenth century, and again in the nineteenth century, so that little of the original remains. See H. Logvin, *Kiev's Hagia Sophia* (Kiev's Holy Wisdom Cathedral) (Kiev, 1971); V.N. Lazarev, *Mozaiki Sophii Kievskoi* (The Mosaics of the Kiev Holy Wisdom Cathedral) (Moscow, 1959); A. Poppe, "The Building of the Church of St. Sophia in Kiev," *Journal of Medieval History,* 7 (1981), pp. 15-66.

24. See above, Note 5.

25. In this passage, Baranovich is playing around with, or showing off his command of Aristotelian concepts and categories. The telos of the word is the deed or act it signifies, and only the deed completes or perfects the word. The Russian original is rather strained and therefore the English translation is a free one. Perhaps the most important sources for the wider dissemination of Aristotelian philosophy (through scholastic theology) and concepts in the Ukraine, and by the second half of the seventeenth century in Russia, were the Jesuit academies which flourished in the Commonwealth with the successes of the Counter Reformation. This Catholic penetration stimulated a response from the Orthodox, the creation of schools that were Jesuit in form and Orthodox in spirit. For early schools founded by the confraternities and the Kiev Academy see below, Notes 40 and 50. It was only later in the seventeenth century that Aristotelian philosophy and scholastic theology began to exert a significant attraction on the educated elite in Russia. The influx of Ukrainian and Belorussian churchmen into Russia as a result of turmoil on the western frontier contributed to the spread of new ideas and books, both theological and secular. In addition, Greek churchmen of the diaspora frequently appeared in Moscow, hat in hand, and more than willing to share their knowledge and learning for a price. Despite their Orthodox credentials many of these Greeks were educated, at least in part, in Western universities such as Padua (a center of neo-Aristotelianism) or Rome. In addition to the works cited in Notes 40 and 50, below, pertaining to the Kievan Academy and the brotherhood schools, interested readers might turn to Harry T. Hionides, *Paisius Ligarides* (New York, 1972), which examines the career of a somewhat unsavory Greek churchman in Moscow. Potter, *Russian Church,* Vol. 2, pp. 384-394, 412-505, discusses the struggle over the founding of an academy in Moscow and the content of the curriculum as well as the eucharistic controversy, one example of the impact of Aristotelianism and scholastic theology in Russia. William K. Medlin and Christos G. Patrinellas, *Renaissance Influences and Religious Reforms in Russia. Western and post-Byzantine Impacts on Culture and Education (16th-17th Centuries)* (Geneva, 1971) and Max J. Okenfuss, *The Rise and Fall of Latin Humanism in Early-Modern Russia. Pagan Authors, Ukrainians and the Resiliency of Muscovy* (Leiden, 1995) are also useful and offer other perspectives on these issues. The patriarch who first approved Baranovich's work was Joasaph II. In 1667 he was archimandrite of the

Trinity-St. Sergius monastery in Zagorsk when he was chosen patriarch to replace the deposed Patriarch Nikon. He served as patriarch for five years before his death in 1672.

26. "New Rome" or Constantinople. By the fourth century the center of the Roman empire had shifted east. Constantinople was founded by Constantine I in 324 on the site of the Greek city of Byzantion and dedicated on May 11, 330. It served as the seat of the imperial government, replacing "Old Rome" in that capacity.

27. Osmachok or osmina, a dry measure (an eighth), equal to one-half a chet' or chetvert'. In the seventeenth century the official chetvert' was equal to eight puds of rye (one pud equals thirty-six American pounds). Thus one osmina or osmachok was officially equivalent to eighteen American pounds. In practice, there were many deviations.

28. When the Israelites were wandering in the wilderness some members of the band, including Dathan and Abiram the sons of Eliab, challenged Moses, thus rebelling against God. For their hubris and disobedience the Lord ordered them swallowed by the earth with all their goods and chattels. Numbers 16:3-31, and referenced again in Deuteronomy 11:6.

29. This is the first Council of Nicea (325) convened by the Emperor Constantine I to address the problem of Arianism. The exact number of bishops attending is unknown. Church tradition sets the number at three hundred and eighteen. The council's creed was the first dogmatic definition of the church to have more than local authority. The council also established the computation for Easter and recognized the jurisdiction of Rome, Alexandria and Antioch. See E. Boularand, *L'Héresie d'Arius et la 'Foi' de Nicée* (The Arian Heresy and the Faith of Nicaea), 2 vols. (Paris, 1972); C. Luibhéid, *The Council of Nicea* (Galway, 1982).

30. See above Chapter II, Note 2.

31. The Camp (Sech) of the Zaporozhian Cossacks was located originally on the island of Little Khortitsa in the Dnieper river, south of the cataracts below the river's first major bend. The Camp subsequently moved but always remained south of the cataracts, thus za porogami, beyond the cataracts, provided the name for the area, Zaporozhia, and the cossacks in this area. The Zaporozhian Camp was the center of the Zaporozhian Cossacks although some lived further north in towns while others were based in or near the Camp itself, on the lower reaches of the Dnieper. These latter were known as the cossacks of the Lower Reaches. By the seventeenth century the distinctions and differences between the "town cossacks" and those of the Lower Reaches were becoming more pronounced. See Edward Sokol, "Sech'," MERSH, Vol. 33, pp. 161-168; Subtelny, *Ukraine,* pp. 110-111; Magocsi, *A History of Ukraine,* pp. 179-181.

32. Pavel Ivanovich Teteria (died c. 1670) was involved in the tortuous struggles that racked the Ukraine in the third quarter of the seventeenth century. A noble by birth and well-educated, his policies were pro-Polish in their direction. In the 1640s he was a close associate of Bogdan Khmelnitsky and by 1653 he had been named colonel of the Pereiaslav Regiment. He was active in his opposition

to Russian efforts to annex the Ukraine, instead supporting Polish claims. In 1658 he was involved in negotiations over the Union of Gadiach. In 1663 he succeeded Yury Khmelnitsky as hetman of the Right Bank Ukraine. In 1665, fearing he would be turned over to his enemy Hetman Briukhovetsky on the Left Bank, Teteria fled to Poland. Dissatisfied with his treatment in Poland he left, shifting his allegiance to the sultan. See "Teteria, Pavel Ivanovich," MERSH, Vol. 39, p. 23; Gajecky, *Cossack Administration*, Vol. 2, p. 654; Subtelny, *Ukraine*, 145-146; Z. Wójcik, "The Early Period of Pavlo Teterja's Hetmancy in the Right-Bank Ukraine (1661-1663)," *Harvard Ukrainian Studies*, 3-4 (1979-1980), pp. 958-972.

33. The term Soloviev uses here and in other places is "Tsargrad", "the tsar's city," a term frequently used in early Russian sources for Constantinople, today Istanbul.

34. The term I have translated as "official" is kaimakam or kaymakam signifying a governor of an administrative district in the Ottoman empire, or more generally a high official in the bureaucracy, in this case in the central bureaucracy in Constantinople. Pasha is the highest title of civil and military officials under the padisha or sultan. Mustafa is too common a name to identify this individual with any certainty, based on the information given.

35. The Hagarites were the descendants of Abraham through Ishmail, his son by the Egyptian servant Hagar. Here this term refers to the Muslim Arabs. See Genesis 16 and 25:12-18.

36. Italics and exclamation point in parentheses are Soloviev's.

37. "[A]mong Rus Christians" here translates mezhdu russkimi khristianami, indicating Christians living in the area now known as Ukraine. Below, "good of the Russian churches" translates dobra tserkvam rossiiskim. Soloviev was a man of the nineteenth century, not the twentieth. He more frequently uses russkii to mean Russian, not making a distinction among Great Russians, White Russians and Ukrainians. When he requires an adjective that refers specifically to the area now known as Ukraine, he generally uses the term malorossiiskii or Little Russian.

38. The term translated here as "Lieutenant...of the musketeers" is streletskii polugolova. He served as assistant to the golova streletskii, in this translation project rendered as musketeer captain. By the end of the seventeenth century polkovnik was beginning to replace the term golova as a musketeer rank. At the beginning of the eighteenth century the musketeers were abolished by Peter I. See Pushkarev, *Dictionary*, pp. 149-150.

39. For Little Russian Chancellery, see Chapter I, Note 63.

40. Most educated cossacks during the hetmanate would have received their education at the Kiev Mogila Academy, although some were educated in academies in the Commonwealth. In the 1640s Ivan Vygovsky, Ivan Samoilovich and Pavel Teteria were students at the academy, as were others who later became officers in the companies and on the general staff of the hetmanate. The academy was a defender of Orthodoxy but its curriculum was essentially Jesuit and it

taught the Polish and Latin languages. Educated cossacks of the period would have been familiar with, and probably used Latin script, not Cyrillic (Russian). Their religious orientation was firmly Orthodox, their political orientation was in flux, their cultural orientation indisputably influenced by Polish culture. See Omelian Pritsak, "The Kiev Mohyla Academy in Ukrainian History," Ihor Ševčenko, "The Many Worlds of Peter Mohyla," George Gajecky, "The Kiev Mohyla Academy and the Hetmanate," and Ryszard Łużny, "The Kiev Academy in Relation to Polish Culture," all in *The Kiev Mohyla Academy,* Harvard Ukrainian Studies, Vol. VIII, Number 1/2 (June 1984), pp. 5-44, 81-92, 123-135.

41. Neither Gajecky, *Cossack Administration*, nor D.I. Iavornits'kii, *Istoriia Zaporozhskikh Kozakov* (History of the Zaporozhian Cossacks), 3 vols. (St. Petersburg 1897; reprint Kiev 1991) identify a Voroshilov regiment. Soloviev may mean the Voronezh company, organized in 1654 as part of the Nezhin Regiment. Subsequently it was made part of the Hetman Guards and transferred from the jurisdiction of the Nezhin Regiment to the General Military Chancellery of the hetmanate. The presence of cossacks of this company in Baturin, the headquarters of the hetman in this period, would not be remarkable. For the Voronezh company, see Gajecky, *Cossack Administration*, Vol. 1, p. 188.

42. The phrase Soloviev uses here is da pust' nezdorov priedet, literally "Well, let the sickness come."

43. Mnogogreshny is threatening to seize the messenger, Musketeer Lieutenant Alexander Tikhonovich Taneev, and send him to the Crimean khan as a captive or slave, should he come again with unwelcome news.

44. Gates translates, fortki, singular fortka, a usage more common in the southern regions of Russia and the Ukraine than in the center or north. See Dal', *Tolkovyi slovar'*, Vol. 4, p. 538.

45. Family networks and linkages are important to all cultures, but the way these links are conceptualized and relationships defined differ according to time and place. As a result, kinship and family terminology can be difficult to translate. Ziat' (plural ziatia) is used in the plural here and translated as "in-laws," a term more commonly known than affine or affinal relations (people related through marriage). Ziat' is a term used generally and inclusively but one that also has specific meanings. Ziat' may be translated son-in-law, the husband of a daughter, but also include the husband of a sister (brother-in-law), and the husband of a husband's sister (brother-in-law). Further, it encompasses the relationship between a man and the parents of his wife (father- and mother-in-law), and the brother and sister of his wife (brother- and sister-in-law). Approached from another perspective, the English term, brother-in-law, may be translated shurin (a woman's brother is shurin to her husband), svoiak (the husband of a woman's sister is svoiak to her husband), or dever' (a man's brother is dever' to his wife). Sister-in-law may be translated nevestka (the wife of a brother), as zolovka (a man's sister is zolovka to his wife), or svoiachenitsa (a woman's sister is svoiachenitsa to her husband). Nevestka also can be translated as daughter-in-law (a son's wife). In Russian, from the perspective of a man, his

wife's mother is teshcha and her father test', but from the perspective of a woman, her husband's mother is svekrov' and his father svekor. When Soloviev uses ziat' in a plural form, as here, I have translated it as "in-laws." When he uses it in the singular, I have translated it specifically (son-in-law or brother-in-law) if I can identify the individual and the relationship to which Soloviev refers. If I cannot make such an identification, I have retained the general translation of in-law.

46. In this sentence, ziat' is used in the singular. I have translated it as son-in-law because Andrei Nesterenko, Mnogogreshny's son-in-law, was colonel of the Lubny Regiment at this time. Gajecky, *Cossack Administration*, Vol. 2, p. 400.

47. A Stepan Grechany-Potrebnich was general chancellor on the general staff of the hetmanate from 1663 to 1665, later serving as a justice in the Gadiach Regiment from 1675 to 1677. This is probably the same Stepan Grechany, sometimes Grechanov according to Soloviev, noted here but his exact position in 1672 is uncertain. See Gajecky, *Cossack Administration*, Vol. 1, p. 362; Vol. 2, p. 665.

48. This is probably Yeremey Andreevich, who served as captain of the Baturin company from 1676 to 1689. Here he is identified as ataman, probably city ataman of Baturin. Gajecky, *Cossack Administration*, Vol. 1, p. 156.

49. The word translated as farmstead is khutor, a farmstead or a small village in the Ukraine and areas of cossack settlement in South Russia.

50. Founded in 1615, the origins of the Kiev Brotherhood monastery were closely tied with the emergence of confraternities in the Ukraine in the late sixteenth century. These confraternities were formed in response to the encroachments of the papacy and the Jesuits in the region. The best way to meet the Catholic challenge was by way of a renewal and a reform of Orthodoxy, thus the confraternities were closely linked to education and the foundation of schools and academies. The Kiev Brotherhood and its school zealously participated in the struggle against assimilation into the Western church. For the confraternities, see Ia.D. Isaievych, *Bratstva ta ikh rol' v rozvytku ukrains'koi kul'tury XVI-XVIII st.* (The Confraternities and Their Role in the Development of Ukrainian Culture from the Sixteenth to the Eighteenth Centuries) (Kiev, 1966).

51. A thaler or Joachimsthaler was a unit of foreign currency, equivalent to about 1 ruble. See also efimok, Chapter II, Note 28.

52. Konstantin Stryevsky was general standard-bearer (1669-1672), acting colonel of Chernigov Regiment for a short period in 1669, and acting colonel of the Pereiaslav Regiment for two months in 1671 while Dmitrashko-Raich was under arrest by Hetman Mnogogreshny. The general standard-bearer originally was an officer of the hetman's court. In 1675 he became a full-fledged member of the general staff council. His duties included displaying the standard of the hetman during ceremonies and on campaigns, and other duties as assigned by the hetman. See Gajecky, *Cossack Administration*, Vol. 1, p. 72, 294; Vol. 2, pp. 676-677.

53. Maksim Alekseev was a clerk in the Chancellery for Foreign Affairs. He appears to have been a specialist in Polish affairs. In 1667 he was clerk in the delegation headed by Ordin-Nashchokin for negotations with the Poles and in 1683 he was clerk in the delegation headed by Prince Yakov Nikitich Odoevsky to Poland. There is no record of his promotion beyond the rank of clerk. See Veselovskii, *D'iaki*, p. 17.

54. Cherkassians or Cherkasy were other terms used to designate Ukrainians. See Chapter I, Note 81.

55. The phrase "by blood and marriage" translates bratstvo i svatovstvo, with bratstvo indicating a kinship relation and svatovstvo indicating an affinal relation. Soloviev introduces the family ties linking Mnogogreshny and Doroshenko abruptly and rather cavalierly, with no explanation or elaboration. He identifies both Mikhail Zinoviev and Kunitsky as cossacks, but neither they nor their family names are included in Gajecky, *Cossack Administration*. Iavornitskii, *Istoriia Zaporozhskikh Kozakov*, Vol. 3, p. 34 and Note, p. 390, refers to a Kunitsky who was a Polish noble (shliakhtich) appointed by the Polish king as acting hetman of the cossacks on the Right Bank (1683-1684). Pasek speaks of a Stepan Kunicki, identifying him as a nobleman from Lublin who was appointed hetman of the cossacks by the Polish king and led an invasion into Tatar lands in 1683. According to Pasek, Kunicki later was killed by the cossacks themselves. Leach, *Memoirs. Pasek,* p. 278. Below, p. 117, Mikhail Zinoviev is identified as a nephew (plemiannik) of Mnogogreshny.

56. The verb I have translated here as "raze" is rubit', literally "to chop, or to cut down."

57. The term used here is korolik, a diminutive and derogatory form of king. See Chapter I, Note 92.

58. A "Black Tatar" was a free Tatar, a member of the Tatar aristocracy, but nonetheless greatly inferior to the Turkish sultan in rank at least in the eyes of the Turkish sultan.

59. "Na ochnoi stavke" was a legal procedure, common to early Russia, wherein an accused was confronted by the accuser.

60. Vasyl (Vasiuto) Zolotarenko, Yakim Samko and Aniky (Ioaniky) Silich were executed by Briukhovetsky upon his election as hetman in 1663. Although the tsar's government was deeply involved in the political struggles in the Ukraine and in the Zaporozhian Host, seeking to shape the situation to its own advantage, the insinuation here that Prince Velikogo-Gagin and the tsar's army were directly involved in the murder of these unsuccessful candidates for the hetmancy is not supported by the evidence. See above, Chapter I, Notes 46-49.

61. Senka is a diminutive for Semeon. See Chapter I, Note 92.

62. A levok or "lion dollar" or rijksdaler was a Dutch silver coin equal to two and one half guilders.

63. Vaska is a diminutive for Vasily, here used affectionately. See Chapter I, Note 92.

64. Grigory Karpovich Bogdanov enjoyed a long and distinguished career in the chancellery system, with important assignments in the Ukraine. He was a member of the delegation led by Ordin-Nashchokin to Poland in 1662-1663, a participant in the negotiations leading to the conclusion of the Andrusovo treaty and was in the delegation led by Prince Grigory Grigorievich Romodanovsky to Little Russia for the election of the hetman in 1669. At the end of 1671 he was promoted from secretary to conciliar secretary. There is some uncertainty and confusion, owing to another Bogdanov, Grigory Kuzmich, who served in the chancellery system at this time. One of these two was a victim of the musketeers rebellion in 1682. The musketeers demanded execution but Bogdanov escaped with exile. See Veselovskii, *D'iaki,* pp. 56-57.

65. In other words, the clerk and his fellows were present at the execution of Yakim Samko in 1663 (see above, Chapter I, Note 48) and shared in the spoils, reminiscent of the Roman centurions who cast lots for Christ's robe after his crucifixion.

66. Ioanniky Galiatovsky was one of the first monk-clerics in the Ukraine to advocate and propagate sermons. He was rector of the Kievan Academy from 1657 to 1669 and archimandrite of the monastery of the Virgin at Elets from 1669 until his death. He was also the author of several collections, including *Kliuch razumeniia* (Key to Understanding) first printed in 1659, a collection of sermons intended for the parish clergy, and *Nebo novoe* (The New Heaven) first printed in 1669, a collection of edifying miracles. There is no substantive work on Galiatovsky in English.

67. Perhaps Feodosy, who was in Moscow for the trial of Patriarch Nikon, and who briefly served as acting patriarch of Moscow and All Russia. See Makarii (Bulgakov), *Istoriia russkoi tserkvi* (History of the Russian Church), 12 volumes (St. Petersburg, 1877-1891), Vol. 12, pp. 758-759.

68. For Konstantin Stryevsky, see above, Note 52.

69. To take monastic vows was to remove oneself from the political sphere and disqualify oneself from any participation in political affairs permanently, at least in theory. In practice this was not always the case, as the example of Yury (the monk Gedeon) Khmelnitsky illustrates.

70. Fedor Zhuchenko served as colonel of the Poltava Regiment from 1659 to 1661 and again from 1670 to 1672. Gajecky, *Cossack Administration,* Vol. 2, pp. 515, 517.

71. Probably written in Latin script. See above, Note 40.

72. This is of course the future Peter I, the Great (1672-1725, reigned 1682-1725), the first son of Tsar Alexis Mikhailovich and his second wife, Natalia Kirillovna Naryshkina.

73. The companies (kompaniia) referred to here consisted of mounted merce-naries (kompaniitsi), often cossacks coming from the Right Bank. Like all merce-naries they were loyal to the person who paid them, in this case the colonels of the different regiments. Iavornits'kii, *Istoriia Zaporozhskikh Kozakov,* Vol. 3, p. 490.

74. In June "the third hour in the morning," would be approximately 7:05 a.m. Moscow time. The hours were based on the time of beginning of the church service, which depended on the month, the time of the year, and the time of sunrise. See E.I. Kamentseva, Khronologiia (Chronologies) (Moscow, 1967), Table 13, p. 108 and p. 110. I thank Professor Daniel Kaiser for giving guidance on this question, and for the citation.

75. For chaika, see above, Chapter II, Note 66.

76. See text, Chapter II, p. 38 and *passim*.

77. Ekten'ia, or litany is a prayer incorporated in the liturgy consisting of versicles and responses, each response generally ending with the phrase "Lord, have mercy."

78. The seventh year of the indiction (a fifteen-year cycle) is meant here. In this case the year indicated is 1672, the cycle beginning in 1665. See Grigorii D'iachenko, *Polnyi tserkovno-slavianskii slovar'* (A Complete Church-Slavic Dictionary) (Moscow 1993), p. 222.

79. The golden gates were monumental gates situated at the south end of the land walls of Constantinople, used for imperial triumphs and other great state occasions. It probably was constructed during the reign of Theodosius II (died 450). The gates were incorporated into the Castle of the Seven Turrets erected by Sultan Mehmed II in 1457-1458. See above, this chapter, Note 19.

80. The name of this false prophet, Vdovichenko, means "son of a widow" (vdova, or the older term, vdovitsa meaning "widow").

CHAPTER IV

1. For the Wiśniowiecki family and Michał Korybut, king for four years (1669-1673), see Chapter I, Note 45. Davies' assessment (*God's Playground*, Vol. I, pp. 470-472) of the status of the family, particularly its financial standing, differs from that of Soloviev.

2. For Jan Sobieski see Chapter I, Note 31.

3. For Sultan Mehmed IV (reigned 1648-1687), see Chapter I, Note 5.

4. The Ottoman victory in the siege of the fortress of Candia in 1669 ended the Cretan War between Venice and the Ottoman empire and completed the conquest of the island of Crete, the largest Mediterranean island remaining in Venetian hands. The bulk of the island was conquered by 1646 but the war dragged on, primarily because of internal political struggles in Constantinople, and the fortress of Candia did not fall until 1669. See Ekkehard Eickhoff, *Venedig, Wien und die Osmanen. Umbruch in Südosteuropa, 1645-1700* (Venice, Vienna and the Ottomans. Revolution in Southeast Europe, 1645-1700) (Munich, 1970), pp. 228-264.

5. The Pruth river flows along the boundary between Rumania and Moldavia, then continues south, dividing into two branches. One branch flows west to become the Danube. The other, the Dunay river, flows southeast towards the Black

Sea. When translating from Russian into English translators frequently translate Dunay as Danube, blurring the distinction between the two courses. When there is doubt, I have used the less specific Danube. Otherwise I have used Dunay.

6. Karol Stanisław Lużecki was castellan of Podlasie in 1672 and later governor of Podolia. Pasek mentions this campaign, and Lużecki's role in it. According to him, the Turks' victories in Podolia and the Ukraine in this campaign were not the result of military prowess, rather of bribery and treason. Leach, *Memoirs. Pasek*, p. 221.

7. Yanychar or janissaries were soldiers of an elite corps of Turkish troops. Organized in the fourteenth century to serve as guards to the sultan, originally janissaries were selected from subject Christian boys taken as tribute. The janissaries continued as the largest unit of the Ottoman army until they were abolished following a rebellion in 1826. By the late seventeenth century and early eighteenth century the coherence and discipline of the force was in decline, although sufficient to rout this cossack contingent. The term aǧa designates a military or civil officer in the Ottoman empire. In this instance it is a military officer.

8. A pomest'e (service landholding) was an inhabited holding, granted on condition of service, originally military service to the sovereign. The first mention of a conditional landholding, although without the term pomest'e, occurs in the testament of Ivan Kalita in 1327. The system developed in the centuries following. Service landholdings may be contrasted to votchiny (patrimonial estates) which belonged to the holder and could be alienated through sale, exchange, etc. In theory distinct, in practice service landholdings exhibited a tendency to meld with patrimonial estates, despite the efforts of the government to keep them separate. The Ulozhenie or Law Code of 1649 permitted regulated exchange of service landholdings. By the end of the seventeenth century the distinctions had become even more blurred. See Jerome Blum, *Lord and Peasant in Russia from the Ninth to the Nineteenth Century* (Princeton, N.J., 1961), p. 85; Pushkarev, *Dictionary*, pp. 93, 181-182.

9. A poltina is a unit of Old Russian money. One poltina equals fifty copecks or one-half a ruble. "A tenth of their income" translates desiataia den'ga. This was an extraordinary income tax introduced in the seventeenth century to cover war expenses, as here. See Pushkarev, *Dictionary*, pp. 92, 10-11.

10. Buczacz is near Tarnopol in Galicia. Here on October 16, 1672 Polish envoys signed a treaty of capitulation with the Turks. In addition to the annual tribute all districts of the Ukraine still in Polish hands by the Treaty of Andrusovo were relinquished to the Turks. See Davies, *God's Playground*, Vol. 1, p. 471. Ducats translates chervonnye and refers to a gold coin, valued at about three rubles.

11. In this passage Simeon Adamovich evokes Psalms 22:6. "But I am a worm, and no man; scorned by men, and despised by the people."

12. The word here translated as "Germans" is nemtsy (singular nemets). This can mean foreigners in general, or it can mean Germans or, more accurately,

Northern Europeans. Here the context suggests the narrower meaning, See Chapter I, Note 70.

13. For the seige of Candia, see above, Note 4.

14. Yakov Kondratievich Lizogub was colonel of Kanev from 1666 to 1669 and one of two aides-de-camp on Doroshenko's general staff from 1669 to 1674. Gajecky, *Cossack Administration*, Vol. 2, pp. 610-611, 671.

15. The reference here is to the Treaty of Buczacz (Buchach). See above Note 10. The town of Belaia Tserkov was one of the towns to be handed over to the sultan in accordance with that treaty.

16. Cavalry equipment translates konskie zheleza, a phrase whose precise meaning eludes me, but perhaps is intended to include horse shoes, bits and bridle parts, stirrups, and possibly protective armor.

17 Kodak or Koidak was an important fortified town in Zaporozhia. See "Kodak, Fortress of" MERSH, Vol. 17, p. 93. For the Camp, see above, Chapter III, Note 31.

18. This is a paraphrase of Psalms 42:1. "As a hart longs for flowing streams, so longs my soul for thee, O God."

19. Lebedinye ozera, Swan Lakes, are north of Lokhvitsia near the headwaters of the Sula river. They are a resting and breeding place in the migratory cycle of the swans. They served as an inspiration for Peter Ilich Tchaikovsky's famous ballet.

20. Khokhly, translated here as "topknots," was the customary hair arrangement for men in the Ukraine, the sides shaven and the top drawn up and bound into a ponytail.

21. Volunteer regiments translates the Ukrainian term okhochi. These were composed of mercenaries. Originally they were maintained only by the hetman, and were at his personal disposal. Later some of the colonels began to maintain their own mercenary companies, which led to more problems and complaints (see text, p. 119). The okhochi were divided into kompaniia or kompaniitsi (cavalry regiments), and serdiuki (infantry regiments). The phrase "little band of mercenaries" translates kompaneishchina and is another form, somewhat derogatory, of kompaniia, or company. A member of such a company is a kompaneishka. See Gajecky, *Cossack Administration*, Vol. 2, pp. 631-632 and Chapter III, Note 73.

22. The incorporation of "Bolshoy" (the Elder) or "Menshoy" (the Younger) in a name, indicates that there is another sibling of the same name in the immediate family.

23. The Kalinchinsky towers were an important part of the Ottoman fortifications in Azov. See Alan W. Fisher, "Azov in the Sixteenth and Seventeenth Centuries," *Jahrbücher für Geschichte Osteuropas*, 21, No. 2 (1973), pp. 161-174.

24. For janissaries, see above, Note 7.

25. The term translated as "navigation channel" is erik or erichek. This is a narrow and deep channel, sometimes called a thalweg, where a river flows into a sea.

26. The Don Cossacks were a host located further east and south, in the region of the lower Don river and along the northern shores of the Sea of Azov. See Edward D. Sokol, "Don Cossack Host" MERSH, Vol. 9, pp. 218-221.

27. Pretenders, impostors claiming to be long-lost tsars or tsareviches, appeared in great number in Russia, beginning in the early seventeenth century during the era of chaos known as the Time of Troubles. The phenomenon was not unique to Russia, although perhaps the Russian examples, in particular the first False Dimitry, are more widely known. For a recent work on the phenomenon which includes an excellent discussion of the historiography see Maureen Perrie, *Pretenders and Popular Monarchism in Early Modern Russia. The False Tsars of the Time of Troubles* (Cambridge, 1995).

28. "a pod ispodom kaftnets chervchatyi kitaikovyi." Kitaika is generally translated as nankeen, a durable and tightly woven fabric manufactured in China of locally grown cotton, which gave the fabric a distinctive yellow color. Here the adjective chervchatyi indicates a deep crimson, almost purple color. The shorter under caftan described probably was of a nankeen-like weave, dyed to the "royal purple" color.

29. The term translated "little father" is batiushka, a colloquial form for father.

30. Solovetsk is a small island located in the White Sea approximately three hundred versts by water from Arkhangelsk. In the early fifteenth century Sts. Savvaty and German, and somewhat later Zosima, founded a monastery on this remote island. The Solovetsk monastery grew and flourished. In the seventeenth century the leading monks of the monastery stubbornly opposed the reforms introduced by Patriarch Nikon. From 1669 to 1676 the monastery withstood siege by government troops rather than accept the church reforms and the reformed books and ordo. Throughout its history the monastery served as a place of exile and incarceration for those out of favor with the government, becoming particularly notorious in this regard in the modern period. See V.I. Buganov, "Solovetskii Monastery" and Orchard, "Solovetskii Uprising of 1668-1676" in MERSH, Vol. 36, pp. 140-144; Georg Michels, "The Solovki Uprising. Religion and Revolt in Northern Russia," *Russian Review,* 1 (January 1992), pp. 1-15.

31. Stenka Razin was not exiled to Solovetsk although some of his followers did escape the suppression following the rebellion to join the defiant monks at the Solovetsk monastery. See preceding Note 30, and Chapter I, Note 52.

32. Here Soloviev uses Khvalynskoe more to designate the Caspian Sea. The origin of the term remains a subject of speculation but most scholars agree that the name is ultimately Iranian in origin and associated with Khwarazm/Khwarizm, or one of the peoples associated with this ancient state. See Max Vasmer, *Etimologicheskii slovar' russkogo iazyka* (Etymological Dictionary of the Russian Language), translated from the German and supplemented by O.N. Trubachev, 4 volumes (Moscow, 1986-1987). Volume 4, p. 229. For a discussion in English, Norman Golb and Omeljan Pritsak, *Khazarian Hebrew Documents of the Tenth Century* (Ithaca, N.Y., 1982), pp. 154-155. I thank colleagues of the

Early Slavic Studies Association internet list for their expert and prompt assistance on this question.

33. Boyar Ilia Danilovich Miloslavsky was the father of Tsar Alexis Mikhailovich's first wife, Maria. See Hughes, "Miloslavskaia, Mariia Il'inichna," MERSH, Vol. 22, p. 135.

34. The term used is gosudaricha, a diminutive form of gosudar', here used affectionately. See Chapter I, Note 92.

35. The word matiushka means "little mother", and parallels batiushka. See above, Note 28.

36. An arshin was a measure of length equivalent to twenty-eight inches or seventy-one centimeters.

37. I have translated siposhi as reeds. Chaikas had bundles of reeds tied to their sides to improve flotation and protect the occupants from hostile fire. I assume the supply of reeds mentioned here were for the chaikas. See Chapter II, Note 66.

38. Like an ell, a lokot is an obsolete measure used chiefly for cloth, originally based on the length from the elbow to the tips of the fingers. In this period it was equivalent to two-thirds of an arshin, forty-six centimeters or eighteen inches.

39. The general aide-de-camp Pashka or Pavel Gribovich was implicated in the downfall of Mnogogreshny and exiled to Siberia. On the way to Siberia he escaped. See text, Chapter III, pp. 116-117. The meaning here is somewhat unclear. The Russian is Pashka, byl s nami, uznal by ia, kak v Sibir' cherez pole posmotret', uznali by, kakoi zholnyr' Serko. It would suggest that Gribovich and Serko were close friends or associates before Gribovich's disgrace, but I can find no firm evidence to support or negate this hypothesis. For zholnyr' as "front-line soldier," see Dal', Tolkovyi slovar', Vol. 1, p. 526.

40. The term translated here as district is voevodstvo, the military and administrative area under a voevoda, generally translated as governor in this volume, unless the individual's duties were clearly and predominantly military, in which case it is translated as commander.

41. Timofey or Timish Tsytsura was colonel of the Periaslav Regiment in 1660. During the Chudnov campaign of 1660 he was acting hetman. In that campaign he switched sides with the rest of the cossacks, abandoning Moscow and joining the Poles. As a result the Poles defeated a Russian army of 36,000 soldiers, killing or taking captive all of them. Gajecky, Cossack Administration, Vol. 1, pp. 292, 315. For Yakim Samko, see Chapter I, Note 48; for Mikita Bezpaly, Chapter I, Note 41; for Yakov Barabash, Chapter I, Note 42; for Martyn Pushkar (Pushkarenko), Chapter I, Note 40; for Vasyl Zolotarenko, Chapter I, Note 49.

42. The picturesque phrase Soloviev used is "plevely vsiakie v narod (eti poslantsy budyt) puskat'."

43. The editors of the Mysl' edition of Soloviev's History (Moscow, 1993) identify this as Ivan Sulima. Gajecky identifies several individuals by the name of Ivan Sulima, but none for this period. The reference here probably is to Ivan

Sulymenko (Sulimka not a diminutive, but an error in transcription), colonel or acting colonel of the Belaia Tserkov Regiment in 1657. Gajecky, *Cossack Administration*, Vol. 2, p. 576.

44. Hetman Samoilovich here is referring to the disintegration in the Ukraine following the death of Hetman Bogdan Khmelnitsky (July 27/August 6, 1657). Ivan Vygovsky was confirmed as acting hetman in August 1657 but soon resigned in anger over Russian interference in the Ukraine. Vygovsky's resignation was not accepted by cossack officers and he returned to the post with an exacerbated anti-Russian orientation. Pro-Russian factions emerged in the Zaporozhian Host, including Yakov Barabash, Martyn Pushkar and others. The pro-Russian faction was supported and encouraged by Moscow. By 1658 a rebellion broke out, led by Pushkar and Barabash (See Notes 40-42). Vygovsky suppressed the rebellion, but relations with Moscow declined. At the same time, Vygovsky engaged in diplomatic struggles with the Polish Commonwealth, becoming increasingly anti-Polish as well as anti-Russian. In 1659 Vygovsky was removed as hetman and replaced by Yury Khmelnitsky. He continued both his anti-Russian and anti-Polish agitations until in 1664 he was shot by the Poles, apparently with cossack assistance. See Basarab, *Pereiaslav 1654*, pp. 13-15, 194, and 223 for different interpretations of these events leading up to, and part of this confusing and tragic period in Ukrainian history known as "The Ruin." For Soloviev's discussion of these events, see Volume 20 in this series.

45. For two months in 1665 Stepan Opara was hetman, or aspiring hetman, on the Right Bank, with the support of the Tatars. Gajecky, *Cossack Administration*, Vol. 2, p. 654.

46. The term used here is chernetskaia rada, synonymous with a black council, or general council. For black council, see above, Chapter II, Note 2.

47. There is no one word in English which will translate the Russian word posad. These were settlements which grew up around a town's kremlin or citadel and usually included government offices and the main churches of the town. The posads were inhabited by trading men, craftsmen, hired laborers and the like. In this series, it is translated as "town quarter." See Pushkarev, *Dictionary*, p. 95.

48. Here Soloviev writes k voevode i getmanu poskakal polkovnik i streletskii golova Kolobova. The verb indicates that the polkovnik (or colonel as translated in relation to cossack ranks) and the streletskii golova (translated as musketeer captain) are one and the same individual. The seventeenth century was a time of transition and reform, not least in the military. In the second half of the century the older term golova was being replaced by the term polkovnik in relation to the musketeers. See Pushkarev, *Dictionary*, pp. 149-150. At the beginning of the eighteenth century the musketeers along with their ranks were totally abolished. It would appear that here Soloviev encountered in the sources, and transferred to his own work, a very vivid example of a transition in process. To avoid confusion the double title here is not translated and the translation of captain for the head of a musketeer regiment is retained. In addition, the editors of the Mysl' edition of Soloviev do not identify Kolobov beyond what Soloviev

himself offers in this passage. I believe it is likely that Kolobov is a faulty transcription and this is the same Captain Mikhail Kolupaev of the Moscow musketeers, first mentioned in the text, p. 101.

49. *moskovskii polkovnik Tseev* commanded new-style regiments, thus I have translated his title as colonel. For the new-style regiments and military reforms, see above Chapter III, Note 14.

50. In the Russian Orthodox church, in theory, children received the name of a saint whose festival coincided with the date of baptism, normally eight days after birth. This became their "name-day." In practice there was much variation, not only in the interval between birth and baptism, also in the actual name given to the child. See Daniel H. Kaiser, "Naming Cultures in Early Modern Russia," *Harvard Ukrainian Studies,* 19 (1995), pp. 271-291.

51. Konstantin Solonina served as colonel of the Kiev Regiment from 1669 to 1682, and again from 1687 to 1690. In 1674 Yakov Solonina replaced his brother, serving as acting colonel of the regiment. The person referenced here is probably Konstantin, although that is not certain. Gajecky, *Cossack Administration,* Vol. 1, p. 206.

52. The editors of the Mysl' edition of Soloviev identify Chief Justice Petrov as Yakov Petrov. According to Gajecky, *Cossack Administration,* Vol. 2, p. 662, Doroshenko's chief justice in 1674 was Yakov Ulezko. The only close reference in Gajecky (p. 645) is to Yakov Petrovich, a justice on the staff of Acting Hetman Ivan Zolotarenko in 1654-1655. I am inclined to think that Chief Justice Yakov Ulezko is intended here.

53. The editors of the Mysl' edition of Soloviev do not identify this Migalevsky. In Gajecky, *Cossack Administration,* Vol. 2, pp. 620-622, there is no similar name listed among the colonels of the Pavolochie Regiment. In 1674 Andrei Doroshenko and Yakov Gamaleia are identified as colonels. The information about this regiment is very scarce. There was a Konstantin Migalevsky who was appointed by Hetman Samoilovich to serve as colonel of the restored Lisianka Regiment (Right Bank). The restoration of the regiment was not successful and Migalevsky only served from August to November of 1674. This may be the Migalevsky referenced here, and given the paucity of information, he may have been transferred from the Povolochie Regiment. Gajecky, p. 639.

54. Ivan Mazepa came from an important Ukrainian noble family. He received a broad education, studying at the Kiev Academy and later at a Jesuit college in Warsaw. As a gentleman-in-waiting to the Polish king he traveled extensively in Western Europe and served as royal emissary to the Zaporozhian Host. In 1687 he was elected hetman. While protecting his own interests and those of the Zaporozhian Host he was able to maintain good relations with the Moscow government, forging a close relationship with Peter I after he came to the throne in 1689. The Great Northern War placed unbearable strains on this relationship. In 1708, angered by encroachments on cossack autonomy and Peter I's refusal, when faced with an imminent Swedish invasion, to defend the cossacks from the Poles, Mazepa went over to the side of King Karl XII of Sweden

hoping to protect Ukrainian lands. Angered by Mazepa's "betrayal," Peter I's commander in the Ukraine, Prince Alexandr Danilovich Menshikov, attacked Mazepa's capital of Baturin and massacred its entire population. The defeat of the Swedish army at the battle of Poltava in 1709 spelled the end for Mazepa, as well as for Zaporozhian autonomy. Mazepa himself fled with King Karl XII of Sweden, taking refuge in Ottoman-ruled Moldavia. He died September 21, 1709. See James Cracraft, "Mazepa, Ivan Stepanovich," MERSH, Vol. 21, pp. 150-154; Orest Subtelny, "Mazepa, Peter I and the Question of Treason," *Harvard Ukrainian Studies,* 2 (1978), pp. 158-183; C. Manning, *Ivan Mazepa, Hetman of Ukraine* (New York, 1957); T. Mackiw, *Prince Mazepa, Hetman of Ukraine* (Chicago, 1967).

55. Patriarch Paisios of Alexandria was still in Moscow in 1669, having come to participate in the church councils of 1666-1667 which brought the Nikon affair to a close. Joasaph was selected patriarch of Moscow and All Russia at the conclusion of the church councils of 1666-1667 which formally deposed Nikon. He served as patriarch until his death in 1671. See above, Chapter I, Note 2.

56. The term translated here as "Ukrainian" is khokholach, referring to the hairstyle commonly worn by men in the Ukraine at that time (see above, Note 20).

57. Sable and other animal pelts were bundled together in groups of forty ("timbers" in English) for valuation, sale and exchange.

CHAPTER V

1. Regarding the Serdeniats, Soloviev's usage is obscure. Iavornits'kii, *Istoriia Zaporizhskikh Kazakov,* Vol. 3, p. 185, mentions a Serdeniat regiment (Serdeniatskii polk). According to Iavornits'kii, on October 4, 1696 Hetman Mazepa was instructed by the tsar to send a new regiment to the town of Tavan, a fortress on the southern reaches of the Dnieper river, to replace the Serdeniat Regiment. Colonel Dmitro Chechel commanded the new regiment, composed of serdiuki, or mercenary foot soldiers. Iavornits'kii capitalizes Serdeniatskii, suggesting a regiment, rather than a type of soldier, like the serdiuki. The regiment is not referenced by Gajecky, *Cossack Administration,* but this is not decisive. The composition of many of the regiments and companies of the hetmanate varied, particularly on the Right Bank, and for many of them there is very little information. Soloviev's usage suggests a group of people associated with an area I have been unable to identify, or ethnically distinct, like the *Cheremis.* Regarding the *Cheremis,* in his own footnote Soloviev identifies them as "the so-called Polish Tatars who betrayed the king." This could be the same group Pasek refers to as "Lithuanian Tatars," a group of Tatars who emigrated from Lithuania to Bessarabia during the short reign of King Michał (Korybut). In this period Bessarabia was subject to Turkish rule. According to Pasek, in 1672 it was the betrayal of these Tatars which assured the victory of the Turks in Podolia and the Ukraine. See text, pp. 125-127 and Chapter IV, Note 6, and

Leach, *Memoirs. Pasek*, p. 221, Note 3. The Cheremis, as an ethnic group, are more commonly called the Mariitsy or Mari, a Finno-Ugrian people incorporated into an expanding Muscovy in the sixteenth century. One group of Mari were located in the area around Kazan. In the second half of the seventeenth century they were drawn into the struggles among Russia, the Polish Commonwealth and the Ottoman Porte, along with the Kalmyks, Bashkirs and Nogay. The alliances were fluid. Soloviev may be referring to this group of Mari. See James S. Olson, ed., *An Ethnohistorical Dictionary of the Russian and Soviet Empires* (Westport, Conn., 1994), pp. 465-466.

2. A murza or mirza was a Tatar noble.

3. Soloviev reports this rumor about Mazepa, Lord Falibowski and his wife based on the account given by Jan Pasek. See Leach, *Memoirs. Pasek*, pp. 153-156.

4. For Pavel Ivanovich Teteria, see Chapter III, Note 32.

5. From 1660 to 1663 Yakim Samko, colonel of the Pereiaslav Regiment, was acting hetman. See Chapter I, Note 48.

6. For the council at Pereiaslav, see text, Chapter IV, pp. 153-154.

7. Chertomlik island is in the Chertomlik river, the right tributary of the Dniester river which flows into Zaporozhia.

8. Orekhovsky, or perhaps Orechowski, was an envoy from the Commonwealth to Doroshenko. I have been unable to identify him more precisely, or to verify the proper spelling of his name.

9. Quarter troops (Kwarciane Wojsko) were the predecessors of a regular army in the Polish Commonwealth. The name was derived from the fact that they were financed with one-quarter of the revenue produced by the royal estates. The force was established in the mid-sixteenth century by King Sigismund II Augustus to defend the southeastern borders from the encroachments of Tatars and Moldavians. In the late seventeenth century the quarter troops were merged with other mercenary troops. See Lerski, *Historical Dictionary of Poland*, p. 487.

10. The term is praporshchik, a rank in the Muscovite army, rather than a cossack rank.

11. The editors of the Mysl' edition of Soloviev (pp. 637, 642) identify Murashka as Colonel Andrei Murashka of the Chausy Regiment and Savva as the archpriest of Ladyzhin, referred to later in the paragraph. Gajecky, *Cossack Administration*, does not report a Colonel Andrei Murashka, and in fact there is little information about the Chausy Regiment. There is a Denys Murashka who served as colonel of the Cherkassy Regiment from 1662-1663 (Gajecky, Vol. 2, p. 590), confirming a cossack family with the surname Murashka. If we accept that Savva was the archpriest of Ladyzhin, then the identity of the sotnik (captain) who fled to the enemy camp with Murashka and the archpriest is a mystery. The context of this sentence suggests that Savva was the captain, probably of a cossack company. Gajecky, *Cossack Administration*, does identify a Sava who was captain of the Kyselivka company in 1649 (p. 94) and another (or perhaps

the same) Sava who was captain of the Kremenchuk company in 1666 (p. 491). There is insufficient information to equate all the Savas and Savvas, although a cossack captain Sava at this time is possible.

12. "From the second hour of the day," would be approximately 5:30 a.m., Moscow time. See Chapter III, Note 71, and Kamentseva, *Khronologiia*, Table 13, pp. 108, 110.

13. See Chapter II, Note 15.

14. Grishka is a diminutive of Grigory, brother of Petro Dorofeevich Doroshenko. See Chapter I, Note 92.

15. Colonel Lazicki was a Pole, probably with a Polish regiment. I have been unable to identify him more specifically, or to verify the spelling of his name.

16. Mikhail Grigorievich Romodanovsky was one of the sons of Prince Grigory Grigorievich Romodanovsky. See Chapter I, Note 82.

17. Mishka is a diminutive for Mikhail, here used affectionately. See Chapter I, Note 92.

18. Andriushka is a diminutive for Andrei, here used affectionately. See Chapter I, Note 92. For the capture and captivity of Andrei Grigorievich Romodanovsky, see text, pp. 32, 79-80.

19. It is not clear from Soloviev's wording whose wedding the young Mikhail Grigorievich Romodanovsky was to attend in Moscow. In 1674 it is too late for it to be the marriage of the tsar and Natalia Naryshkina. If he were referring to the marriage of Mikhail himself, presumably Soloviev would have indicated this unambiguously.

20. Feodora Alekseevna (1674-1678) was the third child, and second daughter of Tsar Alexis Mikhailovich and his second wife, Natalia Kirillovna Naryshkina.

21. *Spiritual Trumpets* translates *Truby dukhovnye*. This is the same book earlier entitled *Truby sloves (Words of the Trumpets)*. See Chapter III, Note 5.

22. For the printing office in Chernigov, see Chapter III, Note 5.

23. Mikhail Lezhaisky was made archimandrite of the Savior monastery in Novgorod-Seversk on February 2, 1670. Evidence places him in that post until June 9, 1677. Stroev, *Spiski ierarkhov*, p. 519.

24. By the end of the fourteenth century the lands later called the Ukraine were incorporated into an expanding Lithuania. A series of dynastic unions with Poland culminated in 1569 with the Union of Lublin which united Poland and Lithuania into the Rzeczpospolita, or the Commonwealth of Two Nations (see Chapter II, Note 45), and ceded the Ukrainian lands of Lithuania to Poland. Until the changes catalyzed by the Khmelnitsky uprising of 1648 the Polish king was the sovereign of the Zaporozhian Cossacks.

25. For Serko's release in response to a petition from the Zaporozhian Cossacks to the tsar, see text, pp. 128-129.

26. Slobodskaia Ukraine or Settlement Ukraine was an area of free settlement on Russian territory, including Kharkov province and parts of Kursk and

Voronezh. Arable land and tax exemptions were offered to those who fled Polish Ukraine. See Magocsi, *A History of Ukraine*, pp. 198, 205.

27. For Michał Korybut, see Chapter I, Note 45.

28. Zawisza was the ambassador of the Polish Commonwealth in Zaporozhia. His given name is uncertain, but the Zawisza family was an important magnate family, with eminent ancestors going back to the fourteenth century. A Krzysztof Zawisza was marshal of the Grand Duchy of Lithuania in the 1660s.

29. As noted earlier, Chapter II, Note 72, a yurt was the tent used by the nomads of the steppes, including the Crimean Tatars, as a dwelling. It was also the territory over which a nomadic group claimed grazing rights. In this context, probably both the territory and the tents, or camp, is meant.

30. The term Soloviev uses here is iazyk. It means "tongue," or "heathen," or a captive from whom information might be extracted. Here it is meant in the last sense, and as there is no one English word to convey the meaning it is translated "captive-informant."

31. The Russian regiment in Kanev under the jurisdiction of Governor Volkonsky was one of the reformed, or new-style infantry units, since the regimental clerk is identified as soldatskii polkovyi pod'iachii. For military reform and the new-style regiments, see above Chapter III, Note 14.

32. Ivan Gursky was colonel of the Kanev Regiment from 1672 to 1676. See Gajecky, *Cossack Administration*, Vol. 2, p. 611.

33. The editors of the Mysl' edition of Soloviev identify Adzhi-Girey as Adil-Girey. By 1675 Adil-Girey was replaced by Selim-Girey as khan of the Crimean Tatars. Haji-Girey, named after the first and one of the most illustrious khans of an independent Crimean khanate, was most likely a kalgay or nurredin sultan. See Chapter II, Note 15.

34. Savva Prokopov (or Prokopovich) was general chancellor of the general staff of the hetmanate from 1672 to 1687. After his tenure as chancellor he became a chief justice. See Gajecky, *Cossack Administration*, Vol. 2, pp. 665, 662.

35. Stanisław Jan Jabłonowski was governor of Ruthenia. In 1676 he was named field hetman, and in 1682 hetman for Crown Poland. Mikołaj Hieronim Sieniawski (died 1683) was governor of Volyn and named field hetman for Crown Poland in 1682. The feats and promotions of both are mentioned by Jan Pasek (Leach, *Memoirs. Pasek*, pp. 177, 242, 259, 261, 272, 276-278). Both Jabłonowski and Sieniawski were members of the Senate, the upper house of the Diet. Senators in the Commonwealth were appointed by the king, and selected from among the wealthiest and most powerful nobles in the realm. Senators were appointed for life.

36. The division of the Ukraine into Right Bank (Russia) and Left Bank (Poland) by the Treaty of Andrusovo meant that Polish magnates who had landholdings on the Right Bank lost them. Although they received compensation from the

Polish government they did not give up hope that these lands might be reclaimed. For the Wiśniowiecki family, see Chapter I, Note 45.

37. Major General Franz Wulf or Wolf or Wolfe evidently was one of the many foreigners who served as officers in the new-style regiments as part of the military reforms of the seventeenth century. I have been unable to identify him precisely, to find further information about him, or to verify the spelling of his name. Therefore in the text I have transliterated it directly from the Russian: Frants Vulf.

38. Serdiuki were infantry units composed of mercenaries who were at the personal disposal of the hetman. Their counterparts were the kompaniia or kompanitsii, the cavalry units composed of mercenaries, discussed in Chapter III, Note 73, Chapter IV, Note 21, and Chapter V, Note 1.

39. A iasyr' was a captive, considered a slave. The origin of the term is Asiatic. See Dal', Tolkovyi slovar', Vol. 4, p. 681.

40. The Host of the lower rapids refers to the cossacks centered around the Zaporozhian Camp (Sech), living below the cataracts, as opposed to the town cossacks.

41. The term translated as "Turkish officials" is sanzhak (plural sanzhaki). The Turkish term sanjak here refers to the Turkish official of an administrative district in the Ottoman empire. The same term also is used to designate an administrative district.

42. For different redactions of the tale of Jesus healing the paralytic, see Matthew 9:2-7; Luke 5:18-25; John 5:5-9.

43. Pavel Yanenko-Khmelnitsky was a cousin of Bogdan Khmelnitsky. He served as captain of the Kiev Regiment in 1650, then as colonel (1654-1656, 1657-1659). Gajecky, Cossack Administration, Vol. 1, pp. 200, 203, 204, 218, 219.

44. The phrase is idti na kozachii erek. I believe this is a misprint and should be kozachii erik, or cossack navigation channel. See Chapter IV, Note 25.

45. The Don Cossack assembly was called the krug, or circle, and was equivalent to the rada of the Zaporozhian Cossacks. There is some confusion in Soloviev's discussion here. Initially, Soloviev notes that Yakovlev "gathered **circles** (krugli)." Two sentences below, he notes the **circle** (iz kruga) broke up. This confusion may be Soloviev's or it may be a typographical error. The context suggests one circle or assembly, singular, and the text is thus corrected.

46. Mikhailo Samarenin and Kornilo Yakovlev were Don Cossacks and in the years preceding the Razin rebellion alternated in the position of ataman. Despite the fact that Kornilo Yakovlev was godfather to Stepan Razin, during the Razin rebellion he and Mikhailo Samarenin were leaders of a loyalist party in Cherkassk. It was Yakovlev who led the forces that seized Razin and his brother and burned their holdout at Kagalnik. Yakovlev and Samarenin led a contingent which delivered the two prisoners to Moscow. Avrich, Russian Rebels, pp. 111-112.

47. Semeon Buianko, identified here with the diminutive Senka, was a renegade Don Cossack. See Chapter I, Note 92.

48. Stenka Razin was brought into Moscow shackled to a scaffold mounted on the rear of a wagon. He was interrogated by Tsar Alexis Mikhailovich himself, put through a series of horrible tortures, and then taken to the execution block on Red Square. He was quartered, his head and limbs were displayed on stakes, and his torso was thrown to the dogs. Avrich, *Russian Rebels*, pp. 112-113.

49. Literally, kovshi da soboli, or "ladles and sable pelts."

50. Literally, "na ruku posadim, a drugoiu razdavim," or "on one hand we sit, and with the other we divide."

51. Yakovlev and Samarenin were responsible for the seizure of Razin and his deliverance to Moscow. See above, Note 46.

INDEX

Abiram, 89, 228
Abraham, 229
Adamovich, Simeon, archpriest of
  Nezhin, 32, 34, 40, 43, 44, 46, 48,
  86, 89-91, 95, 96, 98, 104, 106,
  107, 109, 112, 113, 115, 127, 129-
  131, 147, 150, 170, 172, 235, 226
Adil-Girey, Crimean khan (1666-
  1671), 79, 80, 200, 212, 244
Adrianople, 30
Adzhi-Girey, 244
Africa, 72
aga, 235
Akinfov, Ivan Pavlovich, 29, 54
Alekseev, Maksim, 108, 232
Alexander Nevsky monastery, 209
Alexander of Macedon, 109
Alexandria, 228
Alexandria, patriarch of, 63
Alexis Alekseevich, tsarevich, 54;
  candidate for Polish throne, 56
Alexis Mikhailovich, tsar, 91, 137,
  199, 202, 205, 215-216, 221-223,
  233, 238, 246
alliance, Moscow and Poland, 16, 76;
  anti-Muslim, 70
Almazov, Semeon Yerofeevich, 177-
  178, 186
ambassadors, cossack, 83; Crimean,
  62; Dutch, 65; English 65; foreign,
  142; Polish, 62, 68, 71-73, 75-77,
  97-98, 100-101, 105, 120, 220;
  Russian, 52, 62, 86, 145
America, 72
Andreev, Ivan, "The Sparrow," 157
Andreev, Lukian, 122, 128
Andreev, Yeremey, 104, 113-114, 231
Andrusovo, town, 57, 69
Andrusovo, truce, 14, 16, 27, 57
Andrusovo, Treaty of, xiii, xiv, xvi, 2,
  11, 13, 14, 16, 24, 29, 46, 49, 57,
  61, 63, 70, 73, 74, 90, 198, 202,

204, 205, 207, 211, 212, 216, 233,
  235, 244
Antioch, 228
Apostolenko (Apostol), Grigory
  (Gritsko), 20
aqueducts, 136
Arabian horse, 79, 224
Archangel cathedral, Moscow Kremlin,
  223
Archangel wharf, 143
archimandrites, Kiev, 36
Archive of the Ministry of Justice,
  xviii
archpriest, Braslavl, see Rakushka-
  Romanovsky, 89; Gadiach, 25;
  Romanov, see Rakushka-Romanov-
  sky) 48
argamak, see Arabian horse
Arianism, 228
Aristotle, 227
Arkhangelsk, 237
Armenians, 3, 130
armies, Polish, 167; Polish and
  Lithuanian 178; Russian, of the
  tsar, 163-164, 166, 169, 179, 191
Articles of Bogdan Khmelnitsky, 42
assembly of elders, cossack, 2
Assyrians, 71
Astrakhan Tatars, 78
Astrakhan, 137, 171
Austria, 218
Avdeevsk grain mills, 21
Azerbaijan, 222
Azov, town, fortification, 136-137,
  166, 189-191, 236; Sea of, 237

Bakhchisaray, 79, 197
Balaban, Dionysios, metropolitan of
  Kiev, xv, 197, 205
Balakleia, 159
Balkans, 199
Baltic, 200

248 INDEX

bandits, iv, 191
Bar, 132
Barabash (Barabashenko), Yakov
Fedorovich, 13-14, 19, 148, 207,
209, 238-239
barabasha, 54
Baranovich, Lazar, archbishop of
Chernigov, xv, 22, 33-35, 39, 40,
41 43, 44, 46, 48, 51, 53, 81, 82,
83, 86, 88, 89, 91, 95, 110, 111,
119-121, 114, 170-171, 196-197,
201, 210, 215, 217, 225, 227
barber, 25
barracks, 191
Baryshevka, 116, 124
Baryshpole, 46
Basan, 116
Basarab, John, author, 196
Bashkirs, 78, 242
Bashmakov, Dementy Minich, 48, 217
Batman district, 21
Batog, Battle of, 1672, 125
Batu, 13c. Mongol khan, 72, 222
Baturin, 21, 28, 48, 50, 52, 82, 84-85,
95-100, 102-104, 108-110, 113,
115-118, 129, 134, 151, 169, 175,
178-179, 230-231, 241
Bayezid II, Ottoman sultan (1481-
1512), 77
beekeeper, 84
Beklemishev, Moisey, 159
Belaia Tserkov, 11, 71, 132, 153, 163,
204, 206, 236, 239
Belaia Vezha (Sarkel), 32
Belgorod, 71, 134, 169, 176
Belitsky, Alexis, 141
Belogrud, Grigory, 153
Belorussia, xiii, 204
Belozerie, 185
Bely, Stepan, 140
Beniewski, Stanisław, 63, 73, 220
Berezna, 43
Besarabia, 241
beschest'e, 210
bey, 212
Bezpaly, Ivan, 30
Bezpaly, Mikita, 13, 14, 148, 206, 238

black council, cossack, 38-39, 47-48,
87, 90, 183, 214, 226, 239; see
also general council, cossack)
black people, 214
Black Sea, 75, 78, 136, 223, 234-235
Black Forest, 23, 210
Black Tatar, 80, 110, 232
Blokh, Andrei Bilokin(?), 164
bogatyr, iv, 195
Bogdanov, Grigory Karpovich, 47,
114, 216, 233
Bogoslavl, 179
Bohemia, 217
Book of Exodus, 215
booty, 173, 189
border, Kiev and Lithuania, 96; Little
Russia (Ukraine) and Lithuania,
94, 104-105; see also boundary
border towns, 65; settlers in, 19
borderland, Russia 176, 188
Boriatinsky, Prince Ivan Petrovich,
130
Boris and Gleb monastery, Chernigov,
215
Borona, ---, 28
Borovitsa, 185
Bosphorus, 223, 224
boundary, Poland and Ukraine, 109,
146; Ukraine and Lithuania, 111
boundary commissioners 75, 78
Braslavl, 125, 146, 152-153, 163, 214,
217, 226
brigandage, 137
British Library, London, 200
Briukhovetsky, Ivan Martynovich,
hetman on Left Bank (1663-1668),
xv, xviii, 1-3, 4-7, 9, 12, 15-17,
21-25, 28, 35-38, 41, 48, 50, 53,
73, 83-84, 87, 93, 100-103, 106-
107, 112, 114, 121, 148, 150, 172,
184, 199, 201-202, 208-209, 211-
213, 214, 217, 223-226, 229, 232;
conspires with Methodios, 17-19;
leads rebellion, 19-23; appeals to
Don, 27; downfall and murder of,
30-32
brotherhood schools, 227

Brotherhood monastery, Kiev, 37, 105,
    116, 210, 231
Brovory (Brovary), 27
Brukovsky, Vasily, 107
Brzostowski, Cyprian Paweł, 54, 56,
    69, 71, 218
Buczacz, 128, 235; Treaty of, 236
Bug River, 125, 207
Bugay, Ivan 25
Buianko, Semeon (Senka), 190, 246
Bukhvostov, Leonty, 149, 170
bunchuk, 193
burgher(s), 3, 5, 8-9, 12, 15, 18, 21,
    28-29, 37, 40-41, 45, 48, 61, 78,
    107, 133, 144,157, 165, 170, 177,
    196, 202
burgomasters, 174
Butenko (Buzhenko), Stepan, 153
Butter week, 21, 110, 209
Buzhin, 185
Bychok stream, 166
Byzantine patriarch, 91; see also Con-
    stantinople, patriarch of
Byzantion, 228
Byzantium, 223

Canadian Institute of Ukrainian
    Studies, University of Alberta,
    xviii
Candia, fall of (1669), 125, 130, 234,
    236
canon law, 220
captive-informant, 173, 244
captives, freed, 47, 48, 159
Cardis, see Kardis
Carlos II, king of Spain (1665-1700),
    222
Carpathian mountains, 210, 215
Caspian Sea, 138, 208, 237
castellan, 220
Castle of the Seven Turrets, 87, 226,
    234
Catholic bishops, 204
Catholics, 13
Causasus, 222
cavalry and lancers unit, Russian
    army, 165

Caves monastery, Kiev, 2, 10, 16-17,
    36, 47, 97, 105, 110-111, 135, 203,
    209, 225
Caves lavra, see Caves monastery,
    Kiev
Cecora (Tsetsora), battle of (1620), 213
Central Asia, 222
Central State Military-Historical
    Archive, Moscow, 200
Chaadaev, Ivan Ivanovich, 71
Chaduev, Vasily, 138-140, 142-143,
    155
chaika, 77, 122, 128, 143-144, 155,
    223, 234, 238
Chalcedon, 223
chancellery officials, 51, 65, 67, 87
chancellery system, 210, 219, 233
Chancellery for Foreign Affairs, xvi,
    55, 58, 59, 61-68, 111, 130, 205,
    216, 220, 232
Chancellery for Military Tenures, 219
Chancellery for Kazan, 216, 217
Chancellery for Kiev, 21, 210
Chancellery for Little Russia, 161
Chancellery of the Apothecary 216
Chancellor, Lithuanian, 54; see also
    Pac, Krzysztof
charters, of confirmation to new
    hetman, 52; granted to cossack
    elite for service, 51
Chausy, 37, 242
Cheli-bey, 30
Chelm, bishop of, 218; see also
    Olszowski, Andrzej
Cheremis, 159, 241-242
Cherkassian, 29-30, 65, 81, 108, 130,
    212, 232; towns, 33
Cherkassk, 188-189, 245
Cherkassy, 133, 149, 151, 159, 162,
    166, 179, 183, 185, 242
Cherkassky, Prince Kaspulat Mutsa-
    lovich, 180
Chernaia Kalitva tributary, 137
chernetskaia rada, see black council
Chernigov, archbishop of, 22, 89, see
    also Lazar Baranovich; citadel of,
    28; governor of, 115; (cont.)

Chernigov (continued)
    metropolitanate in, 49; principality
    of, 49; printing office in, 171, 243;
    town of, xiii, 20, 28, 32, 34-35, 42,
    44, 48, 51, 81-82,100, 102, 105-
    106, 115, 117, 121, 127, 146, 153,
    199, 208-210, 217-218, 222, 231
Chernushenko, Klim, 8- 9
chernye liudi, see black people
Chertomlik island, 162, 242
Chertomlik River, 139, 242
chervonnye, see ducats, 235
chervonnye zolotye, see ducat
Chigirin, citadel, 52; cossack council,
    22-23; hetman, 37, 125, 148, and
    see also Mnogogreshny, Demian
    Ignatovich; monastery, 36; town,
    1-2, 12-13, 15, 20, 30, 32. 37-38,
    41, 93,133, 149, 151-153, 158-159,
    162-167, 173, 179-180, 182-187;
    cossack council in, 22-23; as slave
    market, 179; granted to Demian
    Ignatovich Mnogogreshny with all
    its settlements, 187
children of Ivan Samoilovich, 130-131
Christendom, 23, 93
Christian alliance, 77
Christianity, 72, 203
Christians, 43, 53, 126, 129, 135, 156;
    Orthodox, 27, 56, 89, 101, 196,
    204; Roman Catholic, 74; Rus, 229
Christmas, 132
Chudnovo, battle of (17 September
    1660), 32, 224; campaign 238
Chuguev, 156
Chuguy, Ivan, 31
church, 114, 132, 141; Armenian, 126;
    Christian converted to mosques,
    126; Eastern Orthodox, 62, 76, 93-
    94, 100, 126, 133, 158, 163, 187;
    Orthodox turned into Roman
    Catholic, 42, 47; Polish Catholic,
    Kiev, 47; Roman Catholic, 11, 78,
    126; Russian Orthodox, 11, 13, 94,
    126, 199, 203-204, 208-209, 211,
    246; Ukrainian Orthodox, xv, 87,
    196, 206; Uniate, 11, 204;

church council, 92; of 1666-1667, 1,
    199, 201, 211, 219-220, 225, 241
Church of the Annunciation, 55
Church of Michael the Archangel, 155
Church of the Forty Martyrs, Konotop, 1
churchmen, Ukrainian and Belorussian,
    227
circle, Don Cossack, 188, 190
city hall, Moscow, 156
coenobitic monastery, 208
Collins, Samuel, xviii
commissioners, Polish, 49, 61, 68-69,
    70-71, 86
Commmonwealth, see Commonwealth
    of Two Nations
Commonwealth of Poland and
    Lithuania, see Commonwealth of
    Two Nations
Commonwealth of Two Nations, xiii-
    xiv, xvii, 63, 76-77, 101, 153, 163,
    195-6, 198, 204, 207, 213, 218,
    220, 227, 229, 239, 241-244
Condé, Prince de, 218
confraternities, 227, 231
confrontation, judicial, 174, 232
Constantine I, Roman emperor (b.306–
    d.337), 228
Constantinople, 30, 65, 79, 91, 93,
    133, 161-164,189, 204, 219, 226,
    228-229, 234
Constantinople, patriarch of, 34, 63,
    91-93, 196-197, 220, 226
copper money, 44, 200
Copper Riot, 1662, 200
2 Corinthians 9:6, 221
cossack companies, 212
cossack compensation, 218
cossack council, xiv, 6, 80, 98, 120,
    139-142, 150, 162, 181, 185-186,
    192, 206, 208, 214; Glukhov, 48;
    Gadiach, 20; Kozachaia Dubrova,
    118; Nezhin, 201; Pereiaslav, 153,
    181; of elders, 25, 34, 96, 98, 102-
    104, 107-113, 118-119, 132. 153,
    161, 164, 173, 177, 185, 191; see
    also black councils
cossack deserters, treatment of, 52

cossack elders, 7, 14, 22-24, 39-40,
  43-44, 47, 50-51, 53, 85-86, 93,
  97-98, 101-104, 107-109, 113-114,
  117-120, 131-132, 147, 151, 153,
  158-159, 162, 168, 185, 188-191,
  217, 226
cossack hetmanate, v, xiv, 192, 196,
  200, 204
cossack nicknames, 8
cossack registers (lists), 8-9, 21, 23,
  51
cossack regiments, 33, 35, 103, 145,
  150-153, 159, 182, 212; Chigirin,
  159; Gadiach, 203, 231; Kalnik,
  81, 152, 207; Kalnyk-Vynnitsia,
  214; Kanev, 244; Kiev, 99, 209,
  214, 240, 245; Korsun, 81, 152;
  Lisianka, 240; Lubny, 81, 145,
  224, 231; Mirgorod, 39, 81, 145;
  Nezhin, 2, 81, 96, 201, 208, 271,
  230; Pavoloch, 224; Pereiaslav, 21,
  81, 133, 153, 202, 209, 228, 231,
  238, 242; Podolsk, 152; Poltava, 5,
  9, 39, 81, 118, 145, 157, 172, 182,
  206-207, 233; Povolochie, 240;
  Priluki, 39, 81, 145; Settlement
  Ukraine, 172; Sevsk, 71, 169, 176;
  Starodub, 81, 99, 212-213;
  Targovitsa, 200; Uman, 81, 152,
  154, 225; Voroshilov, 103, 108,
  230
cossack navigation channel, 189-190
Council of Nicea, 325, 90, 228
Counter Reformation, 227
courier service, see postal service
Courland, 55-57, 63, 69
court service register, 71
Cracow, 164
Cretan War, 234
Crete, 164, 234
Crimea, 4, 38, 41, 79-80, 101, 123,
  127, 129, 130-131. 139, 144, 161,
  167, 173, 177, 182, 191, 214, 222
Crimean horde, 157
Crimean khan, xv, 1, 4-7, 84, 86, 109,
  133, 144, 158, 162, 165, 167, 181,
  187, 201, 212, 230

Crimean khanate 200, 215, 244
Crimean Tatars, 112, 207, 212, 214,
  222-223, 244
Crimeans, 54, 173, 185
cross-kissing, 20, 33, 61, 82, 104, 209
crown hetman, Poland, 29
crown lands, 217
crown secretaries, 68, 69, 184
customs duties, 66-68, 221
Cyrillic alphabet, 211

Daniłowicz, Maria, 204
Danube River, 199, 234-235
Dathan, 89, 228
Daudov, Vasily Alekksandrovich, 78
Denmark, 220
Desna River, 47, 109, 115, 209
Deuteronomy 11:6, 228
Devitsa, 33
diadem, 137-139, 145
Diet, 195, 244
Dikanka, 30
diminutives, Slavic names, 213
Dmitrashko-Raich, Rodion, 20, 40, 85,
  97-98, 102, 104, 106-108, 110,
  113, 116, 121, 132-133, 147, 153,
  159, 168, 209, 214, 231
Dmitriev, Anastas, 165
Dnieper River, xiii, 3-5, 7, 9, 11-12,
  22, 27, 29, 31, 35-37, 45-46, 49,
  53, 70, 82, 86-87, 93, 95, 97, 101,
  103, 111, 131, 133-134, 136, 144,
  146, 150-151, 154, 157-158, 161,
  165, 167, 170, 176, 178-179, 182-
  183, 188, 202, 223, 228; eastern
  side/bank, East Bank, Left Bank,
  xiii, 6, 15-16, 20, 30, 32, 36, 40,
  54, 75-76, 82-84, 86-91, 94-95,
  100, 113, 121, 124, 131, 134, 136,
  146-148, 153, 163, 166, 168-169,
  179, 181, 184-185, 187,197, 208;
  western side/bank, West Bank,
  Right Bank, 6, 14, 20, 30, 32, 82,
  86, 88, 94, 110, 124, 131, 133-134,
  136, 141, 144-147, 152-153, 162,
  165, 168-169, 172, 181, 184, 186-
  187, 239-241

Dniester River 70, 166, 182, 242,
Dokhturov, Cyril, 219
Dokhturov, Gerasim Semeonovich, 59, 219
Dokhturov, Semeon Kirillovich, 219
Dolgorukaia, Daria Dmitrievna, 223
Dolgorukov, *see* Dolgoruky
Dolgoruky, Boyar Prince Dmitry Alekseevich, 72, 222
Dolgoruky, Boyar Prince Yury Alekseevich, 72, 129, 222
Dolgoruky (Dolgorukov) family, xiv, 222
Dolzhikov, Russian cavalry ensign, 9
Domontov (Domontovich), Ivan, 41, 97, 102, 108, 139
Don Cossack Host, 136, 138, 181, 189
Don Cossacks, 26, 136-137, 143, 189, 191, 208, 211, 237, 245
Don River, 26-27, 72, 136-138, 143, 156, 162, 188-190, 211, 222, 237
Donets River, 80, 137, 156
Donets, Fedor, 6-7, 203
Donets, Grigory, 166
Donets, Ivan, 203
Dormition cathedral, Moscow, 55
Doroshenko, Andrei Dorofeevich, 152, 158-159, 165, 185, 240
Doroshenko, Grigory Dorofeevich, 10, 12-15, 39, 152, 167-168, 187, 243
Doroshenko, Mikhail, 38, 214
Doroshenko, Peter Dorofeevich, hetman, Right/West Bank (1665–1676), xvi, 1, 5-7, 10-13, 15, 19-20, 22-23, 28-32, 36-41, 45, 47, 49-51, 62, 64, 70-77, 81-87, 90-94, 97-98, 100-104, 108-109, 111-114, 116-117. 119-120, 124-125, 127, 130-134, 142, 144-149, 151-152, 154-156, 158, 160-164, 166-167, 170, 174, 177-187, 204, 214, 221, 224-225, 323, 236, 242
double-headed eagle, 139, 145
dragunskie polki, 225
Drozdenko (Drozd?), 31
ducat, 30, 45, 51, 79, 128, 143, 145, 215, 235
duma, 216

Dunay River, 125, 127, 234-235
Dunin-Borkovsky, Vasily, 149, 153, 165
Dutch, 59
Dvina River, 72
Dvoretsky family, 209
Dvoretsky, Vasily, 2, 19, 28, 41, 209, 214
Dzik, Melety, 37, 201

Early Slavic Studies Association, 237
East Slavs, 203, 223
Easter, 84, 203, 228; Easter Sunday, 101; Easter holidays, 117
Eastern Europe, 198
Eastern patriarchs, 1, 56, 219
Edisan Tatars, 78, 223
efimoks, 51, 79, 102, 112, 217, 231
Egypt, 72, 215
Egyptians, 44
ekten'ia, 234
Eliab, 228
England, 220
English, 59
erik, or erichek, 236, 245; *see also* cossack navigation channel
Essar, Dennis F., author, xviii
Estonia, 219
eternal peace, Russia and the Commonwealth of Two Nations (1686), xvii, 56,-57, 66-67, 69-70, 90, 197, 211
Eucharist, 90
Eucharistic Controversy, 210, 227
Europe, 72, 222
exarch, 89, 226

faith, Christian, 130, 156; Muslim, 79; Orthodox, 1, 76-78, 100-101; Roman Catholic, 77
Falibowski, Lord, 160, 242; wife of, 160
Fedor Alekseevich, tsar, 212, 216
Fedor Ivanovich, tsar, 219
Feodora Alekseevna, tsarevna (b.1674–d.1678), 170, 243
Ferapont monastery, 199
ferry at Perevoloka, 156-157, 173

figs, 84
Filimonov, or Filimonovich, Maksim, *see* Methodios, bishop of Mstislavl
First False Dmitry, 223, 237
First Northern War (1654-1660), 219
foreign mercenary officers, 211
foreign regiments, 26
foreigners, 26, 59, 68, 130, 156
fort, 188, 190-191
fortka, 230
fox pelts, 171
France, 54
Friedrich III, Duke of Holstein Gottorp, 219

Gadaich, 2-4, 8, 17, 20, 26, 30-32, 37, 45, 151, 229; governor of, 28; rebellion in, 24; Treaty of, 13, 196, 206-207; Union of, 229
Gajecky, George, author, v, 192
Galiatovsky, Ioanniky, 115, 233
Galicia, 128, 222, 235
Galitsiia River, 179
Gamaleia, Grigory, 30, 81, 152, 224
Gamaleia, Yakov, 240
Gandza, Demian, 225
Gosiewski, Jan, 57
Gdansk, 219
Gedeon, monk, 205, 233; *see also* Khmelnitsky, Yury Bogdanovich
Gediminas, 207
Genesis 16, 229; 25:12-18, 229
Genghis Khan, 222
Genoese colonies, 222
gentry, 14, 177
Germans, 130
Girey, clan, 215
Gizel, Innokenty, 10, 12, 16-17, 36, 47, 63, 111, 135, 204
Glinsk, 134
Glukhov, 28, 45, 48, 86, 103, 150, 156; council of, xvi, 48, 81, 99, 121, 225; treaty and articles, 51-52, 82-84, 90, 104, 119
Glukhovsky, Filipp Umanets, *see* Umanets, Filipp
Gniński, Jan, 57, 69, 71-72, 222
Gogolev, 27, 99

Golden Gates, Constantinople, 226, 234
Golden Horde, 223
Golosov, Lukian Timofeevich, 59, 219
golut'by, 212
Gomel, 101, 106, 111, 114
Gordon, Patrick, 200
Gorlenko, Lazar, 20, 153
gospel, 185
gosti, 221
government officials, Russian, 208
governor, Russian, 2-3, 8, 34-36, 87, 175
grain mills, 45
Grain Chancellery, 217
gramota, 205
grand vizier 78, 151
Great Russia, 45, 57, 66, 83
Great Northern War (1700-1721), 240
Grechany-Potrebnich, Stepan, 103, 113, 121, 231
Greece, 77
Greek empire 72
Greek Catholic church, *see* church, Uniate
Greek merchants, 1
Greek diaspora, 227
Greeks, 130
Gribovich, Pavel, 96, 104, 114, 116-117, 144, 149, 238
Gulak, Ivan, 153
Gulianitsky, Grigory (Grishka), 201; daughter of, 2
Gults, Yagan, 24, 211
Gursky, Ivan, 151, 153, 174-175, 244; wife of, 175
Gvintovka, Fedor, 117
Gvintovka, Irina, 117
Gvintovka, Matvey, 2, 20, 32-33, 40-41, 44, 46-47, 86, 96, 99, 104, 107, 114, 117, 201-202, 208, 225
Gvintovka, Yefim 117 225

Habsburg family, 215
Hagar, 229
Hagarites, 93, 229
Haji-Girey, 177, 244
harem, 125

Harvard Ukrainian Studies, xix
Harvard Ukrainian Research Institute,
    xviii
Hedvig Eleonora, queen of Sweden,
    (b.1626–d.1715), 56, 219
Henri Bourbon, 218
hetmanate, 217, 226, 229; general
    council of officers, 193; general
    court, 192; general military chan-
    cellery, 230; general staff, 192-
    193, 212, 292; hetman's chan-
    cellery, 192; hetman's guards, 230
historiography, Russian, 195
Holland, 220
holy man, 123
Holy Gospels, 50, 77, 181
Holy Roman empire, 45, 215, 220
Holy Spirit, 26, 203
Holy Trinity, 56
Holy Wisdom cathedral, Kiev, 89, 226
Holy Wisdom monastery, Kiev, turned
    into Catholic cloister, 47
Holy Trinity-St. Sergius monastery,
    Zagorsk, 209
homesteads 135
horde, 26, 39, 177
horses, 29, 30, 45
hospodar, 199; Wallachian, 168
hostages, 158, 162-163, 176-177
House of Austria, 72, 222; see also
    Habsburg family
Hrushevsky, Mykhailo Sergeevich,
    author, xvii, 197

iasyr, 245
iazyk, see captive-informant
Ichnia, 108
icon, 74, 98, 110, 117, 126
icon of Christ Pantocrator, 55
icon of the Savior, 60, 64, 97, 102,
    104, 107, 120; and the most holy
    Mother of God, 154
Ilia, Trinity priest, 22
infidels, 89, 122
Isaac, priest of Gogolev, 99
Isaac, vicar of the Baturin monastery,
    129

Ishmail, 229
Iskra, Ivan, 14, 207
Islam, Crimean town, 7
Israelites, 44, 215, 228
Istanbul, 229
Ivan Kalita, grand prince, 235
Ivashka, young man, 115

Jabłonowski, Stanisław Jan, 177, 244
Jagiellonian dynasty, 196
Jan II Kazimierz (Waza), Polish king
    (1648-1668), 29, 56-57, 124, 150,
    160, 205, 218
Jan Olbracht, Polish king (1492-1501),
    77
janissaries, 126, 136, 235
Jassy, 91
Jesuit college, 240
Jesuit academies, 227
Jesuits, 231
Joachim, patriarch of Moscow and all
    Russia (1674-1690), 157, 210
joachimsthaler, 106, 217, 231
Joasaph, patriarch of Moscow and all
    Russia (1667-1671), 89, 155, 227,
    241
John 5:5-9, 245; 15:5, 219
Joseph, monk, 92
Journal of Ukrainian Studies, xix
Juchi, 222
Judas Iscariot, 84

Kagalnik, 245
kaimakam or kaymakam, 229
Kalanchinsky (Kalinchinsky) towers,
    136, 236
kalgay, 46, 86, 167-168, 215, 224-225
Kalmyks, 75, 77-78, 122, 128, 171,
    180, 222-223, 242,
Kalnivka River, 207
Kaluga, 106
Kaluzhanin, Rodion, 188-190
Kama Bulgars, 222
Kamienic, 2
Kamieniec Podolsky, 2, 101, 126, 130,
    132-133, 164, 178
Kanev 1, 81, 94, 110, 132, 134, 139,

149, 151, 153-154, 166, 173-175,
    179, 187, 244
Karandeev, Alexander, 174-175
Kardis, Treaty of (1661), 55-57, 219
Karl IX, king of Sweden, 56
Karl X Gustavus, king of Sweden, 219
Karl XI, king of Sweden (1660-1697),
    219
Karl XII, king of Sweden, 219
Karl XIII, king of Sweden, 240
Karpovich, Grigory, 110, 117
Kasogov, Grigory, 136
Kazan, 242
Kazan Tatars, 78
Kellerman, Heinrich, Andrei, 220
Kellerman (Kelderman), Thomas, 64
    220
Kereberda, 138, 157, 172, 182
khan, Crimean, 22, 28-29, 38, 57, 77-
    78, 103, 127, 133-134, 161, 163,
    166-168, 176, 178, 185
Khanenko, Mikhail Stepanovich,
    hetman Right/West Bank (1669–
    1674), 82, 85, 87, 91, 94, 118, 125,
    133, 144, 151-154, 173, 225
Kharkov, 123, 156, 166, 243
Khitrovo, Ivan Savostianovich
    Bolshoy (the elder), 136-137, 188
Khitrovo, Bogdan Matveevich, xviii,
    47-48, 59, 205, 215-216, 221
Khmelnitsky, Bogdan Mikhailovich,
    hetman (1648–1657), xiii, xiv, 2,
    9, 13, 20, 35, 40, 42, 65, 94, 148-
    149, 162, 193, 196, 201, 205-208,
    216, 228, 239, 245; uprising 1648,
    243; wife of, 2
Khmelnitsky, Yury Bogdanovich, as
    the monk Gedeon, 12, 22-23, 50,
    81-82, 86-87, 133, 142, 164, 197,
    205-208, 216, 226, 229, 233, 239
khorunzhyi 194
Khotin, battle of (1621), 35, 213
Khovansky, Peter Ivanovich, 188-191
Khovansky, Semeon Andreevich, 127
Khristoforov, Magnus, 91-93
Khrushchev, Stepan Ivanovich, 127
khutor, 231

Khvalynskoe more, see Caspian Sea
Kiev, xiii, xvi, 3, 11-12, 15-16, 18,
    20, 22-24, 27-28, 36, 42-43, 45-47,
    49, 51, 54, 57, 62-63, 68-69, 70,
    74-77, 86-87, 89-91, 94, 96-101,
    103, 105-106, 108-109, 111, 114-
    115, 123, 127, 131, 133, 135, 144,
    146, 150, 152- 153, 156, 163-169,
    170-171, 177-178, 201-202, 207,
    209-211, 217, 222, 225; city
    fortifications, 177; metropolitanate,
    xv, 2, 34, 36, 196, 201-202, 209-
    210, 220; metropolitan of, xv, 47,
    74, 88-89; metropolitanate, 16, 20,
    54; root of piety, 47; shrines, 18;
    urban parish clergy, 34
Kiev Academy, 210, 227, 229, 233,
    240
Kievan see, see Kiev, metropolitanate
Kikin, Vasily Petrovich, 4, 7-9
king, Polish, 13, 18, 19, 23-24, 29-30;
    election of, 56
Korybut, Michał, see Wiśniowiecki,
    Prince Michał Korybut
kinship, terminology, 230, 232

kiosks, 170
Kipchaks, 222
Kirgiz, 224
Kishenka, 139
Kliuch razumeniia, Key to Under-
    standing, 233
Klokachev, Timofey Dmitrievich, 28
Kochubey, Vasily Leontievich, 182
Kodak (Koidak), 3, 133, 139, 202, 236
kokhly, 236
Kolchitsky, Grigory, 98-99
Kologrivov, Miron Lavrentievich, 28
Kolomna, 222
Kolomyk, 134
Kolupaev, Mikhail, 101, 106-107, 115,
    151-152, 240
Komar, or Kamar, Jarema, 71
kompaneishchina, kompaneishka, 236
kompaniia, kompaniitsi, 233, 236,
    245; see also mercenary troops,
    cossack

Konotop, 1, 32, 104, 117-118; battle
 of (1659), 1, 65, 200-201, 206
konskie zheleza, 236
Korobovo, 33
korolik, 232
Korostyshev, 176
Korsun, 41, 152-153, 161-162, 179
koshevoi, 203
Kostelets, 46
Kostomarov, Nikolay Ivanovich, au-
 thor, xvii, 197, 214
Kostroma River, 220
Kotelva, 30, 32
Kozelets , 21, 39, 44
Kozlovsky, Prince Grigory Afanasie-
 vich, 99, 105, 111, 127
Krasena stream, 118
Kremenchug (Kremenchuk), 3, 8, 243;
 port, 202
Krolevets, 103
Krylov, 151, 162, 185
Krypetsk monastery, 71
Kuban, 222
Kublitsky, Kostia, 20
Kulish, Panteleimon, author, 214
Kunitsky (Kunicki), Stepan, 109, 232
kuren, 203
Kursk, 169, 178-179, 184, 243
Kvashin, Isay Maksimovich, and wife, 28
kwarciane wojsko, see quarter troops,
 Polish)
Kyselivka, 242

Ladyzhensky, Fedor Abrosimovich, 4,
 6-7, 15; murder of, 5-6, 15
Ladyzhin, 126, 165-166, 242
Last Judgment, 89-90, 158
Latin alphabet, letters, script, 27, 211,
 230, 233
Latin heresy, 27, 211
Latin churches, see church, Roman
 Catholic
Latin language, 230
latinstvo, 211; see also Latin heresy
Lavrinko, Zaporozhian cossack, 30,
 212
Law Code of 1649, 222, 235

Lazicki, Polish colonel, 168, 243
Lebedinye ozera, see Swan Lakes
Lent, 109, 143, 171, 209
Leontiev, Ivan Yurievich,180
Leopold I Habsburg, Holy Roman
 emperor (1658-1705), 215, 222
Letopis' Samovidtsa, 226
levok, see lion dollar, 232
Lezhaisky, Mikhail, archimandrite,
 171, 243
Likhachev, Vasily Bogdanov 28
Likharev, Ivan Petrovich 30
lion dollar, 112, 232
Lipovaia Dolina, 39
liquor franchise, 21, 68
Lisitsa, Pavel, 153
Lithuania, 13, 18, 35, 54, 61, 64, 77,
 146, 148, 163, 195, 205, 220, 243-
 244
Lithuanian dynasty, 207
Lithuanian referendary, see
 Brzostowski, Cyprian Paweł
Lithuanian hetman, 176; see also Pac,
 Michał
Lithuanian Tatars, 241
Little Russian Chancellery, 62, 65, 98,
 210, 216, 229
Little Khortisa, island, 228
Livonia, 219
Lizogub, Yakov Kodrantievich, 1,
 131-134, 144, 151, 153, 178, 236
Loev, 37
Lokhvitsa, 134, 157, 236
Longworth, Philip, author, xix
Lopatin, Ivan Timofeev, 18
Lopukhin, Larion (Illarion) Dmitrie-
 vich, 4, 216
Lords of Cherry Village, see
 Wiśniowiecki family, 207
Lorraine, 218
Louis XIV, king of France, 218
lower rapids of the Dnieper River,
 180-181
Lower Reaches, of the Dnieper River,
 91; cossacks of, 228
Lublin, 13, 78, 232; Union of (1569),
 220

Lubny, 86, 102-103, 108, 112, 134, 153
Lubomirski, Jerzy, 224
Luchka, Hetman Mnogogreshny's retainer, 139
Luchka, dwarf, 24
Ludwika Maria, Maria Louise Gonzaga (1611–1667), widow of Polish King Władisław IV, 218
Luka, archpriest, 8, 17
Luke 5:18-25, 245; 19:26, 221
Lukoshkin, Russian musketeer captain, 180
Lutokhin, Russian musketeer captain, 68
Łużecki, Karol Stanisław, 125, 235
Lvov, 13, 92, 177; Orthodox bishop of, 92
Lvov, Semeon Petrovich, 201
Lysenka, 152, 161
Lysenko Ivan, 17, 105, 152, 179

Machowski, Sebastian, 150
Magosci, Paul Robert, author, xviii
Makarios, patriarch of Antioch 199
Maksakov monastery of the Transfiguration of the Savior, 41, 105, 115-116, 215
Maksim Filimonov, see Methodios, bishop of Mstislavl
Manasios, Greek prelate, 93-94
Mari, 242
Maria Elizabeth of Saxony, duchess of Hollstein Gottorp, 219
Marienburg, 150
Mariitsy, see Mari
Marselis, Leonty Petrovich, 64, 66, 220
Marselis, Peter Gavrilovich, 220
Marselis family, 220
Martynov (Martynovich), Artem, 2, 20, 32
Maslenitsa, see Butter Week
Matskeevich, Hetman Doroshenko's courier, 64, 221
Matthew 7:9, 203; 8:20, 221; 9:2-7, 245; 9:20-22, 213; 15:8, 299

Matveev, Artamon Sergeevich, 47, 71-72, 82, 85, 91, 96, 98, 104, 109, 114-115, 127-131, 136, 150, 161, 171, 175, 182, 191, 216, 221
Mazepa, Ivan Stepanovich, 154, 159-164, 182, 240-242; wife of, 161-162
Mazin, Kalmyk murza, 180
Medvedovka, 185
Mehmed II, Ottoman sultan, 226, 234
Mehmed IV, Ottoman sultan (1648–1687), 30, 78, 125-126, 199, 234
Menshikov, Alexander Danilovich, 241
mercenary troops, cossack, 119, 179, 193; see also kompaniia
merchants, 66, 78, 156; English, 220; German, 130; Greek, 130; Persian, 130; Russian, 55; Ukrainian, 94
Merekhva, 180
Mereshka, 139
Meshcherinov, Ivan Alekseevich, 37
Methodios III, patriarch of Constantinople, 88-89, 226
Methodios, bishop of Mstislavl, xv, 2-3, 12, 16-19, 24, 34, 36-38, 40-41, 43, 46-48, 83, 196-197, 201-202, 207, 209, 225-226; conspires with Hetman Briukhovetsky, 17-19; daughter of, 17; downfall and death of, 36-38
metropolitan, Serbian, 116
metropolitans, Greek, 116
Mezhibozh, 132, 168
Mezhigorie monastery, 37
Midians, 71
Migalevsky, Konstantin, 60. 153
Mignovichi, 60, 66, 68
Miius River, 188
Miiuska, Ivan, 137, 155-157, 182
Mikifor, cossack artillary clerk, 48
military campaign, 1675, 176
Miloslavskaia, Maria Ilinichna, tsaritsa, 142-143, 145, 223, 238
Miloslavsky family, 216
Miloslavsky, Ilia Danilovich, 138, 142-143, 238

Minaev, Frol, 180, 182-183, 190
Minin, Nikita Minich, *see* Nikon,
    patriarch of Moscow and all Russia
Minsk, 67- 68
Mirgorod, 20-21, 28, 50, 84-86
Mnogogreshnaia, Elena Demianovna,
    117
Mnogogreshnaia, Natasia, 117
Mnogogreshny, Demian Ignatovich,
    xvi, 32-33, 35, 39-41, 43, 45, 47,
    52-53, 73-75, 81-99, 101-105, 107-
    111, 113-116, 119, 121, 135-136,
    138, 144, 148, 150, 163, 169, 202,
    213-214, 225, 230-232, 238; ac-
    cused of treachery, 106; curse
    against, 87-88; made hetman, 48,
    52; seized and sent to Moscow, 105
Mnogogreshny family, 117, 149
Mnogogreshny, Ivan Demianovich,
    117
Mnogogreshny, Peter Demianovich,
    117
Mnogogreshny, Savva (Shumeiko,
    Shumka) Ignatovich, 97, 99, 105,
    107, 116
Mnogogreshny, Vasily Ignatovich, 32-
    33, 40, 42, 44, 102, 105, 107, 114-
    116, 139
Mogilev, 37
Mohammed, 166
Mokrievich, Karp, 1, 105-109, 111-
    113, 119, 128, 199
Moldavia, 78, 167, 199, 234, 241
Moldavian hospodar, 1
Moldavians, 77, 81, 242
Monastyrishche, 179
Mongol empire, 222
Mongol yoke, 222
Moscow, city, 4-5, 8-9, 21, 23, 26-27,
    32, 37, 39, 41, 43-46, 48, 52, 54,
    61-62, 64-68, 71, 73, 75-76, 79,
    81-83, 86, 91, 96, 98-99, 101, 103,
    105-107, 108-110, 113-115, 117-
    118, 124, 126-127, 129-130, 133,
    138, 141, 144, 146, 149, 151, 154,
    156, 158, 161-165, 169-170, 172-
    173, 175-176, 180-182, 185-187,

189-192, 196, 202, 206-210, 213,
    215-217, 219-223, 225, 233, 238,
    241; government, xiv, 55, 81, 94,
    128, 197, 218-219, 240; metro-
    politan, 36; musketeers, 85, 98-99,
    101-103, 108, 112, 135, 156, 174,
    190-191, 212, 216, 240; patriarch
    of, 2, 33-34, 63, 129, 196, 220;
    tsardom, 44, 57, 61
Moscow Articles (1665), 2, 201
Moscow Archive of the Ministry of
    Foreign Affairs, xviii
Moses, 228
Moshny, 179
Muslims, 77
moskali, 203
mosques, 77, 126, 132-133
Motovilovka, 176
Mount Batog, 125
Mozyr, 78
Mstislavl, 3, 74, 78
Murashka, Andrei, 81, 110, 165-166,
    242
Murashka, Denys, 242
murza (mirza), 159, 166, 242
Muslim council, 80
Muslims, 1, 10, 23-24, 40, 57, 70, 74-
    76, 82, 84, 123, 126, 128-129, 133,
    135, 146, 154-155, 158, 182, 185
Mustafa Pasha, 92, 229

na ochnoi stavke, *see* confrontation,
    judicial
name-day, 153, 240
Naryshkina, Natalia Kirillovna,
    tsaritsa, 216, 221, 233, 243
national consciousness, Ukrainian,
    xvii
navigation channel, 136; *see also* erik
New Rome, *see* Constantinople
Nebo novoe (The New Heaven), 233
Neelov, Grigory, 95, 97-99, 101, 103-
    104, 108, 112, 118, 120
Neliubovich-Tukalsky, Joseph, *see*
    Tukalsky, Joseph, metropolitan, 205
nemets, nemtsy, 211, 235
neo-Aristotelianism, 227

Nesterenko, Andrei, 231
Nevl, 74
New Rome, archbishop of, *see*
Methodios III, patriarch of Con-
stantinople
New Savior monastery, Moscow, 37
Nezhin, 2, 17-18, 20-21, 28, 32-33,
35-36, 42-44, 48, 51, 81, 88, 99,
106, 116, 127, 153, 170, 172, 201,
210
Nicene Creed, 228
Nikon, patriarch of Moscow and all
Russia, 1, 16, 27, 199, 201, 211,
221, 228, 216, 233, 237, 241
Nogay, 75, 77-78, 222-223, 242
Novaia chetvert', 221
Novgorod, 217, 222
Novgorod Chancellery, 217
Novgorod-Seversk, 28, 30, 32, 44, 95,
171, 210
Novgorod-Seversk hetman, 39, 43; *see
also* Mnogogreshny, Demian
Ignatovich
Numbers 16:3-31, 228
nurredin, 81, 215, 244

Obechevskaia marsh, 179
Odoevsky, Prince Yakov Nikitich, 232
Ogarev, Yury Postnik Grigorievich,
24; wife of, 25
Ogloblia, Ignat, 139
okhochi, 236; *see also* volunteer regi-
ments, cossack
Old Belief, 199
Oliwa, Treaty of, 1660, 56-57, 219
Oliwa monastery, 219
Olonets, 220
Olshovka, 108
Olszowski, Andrzej, 54, 218
Opara, Stepan, 150, 239
Oposhnia, 30
Ordin-Nashchokin, Afanasy
Lavrentievich, xvi, xviii, 12, 15-16,
18-19, 48, 54-60, 63, 66-68, 84,
205, 211, 216, 219, 220-221, 232-
233, 242; attitude towards Chan-
cellery of Foreign Affairs, 58-59;

dismissed from post, 70-71; named
head of Chancellery of Foreign
Affairs, 58; personality of, 58-59;
tonsured as monk Antony, 71
Ordin-Nashchokin, Voin Afanasievich,
219
Orekhovskky (Orechowski), Polish
envoy, 163, 242
Orenburg, 222
Orlovka, 159
Orthodox liturgy, 204
Orthodox tsar, 45, 93, 177
osmachok, osmina, 228
Oster, 28, 44, 46, 48, 51, 127, 209
Ostrog, 71, 73
Ottoman empire, 199, 229, 234-235,
245
Ottoman Porte, 199, 204, 242
Ottoman Turks, 213, 215, 221

Pac, Bonifacy, 212
Pac family, 212
Pac, Michał, 29, 56, 212
padisha, 229
Paisios, patriarch of Alexandria, 82,
114, 155, 199, 220, 225, 241
Pasek, Jan Chryzostom, xviii, 198,
232, 235, 241, 244
pasha, 126, 229
patrimonial estates, 127, 235
Pavoloch, 176
peasants, 8-9, 21, 83, 103, 120, 143,
167, 208; homesteads, 127; tax-
paying, 12, 45; rebellion, 37
Pentecost, 203
Pereiaslav, 3, 12-13, 18, 20, 28, 35,
40, 42, 44, 48, 50-51, 85, 97, 99,
106, 127, 132, 135, 141, 152-154,
158, 160-162, 169, 202, 217, 242;
bishop of, 89; metropolitanate in,
49; Treaty of (1654), xiii, 35, 196,
201
Perekop, 79, 122-124, 144, 180
Perevolochna, 81
Perevoloka, 156-157, 173
Pernal, Andrew B., author, xviii
Persia, 208

Persians, 71, 130
Persian shah, 78
Peter I Alekseevich, tsarevich, tsar,
  emperor, 119, 207, 226, 233, 240-
  241
Petrov, Yakov, 153, 240
Petrovich, Yakov, 240
pilgrimage(s), 74, 103
Piwo, Jan, 70, 96, 101, 105
plenipotentiaries, Polish, Russian and
  Swedish, to meet at Andrusovo,
  55-57
Pliusa, Treaty of (1666), 55-56, 219
Pochaev monastery, 209
Pochep, 30, 213
Podlasie, 125, 235
Podolia, 125, 128, 235, 241
Poland, xiii, 12-14, 18, 23, 26, 31, 35,
  39, 41-42, 54-57, 61, 65, 67-68,
  71, 76-78, 91, 124-126, 134, 146-
  148, 156, 160-161, 163, 167, 169,
  195, 200, 205, 207, 209, 211, 216,
  219-220, 229, 232-233, 243; see
  also Commonwealth of Two
  Nations
Poland-Lithuania, see Commonwealth
  of Two Nations
Polianovka, Truce of, 223
Polish commissioners, 25, 52
Polish Commonwealth, see Common-
  wealth of Two Nations
Polish gentry, 124, 177
Polish king, 5-6, 10-11, 37, 39, 41-42,
  49, 56, 72-77, 84, 90, 93, 96-97,
  100, 110, 122, 129, 132-133, 138,
  153, 158, 161, 168, 171-173, 177,
  185, 187, 232, 240, 243; election
  of, 55; expected to abdicate, 54-55
Polish language, 168, 230
Polish script, 99
Polish Ukraine, xvi, 201, 204
Polish Tatars, see Cheremis
Polish-Lithuanian Commonwealth, see
  Commonwealth of Two Nations
Polkov, Stepan, 29
Polkova Rada, Cossack hetmanate,
  194

polkovi suddi, 194
polkovnik, 193
polkovyi pysar, 194
polkovyi oboznnyi, 194
Polotsk, 74, 115
Poltava. 5, 8-9, 20, 28, 50, 84-85, 133,
  207; battle of (1709), 241
Polubotok, Leonty, 107, 114, 165
pomest'e, see service land holding
Pope, 204
Popovich, cossack standard bearer,
  48
Poret, district, 58
posad, 239
postal service, 64, 66, 68
postal system, 220
Potocki, Stanisław, 224
Povolochie, 153
Pozharsky, Semeon Romanovich, 201
prelates, Muscovite, 36
priest, Romanovsky, see Rakushka-
  Romanovsky, Roman
priests, Roman Catholic, 27, 211
prikaz system, see chancellery system
Priluki, 20-21, 28, 153, 179
Printing Office, 170
prisoners, 37, 189
Prokopov (Prokopovich), Savva, 177,
  244
Protasiev, Peter, 1
Protestants, 196
Prussia, 218
Pruth River, 199, 234
Poryvay, Zaporozhian cossack, 162
Psalms 22:6, 235; 42:1, 248
Pskov, 71
Pushkar (Pushkarenko), Martyn, 13-14,
  148, 206-207, 238-239
Pushkar rebellion, 206-207
Putivl, 39, 45, 70, 81, 104, 106-107,
  109, 127, 169

quarter troops, Polish, 163, 242
quitrent, 8-9, 42

Raicha, Dmitry, see Dmitrashko-
  Raich, Rodion

Rakushka-Romanovsky, Roman
 Orisimovich, 88-89, 92, 193, 217,
 226
ranks, Muscovite, 173
ransom, to Turks for Russian captives,
 80
Rassava, council at, 81
ratusha, 209
Razin, Stepan, Stenka, 16, 27, 85-86,
 94, 137-138, 140, 143, 149, 154,
 156-157, 190-191, 208, 225, 237,
 246; rebellion, 245
Rechitsa, region, 78
Red Square, Moscow, 157, 246
reform, Russian church, 199, 211
regalia, Zaporozhian Host; banner,
 mace, staff, standards, 14, 20, 30-
 31, 48, 52, 84, 118, 120-121, 124,
 142, 148, 150, 153, 161-162, 181-
 182, 185-186
regimental chancellery, Cossack
 hetmanate, 194
registered cossacks, 203
reitarskie polki. 225
Rej, Jan, governor of Lublin, 54
relics, 42, 74
religious schismatics, 1
Republic of Two Nations, see
 Commonwealth of Two Nations
resident-agent, Swedish ,65, 67
Riurik, 207, 222
rjiksdaler, see lion dollar
Rog, Zhdan, 4
Rom 11:16, 215
Roman Catholics, 196; see also
 Christians, Roman Catholic
Roman empire, 72
Roman Catholic church, see church,
 Roman Catholic
Roman centurions, 233
Roman empire, 228
Romanov, 217
Rome , 204, 227-228
Romny, 81
Romodanovsky, Andrei Grigorievich,,
 Andriushka, 32, 79, 169, 212, 243
Romodanovsky, Prince Grigory

Grigorievich, 30, 32-33, 39-40, 45,
 47-50, 52-53, 82, 86, 117-119,
 123-124, 129, 131, 133-135, 142,
 144-146, 148, 150-151, 152-154,
 156, 158-159, 161-162, 164-167,
 169, 172, 176-179, 181-187, 212,
 233, 243
Romodanovsky Mikhail Grigorievich,
 169, 184, 243
Romodanovsky, Grigory Petrovich 212
Roslavets, or Roslovchenko, Ivan 86
Roslavets, or Roslovchenko) family
 213
Roslavets, or Roslovchenko, Peter, 33,
 43, 85-86, 97, 106, 108, 116, 153,
 212-213
Ruin, xvii, 206-207, 214, 224
Rumania, 199, 234
Runciman, Sir Stephan, author, 226
Russian army, xvi, 75, 131-132, 135,
 206-207, 211, 224, 238
Russian chancellery system, 210
Russian government, 55, 170, 192,
 206, 210, 220
Russian Orthodox church, see church,
 Russian Orthodox
Russian regiments, 151; musketeer,
 86; new formation, 86
Russian script, Cyrillic, 99, 230
Russian State Archive of Ancient
 Acts, RGADA, xviii
Russo-Polish War, 1654-1667, see
 Thirteen Years War
Russo-Swedish War, 1656-1658, 219
Rusyn, 76, 223
Ruthenia, 204, 244
Ruthenian Principality, 206
Rylsk, 45
Rzeczpospolita, see Commonwealth of
 Two Nations
Rzeczpospolita obojga narodow, see
 Commonwealth of Two Nations
Rzhevsky, Ivan Ivanovich, 17, 21-22,
 43, 96, 99, 118, 127

sable pelts, timbers, 52-54, 157, 159,
 162, 218, 241

Safonovich, Feodosy, abbot, 37
St. Kallistratos (Callistratus), 78, 223
St. Cyril's monastery, Kiev, 37, 201
St. George, 227
St. German, 237
St. Nicholas gates, Moscow, 130
St. Nicholas hermitage, 37
St. Nicholas of Krupitsk, monastery
    of, 102-103, 115
St. Nicholas, church of 226
St. Petersburg, 209
St. Savvaty, 237
St. Zosima, 237
Samarenin, Mikhail Fedorovich, 110,
    188, 190, 245
Samko, Yakim, 14, 44, 112, 114, 116,
    148, 161, 184, 207-208, 232-233,
    238, 242
Samoilovich, Grigory Ivanovich, 129
Samoilov(-ich) Ivan, hetman (1672-
    1687), xvi, 20, 28, 53, 102, 107,
    109. 121, 127-129, 130-135, 137-
    139, 142, 144-146, 147-154, 156,
    158-161, 164-169, 171-173, 175-
    179, 181-187, 209, 212-213, 218,
    229, 238, 240; made hetman of
    both sides of the Dnieper, 153;
    sons of, 164
sanzhak (sanjak), 245
Sasimov, Petrushka, 22
Sasov, Muscovite colonel, 165
Savin, Mikhail, 84-85, 94-95
Savior gates (Moscow), 130
Savior monastery (Novgorod-Seversk),
    171, 243
Savostianov, Mikhail, 143, 145
Savva, cossack captain(?), 165, 242
schism, Orthodox Ukrainian Church,
    87
seal of Zaporozhian hetman, 38, 168,
    173, 181
Sebezh, 74
Sech, xiii, 4-7, 133, 139, 163, 202-
    203, 207, 228, 245
Secret Chancellery, 62
Sednevo, 33, 102
Seim River, 109

Sejm, 11, 42, 55-56, 67, 76, 84, 105,
    195, 204
Selim-Girey, Crimean khan, 79, 244
Semeonov, Prokopy, 154
Semeonov, Vasily, 86, 90
Senate, Polish, 73-74, 244
senators, Polish, 14, 27, 29, 54
Senkeevich, Ivan, 184-185
Serapion, monk, 146
Serbin, Ivan, 153
Serdeniats, 159, 241
serdiuki, 236, 241, 245
Serko, Ivan Dmitrievich, 39, 94, 118,
    121, 128-129, 137-145, 150, 154-
    159, 162-163, 168, 171, 173, 180-
    182, 185-186, 207, 214, 243
service land holding, 127, 235
Settlement Ukraine, 172, 182, 243
Severia, xiii, 44-45
Severian hetman, 91
Sevsk, 45, 82, 86, 106-107, 150, 155
shah, 130, 203
Shamay, 39; see also Sukhovey, Peter
Shashol, Yevsevy, 123
Shchegolev, Semeon 121-122, 138-
    140, 142, 155, 167
Shcherbak, Maksim, 138
Shcherbaty (Shcherbatov), Prince
    Konstantin Osipovich, 30
Shcherbina, Stepan, 153
Shcherbyna-Koshevyi, Ivan, 39, 214
Sheksna River, 220
Sheremetev family, 202, 224
Sheremetev, Peter Vasilievich, 3, 10-
    12, 18-19, 22, 28, 36-39, 41, 46,
    99, 202, 209
Sheremetev, Vasily Borisovich, 23,
    79-80, 179, 202, 224
Shirkevich, Jeremiah, abbot, 41, 83,
    105, 113, 115, 215
Shrovetide, see Butter Week
Shuisky, Vasily Ivanovich, tsar, 75,
    223
Shumeiko, Savva, see Mnogogreshny,
    Savva Ignatovich
Siberia, xvi, 26, 103-104, 103, 113,
    117-118, 144, 171-172, 238

Sicily, 72
Sieniawski, Mikołaj Hieronim, 177, 244
Sigismund III Augustus, king of Poland, 242
Silich, Aniky (Ioanikii), 14, 112, 208, 232
Silka, 13; *see also* Serko
Simbirsk, 208
Simeon Alekseevich, tsarevich/Pretender, *see* Zaporozhian pretender
Simeon ("some Latin"), 92
Siniavin, Grigory, 119
Skuratov, Alexander Petrovich, 32, 79
Skuratov, Peter Dmitrievich, 151
slaves, 185, 190
Slobodskaia Ukraine, *see* Settlement Ukraine
Smelaia, 16, 81, 159
Smolensk, xiii, 37, 54, 60, 63, 70, 77, 101, 206
Smolensk cathedral, 78
Sniatin, 132
Sobieski Jan III, 11, 29, 73, 124-125, 153, 163-164, 167-168, 204, 234
sokha, 215
Sokha, cossack colonel, 25, 28
soldatskie polki, 225
soldiers, Polish and Lithuanian, 178
soldiers, Russian, 1, 3, 9, 149, 162, 166, 178, 181, 187-191; deserting, 188, 191
soldiers, Russian and Polish, unified, 179
soldiers, Turkish and Crimean, 167
Solonina family, 209
Solonina, Konstantin, 73, 95-99, 101, 103, 120-121, 135, 153, 240; wife of, 98-99
Solonina, Yakov, 240
Solovetsk island, 138
Solovetsk monastery, 237
Solovey, Mikhail, 153
Soloviev, Sergei Mikhailovich, author, iv, xv, xvii, 195, 197, 199, 209, 212
Soroki, 165

Sosnitsa, 21, 28, 43, 102-103
Sosnitsa River, 131
sotniki, sotnyky, 194, 212
Sozh River, 94-95, 111, 120
Sparrow, *see* Andreev, Ivan
Spiritual Trumpets, see *Words of the Trumpet*
Spitsyn, Moscow musketeer, 21
Stanislavsky, Ivan, abbot, 37
Starodub, 28, 33, 77, 85-86, 97, 116, 153, 226
Stary Bykhov, 37
Stary Koliadin, 121
steppe, 95, 118, 137, 140, 144, 147-148, 154-155, 167, 173, 178, 222
Stockholm, 55
Stolbovo, Treaty of (1617), 219
stolnik, 211, 216
Strakh, cossack, 7
Streletskie prikazy, *see* Russian regiments, musketeer
Stryevsky, Konstantin, 107, 116, 231, 233
Stryjkowski chronicle, 77, 223
Subbotovo, 185
Subtelny, Orest, author, xviii
Suceava, 92
Sudzha, 134, 178
Sukhovey (Sukhoveenko), Peter, xv, 38-39, 45, 81-82, 87, 144, 214, 224
Sula River, 134, 236
Sulima (Sulimka), Ivan, 150, 238
Sulymenko, Ivan, 238-239
Sumy, 87, 134, 177
Suzdal, 222
Swan Lakes, 134, 236
Sweden, xiii, 219- 200
Swedes, 55-56, 62, 65
Syniukha River. 199
synod, 205
Sysyn, Frank, author, 196-197

Tamerlane (Timur the Lame), 72, 222
Taneev, Alexander Tikhonovich, 95, 97-98, 100-101, 104, 111, 113, 230
Targovitsa, 1, 153, 199
Tarnopol, 235

Tashlyk stream, 159
Tatar horde, 81-82, 86, 147, 150
Tatar language, 80
Tatar tribe, 224
Tatars, xv, xvi, xviii, 4, 7, 11-14, 23,
    29-32, 38-39, 41, 46, 54, 70-71,
    75, 79-81, 86, 93-94, 101, 103,
    107, 125-126, 128, 134-135, 148,
    152, 159, 165-166, 176-182, 204,
    212, 224, 239, 242
tax, 3, 11, 15, 21, 25, 30, 44, 116,
    135-136; alcohol, 121; collections,
    24, 49, 51, 202; collectors, 21, 24;
    exemption, 50, 53; paying people,
    15
Tchaikovsky, Peter Ilich, composer,
    236
Telepnev, Ivan, 2-3
Terekhtemirov monastery, 99
Terpigorev, Elizar, 158-159
Teteria, Pavel Ivanovich, 91, 150, 161,
    228-229, 242
thaler, see Joachimsthaler
thalweg, 236
Theodosius II, Roman emperor
    (d.450), 234
theology, scholastic, 227
Thirteen Years War (1654-1667), xiii,
    1, 198
Tiapkin, Vasily Mikhailovich, 12-15,
    18, 20, 206
Tiasmin River, 159, 183
Tichanowiecki, Mikołaj, 69
Tikhy (Tikhonov), Semeon, 110, 112
Time of Troubles, 200, 223, 237
Timofeev, Gavril, 22
1 Timothy 6:10, 221
Timur lenk, see Tamerlane (Timur the
    Lame)
Tobolsk, 117
Tokhtamysh, 222
Tolstoy, Andrei Vasilievich, 28, 79
Tolstoy, Mikhail Andreev, 32
Torets, 166
town cossacks, 245
town prefects, 174
towns, border, 45; Crimean 4; Muslim,
    123; Polish, 45, 101; Russian, 82,

87, 93, 130; Siberian, 102, 117;
    Ukrainian/Little Russian, 35, 45-
    46, 49, 53, 57, 82, 85-86, 95, 97,
    100-101, 114, 130, 237,
town cossacks, 228
town elders, 159, 161
townsmen, 127, 152, 164, 208
trade statutes, 66
Transcarpathia, 215
Transylvania, 210, 215
Trinity Sunday, 6, 203
Trinity-St. Sergius monastery
    (Zagorsk), 228
Trubchevsk, 30
Trubetskoy, Prince Yury Petrovich,
    127, 131, 135, 150-152
Truby sloves, see Words of the
    Trumpet
Truby dukhovnye, see Words of the
    Trumpet
Trumpets see Words of the Trumpet
tsareviches, 189
Tsargrad, see Constantinople
Tseev, Muscovite colonel, 152
Tsytsura, Timofey (Timish), 148,
    238
Tukalsky, Joseph, metropolitan, xv,
    12, 15, 19-24, 30, 36, 47, 54, 62,
    81, 87-88, 92, 94, 110, 114, 116,
    127, 133-134, 146-147, 150, 154,
    162, 165, 168, 205
Tur, Alexis, abbot, 37
Turansky, Iliash, 9
Turkey, 124, 177
Turkish affairs, 71
Turkish army, xvi, 125-126, 165
Turkish garrison, 166
Turkish officials, 184-187, 229, 245
Turkish sultan, 6, 13, 20, 22, 29-30,
    39, 49, 75-77, 79, 87, 89, 91-93,
    101-102, 109-110, 117, 120, 125-
    128, 130, 132-134, 144, 149, 158-
    159, 163, 165-168, 170, 173, 176,
    179, 181, 185-187, 224, 229, 232,
    235
Turkish vizier, 93, 126-127, 162, 166-
    168, 178
Tver, 222

Tver gate (Moscow), 55
Tver street, 156

Uglitsky, Feodosy, abbot, 37
Ukrainian Orthodox church, see
    church, Ukrainian Orthodox
Ukrainian Quarterly, xix
Ukrainian Review, xix
Ulezko, Yakov, 240
Ulozhenie of 1649, see Law Code of
    1649
Uman, 41, 82, 125, 149, 153, 165-166,
    168, 199, 225
Uman monastery, 36
Umanets, Filipp , 44, 153
Umanka River, 225
Uniate church, see church, Uniate
Uniates, 163, 196
Union of Brest (1596), 204
Union of Lublin (1569), 195, 243
universal(s), 11, 29, 81, 86, 103, 205
Ushakov, Vasily, 46-47

Vaga River, 220
Valuiki, 62
Vasiutenko, Astap (Ostap), 4-5, 7
Vasseur, Guillaume le, Sieur de
    Beauplan, xviii, 223
Vasvar, Treaty of (1664), 215
vdova, vdovitsa, 234
Vdovichenko, Nikita, 121-124, 234
Velichko, Samoil, xviii, 198
Velikogo-Gagin, Prince Daniel
    Stepanovich, 232, 112
Venetian war, 125
Venice, 220, 234,
Veniukov, Nikifor Dmitrievich, 78
Veprik, 121
Verderevsky, Ivan Ivanovich, 159
Vernadsky, George, author, 197
Vestov, Muscovite colonel, 184
Vienna, 211
Virgin at Eletsk, monastery of the, 115,
    233
Vistula River, 156
Vitebsk, 74,
Vitiazenko, Grigory, 8-9
Vladimir, 222

vodka, 45
voevoda, voevodstvo, v, 238
Voikheevich, Mikhail, 116
Volga River, 72, 137, 208
Volhynia, 13, 160, 207, 209
Volkonsky, Prince Vladimir Andree-
    vich, 127, 244
Volkonsky, Prince Mikhail Ivanovich,
    5, 8, 174-176
Volkonsky, Prince Ignaty Grigorie-
    vich, 28
volunteer regiments, cossack, 135-136,
    176, 236
Volyn, 244
Volynsky, Vasily Semeonovich, 55, 71
Voronezhh, 137, 230, 244
Voronovka, 185
votchiny, see patrimonial estates
Voyn, district, 220
Vulf, Frants, 179, 245
Vydubits monastery, 37
Vygovsky, Ivan Astafievich, 13-14, 20,
    50, 150, 158, 201, 206, 229, 239
Vynnetsky, Anthony, bishop, 205

Wallachia, 78, 167, 199
Wallachian hospodar, 1, 92
Wallachian hussar regiment 108
Wallachian prince, 23
Wallachians, 30, 77, 81, 165
Warsaw, 29, 54, 61, 66, 75, 101, 113,
    156-157, 163, 206, 223, 240
Western Europe, 240
White Rus, White Russia, 13, 200,
    205
White Russian script, 119
Whitsunday, 203
Wilno, 66, 220
Wiśniowiecki family, 156, 234, 245
Wiśniowiecki, Prince Dymitr, 157,
    178
Wiśniowiecki, Prince Jarema, 66, 156,
    207, 204, 207, 218
Wiśniowiecki, Prince Michał Korybut,
    66, 124, 173, 234, 244
Wiśniowiecki princes, 14
Words of the Trumpet, 82, 89, 91, 151,
    170, 224, 243

Yakovlev, Andrei, 140
Yakovlev, Kornil, 188, 190, 245
Yanenko-Khmelnitsky, Pavel, 158,
    185-186, 245
yanichar, *see* janissaries
Yanov, captain Muscovite musketeers,
    156
Yaroslavl, grand prince, 226-227
Yaroslavl, town, 222
Yasilkovsky, Pavel, 129
Yasinsky, Varlaam, abbot, 37, 105
yasyr, 224
Yazlovets, 132
Yermelenko, Daniil, 202
Yezych River, 201
Yuditsky, Muscovite officer, 37
Yuriev, Efim Rodionovich, 59, 220
yurt, 80, 173, 224, 244

za porogami, 228
Zabela Peter, 3, 41, 44, 46-47, 50, 52,
    97, 101-102, 104-105, 108-109,
    121, 139
Zagriazhsky, Kirill Alexandrovich, 28
Zaporozhia, 3-4, 6, 8, 15, 23, 25-27,
    35, 38-39, 77, 82, 85-86, 106, 116,
    121-123, 137-139, 142, 144-145,
    147, 155-156, 161-162, 172-173,
    178, 180-181, 185-186, 202, 206,
    216, 234-235, 242, 244

Zaporozhian chancellor, 171
Zaporozhian Host, xiii, 1, 4, 9, 11, 14,
    18, 23, 26, 28, 34-35, 39-42, 45,
    50, 53-54, 83-84, 88, 91, 98-101,
    111-112, 118-120, 122-123, 128-
    129, 131, 137-138, 141-142, 144-
    145, 147-148, 153-155, 159, 163,
    169, 171, 175-176, 178, 180-182,
    185-186, 211, 232, 239-240, 245,
Zaporozhian pretender, 137-145, 154-
    157, 162-163, 172, 182
Zaporozhian Sech, *see* Sech
Zawisza, Polish ambassador, 173
Zawisza family, 244
Zawisza, Krysztof, 244
Zhabotin, 185
Zhdanov, Yakov, 22
Zheliabuzhsky family, 210
Zheliabuzhsky, Ivan Afanasievich, 24,
    68-69, 210-211
zholnyr, 238
Zhuchenko, Fedor, 118, 233
Zhvanets, 132
Zinoviev, Mikhail, 109, 117, 232
zloty, Polish or Lithuanian, 217
Zolotarenko, Ostap, 44
Zolotarenko, Vasyl (Vasiuto)
    Nikiforovich, 14, 112, 116, 148,
    208, 232
Zvenigorodsky, Semeon, 127

THE EDITOR AND TRANSLATOR

Cathy Potter is an Associate Professor in the History Department of the Chinese University of Hong Kong. She received her doctorate in Russian History from Yale University in 1993. Her dissertation examined the process of reform in the Russian church during the second half of the seventeenth century, focusing on ecclesiastical politics and the goals of reform. She has published articles on the eucharistic controversy in the 1680s, church reform during the patriarchate of Joachim and on corruption in pre-Petrine Russia, a current project.

FROM ACADEMIC INTERNATIONAL PRESS*

THE RUSSIAN SERIES

1 S.F. Platonov History of Russia **
2 The Nicky-Sunny Letters, Correspondence of Nicholas and Alexandra, 1914-1917
3 Ken Shen Weigh Russo-Chinese Diplomacy, 1689-1924
4 Gaston Cahen Relations of Russia with China…1689-1730
5 M.N. Pokrovsky Brief History of Russia
6 M.N. Pokrovsky History of Russia from Earliest Times
7 Robert J. Kerner Bohemia in the Eighteenth Century
8 Memoirs of Prince Adam Czartoryski and His Correspondence with Alexander I
9 S.F. Platonov Moscow and the West.
10 S.F. Platonov Boris Godunov
11 Boris Nikolajewsky Aseff the Spy
12 Francis Dvornik Les Legendes de Constantin et de Methode vues de Byzance
13 Francis Dvornik Les Slaves, Byzance et Rome au XIᵉ Siecle
14 A. Leroy-Beaulieu Un Homme d'Etat Russe (Nicholas Miliutine)…
15 Nicolas Berdyaev Leontiev (In English)
16 V.O. Kliuchevskii Istoriia soslovii v Rossii
17 Tehran Yalta Potsdam. The Soviet Protocols
18 The Chronicle of Novgorod
19 Paul N. Miliukov Outlines of Russian Culture Vol. III Pt. 1. The Origins of Ideology
20 P.A. Zaionchkovskii The Abolition of Serfdom in Russia
21 V.V. Vinogradov Russkii iazyk. Grammaticheskoe uchenie o slove
22 P.A. Zaionchkovsky The Russian Autocracy under Alexander III
23 A.E. Presniakov Emperor Nicholas I of Russia. The Apogee of Autocracy
24 V.I. Semevskii Krestianskii vopros v Rossii v XVIII i pervoi polovine XIX veka
25 S.S. Oldenburg Last Tsar! Nicholas II, His Reign and His Russia
26 Carl von Clausewitz The Campaign of 1812 in Russia
27 M.K. Liubavskii Obrazovanie osnovnoi gosudarstvennoi territorii velikorusskoi narodnosti. Zaselenie i obedinenie tsentra
28 S.F. Platonov Ivan the Terrible Paper
29 Paul N. Miliukov Iz istorii russkoi intelligentsii. Sbornik statei i etiudov
30 A.E. Presniakov The Tsardom of Muscovy
31 M. Gorky, J. Stalin et al., History of the Civil War in Russia (Revolution)
32 R.G. Skrynnikov Ivan the Terrible
33 P.A. Zaionchkovsky The Russian Autocracy in Crisis, 1878-1882
34 Joseph T. Fuhrmann Tsar Alexis. His Reign and His Russia
35 R.G. Skrynnikov Boris Godunov
36 R.G. Skrynnikov The Time of Troubles. Russia in Crisis, 1604-1618
38 V.V. Shulgin Days of the Russian Revolutions. Memoirs From the Right, 1905-1907. Cloth and Paper

39 A.E. Presniakov The Formation of the Great Russian State.
40 J.L. Black "Into the Dustbin of History"! The USSR From August Coup to Commonwealth, 1991. A Documentary Narrative
41 E.V. Anisimov Empress Elizabeth. Her Reign and Her Russia, 1741–1761
42 J.K. Libbey Russian-American Economic Relations, 1763–1999
43 Nicholas Zernov Three Russian Prophets. Khomiakov, Dostoevsky, Soloviev
44 Paul N. Miliukov The Russian Revolution 3 vols.
45 Anton I. Denikin The White Army
55 M.V. Rodzianko The Reign of Rasputin—An Empire's Collapse. Memoirs
56 The Memoirs of Alexander Iswolsky

THE CENTRAL AND EAST EUROPEAN SERIES

1 Louis Eisenmann Le Compromis Austro-Hongrois de 1867
3 Francis Dvornik The Making of Central and Eastern Europe 2nd edition
4 Feodor F. Zigel Lectures on Slavonic Law
10 Doros Alastos Venizelos—Patriot, Statesman, Revolutionary
20 Paul Teleki The Evolution of Hungary and its Place in European History

FORUM ASIATICA

1 M.I. Sladkovsky China and Japan—Past and Present

REFERENCE SERIES

The Modern Encyclopedia of Russian, Soviet and Eurasian History 60 vols.
The Modern Encyclopedia of East Slavic, Baltic and Eurasian Literatures 50 vols.
The Modern Encyclopedia of Religions in Russia and the Soviet Union 30 vols
Russia & Eurasia Military Review Annual
Russia & Eurasia Facts & Figures Annual
Russia & Eurasia Documents Annual
USSR Calendar of Events (1987- 1991) 5 vol. set
USSR Congress of Peoples's Deputies 1989. The Stenographic Record
Documents of Soviet History 12 vols.
Documents of Soviet-American Relations
Gorbachev's Reforms. An Annotated Bibliography of Soviet Writings. Part 1 1985–1987
MilitaryEncyclopedia of Russia and Eurasia 50 vols.
China Facts & Figures Annual
China Documents Annual
Encyclopedia USA. The Encyclopedia of the United States of America Past & Present 50 vols.
Sports Encyclopedia North America 50 vols.
Sports in North America. A Documentary History
Religious Documents North America Annual
The International Military Encyclopedia 50 vols.
Nationalities and Ethnicity Terminologies. An Encyclopedic Dictionary and Research Guide 2 vols.

SPECIAL WORKS
S.M. Soloviev History of Russia 50 vols.
SAFRA Papers 1985-

*Request catalogs. Sample pages, tables of contents, more on line at www.ai-press.com